TEACHING AND LEARNING LATIN
IN THIRTEENTH-CENTURY ENGLAND

Volume II

Glosses

TEACHING AND LEARNING LATIN
IN THIRTEENTH-CENTURY ENGLAND

VOLUME I: TEXTS
VOLUME II: GLOSSES
VOLUME III: INDEXES

TEACHING AND LEARNING LATIN
IN THIRTEENTH-CENTURY ENGLAND

TONY HUNT

Fellow of St Peter's College, Oxford

Volume II

Glosses

D. S. BREWER

First published 1991 by D. S. Brewer, Cambridge

D. S. Brewer is an imprint of Boydell & Brewer Ltd
PO Box 9, Woodbridge, Suffolk IP12 3DF
and of Boydell & Brewer Inc.
PO Box 41026, Rochester, NY 14604, USA

ISBN 0 85991 338 4 (Volume II)
ISBN 0 85991 299 X (three-volume set)

British Library Cataloguing in Publication Data
Hunt, Tony
    Teaching and learning Latin in thirteenth-century England.
    1. England. Latin language. Teaching
    I. Title
    478.007042
    ISBN 0–85991–299–X

Library of Congress Catalog Card Number 89–71269

Publication of this work
was assisted by a grant from
the British Academy

This publication is printed on acid-free paper

Printed and bound in Great Britain by
Woolnough Bookbinding Ltd, Irthlingborough, Northants

CONTENTS

CHAPTER THREE

THE *AUCTORES* AND THE 'LIBER CATONIANUS'

MS LINCOLN CATHEDRAL CHAPTER LIBRARY 132

1. Theodolus, *Ecloga* ff.11ra–19vb and 31ra–36va
[f.11va] (15) *littoris*: ruve [corr. rive] / [f.13ra] (51) *ne . . . temeremur*: que ne folum / [f.14va] (89) *arce*: forteresce / [f.14vb] (96) *pecoris*: de betaly / [f.15va] (110) *suber*: ascoce / [f.17rb] (137) *magicas*: encha[n]tereces / [f.17vb] (148) *infula*: chesible / [f.18ra] (151) *specus*: fose / [f.18rb] (157) *oestro*: de tau[n]z / (159) *sitis*: pursisze / [f.19vb] (196) *exortes*: forpartyez / [f.31ra] (211) *humo*: arosabel / [f.31vb] (222) *cicadam*: grisilun / [f.32ra] (232) *pompa*: lossungrie / [f.33rb] (254) *ceris* (=seris): de baris / *obstruxit*: astopaz / [f.34ra] (272) *peremptis*: tuez / [f.34rb] (top of page) ***: scharricer / *upupa vel popina*: lepwincz [1] / [f.35vb] (321) *subsidat*: abese

2. Cato, *Disticha* ff.20ra–28vb
[f.23rb] (II, pref.9) *semotum*: aloiniez / [f.25ra] (III,1) *discere*: apre[n]dre / [f.27ra] (IV,20) *loquatur*: parlaz / [f.27vb] (IV,31) *demissos*: abessez / [f.28vb] (IV,48) *vita*: achuez

3. Persius, *Satirae* ff.109r–114v
[f.109v] (I,40) *uncis*: crochés / [f.111r] (I,133) *petulans*: way / [f.112v] (III,9) *rudere*: recaner / [f.113r] (III,44) *olivo*: elye [2] / (III,59) *oscitat*: baelet / [f.113v] (III,75) *monumenta*: chencele / [f.114r] (IV,2) *sorbicio*: devour / *cicute*: cigue, anglice wodeyonge [3] / (IV,24) *mantica*: faredel / [f.114v] (IV,32) *pannosam*: cremuse / *fecem*: lye / (IV,35) *despuat*: eschopet / (IV,38) *inguinibus*: de penuls

4. Avianus, *Fabulae* ff.115r–123v [4]
[f.115r] (IX,10) *relisus*: ajené / (IX,19) *sodes*: escheles (adverbium comicum est) / [f.116r] (XIII,3) *speluncam*: fosse [5] / [f.117r] (XVIII,12) *pecus*: bestaly(l)z / [f.117v] (XIX,1) *abies*: sap / [f.118r] (XX,7) *antris*: fosses / (XXI,2) *cespite*: bleste / [f.119v] (XXVI,4) *jugis*: teretres / (XXVI,5) *cytisi*: cheverefolez / [f.120r] (XXVII,6) *dolos*: quintiscez / (XXIX,1) *conjestis*: monzelés / (XXIX,2) *durato*: dursye / (XXIX,5) *antro*: fosez / [f.120v] (XXIX,15) *cratera*: hanap / (XXIX,19) *obstupuit*: abayt / [f.121r] (XXXII,9) *congressum*: avay / [f.121v] (XXXIV,5) *labores*: travays / (XXXIV,6) *casis vel cavis*: creves / [f.122v] (XXXVIII,5) *non tulit*: ne sufri pas / *phoca*: un porpiés / [f.123r] (XL,5) *sordenti*: soylé / [f.123v] (left-hand margin) *aprina*: .a. braun [6] / [f.123v] (XLI,16) *pharetratis*: quiverés / (XLII,1) *edus*: cheverel

5. Statius, *Achilleis* ff.134r–150v
[f.134r] (I,14) *Itala*: de Lumbardye / [f.135r] (I,79) *eam invitat*: la pryt / [f.135v] (I,96) *ratibus*: a nefs / (I,101) *letantur*: se lesynt / (I,102) *antra*: fosz / (I,111) *stabula*, *solia*: solerz / [f.136r] (I,123) *motaque*: mové / (I,124) *submissus*: abesez / (I,135) *magici*:

---

1   See MED sub *lapwink(e n.*
2   See MED sub *ele n.(1)*.
3   This word glosses *suffonia* (Helleborus niger) in a number of plant glossaries.
4   The text starts at IX,6.
5   Following XIII,12 there are two extra lines, as follows: 'Dum cupis illatum tibimet persolvere dampnum / absque tuo dampno hocque caveto fore' to which is appended 'malement sen veint que sun damage anoyte'. See Walther, *Initia* 6485.
6   See MED sub *braun n.*

enchaunteresse / [f.136v] (I,162) *purpureus*: vermayl / (I,168) *fetam*: founyse[7] / (I,177) *saltu*: par saut / (I,180) *hanelo* (=anhelo), laborioso: chaud / [f.137r] (I,190) *cestu*: eskyrmye, talevaz (right-hand margin: .i. quo ludo cestuum gallice eskymrye) / (I,195) *saxo*: .i. roche / (I,195) *collabitur*: escolurge / [f.137v] (II,229) *rupibus*: roche / (II,232) *recursus*: repeyrys / (II,239) *spelunca*: fosez / (II,240) *querunt*: demaundeyt / (II,241) *connubia*: mariagez / (II,245) *emensa*: mesurez / [f.138r] (II,256) *genus*: lyne / (II,256) *preclusa*: forclose / (II,258) *metis*: boundes[8] / (II,263) *induit*: enfubla / [f.138v] (II,283) *(h)astum*, calliditatem: qunytiscez / (II,289) *hastam*: lanse / (II,315) *juvencam*: torrel, genize / [f.139r] (II,330): *limbo*: orné / (II,332): *artificis*: engynere / (II,332) *iuncture*: a joyndre / [f.139v] (II,384) *cure*: garde / (II,385) *haustu*: (=astu) astuze (misplaced under *depositumque*) / [f.140r] (III,407) *bimari*: duble mer / (III,412) *erigit*: adresce / (III,413) *ora*: cunterey / (III,416) *stipare*: enviruner / (III,417) *juvencis*: torelys / (III,418) *pedites*: poyners / [f.140v] (III,426) *sidunt*: abe-synt / (III,429) *lax*: est alaché / (III,439) *fata*: destinez / (III,443) *operta*: covertys / [f.141r] (III,466) *cerva*: bisez / (III,484) *choirent*: asembla (corr. asemblé) synt / (III,488) *hanela* (=anhela): chaufez / [f.141v] (III,494) *cupido*: covetyse / (III,508) *laxa*: alatché / [f.142r] (III,537) *tremefactus*: espaunté / (III,543) *secretumque*, vel *facundum*: estre renable / (III,553) *stimulat*: enaguse / [f.142v] (III,565) *exsolvit*: delyat / (III,565) *di(s)gressa*: departy / (III,583) *pensa*: fisyls / [f.143r] (III,592) *astus*: cuuyntyse / (III,601) *temerator*: enfobere / (III,617) *serta*: garlandis / (III,618) *invasit*: envayt / [f.143v] (III,621) *orbem*: mu[n]dez / (III,628) *queris*: demaundis / (III,636) *pampineis*: de vyne / (III,636) *tirsis*: a braunchis / (III,647) *fragor*: fru(r)isur[9] / [f.144r] (III,655) *tympana*: taburs / (III,662) *exter[r]ita*: espaunté / [f.144v] (IV,690) *pene-trabile*: herbergable / (IV,692) *rudentes*: cordes / [f.145r] (IV,739) *hospicio*: herbergage / (IV,741) *famularis*: servable / (IV,745) *penates*: privez chaumbris / (IV,750) *iamdu-dum*: ja peza / [f.145v] (IV,756) *strepitu*: noyse / (IV,756) *picto*: depeynt / (IV,757) *comites*: compaynys / (IV,774) *placata*: enpeysé / (IV,777) *adorsos*: envays / [f.146r] (IV,794) *intentum*: ententif / (IV,796) *proavis*: est de besaeus / [f.146v] (IV,833) *orbe*, rotunditate: turnez, tournys / (IV,850) *timpana*: taburs / (IV,850) *tempora*: tempres / [f.147r] (IV,859) *pecti*: estre pyné / (IV,882) *perfudit*: espaundi / (IV,889) *limina*: soyls / [f.148r] (IV,932) *dignabere*: dedeyneras tu / (IV,949) *quin age*: hey gallice, a me anglice / (IV,949) *comitem*: compayne / (IV,950) *pensa*: fuseys / [f.148v] (V,7) *invasit*: envay / (V,15) *juvenca*: torrele (V,19) *orsus*: parlez / (V,31) *aggressus*: envay / [f.149r] (V,43) *componere*: espoundre / (V,53) *sociam*: companye / (V,60) *cedit*: copey / [f.149v] (V,84) *capulum*: pomel / (V,90) *augere*: acreytre / [f.150r] (V,110) *torserat* aveytt purs / (V,110) *orbes*: rundescys / (V,120) *saltus*: laundes / (V,132) *cestum*: tarche, askerz[10] / [f.150v] (V,148) *tulisset*: sofert / (V,152) *agebat*: demeneyt / (V,155) *nudare*: descoveryr

6. Claudian, *De raptu Proserpinae* ff.151r–162v

[f.151r] (-) *nothus*: suth / *sephirus*: west / *boreis*: north / (I,133) *procis*: dauanneturz(?)

---

[7] This is one of the attested forms from *fetus*, see FEW 3,487a 'fedunuse' and TL 3,ii,1726 sub *feonos*.
[8] The Latin gloss has 'fini tuo apropinquantis'. See MED sub *bound(e n*.
[9] A hapax.
[10] In the left-hand margin of f.150r there is a note 'cestus genus ludi est .s. talevaz'.

/ [f.151v] (I,192) *presaga*: divineresse / (I,197) *ligones*: syes / [f.154r] (I,203) *silex*: pere
/ [f.154v] (I,279) *molitur*: aparalezy / [f.153r] (II, prol.42) *cervam*: bisse / [f.153v] (II,
prol.52) *excutis*: debuteys / (II,19) *arces*: les tures / [f.154r] (II,63) *populata*: degasté /
(II,74) *la[s]civo*: way / [f.154v] (II,96) *aeni*: de chadrunt / (II,105) *soles*: chalurs /
(II,109) *ilex*: cheyne / (II,126) *fagique*: foy / (II,130) *ligustris*: primereloy / [f.155r]
(II,138) *vimine*: de oser / (II,141) *tubarum*: de businez / (II,185) *tellus colonis*: a
cotefyors / [f.156r] (II,295) *aequora*: reunz / [f.157r] (III,325) *flammea*: coverchep /
(III,362) *pronuba*: chambrere, pedestote[11] / [f.157v] (III,12) *canities*: chaneés /
[f.158v] (III,79) *bipenni*: hache denache / [f.159r] (III,113) *exilit*: or saut / (III,17)
caminis: de chimeneys / [f.159v] (III,155) *semirutas*: demi pescez / (III,155) *stamine*: a
stamez / [f.160r] (III,223) *bruina*: geley

MS LONDON, BRITISH LIBRARY, ADD. 16380[12]

Statius, *Achilleis* (ff.128r–143v): [f.128v] (I,55) *cete*: porpeys / [f.129r] (I,78) *ceruleis*:
blou / [f.129v] (I,115) *pharetre*: quiweres / [f.131r] (II,224) *glauce*: gloey[13] / [f.131v]
(II,236) *fuge*: de la fute / [f.132r] (II,283) *attonite*: ebayé / [f.132v] (I,304) *vibrata*:
croulé / (II,308) *puniceo*: vermayle / (II,330) *limbo*: orle / [f.133r] (II,355) *calathos*:
paniers / [f.134r] (III,406) *decrassata* (=degrassata): envaye / [f.134v] (III,437) *conis*:
creytes / (III,459) *indago*: serge / (III,596) *cerua*: bise / [f.136v] (III,596) *revulsas*:
arachés / [f.138r] (IV,682) *cephirum*, occidentalem: west / (IV,691) *scopulosa*: peruse /
[f.138v] (IV,737) *intercipit*, se interponit: se entremet / (IV,741) *famularis*: servisable /
(IV,749) *cespite*: blete / [f.139r] (IV,777) *adortos*, congressus: envays / [f.139v]
(IV,796) *proavis*: per beseus / (IV,802) *stratis*: cuches / [f.140r] (IV,836) *brachia*: coreis
/ (IV,853) *celatum*: taylés / [f.140v] (IV,859) *iubas*: creytes / [f.141r] (IV,905) *possessa*:
[par] forse amé / (IV,925) *consumpta*: demené / [f.142r] (V,16) *exta*: boés / [f.142v]
(V,39) *litui*: de grelet / [f.143v] (V,145) *vulsas*: rachés

MS CAMBRIDGE, PETERHOUSE 215

1. *Disticha Catonis* ff.59v–63r

[f.59v] (Brev. S.) *familia*: ta meynné / *troco lude*: le top fuez / *alias fuge*: autres fuez[14] /
[f.60r] (I,12) *esse locutum*: aver parlé / [f.60v] (Pref. II) *semotum*: anluynné / (II,3)
metum: powr / (II,5) *sumptum*: despense / [f.61r] (II,17) *sumptus*: despense / [f.61v]

---

[11] Cf. Du Cange sub *pedisseca*. The expected gloss is *baudstrot*. *Pedestote* is unattested.
[12] The MS (s.xiii[2]) is essentially a compilation of grammatical texts incl. Ralph of Beauvais's
Liber Titan (ff.111ra–119vb) and *Summa super Donatum* (ff.123vb–127ra), see C. H. Kneep-
kens (ed.), *Ralph of Beauvais, Glose super Donatum* (Nijmegen, 1982) pp.xii–xiii, and an anon.
commentary on 'Priscian minor' (ff.186ra–281rb, 283ra–305vb). The *Achilleis* (ff.128r–143v)
is followed by a commentary on the *Thebaid* with all textual lemmata underlined, ending
incomplete at XII,35. The first half of the MS deserves further study, for it comprises detailed
commentaries on the *Aeneid* (ff.2ra–72ra 'glosule Eneidos'), the *Georgics* (ff.73ra–91vb, incomplete), and Juvenal (ff.92ra–110vb, incomplete).
[13] FEW 4,150b attests only a Provençal reflex of *glaucus*.
[14] The glossator has misunderstood *alias* (= *aleas*).

(III,11) *contenptus*: apaé / [f.62r] (IV,2) *contenptus*: apaé / [f.62v] (IV,30) *complectere*: abracez / (IV,33) *litus*: rivage / (IV,33) *carpere*: prendre / (IV,33) *remis*: par aviruns / (IV,33) *velum*: veyl / (IV,34) *ulci[sci]tur*: venget / (IV,38) *placa*: playset / [f.63r] (IV,34) *aptisima*: tres feyté

2. Theodolus, *Ecloga* ff.63ı–65rb

[f.63r] (12) *a[u]scultando*: acutand / *modulantis*: atempré / (17) *certare*: atriver / [f.63v] (41) *incola*: cutifiere / (47) *succesit*: est sus alé / (51) *ne . . . temeremur*: ke (ne) nus ne sum afolé / (52) *vetat*: deveet / (54) *rimatus*: anserchi / (65) *polluto*: suyllé / (73) *disrupit*: a debrusé / [f.64ra] (77) *exagitat*: demenet / (79) *armiger*: aquier / (101) *aptatis*: afaytés / (110) *suber*: corse / (116) *cautem*: roche / (121) *congressus*: .i. avay[15] / (121) *luctamine*: .i. atrif / [f.64rb] (122) *femoris*: de quisse / (126) *focas*: .i. porpeys / (133) *vestigat*: anserchet / (143) *Agenoris*: .i. prins eurous(?) / (148) *infula*: .s. chesuble / (150) *bacca*: .i. luche[16] / (153) *parere*: .i. obeer / (156) *indagare*: ansercher / (157) *ventulat* (corr. *ventilat*): .i. chascet / (157) *oestro*: de un tauwnz / [f.64va] (173) *clava*: la maçue / (176) *pelex*: .i. rivayle / (189) *orni*: .i. cheynnes (.s. inferni) / (194) *citharista*: harpur / (197) *succos*: lé juus / (204) *confectum*: li ateynt / (209) *obstruxit*: .s. a astupé / (211) *torrente*: russel / (212) *assecla*: messager / [f.64vb] (214) *diriguerunt*: .i. il an reddirunt / (217) *obstruxit*: .i. a astupé / (228) *lora*: lé reyns / (248) *ruminat*: .i. runget / (254) *seris*: .i. par bares / (254) *obstruxit*: .i. a astupé / [f.65ra] (261) *tura*: ansens / (263) *humero*: .i. de la paudle / (263) *spicula*: .i. dars / (272) *infesta*: .i. haynnuse / (279) *rostro*: en un bec / (285) *virent*: .i. anferdisent[17] / (285) *frondent*: .i. anbronchisent / (294) *cithiso*: de un flur / (294) *ulmo*: .i. ulme / (303) *hortos*: curtyls / [f.65rb] (305) *arentibus*: .i. secchisans

3. Avianus, *Fabulae* ff.65rb–69ra

[f.65va] (II,4) *bacta*: .i. nuche / (III,2) *relisis*: ahurté / [f.66ra] (IX,10) *relisus*: engené[18] / (IX,13) *concreto*: amuncelé / [f.66rb] (X,7) *galero*: haume / (XII,6) *depositas*: estuez / [f.66vb] (XVI,11) *stridula*: sonable / (XVI,15) *Austros*: ventos de su / [f.67va] (XXV,7) *improba*: engrés / (XXV,8) *ima*: lé funz / (XXVI,5) *cicici* [= cytisi]: chevrefoyle / (XXVI,6) *glaucas*: bloys / (XXVI,6) *salices*: sauz / [f.67vb] (XXVIII,8) *seva*: .i. cruel / (XXIX,6) *satirus*: forester / [f.68ra] (XXIX,21) *successerit*: eyt entré / (XXX,3) *monumenta*: amonesteme[n]z / [f.68vb] (XXXVIII,5) *phocas*: porpés / (XXXVIII,12) *ere brevi*: de petyt areym / (XXXIX,7) *lituus*: un ruet / (XLI,8) *anphora*: pot

4. Claudian, *De raptu Proserpinae* ff.72vb–78rb

[f.73ra] (I,4) *congesta*: amuncilé / (I,19) *thyrsis*: balatuns / [f.73rb] (I,53) *ferratis*: par durs / (I,53) *pensis*: de fisils, fyn[19] / (I,57) *stamina*: fyls / (I,59) *letum*: le mort / (I,71) *concretus*: amuncelé / [f.73va] (I,132) *formidine*: pöur / [f.73vb] (I,143) *Italie*: de Lumbardye / (I,144) *confinia*: le veysinableté / (I,122) *crastina*: de demayn / (I,228) *lacivis*: way / (I,244) *atria*: les estres / [f.74ra] (Pref. II,5) *feris*: a beytes / [f.74rb] (Pref. II,24) *laurus*: lorer / (Pref. II,35) *sidereos*: d'eteyle / (II,6) *cardine*: la char[n]ere /

---

15 Cf. MS Lincoln Cath. 132 f.121r [Avianus XXXII,9] '*congressum*: avay'.
16 For the form *luche* see Gfry 5,506a sub *noche*. It here translates *bac(c)a monilis*.
17 This appears to be a hapax, though *renverdir*, of course, is well attested.
18 See TL 3,i,1070 sub *esgener*. MS Lincoln Cath. 132 f.115r has 'ajené'.
19 In the right-hand margin is 'hoc pensum -si .i. finis'.

[f.74va] (II,17) *fibula*: une tache / (II,31) *remisso*: .i. detenso, avalé / (II,33) *vestis*: sun rochet / [f.74vb] (II,54) *tempora*: lé temples / (II,57) *saxa*: reynes [20] / (II,62) *peltis* . . . *ademptis*: escu / (II,66) *securi*: de cele coyne / (II,74) *lacivo*: enveysé / (II,74) *volatu(m)*: volement / (II,75) *irroras*: aroseyét / [f.75ra] (II,107) *habies*: de saf (corr. sap) / (II,108) *cuperitus*: ciprés / (II,110) *buxus*: boys / (II,111) *ulmos*: les epuayles / (II,112) *lacus*: ruscel / (II,115) *pervius*: avauntalable / (II,121) *humectat*: amoutet / (II,126) *castra*: herberges / (II,126) *alvo*: ventre / (II,130) *ligustris*: de primeroles / (II,139) *calatos*: paniers / [f.75rb] (II,151) *passim*: comunement / (II,155) *pert[er]lita*: apaunté / (II,164) *effosi*: fuey / (II,169) *devia*: forviableté / [f.75va] (II,199) *torta*: launcé / (II,200) *austri*: vent de seu / (II,203) *inf(l)ecte*: ateyns / (II,207) *stimmula(n)t*: enaguset / (II,210) *fodit*: percet / (II,212) *sanie*: puruture / (II,212) *jubarum*: creytes / (II,214) *deterrime*: trémaveys / (II,217) *infestare*: nerer / (II,219) *coniuge*: barun / (II,220) *linque*: deverpét / (II,222) *proteris*: defulét vus / (II,223) *au[i]dos*: cuvetus / (II,225) *obice*: obstacle / (II,226) *operit*: cuevert / (II,229) *torsisset*: eyt launché / (II,230) *[hi]ulcis*: .i. largis / [f.75vb] (II,243) *sevique*: cruels / (II,242) *pharetras*: quivers / (II,248) *cesariem*: sa chevelure / (II,259) *hiatus*: goleys / (II,266) *dep[r]ense*: aparsçu / (II,268) *buxus*: busine / (II,274) *suspiria*: supyrs / (II,275) *ferrugenio*: de fer / (II,278) *vexare*: traviler / [f.76ra] (II,320) *aulea*: lé cortines / (II,321) *cultas*: atyffés / (II,325) *flamea*: cerchefs / (II,325) *prevelatura*: a cuveryr / (II,327) *luxuriant*: aveysent / [f.76rb] (II,343) *oblite*: obliés / (II,343) *formidati*: duté / (II,344) *cratera*: hanaps / (II,348) *pestiferi*: portant pestilence / (II,353) *perhibent*: temoneynt / (II,354) *stamina*: esteym / (II,355) *obstrepitant*: noysunt / (II,355) *vagatur*: vacret / (II,357) *navite*: le notiner / (II,358) *opida*: chautés / (II,364) *genitalia*: mariablis / (II,366) *sumunt*: yperunt(?) / (II,368) *unanimis*: deu meyn / (II,369) *alternis*: entrechang . . . / (II,369) *innectite*: alacét / (II,370) *proles*: la ligne / (II,371) *expectat*: atent / (III,1) *cinctam*: seynt / [f.76va] (III,7) *agitanda*: a domener / (III,17) *fauni*: folesteus de chemp / (III,23) *stimmulos*: aguluns / (III,25) *favis*: ré de mel / (III,25) *tumerent*: (en)enflyt / (III,28) *desuasor*: amoneyter / (III,31) *exp(o)loret*: encerchet / (III.43) *avia*: le forviableté / (III,52) *indicio*: par la demontrement / [f.76vb] (III,54) *cerulei*: bloy / (III,62) *optabit*: desyrat / (III,72) *nigrescere*: aneyrer / (III,73) *o[r]nos*: cheynes / (III,74) *luco*: de boys / (III,83) *vincta*: lyé / (III,89) *pruinis*: aube geleys / (III,94) *sevitie*: de crueleté / [f.77ra] (III,102) *teror*: ye su defulé [21] / (III,103) *instrepis*: tu noyses / (III,120) *depositum*: estu / (III,120) *vulgata*: de peple / (III,124) *infausta*: maluré / (III,126) *flavencia*: bloysaunt / (III,145) *colubris*: coleverye / [f.77rb] *resupinati*: encliné / (III,150) *con[s]cidit*: elechyt / (III,150) *avellit*: arachit / (III,152) *vibrat*: croillunt / (III,153) *succidui*: decheablis / (III,153) *titubant*: chauncelunt / (III,154) *sedes*: segys [22] / (III,155) *semiratas*: demi freynz / (III,158) *sacrilego*: ecumegé / (III,158) *aranea*: yreyne / (III,161) *radios*: landes / (III,161) *pensa*: fusels / (III,167) *populatrices*: devacceresses [23] / (III,185) *pedes*: peoner / [f.77va] (III,194) *moratur*: target / (III,196) *acies*: batayle / (III,217) *aptavit*: teyset / (III,227) *lubrica*: encullurg-

---

[20] A reflex of *arena*?
[21] Here, as in the gloss to III,435, the MS clearly has 'y' with a point above it.
[22] The gloss has been misplaced above *atria* in the following line.
[23] The fifth letter is obscured. Read *devaçteresses*?

able[24] / (III,235) *mutat*: cauncelet / [f.77vb] (III,239) *rubigine*: de roys / (III,240) *ligustra*: primeroles / (III,241) *lilia*: lys / (III,242) *rauco*: roy / (III,246) *exanimem*: demey mort / (III,259) *sen[i]um*: la veylesse / (III,264) *ludibria*: aveysurus / (III,276) *sopor*: somul / (III,277) *amplexus*: anbracement / (III,361) *explorat*: serchyt / (III,363) *merces*: marchandise / (III,364) *mollitur*: aparaylet / (III,365) *fagos*: lé fous / [f.78ra] (III,371) *cespite*: bleyte / (III,377) *excerta*: depeylé / (III,383) *fastigia*: hautesses / (III,383) *haneli*: echiné / (III,384) *nulli pervia*: non persable / (III,395) *hiatum*: l'abay-ment / (III,399) *strident*: noysent / (III,401) *inocciduos*: nent cheabeles / (III,405) *explicuere*: acheverunt / (III,407) *cedas*: branduns / (III,411) *discrimene*: par la de-severance / [f.78rb] (III,412) *prochorum*: de daneur / (III,421) *instantibus*: apre-cheauns / (III,423) *tihatis* (=thiasis): de feyris[25] / (III,425) *fatescunt*: defaylent / (III,426) *sulci*: reuns / (III,435) *genarum*: de no youes / (III,436) *fortasse*: par avan-ture

5. Statius, *Achilleis* ff.78rb–84va[26]

[f.78rb] (I,1) *mangnanimum*: .i. hardi / (I,1) *formidata*: .i. duté / (I,11) *tempora*: lé temples / [f.78va] (I,17) *trepidum*: .i. dutés / (I,24) *invisis*: .i. haynnuses / (I,26) *auguria*: divinaylles / (I,55) *armigeri*: .i. aquiers / (I,55) *scopulosa*: .i. rochuses / (I,55) *cete*: porpeys / [f.78vb] (I,65) *rupit*: a debrusé / (I,72) *obrue*: .i. agraventét / (I,76) *scopulos*: .i. roches / (I,86) *tepidos*: teves / (I,95) *demissa*: abessé / (I,98) *torquet*: lancet / (I,100) *vada*: lé wes / (I,107) *arcu*: .i. voçure / [f.79ra] (I,108) *ruperat*: debrusé / (I,113) *orni*: de cheynne / (I,131) *infestos*: haynnuses / (I,132) *livere*: .i. abloyr(z) / [f.79rb] (I,168) *leenam*: .i. lyonesse / (I,174) *connexus*: alacé / (I,185) *attonitam*: abayé / (I,190) *cestu*: .i. par talevas / [f.79va] (II,210) *chatenas*: .i. chennes[27] / (II,244) *vada*: wes / [f.79vb] (II,255) *Parcas*: .i. destyneys / (II,261) *pensa*: fusil / (II,262) *palla*: .i. mantel / (II,263) *verrere*: treynner / (II,283) *attonite*: .i. abayé / [f.80ra] (II,304) *vibrata*: croyllé / (II,320) *nectere*: alacer / (II,330) *choibet* (= cohibet): .i. afayteyt / [f.80rb] (II,348) *deducit*: .i. abesset / [f.80va] (III,426) *sidunt*: .i. abeyssunt / (III,428) *ceduntur*: sunt trenchez / [f.80vb] (III,459) *indago*: parke / (III,466) *cerua*: bice / [f.81ra] (III,477) *effosa*: .i. fué / (III,497) *possessa*: .i. pursis / (III,498) *Parcarum*: .i. destyneis[28] / [f.81va] (III,572) *thirso*: .i. baletun / (III,599) *antrum*: fosse / (III,612) *missile*: gaveloc / [f.81vb] (III,623) *era*: .i. clochers / (III,634) *tyrsis*: baletuns / (III,635) *tenuare*: .i. amenuser / (III,655) *tympana*: .i. taburs / [f.82ra] (IV,699) *cetu*: conpanie / [f.82rb] (IV,715) *Bachea*: .i. taburs[29] / (IV,724) *Agipptes* (= Agyrtes): .i. businur / (IV,747) *Moloso*: .i. Molosis .i. brachés / [f.82va] (IV,790) *velorum*: .i. de sigles / [f.82vb] (IV,819) *Agirte*: .i. businur / (IV,829) *terga*: .i. taburs / [f.83ra]

[24] The expected form is *esculurgable*, but prefixes in Anglo-Norman are notoriously unstable (see *aveysurus* for *envoiseure* at III,264).

[25] MS = *feyus*.

[26] Line references are to Clogan's edition. The same references may be applied to H. W. Garrod's edition for the Oxford Classical Texts if it is remembered that his division into two books corresponds to the division between books 4 and 5 in Clogan. Cf. Jeudy and Riou, *Rev. d'Hist. d. Textes* 4 (1974), 150, n.3.

[27] MS = *chonnes*.

[28] On f.81rb the gloss to I,553 *stimulat* is 'antysunt' which presupposes the attested variant *stimulant*.

[29] See the gloss to this and the following entry in Clogan, *ed. cit.*, p.95.

(IV,850) *tympana*: .i. taburs / (IV,853) *celatum*: .i. antayllé / [f.83va] (V,1) *inplicitum*: avolupé / (V,15) *exta*: .i. bowés / [f.83vb] (V,36) *latebris*: .i. repostaylles / (V,60) *penetralia*: secrés / [f.84ra] (V,100) *medullas*: lé meules / [f.84rb] (V,132) *cestum*: .i. talevas

MS CAMBRIDGE, PETERHOUSE 207 [vol.1]

1. *Disticha Catonis* ff.1r–6r
[f.5v] (IV,30) *complectere*: bracez / (IV,33) *velum*: sayl

2. Theodolus, *Ecloga* ff.6v–12v
[f.8v] (126) *focas*: porpays / [f.9r] (137) *magicas*: de sorserye / (141) *calidas* . . . *medullas*: chaude meules / (151) *hausit*: .i. transgluta / (151) *specus*: fosse / (154) *arida*: secke / (155) *sepeliverat*: foué / (156) *indagare*: sercher / (157) *oestro*: un taun / [f.9v] (159) *horrentibus*: hyduse / (159) *setis*: de payl / [f.10r] (189) *demissis*: abesez / [f.10v] (216) *comit*: la payl / (220) *geminatur*: est duble / (228) *lora*: lé reyns / (232) *opida*: chateus / [f.11r] (247) *capellas*: cheveres / (261) *thura*: ensens / [f.11v] (272) *infesta*: par heynouse petilense / (281) *tumido sermone*: par l'enflé parole / (285) *frondent*: branchisent / [f.12r] (294) *ab ulmo*: del ulmel / (308) *exuerit*: eyt depoulé / (308) *placari*: estre ansuagé / [f.12v] (321) *subsidat*: abeset / (337) *adipisci*: purchase / (339) *ultro*: de gré

3. Avianus, *Fabulae* ff.20r–26r [ff.13–19 have been cut out]
[f.21v] :(XXIX,3) *mole*: pesauntune / [f.22r] (XXIX,13) *agrestem* . . . *vitam*: vye de opelande[30] / (XXIX,18) *algenti*: frayt / [f.23r] (XXXIII,6) *exosas*: heynouses / (XXXIV,7) *pruinas*: gelés / [f.24v] (XXXVII,9) *pererras* .i. circuis: vyrounes / (XXXVIII,5) *foca*: porpeys / [f.25r] (XXXIX,7) *lituus*: grelet / (XXXIX,12) *submisso*: basé / (XL,1) *distinctus*: devisé / [f.25v] (XL,16) *pharetratis*: cowerés

MS LONDON, BRITISH LIBRARY, HARLEY 4967

1. Avianus, *Fabulae*: [f.92v] (IV,8) *ymber*: guter / [f.93v] (VII,13) *insultantem*: rechineant / [f.94r] (IX,8) re *fronde*, hic *frondator*: genus titemose[31] / [f.96v] (XVIII,11) *insistere*: assaverer / (XVIII,16) *discere*: aprendre / (XIX,1) *abies*: sapin / (XIX,8) *explicat*: estent / (XIX,9) *spineta*: spine / [f.97r] (XX,14) *vices*: feis / (XXI,3) *culmo*: jame, stele[32] / [f.97v] *popa*: gallice cropt[33] / [f.98r] (XXV,2) *rictibus*: sobing .g.[34] / [f.99r] (XXIX,18) *algenti*: enfredisant . . . *algere* enfreder / [f.99v] (XXXI,7) *fatigans*: enteriant / [f.101r] (XXXVI,12) *cultro*: a cuteel / (XXXVI,13) *indulgencia*: ese / [f.101v] (XXXVIII,4) *eximium*: noble / (XXXIX,13) *crepitantibus*: fere noyse

---

30 See OED sub *upland sb.*[2].
31 See OED sub *titmouse*.
32 *jame = chaume*. See OED sub *steal sb.*[1].
33 This gloss is entered at the top of the page, independent of the text.
34 See OED sub *sobbing*.

3. Treatise on deponent verbs: see vol.1, pp.153ff

6. Virgil, Eclogues: [f.126v] (I,18a) *cava*: crosé / ab *ilice*: du chene / [f.127r] (I,53) *sepes*: haye / [f.127v] (I,61) *finibus*: cuntreye / [f.128v] (II,50) *vaccinia*: primerole / [f.129v] (III,37) *celatum*: entalee / [f.130r] (III,87) *arenam*: gravele / [f.131r] (IV,50) *convexo*: enclin / [f.133r] (VI,16) *serta*: garlondechis / [f.134r] (VI,84) *pulse*: tochié / (VII,1) *ilice*: chene / [f.134v] (VII,28) *mala lingua*: malchrie[35] / (VII,33) *sinum*: chesevet[36] / *liba*: uasteys / [f.135r] (VII,42) *alga*: verc de mer[37] / (VII,49) *tede*: brandun / (VII,53) *castanee*: castenere / (VII,57) *aret*: ensechii / (VII,67) *revisas*: revises / [f.136v] (VIII,86) *bucula*: boveyt / (VIII,87) *ulv(u)a*: vreyc de mer, chrape[38] / [f.137r] (IX,9) *cacumina*: hautesse / (IX,15) ab *ilice*: de cheyne / [f.137v] in *collibus*: en tertris

7. The Satires of Persius: [f.140v] (I,82) *subcellia*: suscelys / (I,94) *delfin*: porpeys / (I,106) *pluteum*: carole / (right-hand margin) *villus* -li: gallice focheym .s. pars velleris[39] / [f.141v] (II,11) sub *rastro*: herse / [f.142r] (II,33) *salivis*: spoleys / (II,42) *tucetaque*: hacys[40] / [f.143v] (III,50) *anguste*: estreit / [f.144r] (III,93) *lenia*: sueif / (III,111) *algente*: fregisaunt / (III,113) *ulcus*: bose / (III,115) *alges*: frigessis / (IV,11) *ancipitis*: duble / *libre*: de balannse / (IV,18) *curata*: garri / *cuticula*: quir / (IV,21) *deterius*: de pis / *pannucia*: reclute / [f.145r] (IV,24) *mantica*: trusse / (IV,28) *computa* (corr. compita): quarfours / (IV,34) *despuat*: et qui ecrascheyt / (IV,40) *nates*: najes / *adunca*: croche / (IV,49) *vibice*: tayle / [f.145v] (V,29) *fibra* .i. martano corde meo: en la veyne / [f.146v] (V,74) *tesserula*: en une mesure / [f.146v] (V,86) *aceto*: de aysel / [f.147r] (V,112) *sorbere*: transg[l]uteer / [f.147v] (V,139) *onoforum*: chostrel / [f.148r] (V,170) *artos*: etreis / *casses*: reys / (V,175) *lictor*: serjang / (V,188) *allii*: des auyis / (re V,183: r.-h. margin) *tumet*: egrossiyt / [f.148v] (VI,35) *cinama*: canele / [f.149r] (VI,43) *a cesare*: de l'emperur / (VI,68) *inpensius*: plu largement / (VI,69) *caules*: cheuus, (olera)

9. Alan of Lille, *Parabolae*: [f.152v] (584A) ab *occasu*: achevement / (584A) *habitare*: menydre (corr. meyndre) / [f.154r] (586C) *fucus*: meloi, dron[41] / [f.154v] (587A) *mutua*: entrechaable / (587B) *luscus*: borne / [f.155r] (587C) *mantica*: trusse / (588A) *ramat*: enbranchit / [f.155v] (588B) *milvus*: coufle / (588B) *exta*: entrellis / [f.156r] (589A) *catellus*: cheel / (589A) *semel*: une fef / (589A) *plaustro*: char / [f.156v] (590A) *vindemianda*: envendenger / [f.157v] (591D) *filices*: feuger / [f.158v] (593A) *argilla[m]*: en arsil / (593A) *figulus*: poter / [f.159v] (extra line) *colum*: conil

---

[35] Cf. S. J. Borg (ed.), *Aye d'Avignon* (Genève, 1976), 1.2930 and see the glossary sub *malescherie*.
[36] See MED sub *chese n.3(b)*.
[37] i.e. 'wrec de mer', see OED sub *wreck sb.*[1]2.
[38] See AND sub *croupe* and OED sub *crap sb.*[1].
[39] The gloss is obscure.
[40] See MED sub *hagis n.*
[41] See MED sub *drane n.*

MS LONDON, BRITISH LIBRARY, ADD. 10089 (s.xv) [42]

Theodolus: [f.9r] (209) *obstruxit*: anglice stopped / (211) a *torrente*: a bek

Aesop: [f.13v] (Prol. 2) *seria*: ernest / (Prol. 7) *inercia*: dulnesse / (Prol. 12) *nucleum*: curnel / (I,1) *rigido*: styffe / (I,3) res . . . *preciosa*: bewte / [f.14r] (II,4) *inpugnat*: steryth / [f.14v] (IV,1) *in causam*: into plee / (V,2) *urget*: suachyth / [f.15r] (V,3) *fenore*: dauntage [corr. advantage?] / (VII,1) *vicinia*: neghburrede / [f.15v] (IX,1) *nectare*: pyment / [f.16v] (XII,13) *inepto*: ungayne / (XII,20) *fellitumque*: ymade bitter / [f.17v] (XVI,1) *ynglaceat*: chelyth / (XVII,1) *studio*: busynes / [f.19r] (XIX,7) *rediere*: rave / [f.20r] (XXII,10) *egens*: nedy / [f.21r] (XXVIII,4) *se metui*: to be adradde / (XXVIII,8) *metui*: to be dradde / [f.22r] (XXXII,3) *Parca*: wyche / (XXXIII,1) *ciconia*: storke / (XXXIII,2) *liquidus*: thynne / [f.22v] (XXXIV,9) *assensor*: clymer / [f.23v] (XXXVII,2) *causa*: plee / (XXXVII,3) *simius*: ape / [f.25v] (XLII,14) *reda*: cart / [f.26r] (XLV,11) *prefert*: preferryth / (XLVI,1) *studium*: busynes / [f.26v] (XLVI,3) *impetit*: assaylyth / (XLIII,9) *extorquere*: to wynde out / [f.27r] (XLIII,15) *perde*: destrue / [f.27v] (LXVI,1) *irretit*: cumbryth / [f.28v] (XLIX,6) *obside*: a borow / [f.29v] (LIII,5) *sculpere*: sckope / [f.30r] (LIV,5) *cribella*: tymbyrs / (LIV,5) *timpana*: tabyrs / [f.30r] (LV,1) *avia silve*: wayles placys / (LV,3) *equora campi*: playne felde / (LV,10) *munit*: storyth / (LV,21) *munit*: storyth / [f.30v] (LV,25) *esse suum*: hys owne man / (LVIII,17) *differt*: dyfferryth / [f.31r] (LXVIII,19) *differt*: dyfferryth / [f.31v] (LXVIII,20) *sollicitat*: travaylyth / [f.32r] (LXVIII,46) *prodiga*: lavase

MS OXFORD, BODLEIAN LIBRARY, AUCT. F. 5. 6 [43]

Claudian, *De raptu Proserpinae*: [f.59r] (I,25) *penetralia*: lé privitez / *pandite*: demou-trét / (I,28) *dotale chaos*: confusiun duarie / (I,29) *genitrix erravit anxia cursu*: le mere errat anguysus curs / (I,32) *dux herebi*: Pluto de enfern / *tumidas*: par gros / *exarsit*: enardat / *iras*: iris / (I,34) *conubiis*: a mariagis / [f.59v] (I,38) *in turmas*: en lé chilez / *aciem*: le host / (I,39) *furie*: ragis de enfern / (I,40) *quatiens*: crulaund / *in fausto* (sic): devinal / (I,43) *penitus*: de tut en tut / *remisso*: rachi / (I,45) *celeste iubar*: celestiene clarté / (I,47) *fulmina*: foudris / (I,48) *Parce*: mes destinez / (I,49) *severa*: le cruel / *fudere*: parplierunt / (I,50) *cum simplice fletu*: par humble gayment / (I,53) *pensis*: par fusilis / [f.60r] (I,69) *turbine rauco*: par roy tempeste / (I,70) *glacie*: par glas / *nivali*: de nif / (I,71) *hispidus*: .i. velu / *getica* . . . *grandina*: par gresil de Gete / [f.61r] (I,112) *intemerata*: nen defolé / (I,128) *torva parens*: bloye mere / (I,131) *pronuba*: baudestrot / [f.64r] (I,276) *humida*: mueli / (I,277) *ceruleis*: blois / *bigis*: chars / [f.64v] (I,282) *stangnaque*: flestisable / *marcida*: estuz / [f.65v] (II,8) *terribilis*: pountable / *mugitibus*: mugicemens / [f.66v] (II,46) *duces*: le gyis / (II,48) *ceruleusque* . . . *radiatur*: le bloyse-runt / *alumpnis*: nefus / [f.67v] (II,103) *in collem*: in le somet / (II,109) *ilex*: chene / *laurus*: lorer (II,110) *denso*: pesse / (II,111) *hulmos*: elme / (II,115) *pervius*: avantal-

---

[42] I have not annotated these exclusively English glosses, which fall strictly outside the scope of the present study. Line references are to Gualterus Anglicus as edited in J. Bastin, *Recueil général des Isopets* 2 (Paris, 1930), pp.7–66.
[43] The *De raptu Proserpinae* is found on ff.58v–81v and the line references are to the edition of J. B. Hall.

able / [f.68v] (II,143) *vellit*: rachit / (II,152) *fragor*: noyse / (II,156) *amfractus* . . . *opacos*: cravase / [f.69r] (II,169) *devia*: forviabletés / [f.72v] (II,360) *remos*: averun / (II,361) *processerat*: aveyt issu.

MS LONDON, BRITISH LIBRARY, ADD.41476 [44]

Persius, *Satyrae*: [f.3v] (III,9) *rudere*: brayer / [f.4r] (III,39) *[a]era*: boceneus / (III,55) *polenta*: de gruel / (III,59) *oscitat*: baleyit / [f.5r] (III,91) *currere*: gallice bater / (III,113) *ulcus*: un boce / (IV,2) *cicute*: herbe mortifere / [f.5v] (IV,38) *inguinibus*: in flankyz / [f.6r] (IV,43) *vivitur*: lev / (IV,49) *vibice*: tayl / [f.6v] (V,31) *bulla*: gallice campornole / (V,53) *vivitur*: lev / [f.8v] (V,190) *crassum*: sein

---

[44] The text of Persius (beginning at II,40) is found on ff.3r–9v. The MS also contains an incomplete copy of John of Garland's *Compendium grammatice* (ff.10r–21v) and an unglossed text, also incomplete, of his *Accentarium* (ff.22r–45v).

CHAPTER FOUR

THE GRAMMARS

Alexander of Villa Dei: Doctrinale

THE LONDON, DURHAM AND DUBLIN MANUSCRIPTS

(–) *reformans*: gallice refetaunt (D) / (–) *rictus*: gallice esshinemens, greninge (D)[1] / (56) *celtiber*: gallice espainel (D) gallice espaineus (T) / (98) *lanx*: esquele (D) / (111) *lienis*: bouel (T) / *lienteria*: menisun (T) / (112) *renis*: gallice ren, anglice nere (D) / (130) *epatis*: gallice feye (T) / (–) *acer*: gallice mapil, anglice arable [sic!] (D) / (143) *ebur*: ewr (T) / (re 158) *obses*: ostage (A) gallice hostage (D) / (164) *cuspidis*: gallice poynte (D) / (166) *exanguis*: pale (T) / (169) *ibidis*: sigoyne (T) / (188) *aceris*: gallice equiralie (D) gallice escurrayle (T) / (191) *grus*: gallice grue (D) / (210) *lodix*: anglice weytyl, gallice lawgel (T)[2] / (211) *mastico, -cas*: anglice chowe (T) / (215) *filicis*: feuger (A) gallice feugere, anglice brake (D) / (–) *lactes*: letenge, anglice rouie (T)[3] / (225) *restim*: anglice corde (D) / (237) *gausape*: nape (D) / *presepe*: gallice creche (D) / *cepe*: gallice huniun (D) / (re 255) *monilia*: gallice nuche, anglice broche (D) / *alvearia*: gallice ruches, anglice hive (D) / (re 274) *menceps*: gallice abay (D) / (303) *acus*: agule (T) / *arcus*: arc (T) / (304) *portus*: haven (T) / *artus*: gallice membre (T) / (304) *lacus*: wé (T) / *verubus*: gallice spitis (D) / (366) *zizania*: garciri (A) jarezel (T) gallice jarzeri,[4] anglice cockil (T, right-hand margin) / (368) *amigdala*: almaunder (T) / (374) *carbasus*: gallice sigle (D) / (375) *arbutus*: gallice cireneres, anglice sirne-tre (D)[5] eglenter (T) aube espine (A) / *intuba*: humeloc (A) humbeloc (T) / *Pergama*: le mur de Troye (A) / (377) *rastrum*: rastel (A) / *porrum*: gallice porré (D) / (384) *suparus*: gallice rochet (D) / (386) *peleus* [= pileus]: hure (A) / (390) *penus*: celer (AT) / *colus*: conil, anglice roke (D)[6] / (391) *cantus, -tus*: chaunsun, *-ti*: felu (A)[7] / (393) *cera* (= sera): lok (A) / *jugum*: yok (A) / *limus*: bouue (A) / *animus*: mag (A) (?) / (399) *lacus*: wé (T) / (400) *humentia*: humur (A) / (403) *lupinus*: gallice vesce (D) / (–) *appello*: gallice ariver (D) / (418) *exta*: gallice bueus (D) / (420) *nuptias*: gallice esposalies (D) / (440) *sospes*: gallice estu (D) / (446) *glis* (terra): arcil (A) arçail, arsil (T) / *glis* (lappa): gleytiner (A) gletener (T) / (447) *glissis*: arcil (A) / (449) *tignus vel tignum*: gallice cheverun vel anglice raftre[8] (D) trepfe (T) / (451) *glomus*: lucel (A) gallice lussel de fil (D) / (512) *siler*: osier (A) / *rubus*: anglice busk (D)[9] / (513) hic *siler*: .a. osier / *vimen*: osyer (T) / hoc *siler*: quedam herba que gallice vocatur mintte (T)[10] oser (A) / (re 511) *ficus*: feg (A)

---

1 See MED sub *grenninge ger.* and AND sub *eschiner*.
2 See TL 5,141 sub *langel* and OED sub *whittle sb.*[1].
3 See FEW 5,112b and OED sub *roe*[2] and *rown*. Cf. MED sub *milk n.3*.
4 See Gfry 4,636a sub *jargerie*. In T's *jarzeri* the 'z' is written over an expuncted 'g'.
5 See MED sub *sirve* and AND sub *cenele*.
6 See OED sub *rock sb.*[2].
7 See MED sub *felwes n.(pl.)*. Singular forms are described as rare.
8 See OED sub *rafter*.
9 See MED sub *bush n.(1)*. Notes at the top of f.55r in MS A include 'domiduca, "acer-buyf"[?]; carduenus, "goldfing"; capiterium, "gibelot"; acromellum, "grut"; granomellum, "malt"; lapatium: "clite'.
10 See MED sub *minte n.(1)*. At the bottom of f.124v MS T has 'brom, siler a. uiker', see OED sub *wicker sb.1*.

/ (513a) *viburnum*: gallice auburne (D) / *vimen*: oser (A) osiere (D) / (519) *ydola*: gallice maumés (D) / (545) *mustela*: wesel, belet (T) / *balena*: anglice wal (D) / (552) *cento*: feuter (A) gallice feuter (T) / (559) *unio* (lapis pretiosus): gallice perle (T) / (–) *mimos*: gallice jugulurs (A) jogelurs (T) / (572) *ren*: gallice renun, anglice kideneir (D)[11] / *pecten*: plaiz (D) / *splen*: anglice milte (D) / (573) *lien*: buel (A) / (576) *delphines*: gallice purpeys (D) / (re 579) *torcular*: gallice pressur (D) / (582) *spinter*: ficail (T) / *ruder*: guter (T) / (583) *campester*: chopeter (T) / (584) *celeber*: vestivable (A) festivable (T) / *celer*: ignel (T) / *saluber*: saluable (T) / (re 578) *geralagodium*: gallice treacle (T) / (–) *lagana et pultes*: cakis ant keris;[12] cake, turtel (T) / (600) *marmor*: marbele (T) / (606) *turtur*: turbut (A) gallice turbot (T) / (607) *furfur*: gallice dicitur bren (A) gallice bren (T) / (–) *pir*: brinston (A) / (617) *teges*: bordés, tegeus, hulet (A) / (618) *compes*: gallice bue de fer, firgis (D) / (621) *hebes*: gallice rebuc (AT) / *prepes*: inel (A) / *teres*: rund (T) / (624) *verres*: sengler (T) / (re 630) *erarius*: cheytur le rei (A)[13] / (632) *caulis*: cholet (T) / *edilis*: senescal (T) anglice meire (D)[14] / (637) *bipennis*: gallice hache daneche (D) hache danesche (T) / (638) *restis*: ruddir (T)[15] / *lactis*: letense, anglice makcroune (D)[16] / (639) *cuspis*: gallice pointe (D) / (640) *glis*: gallice glettunere (D) / (641) *clunis*: croper (A) anglice crupe equi (D) crupe de equo (T) / *ibis*: cigoyne (T) / (642) *orexis*: vomisement (A) / (644) *tricuspis*: anglice treble pointe (D) / (650) *melos*: melodie (T) / (652) *cos*: cheuz, anglice weston (D) / (655) *sinodus*: anglice sene (D)[17] / (657) *smaragdus*: meraude (A) gallice amiraude (D) gallice merroude (T) / *vannus*: fan, wan (T)[18] / *colus*: conil (T) / *jacinctus*: fuit quidam puer et fuit mutatus in florem, anglice bluwed[19] (T) blowet (A) / (656) *cristallus*: cristal (T) / *alvus*: anglice hellerin (T)[20] / *biblus*: gallice bible (T) / (660) *vulgus*: racail (T) / (669) *anus*: veyle (T) / *porticus*: porche (T) / (670) *acus*: aguil (T) / *nurus*: suore, brue (T) / (671) *specus*: fosse (A) / (679) *forceps*: scisurs (T)[21] / *adipatum*: gallice brués (D) / (680) *celebs*: gallice chaste (D) / (681) *effrons*: gallice baud (D) / (685) *pelex*: gallice rivayl (A) rivayle (T) gallice helye (D)[22] / *pulex*: gallice fle (D)[23] / *vibex*: anglice uale (T)[24] /

11 See MED sub *kide-nere* n.
12 See MED sub *cake* n. and Thurot, *op. cit.*, p.530 who cites a gloss 'polenta est potio de farina et aqua, anglice keres'. In MS T the gloss is part of a translation of a Latin phrase and runs 'cakis ant keris makin bare w. . .'
13 The gloss remains obscure.
14 See MED sub *mair(e* n.
15 The gloss is apparently mistaken, see OED sub *rudder* sb.
16 See note 3 above. Presumably *mack-* is a misreading of *milk-*.
17 See OED sub *sene* sb.[3].
18 See MED sub *fan(ne* n.
19 See MED sub *bleuet* n.
20 The lemma has been misread as *alnus*, see MED sub *hilder* n. and *ellern*.
21 In the margin of f.92r MS D has 'gallice cisuris' and *decutit* appears to be glossed 'gallice delochit'.
22 I do not understand this gloss. MS A explains the lemma thus: 'rivayl est quando tres mulieres aderent uno viro, rivales quando tres vel plures homines'[?]
23 The gloss is English, see MED sub *fle* n.
24 See OED sub *wale* sb.[1].

supellex: utilemens gallice (T) / (686) *forpex*: guinole (A) gynole, uinnere (T) [25] / *cortex*: anglice bark (D) / (687) *silex*: cailoe (A) caylou, caylow (T) gallice flint [sic] (D) / *ramex* (mentula): gallice culiuns (D) / (re 687) *filix*: gallice feugere, anglice brake (D) / (688) *frutex*: anglice grene (A) gallice bussun (D) bussun (T) / *sandix*: ueede, anglice tasil (A) anglice madir, gallice warence (D) [26] uede (T) / *carex*: star (T) [27] / (690) *fornix*: gallice bordel (D) *silex* (= Cilix, pirata): gallice robeur de mer (D) / (691) *mastix*: anglice madir (A) / *calx*: anglice brend lim (D) / (–) *fatigat*: anglice woriet (A) [28] / (–) *frigo*: frire (A) gallice frire (D) / *frigeo*: enfreider (A) enfreder (T) / (693) *victrices*: gallice venkeresse (D) / *turbe*: cumpanies (D) / (–) *anguem*: anglice snake (D) / (re 709) *applico*: gallice ariver (D) / (re 714) *frico*: gallice froter (D) / (–) *repungere*: repupuer (A) [29] / (719) *nexo*: gallice alacer (D) / (752) *adultus*: gallice parcru (D) / (769) *neo*: anglice spinnin (D) / (772) *sorbeo*: gallice humer (DT) / *sorbilla*: anglice rope (D) / (803) *ruo*: trebucher (T) / (–) *lacesso*: atarier (T) gallice entarier (D) / (–) *arcesso*: apeler (T) / (re 822) *incus*: gallice emclume, anglice stit (D) [30] / (–) *mandibula*: anglice chanil (T) [31] / (831) *tundo*, *tusum*: gallice batu, anglice stampin (D) / (832) *rudo*: gallice recaner (D) / (re 837) *cedo*: gallice trencher (D) / (re 841) *scindula*: anglice blade (D) [32] / (868) *repetit*: reprent (T) / (869) *salo* (= sallo): gallice saler (D) / (872) *psallere*: saler (T) / (894) *pinso*: pincer (D) / (re 915) hic *campso*: gallice chanjur (D) / (923) *sepio*: gallice fere haye (D) / (936) *fateor*: regeir (T) [33] / (940) *proficiscor*: espleyter (T) / (re 941) *na[n]ciscor*: purchacer (T) / (962) *lingo*: engluer (A) / (964) *scalpo*: gallice grater (D) / *scabo*: grater (A) / (972) *estuo*: bulier (A) bullier (D) / *strideo*: facere noise (A) gallice cruser (D) / (973) *conquinisco*: encliner (A) / (–) *presepe*: cresche (D) / (–) *reno*: pelichun (D) / (980) *largior*: je done, je su duné (T) / *experior*: prover (T) / *veneror*: onore (T) *moror*: more (T) / *osculor*: baise (T) (these glosses to 1.980 in s.xiv hand) / (981) *criminor*: blame (T) / *amplector*: embrace (T) (these two glosses also in s.xiv hand) / (–) *Hesperiam*: gallice Lumbardie (D, citing Lucan *Phars.* 5,533–4) / (–) *juvencus*: gallice bover (D) / (–) *pelex*: rivaile (D) / (re 1021) hec *mala*: gallice goue (T) / (1698) *corea*: gallice charole (D) / (1703) *scabo*: grater (A) / (1704) *labo*: chanseler (A) / (1707) *strabo*: gallice borne (D) / (1709) *acer*: mapyl (T) arable (D) / *acerbus*: egre (T) / (1710) *paciscor*: gallice fere covenaunt (D) / (1713) *graculus*: gay (A) gallice gay (D) / (1714) *vada*, hoc vadum: gallice wé (D) wés (A) / (1715) *suadeo*: amonester (A) / (1716) *traduco*: gallice trahyr (sic!) (D) / (1717) *Gades*: gallice merches (D) / (re 1718) *nafer*: gallice koynte (D) / (1720) *saga*: sorseresse (A) sai (D) gallice say (T) / *vagina*: gallice escaubers (D) / (1721)

---

25 See TL 4,790 sub *guinde* and 791 sub *guinole*.
26 See OED sub *woad sb.*[1] and FEW 17,471b (**waizda*).
27 See OED sub *star sb.*[3].
28 See OED sub *worry v.*
29 I do not recognise this word.
30 See OED sub *stith sb.*
31 The gloss is inaccurate, see MED sub *chanel n.4(a)*.
32 See MED sub *blade n.3(a)*.
33 See TL 8,658 sub *rejehir*. In the right-hand margin of f.61v MS A has 'cambire, chaunger; hoc fartum, gallice pochoun; stertere, anglice routhe'.

lagana: turtel (A) crampecake (DT) [34] / *indago*: gallice parc (D) [35] / (1723) *fragor*: noise (D) / (1726) *phalam*: gallice bretasche (D) / (1729) *palus*: gallice wé (D) / *ales*, *-litis*: gallice hoysel (D) / (1730) *balista*: gallice alblast (D) / (1731) *balena*: anglice wal (D) / (1736) *lamina*: plate (A) gallice plateyn (T) / *lamentor*: waymenter (D) / (1739) *anabatrum*: cortine gallice (T) / (re 1740) *sanies*: gallice purture (D) / (1741) *ganeo*: huler (A) lechur (D) / (re 1737) *canus*: chanue (D) / (1738) *anas*: gallice malard (D) / (1742) *vapulo*: je su batu (D) / (re 1742) hoc *papatum*: anglice pappe (D) [36] / (1743) *lappa*: gletunere (D) / (1744) *mappa*: nape (A) / *rapa*: nep, gallice navet (A) un navet, anglice nep (D) / (1747) *carex*: gallice ros, anglice star (D) gallice glagel (A) / (1748) *naris*: naril (T) / *area*: place (D) / *glarea*: gleyr (A) gallice gleyre (D) / (–) *paraphonista*: hauth chantour (A) / (1753) *casa*: bordel (A) / (1754) *basium*: gallice beyser (D) / (1755) *quaternus*: quaer (D) / (1757) *vates*: gallice poete (D) / *laterna*: gallice launterne (D) / (1769) *nebo*, de neo: gallice filer (D) / (1771) *fecis*: gallice lie (D) lie de vin (A) / *cecus*: visere (A) wgle (D) / (1772) *vecors*: gallice chuard (D) / (1773) *theca*: un dayel (D) / (1777) *sedulus*: ententif (D) / (1778) *seditiosus*: gallice trecherus (sic!) (D) / *seditio*: traysoun (A) / (1786) *scelus*: feluneye (A) / *melus*: tessun, broc (A) [37] / (1800) *venum*: vente (A) vent (D) / (1801) *venor*: adquire vel chaser (T) / *tenia*: gallice frenge (D) / *tena*: gallice koyfe (D) / (1809) *ceraunum*: ponitur pro ceraunium per cincopam et sunt ceraunia elevationes aquarum in mari turbido gallice wawes (D) [38] / (1811) *erumpna* (= aerumna): gallice mesese (D) / *ceruleus*: gallice bloye (D) / (1812) *(h)eruca*: herba vel radix est interitans libidinem, anglice scirewittis (A) [39] / *ceroma*: blaunchet (AT) / (1816) *veru*: gallice gose spit (sic) (D) broche (T) / *veratrum*: gallice eble, uallewort (A) gallice eble, quedam herba anglice waleworth (T) / (1818a) *pera*: gallice scrippe (D) / *pero*: rivelins (D) / (1821) *fretus*: gallice husé (D) / (1827) *bever*, hoc luter: hoter, a broc (A) [40] / (1828) *tribulus*: gallice runce, anglice wede (D) / (1829) *tribula*: schovele (A) scovele (D) / *fibula*: tache (ADT) / (–) *petulium*: gallice bosun (D) / (1830a) *viburnum*: gallice auburne (D) / (1831) *libum*: wastel (A) gastel (D) uastel (T) / *libo*: gaster (D) / *vibex*: uale (T) / (1832) *libra*: inde hec vibrella quodam pondus vel vibra gallice tumbrel (A) / *vibra*: tumberel vel bray, anglice brake (T) [41] / (1834) *spiculum*: broche (D) / (1835) *vicus*: rue (D) / *mica*: mie (D) / (1836) *picus*: anglice notehace (DT) [42] / *vicenus*: vintane (D) / *phicedula*: gallice oriole, anglice wodewale (D) [43] / (1837) *spica*: anglice here (T) [44] / *pica*: pye (D) pie (T) / (1838a) *sicarius*:

[34] See MED sub *cram-cake n.*
[35] In the left-hand margin of f.77r MS A has 'hic gamarus, anglice starpink', the last word being written with what looks like a superscript 'l' over the 'p' (but see OED sub *pink sb²*.) by a late-thirteenth-century hand in darker ink.
[36] See MED sub *pap n.*
[37] See MED sub *brok n.*
[38] See OED sub *wave sb.* and FEW 17,418a.
[39] See OED sub *skirret¹*. In the left-hand margin of f.78v MS A has 'narstucie anglice welle crasses', see MED sub *cresse n.1(a)*.
[40] See MED sub *oter n.* and *brok n.* The latter is an erroneous gloss here.
[41] See MED sub *brake n.(1)(c)*.
[42] See MED sub *note-hach(e n.*
[43] See OED sub *woodwall.*
[44] See MED sub *er(e n.(2)(a)*.

merdrischur (D) / (1840) *fido*: afier (T) / (1844) *strideo*: gallice cruser (D) / (1845) *ydolum*: gallice maumet (D) / (1848) *pige*: gallice nage et hic et hec *depigis* .i. anus, clunus: crowpe (T) / (1849) *migro*: passer (AD) / *frigo*: frier (AD) / (1850) *stigo*: entarier (D) / (1851) *strigilis*: anglice horsekomb (D) / (–) *in horreo*: en la grange (D) / (1853) *filomena*: rusinole (D) ruscinole (T) / *filix*: pheugere (D) brake (T) / *Cilix*: robeur de mer (D) / (1854) *pilus*: peil (T) / *pila*: pelote (D) pelot (T) / (1857) *fimus*: fens, mok (D) / (1858) *simia*: singe (T) / (1862a) *coagula*: macuns, cruddes (D)[45] / (1864) *ciphus* (= cippus): cep (A) / *stipo*: apower (T) / *stipula*: anglice stubbil (D) / *stipes*: gallice trunk (D) / *stipite*: apual (A) / (1868) *pirus*: perer (A) / (1869) *mirica*: genest (D) / *stiria*: gallice glaçun, anglice hichil (D)[46] / (1870) *pirula*: bec (T) / *pirata*: galey (A) robeur de mer (D) galie (T) / (1874) *ambitio*: cuveytise (D) / (1875) *clitella*: cofre (D) fardel (T) / (–) *clenodium*: une juele (D) / (1876) *sitacus*: papegay (A) gallice papingay (D) / *titillo*: katilher, anglice tikelin (D) catellir (T) / (1877) *Italus*: lumbard (D) / *glitis*: gletun (A) / (re 1879) *ritus*: custume (D) / (1880) *vitellum*: muel del of (A) anglice yelke (D) moyl (T) / (1888) *jocor*: enveycer (T) / (1890) *foca*: porpeys (AT) gallice baleyne, anglice wal, porpeis (D) / (re 1894) *modius*: anglice kumbe, et dividitur quartus (D)[47] / (1897) *offa*: soppe (D) / (1898) *toga*: anglice gunel (D)[48] / (1900) *colo*, -is: cotefier (D) / *colo*, -as: coler (D) / (1902) *boletus*: musserun (D) muscerun (T) / (1903) *po(p)lipus*: gallice crabbe (T) / *solum*: base (T) / *cola*: gallice entuneur (D) / *colas*: coler (A) *colum*: sas (MS. sar) (A) / (1904) *sollemnis*: festivable (T) / *sollers*: coymte (sic) (D) / (1906) *omentum*: anglice wyting (A)[49] / *omasum*: tripe (A) / (1908) *glomus*: lucel (AD) / *glomero*: musceler (A) munceler (D) / (1914) *soporus*: gallice endormi (D) / (1915) *opilio*: bercher (A) / (1919) *scopulus*: gallice roche (AD) / *scophinus*: hanaper (A) / (1922) *torax*: hauberc (A) / (1923) *morus*: anglice mulbery (A) / (1926) *provincia*: pays (A) / (1936) *ruber*: bussun (D) / (1937) *tuber*: bose, gallice musse(ce)run (T) / *rubigo*: ruel (A) rul (D) / *suber*: scorce (A) / (1938) *pubes*: penilis (A) gallice penul (T) / (1939) *pronuba*: baustrot (A)[50] / *bubulcus*: bover / (re 1941) *lucus*: pur boys (A) / (1942) *lucerna*: launterne (D) / (re 1943) *cucula*: cuwel (T) / (1945) *rudis*: bustuse (T) / (re 1945) *truda*: genus vehiculi sine rotis, anglice sclide (D) anglice slede, dreye (T)[51] / (1946) *cudo*: batre (A)[52] / (1950) *jugerum*: gallice aker de tere (D) / (1952) *uligo*: mareys (D) / (1953) *fuligo*: gallice sue, anglice sod (D)[53] / *gulio*: glutun (D) / (1954) *fulica*: avis marina, moue (A) gallice blarie (D)[54] / (1956) *humerus*: espaule (D) espaude (T) / (1958) *strumam*: boce (A) bose (T) une boce (D) / (1960) *cuneum*:

---

45 See MED sub *crud* n. The gloss *macuns* is probably a miscopying of some reflex of *mesgua* ('whey'), read *macuus*?
46 See MED sub *ikel* n.
47 See MED sub *coumb* n.(1).
48 See MED sub *gonel* n.
49 The Latin gloss reads 'ventris pinguedo'. I do not know the English word.
50 See MED sub *baud(e-strote* n.
51 See OED sub *slide* sb. I.4a and MED sub *draie* n.
52 In the left-hand margin of f.81v in MS A a fourteenth-century hand has added 'cambucam, cambuk ... sambucam, hellerne ... cuna, hole ... cippus, anglice stokkes'.
53 See OED sub *soot* sb.[1].
54 Confusion of this sort over the identity of *fulica* is common in grammatical MSS.

vehcg (colesio militum, A) weg (A) anglice wegh (D) [55] / (1962) *cupa*: cuve, anglice fat (A) [56] hanap (D) / *stupa*: anglice herdes (D) [57] / *upupa*: lapuhing, wype, vanel (A) *hupapa*: gallice vanele, anglice lepwinkel (D) / *pupa*: gallice venele (T) [58] / (*) *pupa*: anglice puppe, gallice pupie (D) [59] / (1967) *susurro*: grundiller (D) / (1969) *frutex*: busun (D) bussun (T) / *putris*: gallice puaunt (D) / (1971) *puteo*: gallice puer (D) / *glutio*: trangluter (A) / (1972) *futio*: esspaundre (A) / (re 1974) *uva*: grape (D) / (1978) *venabula*: anglice borespere (D) [60] gaveloc (T) / (1979) *cloaca*: une lungayne (D) / (re 1979) *psitacus*: un papegay (D) gallice papingay (T) / (1982) *cicada*: anglice greshop (D) gressop (T) [61] / (1983) *elephas*: olifaunt (A) / (1988) *toral*: gallice tapit (D) / (1997) *aranea*: iraine (D) / (1997a) *balanatum* .i. fimberatum: gallice frengé, anglice raggid (D) [62] / (2000) *Priape*: deus ortorum, gallice babeweyne, qui stat in ortis et in blado et vocatur larva (T) [63] / *sinapis*: seneveye (D) / *sinapium*: mustard (D) / (2001) *barbarus*: estraunge (D) / *zedoare*: gallice cedewale (D) / (2006) *caparis*: gallice cherful (D) [64] / (2009) *omasum* est pellicula unde fiunt scruta: anglice felefold (D) [65] / (re 2011) *dominatus*: seynhurie (D) / (2014) hoc *scema*: ciment, anglice morter (D) / (2019) hic *athelebus*: gallice cattepeluse (D) [66] / (2020) *apoteca*: especerie (D) / (2029) *Alemanea*: Alemayne (T) / (2031) *(h)ebenus*: hauburne (A) / (2035) hec *statera*, lingua trutine: de la balaunce (D) / (2037) *galerus*: haume (A) chapel (T) / (2041) *crateram*: hanap (A) / (2049) *lebete*: caudrun (A) / (2055) *formica*: gallice formie (D) gallice furmeye (T)/ *umbilicus*: anglice navele (D) / (2056) *lorica*: hauberk (D) hauberc (T) / *mirica*: genest, brom (A) genest, anglice brom (D) / (2057) *vescia*: vesie (A) gallice fesie, anglice bladre (D) bleddir (T) / (2062) *filice*: gallice fougere, gallice (sic) brake (D) brake (T) / (re 2062) *silicis*: cayloue (A) / *silex*: gallice calou, anglice flint (D)/ *salice*: saus (A)/ *salix*: anglice salue (D) [67]/ *filicem*: feuger (A) / (2064) *masticem*: wod (A) / (2065) *lodicis*: veluce (A) langel (T) laungel (D) / (2075) *auriga*: gallice karter (D) / (2076) *calige*: gallice chauce (T) / (2080) *nubilis*: gallice mariable (T) / (2086) *caminus*: gallice chimené (D) / (2088) *salinum*: saler (T)/ *cuminum*: gallice comin (D) / (2092) *nundina*: gallice feyre (D) / (2093) *acinum*: marc de grape, marc de le grap (D) / (re 2095) *bombax*: cotun (D) / (–) *apoca* (corr. acopa): tayle (T) / *antipoca* (corr. anticopa): en-

---

55 See OED sub *wedge sb*.
56 See OED sub *vat sb*.
57 See MED sub *herd(e n.(3)*.
58 See OED sub *wype* and MED sub *lap-wink(e n*.
59 Cf. OED sub *puppy* 3[†]b.
60 See MED sub *bor n.1.5*.
61 See MED sub *gras-hoppe n*.
62 See OED sub *ragged a.*[1].
63 See DMLBS sub *babuinus*, MED sub *babewin n.* and Gfry 1,544c (*baboe*) and Compl., 265a (*babouin*).
64 See DMLBS sub *capparis* ('caper', also 'woodbine') and MED sub *chervel n.* and AND sub *cerfoil*. Confusion over plant names is very common, see T. Hunt, *Plant Names of Medieval England* (Cambridge, 1989).
65 I have found this word in several MSS, though it is not in the dictionaries. See, however, the obviously comparable *felo-ferþ* in Toller's Supplement to *An Anglo-Saxon Dictionary*.
66 See DMLBS sub *attelebus* and TL 2,314 sub *chate*.
67 See OED sub *sallow sb*.

cuntre-tayle (T) / (2097) *machina*: enchin (A) / *trutina*: balance (D) / *lamina*: plate (D) / (2098) *buccina*: gallice busine (D) bucine (T) / *fuscina*: gallice havet, anglice algere (D)[68] / (2098a) *fiscina*: gallice fecele, anglice chesefat (D)[69] / (2102) *constipo*: gallice apoer vel acostiver (D) / (2104) *siliquis*: gallice coce, anglice pod (D) / (re 2105) hic *titirus* est maior aries in grege .s. ille qui fert *nolam*: anglice belleweþer (D)[70] / (–) *lacticinium*: anglice witen (D)[71] / (2114) *margarita*: gallice perle (D) / (2115) hec *pituita* (est morbus gallinarum): anglice pippe (D) pipie (A)[72] / (2115) *polimita*: gallice pipelori (T) / (2118) *censu*: gallice chatel (D) / (re 2133) hic *gorges*: gallice gors (D) / (2135) *orobus*: anglice fiche (A)[73] / (2145) *sindonis*: sendel (T) / (2147) *vasconis*, de Vasconia: gaskoine (D) / (2148) *britonis*: gallice bretun (T) bretagne (A) / (2159) *castor*: lutre (A) / (2163) *alosa*: anglice scad fis (D)[74] gallice loche (T) breyne (A) / (re 2168) *eruca*: anglice karloc (D)[75] / (re 2172) *erugo*: anglice rust (D) / *subtellaris*: gallice souler (D) / (2173) *sugo*: sucre, anglice souke (A) sucher (T) / *sanguisuga*: anglice leche (A) / (2179) *alumen*: gallice alwm (T) / (2189) *cerusa*: blaunchet (A) blanchet (T) / (2190) *arbutus*: une cirevere (D) glenter (T) / (–) *Lingones*: gallice lengereys (D) / (re 2373) *ut parlare*, wesseylare (D)[76] / (2506) *piscina*: viver (A) / (2508) *aristas*: stuble (A) / (–) *[H]esperiam*: Lumbardie (A) / (2559) *ircos*: bukes (A) lé bucces (D) / *mulgere*: lettyr (A)

MS CAMBRIDGE, UNIVERSITY LIBRARY Oo. 6. 110 ff.1r–35v

(–) *yscis* (*ysco*): gallice abair / (–) *excessus*: gallice surmuntanse / (–) *Esperiam*: gallice Lumbardie / (–) *orator*: gallice pleydur / (1703) *scabo*: grater / (1704) *labo*: chanceler / (1709) *acer*: mapul / *acesso*: enegrir / (1712) *facundus*: renable / *Dachus*: deneys / (1713) *graculus*: fru, gay[77] / (1715) *spadix*: brun / (1717) *Gades*: merches / (1720) *vagio*: flere vel in vagina apponere waynter gallice / (–) *pera*: screpe / (1721) *indago*: parc / (1723) *plaga*: rey / (re 1722) *fagus*: bech / (1731) *alea*: table / (1733) *clamis* (= chlamys): mantel / (1744) *mappa*: mape / *rapa*: nep / (–) *Japix*, ventus qui dicitur nothus: vent de suy / (1746) *varicosus*: curte(?) / (1747) *carex*: rosel, ros / (1748) *area*: place / (1751) *ara*: autel / *ara*: porcherie / (–) *lacerna*: bifle / (1786) *scelus*: felunie / (1797) *penum*: celir / (1801) *tenia*: frenge / *tena*: coyfe / (1804) *cepa*: oynun / (1811) *cerulus*: bloy / (1812) *eruca*: skirewyt / (1816) *veru*: espey, spite / (1822) *meto*: seir / (–) *lienteria*: gallice munisun / (–) *pillea*: gallice hure / (512) *siler*: hosir / *dumus*: bussun / (re 540) *tibicen*: gallice estivur / *liricen*: gallice harpur / (548) *presepe*: cracche / (550) *cete*: wal anglice / (552) *cento*: feutre / (–) *pillei*: gallice hure / (–) *mimos*: juglurs / (567) *consul*: gallice aldre-

---

68   See MED sub *alger* n.
69   See MED sub *chese* n.3(b).
70   See MED sub *bel(le-wether* n.
71   See note 49 above.
72   See MED sub *pip(pe* n.
73   See MED sub *fecche* n.
74   See OED sub *scad*[3] and FEW 15,i,235a (brahsima) and var. in TL 1,1116.
75   See MED sub *cherlok* n.
76   Cf. OED sub *wassail* v.
77   See MED sub *jai* n.

man [sic] [78] / (re 573) *lienteria*: menisun gallice / (576) *delfin*: gallice porpays / (584) *silvester*: savage / *acer*: egre / *saluber*: gallice salvable / (583) *alacer*: gallice halegre / (591) *cucumer*: curde / hic *cucumer* vel *cucumis*: gallice gurde, wilde popi / (593) *cures*: gallice batel / (618) *compes*: gallice firges de fer / (–) *(h)abies*: sap / (632) *caulis*: cholet / *edilis* est maior ville: gallice mere / (re 633) *axis*: essel / (638) *restis*: hart / (641) *clunis*: crupe / (655) *synodus*: sene [79] / *costus*: ditanie / *carbasus*: sigle / (–) *pulex*: pusse / (685) *pelex*: gallice wale (sic) / *pulex*: gallice puce, nite [80] / (688) *frutex*: gallice bussun / (–) *filex* (sic): virn [81] / (–) *decutit*: delochez / (690) *Cilex*: gallice robur de mar (sic) / (691) *latomorum*: de massuns / (–) *farsio*: gallice farsir / (820) hic *cudex* idem quod faber: gallice abessur / (821) *cudo*: abesser / (848) *ambesus*, ab an, quod est circum, et esus, -sa, -sum: gallice mangé / (–) *ammicina*: anglice tike [82] / (869) *salo* (= sallo): gallice sallir / (892) *lacesso*: gallice entarier / (re 1021) *mala*: gallice jowe / (1829) *fibula*: tache mantelli / (1831) *libum*: wastel / (1832) *vibra*: gallice brake, inde *vibrilla*: petite peyse / (1834) *convicia*: ledenges / *spicula*: dart / (1833) *convicior*: gallice ledenger / (1835) *vicus*: rue / (1836) *ficedula*: gallice oriole, anglice wodewale / (1837) *licea*: helvelyred [83] / (1838) *sica*: gisarme / (1839) *fatidicus*: pleidur / (1845) *ydola*: maumés / (1844) *strideo*: noiser / (1846) *ciphus*: hanap / (1847) *fligo*: turmenter / (1848) *pige*: nages, cuyl / (1849) *migro*: passer / (1851) *stiga*, stigo, -gas .i. lacessito, -tas: gallice entarier / *strigilis*: estrille / (1853) *philomena*: russinole / *filix*: vern / (1854) *pila*: ludus pelote / (1856) *thima*: hunisoke / (re 1859) hec *lineo*, lineonis est vermis: anglice mathe [84] / (1866) *liquor*: decure / (1868) *pira*: pere / *antipira*: gallice echeren / (re 1869) *stiria*: anglice isichil [85] / *mirica*: gallice genet, brom / (1875) *clitella*: trusse / (1876) *psitacus*: papejay / *titillo*: gallice catiller / (1879) *opaca*: flaun gallice / (–) *nisus*: espervir / (1884) *obex* .i. obstaculum: stake anglice vel repagulum, barre / (1890) *phoca*: porpeys / (1967) *susurro*: grundiler / (1969) *frutex*: bussun / *uter*: bussel / *luto*: teynture [86] / (1971) *glutio*: trangluter / (1992) *timiana*: letuarie / (1993) *clibanus*: feyn in pratis vel furnus / (1997) *haranea*: yreyne / (2000) *sinapis*: senevee / (2001) *zeduare*: zedoale / (2009) *amasum* (corr. omasum) parvus mons vel amasum: tripe de berbis / (top of f.27r) *pantera*: anglice werewulf (2035) / *statera*: balance / (2037) *galerus*: haume / (2056) *lectica*: chere / *mirica*: genet, brom anglice / (2062) *filice*: gallice feugire, virn; fugire, anglice bil [87] / (–) *opilo*: astuper / (2086) *caminus*: chemenee / (2088) *cuminum*: cumin / *salvium*: salve, herba .s. ache / *caninum*: dubelir / (re 2093) *acumen*: est

---

[78] See MED sub *alder-man* n.
[79] See OED sub *sene* sb.[3].
[80] See MED sub *nite* n.(1).
[81] See MED sub *fern* n.(1).
[82] See OED sub *tick* sb.[1].
[83] See MED sub *heveld* n.(a) (*heveld-thred*). At line 1836 written over *ficedula picus* is the wild gloss 'nomen cuiusdam avis .s. butor'.
[84] See MED sub *mathe* n.
[85] See MED sub *ikel* n.
[86] In the right-hand margin is the line 'gaudet scropfa / true / luto / tay / gaudet caro scabida luto / colur /'.
[87] Either an element has dropped out before *-bil* or it is an erroneous gloss, *bilre*, see MED sub *biller(e* n.(2).

granum uve quod ponitur in vino, quod dicitur 'raspe',[88] vel granum quod remanet in uva vini, hoc *acumen*: gallice drasche / (2097) *trutina*: balance / (2098) *fuscina*: havet / (–) *fiscina*: [89] chesewat / *narstucium*: karse[90] / (2106) *papiro*: junc / (2107) *vitro*: glas, veys[91] / (2115) *polimita*: pipelori[92] / *pituita*: pippe / (–) *ambitus*: coveytise / (2133) *gurges*: gorz / (2135) *orobus*: gallice vesse / (–) *lens*, lendis: anglice nite / (2144) *amomum*: canele / (2145) *sindonis*: sandel / (–) *globum*: lussel / (2163) *alosa*: gallice turbut / (–) *cambucam*: croce / (2173) *sanguissugum* (sic): samsue / (2179) *alumen*: gallice marle / (2189) *cerusa*: blanket / (2190) *arbutus*: gletunir / at the bottom of f.34r in a hand of s.xiv ex.: *fatigatus*, -ta, -tum: anglice weri, gallice laz; ista via est fatigativa: anglice wersum[93]

MS CAMBRIDGE, PETERHOUSE 215 ff.30v–59r

(56) *lacer*: gallice desyré (hand of s.xiv) / (134) *stater*: balance / (144) *gigas*: giant / (146) *as*: maile / *vas*: gage / (164) *cuspidis*: poynte / (169) *ibis*: sygoynne / (210) *lodicis*: launge / (215) *filicis*: verne / (264) *sacerdotum*: preytre / (264) *custodum*: gardens / *locupletum*: riche / (–) *noctiluca*: glouybert[94] / (375) *arbitus* (= arbutus): eglenter / (375) *intuba*: emeloc / (406) *acies*: cumpaynie / (418) *exta*: buwés / (446) *lappa*: gletinel / (513) *siler*: idem in gallica lingua quod minte, siremuntayne / (538) *pincerna*: butiler / *lixa*: quistrun / (572) *ren*: kideney / (575) *syren*, monstrum maris: merminne[95] / (576) *delphin*: gallice porpas / (582) *spinter*: ficayl / *ruder*: guter, purgamentum coquine / *juger*: tertre / (624) *verres*: sengler / (638) *aspis*: serpente / (639) *cuspis*: poynte / (656) *cristallus*: cristal / *bissus*: chesil / (657) *vannus*: vannee / *colus*: conille / (669) *porticus*: porche / (671) *specus*: fosse / (677) *calibs*: steel .i. asser / (685) *pulex*: fle .i. puce / *pelex*: rivayle / (686) *forpex*: wyndre / (687) *silex*, hic vel hec, lapis: flint / (688) *frutex*: .i. bussun / (690) *fornix*: bordel / (691) *latomorum*: maçuns / (715) *plicat*: preter / (717) *dimico*: cumbatre / (769) *neo*: spinne, idem est quod filer / (867) *vello*: pur arascer / (869) *salo*: saler / (961) *compesco*: refrener / *cremo*: duter / (962) *lambo*: lescher / *metuo*: duter / *urgeo*: destrendre / (964) *scabo*: grater / (–) hec *fulgetra*: orpeter / (–) *aqualicium*: lavur / (964) *scalpo*: grater / (972) *sterto*: runfler / *strido*: grennet[96] / (1709) *acerbus*: egre / (1712) *facundus*: renable / (1713) *graculus*: jay / (1714) *vada*: wés .s. lake / (1715) *spadix*, hic, est color fuscus vel equus ementulatus: ambli[97] / (1717) *Gades*: merks / (1719) *strages*: occisiun / (1720) *vagio*: abraer / *magalia*: lé hulés / *stragula*: vesture raee / *saga*: queute / (1721) *indago*: ensercher / (1722) *flagellum*: flael / (1723) *ora*: cuntre / (1729) *palus*:

---

88 See FEW 16,671a.
89 MS = *fuscina*.
90 See MED sub *cresse n.*
91 corr. *veyr*.
92 See TL 7,966–7 sub *pipoler*.
93 i.e. 'weary', 'wearisome'.
94 See MED sub *glou-berd* n. Cf. K. Bitterling, 'Middle English "glouberd" "a doormouse" ', *Notes & Queries* 220 (1975), 388.
95 See MED sub *mer(e-minn*.
96 See MED sub *grennen v.*
97 Cf. MED sub *ambler(e n.(1)*.

red[98] / (1731) *alea*: table / *caligo*: oscurté / *squales*: devenir led / (1733) *clamis* (= chlamys): mantel / (1736) *amentum*: gaveloc / (1738) *anus*: veil femme / *anasque*: ane / (1741) *ganeo*: lechur / (1742) *papilio*: buterflie / (1743) *crapula*: glutenerie / (1743) *lap[p]a*: gletinere / (1744) *rapa*: nep / (1748) *area*: place / *glarea*: gleire / (1758) *clatros*: barre / (1764) *avia*: forfeabletez / (1770) *m[o]echus*: idem est quod lechere / (1771) *scecus*: anvegle / (–) *fex*: lyes .s. drasce / (1772) *preco*: bedel / (1773) *techa*: wyche[99] / (–) *pedum*: hec cambuca, -ce est 'croce' episcopi .s. baculus / (1782) *tegula*: tiwele / (1786) *melus*: tessun .s. broc / (1787) *spelunca*: .i. fosse / (1788) *spelea*: .i. fosse / (1789) *delubra*: .i. temple / (re 1795) dic *femur* 'quisse de humme' esse viri, *femen* 'quisse de femme' dic mulieris / (–) hec *impedia*, -die: empeynne de soler / hec *solea*, -lee: semele de soller / (1795) *memor*: recordable / (1797) *penum*: celer / *penetro*: percer / (1799) *gena*: chowe / (1800) *venum*: vente / *vena*: veyne / (1801) *tenia*: tingne / *tena*: 'coyfe' dic tyneam 'moþe' vermem,[100] capitis tenam 'coyfe', teneam 'frenge' dic ornatum, teneam quod calces 'enpenne de solers' optinet in se / (1804) *cepa*: oynnun / (1809) *ceraugmon*: .i. claritas maris vel fluctus, (right-hand margin) fallunt mane rubens hera clerica, cana pruina .i. blanche gelee / (1810) *heresis*: heresie / (1811) *erumpna*: meysese / *cerulus*: bloye / (1812) *euruca*: skyrewyt / *cerona*: blanket / (1816) *veru*: spite / *vereor*: duter / (1817) *feretrum*: bere / (1818) (right-hand margin) est testis pera 'scrippe', testem producito pero / (1828–29) *tribulos*: runce / *tribulam*: flael / *tribulum*: truble / (1830) *tibia*: est instrumentum 'astive', sic est quoque tibia membrum 'chambe' / (re 1830) *viburnum*: auburne / (1833) *convic[i]or*: ledenger / (1835) *vicus*: venele / *trica*: trace de femme / (1834) *convicia*: ledenges / *spicula*: dars / (1836) *facedula*, avis: hyere (in right-hand margin a later hand has added 'nothehache')[101] / (1840) *fido*: afier / (1848) *bige*: carette / (1849) *migro*: passer / (1850) *instigare*: antycer / (1853) *philomena*: ruscinole / (1853) *philix*: feugere .s. fern / *hilaris*: heyté / *cilium*: cils / (1854) *pilus*: pestel / *pila*: pelote / (1858) *simia*: cingerel vel cinge .s. hape[102] / (1862) *sinum*: chusevat / *mino*: agarder / (1863) *ripa*: rive / (1864) *stipite*: trunc / *stipo*, -as: apuer, componitur constipare .i. fere chostive / (1867) *lira*: pro sulco, reun / (1868) *lira*: harpe / (1870) *pirula*: bek de naso / *pirata*: robeur de mer / (1872) *tisanam*: tysane / (1875) *clitella*: sumer, ditella est bulge[103] / (1876) *sitacus*: papejay / (1880) (left-hand margin) ovi tres partes: albumen 'wyt', testa 'syulle', vitellus 'yelke'[104] / *vitellum*: moel de efe .s. yelke / (1890) *foca*: porpeys / (1891) *oculo* (= occulo): muscer / (1895) *poderis* est vestis et dicitur a pos, quod est pes, quia vestis est sacerdotis .s. quando cantat missam: aube / (1896) *profor*: parler / *ofella* est diminutivum de offa: pur supe .s. soppe / (1898) *toga*: cote / *rogus*: magnus ignis .s. hode[105] / (1901) *mollior*: aparyler / (1902) *tuber*: musserun .s. tadehat[106] / (1903) *colo*: culer .s. servisiam / (1905) (in right-hand margin) *come*:

---

98 See OED sub *reed sb.*[1].
99 See FEW 4,519a (*hutica*).
100 See MED sub *motthe n*.
101 See Bosworth and Toller, *An Anglo-Saxon Dictionary* sub *higera*.
102 See MED sub *ape n*.
103 See MED sub *bulge n*. The form *ditella* is a commonly attested corruption of *clitella*.
104 i.e. 'white', 'shell' and 'yolk'.
105 See MED sub *hot n.(1)*?
106 OED sub *toad sb.7b* cites 'todyshatte' from the *Prompt. parv.* of c.1440.

planiet / *comas*: cheveus / *comitis*: del cunte / *comis*: curtayse / *cometissa*: cuntesse / *comatim*: planyement / (1906) *homentum*: tripe / *omasum*: tripe / (1907) *coma*: chevelure / (1908) *glomus*: lussel / *glomero*: amunceler / (1911) *nonus*: nevime / (1914) *sopor*: sumil / *soporus*: sumilus / (1915) *olipio* (corr. opilio): berker / (1916) *sopio*: dormir / (1919) *scopulus*: roche / *acopa*: taylle / *anticopa*: cuntre-taylle / (1923) *morus*: murir / (1937) *tuber*: boze / *rubigo*: ruyl / (1938) *puber*: penule / (1939) *pronuba*: baudestrote / (1944) *trudo*: deboter / (1946) *cudo*: batre / (1948) *tuguri*: hulet, domus pastoris / (1949) *pugil*: peunte / (1956) *humerus*: apaulé / (1958) *strumam*: boce / (1960) *cuneum*: cumpayne / (1962) *cupa*: cupe / *stupa*: astupe / (1964) *pupillam*: purnel de oculo / (1967) *susurro*: grundiler / (1969) *putrus* (= putris): puaunt / *cutis*: quir / *uter*: ventre / *lutum*: tay / (re 1970) *mutilo*: aspeuter, hamely hundes[107] / (1971) *putet*: quidet / *putet*: puwet / *mutuus*: entrechaungable / (1972) *futilis*: apantisable / (1973) *utrem*: busseu / (1979) *cloaca*: ganghus[108] / (1982) *cicada*: grisilun / (1986) *Italus*: .s. lumbards / (1988) *thoralis*: chaluns / (1993) *clibanus*: furne / hic *arconius*: mullum de feyn / (1997) *aranea*: hyreyne / (2000) *priape*: vit / *sinapis*: senevey-sed / (2001) *zodoara*: zedewale / (2004) *iubaris*: clarté / (2009) *omasum*: tripe / (2010) *ciatus* (= cyathus): hanap / (2015) *cadaver*: carunye / (2028) *veheemens*: devé / *heremus*: desert / (2035) *statera*: balance / (2037) *galerus*: heume / (2038) *Chimera*: chimere / (2049) *lebete*: caudrun / (2055) *umbilicus*: umblil / (2056) *lorica*: hauberk / *myrica*: genet .s. brom / (2057) *vesica*: vessye / (2058) *urtica*: urtyls / (2062) *salicem*: sauz / (2064) *masticem*: weyde[109] / (–) *posterula*, -le: posterne / (re 2074) *rumigo*: arunger / (2075) *auriga*: chareter / (2076) *calige*: chauces / (2080) *dapsilis*: large / (–) *apes*: .s. dranes, been[110] / *missile*: gaveloc / (2084) *zima*: leveyne / (2088) *salinum*: saler / (2093) *acinum*: drasche / (2097) *trutina*: balance / *lamina*: plate de fer / (2099) *ficina*: chesevat / *patina*: paele / (2098) *buccina*: busyn / *fuscina*: crok / (2104) *siliquis*: coce de fefes / (2106) *papiro*: junc / (2115) *pituita*: pippe / (2131) *aconita*: venym / (2142) *soboles*: lingnage / (2144) *amomum*: .s. canele / (2145) *scindonis*: cendel / (2148) *ligonis*: picoyse / (2167) *coluber*: colefre / *saluber*: saluwable / (2170) *fiducia*: leuteye / *lacunar*: chillé[111] / (2173) *sanguissuga*: leche / (re 2175) *torcular*: pressur / (–) *hircum*: bukerel / (2184) *purpura*: purpre / (2189) *cerusa*: blanket / (2190) *arbutus*: eglenter / (–) *pausat*: reposet / (–) *pauset*: reposet / (2361) *pluribus*: plusurs / *membris*: membris / *figura*: figure / *loquele*: paroles / (2363) *debes*: tu deis / (2369) *associari*: cumpainner / (2431) *servam* (= cervam): .i. bisse / (2479) *umbone*: bucle de talevas / *umbo*: talevas / (2502) *alii*: autre / *similis*: ensemblement / (2506) *piscena*: servur / (2508) *aristas*: arest .s. heile[112] / (2509) *plures*: plusurs / (2516) *si dicas*: si tu dies (a second, later hand) / *bella*: bataille (second, later hand) / (2517) *pro toto*: pur tut / (2525) *tubarum*: de busynes / (2548) *relatu*: par cunte

---

107 See TL 3,i,1205 sub *espieter* and MED sub *hamelen v.* and *hound n.*
108 See MED sub *gang, gong* n.3(c).
109 'Woad' is an error which has probably arisen from a misreading of OE *cwudu* ('code'), cf. MED sub *cud(e n.*
110 See MED sub *be n.* and *drane n.*
111 i.e. *celé*.
112 See MED sub *eile n.*

A number of vernacular glosses are also found in the marginal commentary which accompanies some of the text of the *Doctrinale*:

[f.32v] ebes dicitur ab *ebeto*, -tas: 'rebucher' et *teres*, quod gallice dicitur 'runt' (re 153ff) / hic *pignus*, -neris: gage (cf.183) / [f.36r] *rubus* idem est quod 'runce' gallice (cf.512) / [f.37v] *compes* idem est quod 'manicle de fer' (cf.618) / hec *abies* . . . .i. arbor .s. 'saype'[113] / [f.38r] hic *lepor*, -oris: renable (cf.663) / *pulex*: .i. fle (cf.685) / *lues*: .i. pudre / *pelex*: rivayle (cf.685) / *lumbricus*: .i. angeltwache[114] / *lumbos*: .i. reyns / *lumbago*: .i. gute / [f.40v] *cambio*: changer / *cambium*: change (cf.915) / [f.41v] *mala*: chowe

Eberhard of Bethune: Graecismus

THE LONDON, OXFORD, DURHAM AND DUBLIN MANUSCRIPTS

(Prose prologue) *inopinabile*: gallice nent creable (D) / *coherenti*: herdaunt (T) / *cesariem equinam*: gallice sey de cheval (D)[115] / *apros*: senglirs (T) / *aprina*: gallice braun (D) / *squamas*: escherdes (C) eçkerdes (T) / *retundere*: gallice abatre (D) / *errorem*: gallice foleure (D) / *lima*: file (C) / (beside IV,23) *titubatorium*: anglice kinte (D)[116] / (V,6) *ambages*: trufles vel glutun (T) / (V,22) (re *inmittit*) hoc *missile*: gallice gaveloc (D) / (re V,30) hec *ustrina*: gallice torail, anglice k. . . (D) / (V,36) *fex*: lye, drasce (D) / (VI,10) *cos*: achesur (T)[117] / *falx*: faucile (T) anglice sithe / *falxilla*: anglice sikele (D) / (VI,11) *fax*: gallice braundun (C) tisun (D) / *fex*: lye (CDT) / (VI,14) *merx*: marchaundie (D) marchandise (T) / *sors*: sort, anglice lot (D) / (VI,15) *pix*: pich (D) / *strigis*: anglice strie (D)[118] / (VI,18) *puls*: gruel (C) bolie (D) bule, gruel (T) / *faus*: joue (T) / *plebs*: gallice rascalie (D) / (VI,23) *giht*: idem est quod lolium, hoc gith idem est quod nigella, anglice kokil (D) / (VI,24) *es*: gallice arreim (C) / MS C f.13r *cuculla*: gallice coyfe / (VI,29) *grus*: anglice crane (D) / (VI,31) *lens*: anglice nite (D) / (VIII,9) *arthocopus*: gallice cymenel (C) / (VIII,16) *acrizimus* (panis leviter fermentatus): anglice yerfe bret (D)[119] / (VIII,26) *ancile*: gallice bokiler (C) / *rotundum*: rundel (T) / (VIII,29) *Andigavis*: Anjouhe (T) / (VIII,30) *utrem*: bussel (T) / (VIII,31) *incus*: gallice enclune (C) anglice stithe (D)[120] / (VIII,32) *beta*: gallice burage (C) / (VIII,41) *balista*: arblast (C) / (VIII,58) *calathus*: gallice panier (C) anglice panier (D) / (VIII,62) *catarrus*: gallice le cernu, s[n]evil vel pose, encernure (T)[121] / (VIII,70) *arthocrea*: gallice russoles (C) russeus

---

113   Cf. OED sub *sap* sb¹4 and TL 9,170.
114   See MED sub *angel-twacche n.*
115   See FEW 11,48a ('crin de cheval'). At the top of f.11v MS D has 'hoc miscellenium, gallice mes'.
116   I cannot be sure that I have read the minims correctly. I do not recognise the word.
117   i.e. 'anguiseor'.
118   See OED sub *stry, strie*.
119   The scribe writes 'y' for 'thorn', see OED sub *tharf a.* (*bret* = bread).
120   See OED sub *stith sb.*
121   See TL 3,i,179 (*encerné*) and FEW 2,i,701a, OED sub *snivel v.* and *pose sb.*¹. A faint gloss in a fourteenth-century hand reads 'snevil, morve'.

(T) / (VIII,73) *cubitus*: elboue (C) / (VIII,86) *cepa*: gallice hoynun (C) gallice oynun (D) / (VIII,93) *cytharam*: le harpe / (C) (VIII,123) *epimerides* (cesura in ligno facta): gallice tayle (T) / (re VIII,127) *eliostrofium vel solsequium*: golde (T) / (VIII,148) *fagus*: anglice beche (D) bech (T) / (VIII,154) *fermentum*: le levayne (C) leveyne (T) gallice levein (D) / (VIII,160) *geralogodion*: letuarie, treacle (T) / *geralagodion*: gallice triacle (D) / (VIII,165) *arnoglossa*: gallice plaunteyne (D) / (VIII,179) *ypotha-mus*: gallice chyn de mer (C) / (VIII,181) *ydromellum*: gallice ciser (D) / (VIII,191) *lathomus*: anglice massun (C) / (VIII,200) *lixivum*: anglice leye (C) gallice lese, (and in a second hand) gallice lessie (T) / (VIII,222) *census*: le chatel (C) / (VIII,235) *piropus*: charbucle (T) / (VIII,239) *omentum*: gallice tripe (C) felefolde (T)[122] / (VIII,242) *hostis*: enemi (C) / (VIII,249) *compos*: gallice pusant (C) / (VIII,251) *compita*: gallice quart fur (C) / (VIII,255) *possidenopagus*: villa iuxta portum sicut Bristouwe (C) / (VIII,273) *gazophilatia*: gallice tresorie (C) / (VIII,275) *palinodia*: gallice refreid de chant (C) / (VIII,288) *sarcophagus*: gallice sarcue (T) / MS T f.48r *socors*: gallice couuard, *socordia*: cowardise (C has couuardyse) / (VIII,291) *parasitus*: gallice glotun (C) anglice glutun (D) / (VIII,292) *syrenes*: gallice [sic] mermen (C) sunt monstra marina, unde *sirentorium*: gallice warroc (D)[123] / / (VIII,297) *sospes*: halegre (C) / (VIII,298) *secors*: couward (C) / (VIII,304) *pavere*: gallice paver (T) / (VIII,307) *solemnis*: gallice festivable (C) / (VIII,310) *trochos* (hec troclea): anglice windace (D)[124] / (VIII,313) *hyrcus*: gallice bokerel (C) / (VIII,315) *triumphus*: gallice victorie (C) / (VIII,321) *tela*: web vel dars (C) gallice teyle, anglice web (D) gallice dart (T) / (VIII,328) *tymum*: hunysuke (C) / (VIII,337) *fermentatum*: gallice leveyne (C) / (IX,6) *orphanus*: gallice [sic] stepchil (C) / (IX,13) *coluber*: gallice colevere, anglice snake (C) / (IX,15) *serpo*: gallice raumper (C) / (IX,16) *coluber*: la colevere (C) / (IX,20) *primipilus*: gallice baneur (C) / *vexilla*: gallice baners (C) / (IX,28) *currus*: gallice char (C) char (T) / (IX,31) *dolo*: hewe vel ywyte (C)[125] / (IX,57) *bufo*: gallice crapout (C) / *bubo*: gallice huan (C) / (IX,58) *bubo*: anglice [sic] huan (D) / (IX,73) *apostata*: gallice renyé (C) / *apostata*: gallice reneié (D) / (IX,77) *camelus*: gallice chamayle (C) / (IX,82) *messor*: gallice cyur (C) / (IX,97) *archos* (for arctos): norht (C) / (IX,106) *tribunus*: cunistable (T) / (IX,112) *gibbus*: gallice boce (C) bos (T) / (IX,114) *strumosus*: gallice bozus (D) / (IX,116) *caulem*: cholet (T) / (IX,123) *discus*: gallice coyte (C) / (IX,136) *muto*: gallice motun (C) / (IX,137) *vervex*: gallice chatris, anglice weþer (C)[126] / (IX,142) *sonipes*: gallice runcin (C) / *harena*: gallice gravel (C) / (IX,146) *asturco*: ostur (T)[127] / (IX,147) *succutiendo*: gallice trottan (C) en trottaund (T) / (IX,148) *emissarius*: gallice estalun (C) gallice stalun (D) / (IX,149) *currere .i. in equicio*: haraz (D) / (IX,158) *instat*: bargainet (D) / (IX,163) *columbos*: ramages (T) / T f.51r *suber*, inde *suberamentum*: gallice tan, anglice barric[128] / (IX,170) *compede*: chene (T) / (IX,177) (*latex*) *terra laticosa*:

---

122 See note 65 above.
123 See OED sub *warrok sb.*
124 See OED sub *windas.*
125 See MED sub *heuen v.(1)* and OED sub *thwite v.*
126 See OED sub *wether.*
127 Over *sturnus* MS T has 'eturle', which is probably an error for *esturnel.*
128 See MED sub *bark n.*

anglice wateri heþeye (D) [129] / (IX,181) cignus: gallice cyne (C) / (IX,183) olon: gallice cotun (D) / (IX,185) redam: charette (C) / (IX,187) nothus: bastard (CT) / (IX,209) capriolus: gallice cheveral (C) / (IX,224) radium: gallice [sic] slay (C) [130] / (IX,225) radius: spoke (D) / (IX,235) polipus: gallice moruele (C) / fedacio: ordure (T) / (IX,239) testudo: gallice voute (D) / (IX,244) pollex: gallice deel (T) / (IX,250) ponderis: peys (T) / (IX,253) prochor: wow (A) [131] / procos: gallice dauner (C) gallice douneur (D) dauneour (A) / (IX,256) putator: gallice vinerun (C) / (IX,262) intestinorum: gallice bouell (C) / renunculus: gallice reynuns (C) / (IX,266) mango: gallice kozun (D) [132] / (IX,286) strabo: gallice borne (D) / MS D f.25r capulus: anglice hilte of þe swerd (D) / (IX,288) incantatores: lecheres (A) / MS A f.5r (14th C. hand) hoc braccale, renale, lumbare idem sunt: breis, gurdel / (IX,292) bubalus: bugle (T) / (IX,303a) hastam: gallice la haunte (C) / (IX,304) cuspis: gallice pynte (C) / (IX,312) satirus: sauteroles (C) / (IX,313) faunus: anglice wodewose (D) [133] / (IX,332) pubes: penulis (T) penil gallice (C) / piscis: playis (T) / corea: gallice carole (C) carole (T) / (IX,341) thoros, plicas pendentes in collo tauri: gallice gorjeruns, anglice dewlappe (D) [134] / paliaria: charneus (T) / (IX,349) lampas: gallice laumpe (C) / (X,6) concava: cros (A) / carina: gallice crevesse (C) / (X,11) carchesium, summitas mali: mast (D) / (X,12) cherucus: gallice cochet (A) / (X,14) plaga (regio): gallice reume, anglice forue (D) [135] / (X,20) galea: gallice coyf de quir (A) / (X,30) penoris: gallice celer (C) / valva: weyket (T) / MS C f.26v hoc meremium, -mii: gallice merine / (X,56) decipule: gallice peges (T) / (X,62) strigilis: est[ri]le (T) / (X,64) plectrum: gallice wrestel (C) [136] / (X,65) strigile: spole (D) / stamina: warp (D) / (X,66) strigilis (cremium): anglice crauke (T) [137] / (X,67) strix: fresey (T) / (X,69) nurus: gallice brus (C) / (X,74) strues: uode cas (T) [138] / (X,76) testa: scale (D) / (X,79) vitta: bende (T) / (X,80) furcula: furche (T) / (X,84) resipiscentem: gallice repentan (C) / (X,94) turtur (piscis): turbut (T) / (X,95) fex, inde defecatus, -ta, -tum: gallice escolé (MS = escalé) (D) / (X,97) scoriam: gallice arsun, anglice cinder (C) / (X,105) pestis: gallice poysun (C) / (X,111) ydolis: gallice maumest (C) / (X,148) plectro: gallice [sic] wrastel (C) [139] / (X,151) cartilago: gallice [sic] gristel (C)[140] / legua (for legia): de wlaspe (D) [141] / (X,166) forcipe: tenail, to[n]ges (D) tenalis (T) / (X,168) lappa: clote (C) clete (D) gletunere (T) / (X,174) juventus:

[129] See MED sub heth n.
[130] corr. 'anglice' and see OED sub slay sb.[1].
[131] See OED sub woo v.
[132] See TL 2,516 sub coçon.
[133] See OED sub woodwose, woodhouse.
[134] See MED sub deu-lap(þe n. At the bottom of f.5v MS A has the gloss 'polio, anglice plane'.
[135] See MED sub forwe n. The English gloss renders a different sense from the French (= 'royaume').
[136] See OED sub wrest sb.[1]5. The form with final -l is not attested.
[137] See MED sub craukan n. Graec. X,66 runs 'Strigilis est cremium, venit hoc a strideo strides'.
[138] = woodcast, see OED sub wood sb.[1] III.10.
[139] See OED sub wrest sb.[1]5.
[140] See MED sub gristel n.
[141] See MED sub lap(þe n. See Du Cange sub *5 legia ('tendre cuir d'oreille, dur et mol').

bachilerie (D) / (X,177) *situla*: buket (C) bochet (D) / (X,182) *scobs* (corr. *scoba*): balayse, besme (C)[142] scovele (T) / *scoba*: bayleys (T) / (X,185) *cute*: quyr (C) / (X,189) *capitale*: chatel (T) / (X,191) *laterna*: lantern (C) / (X,192) *lacerna*: bifle (T) / (X,199) *subula*: aleyne (D) ellen, gallice allerne (T) / (X,204) *penus*: celer (C) / (X,209) *bipennis*: twibile (C)[143] / (X,214) *Italie*: Lumbardie (T) / (X,227) *pistrin*: gallice baleine (D) / (X,229) *fax*: gallice braundun (C) tisun (D) / (X,231) *tedas*: gallice tysun (C) branduns (T) / (X,243) *toga*: gallice gunel (C) / (X,249) *examitum*: gallice amyce (C) / (X,252) *syren*: mermen (C) / (X,262) *occasio*: aventure (T) / *causa*: chesun (T) / (X,264) *tuba*: gallice busine (CT) / (X,268) *abies*: gallice sap (C) / (X,277) *fex*: gallice la lye (C) / (X,279) *adeps*: gallice gres (C) / (X,280) *aruina* .i. *uligo*: anglice marle (D)[144] / (X,281) *alga maris*: wrec bom (C)[145] / *ulva paludis*: gallice canne, chenaupie (C)[146] / (X,282) *algeo*: enfreder (T) / (X,283) *ornix*: gallice fesaunt (C) fesan (T) / (X,284) *aurificina*: gallice la forge (C) / (X,285) *aurifodina*: goldbore (C)[147] / (X,286) *antela*: peytrel (C) peterel (T) / (X,287) *postela*: taylrop (C)[148] / (X,290) *nuge*: gallice trufes (C) / (X,291) *nugari*: trufler (T) / (X,292) *sagana*: gallice sarge (C) anglice sarge, sai (D) sarge, say (T) / (X,294) *lamina*: gallice unne pece (C) / (X,296) *bracteole*: gallice blate (C) / (X,300) *croceo*: gallice gaune (C) / (X,293) *arundo*: gallice rosel (C) / (XI,2) *est cognominis agnomen dic significare*, ut aliquis vocatur *bursirapus*: anglice cutteburs (C)[149] / (XI,4) *indictum*: gallice ban (C) / *edictum*: ban (C) / (XI,14) *jaculum*: gallice dart (C) / (XI,20) *cuticula*: quier (T) / (XI,27) *velum*: seyl, (vestis monacarum) anglice kercheve (T)[150] / (XI,32) *ocillum*: gallice braundele (T)[151] / (XI,45) *epicauterium*: haytre (D) / *ollas*: les poss (T) / (XI,49) *presagia*: gallice devinement (C) / (XI,56) *citato*: gallice somuns (T) / (XI,57) *penus*: gallice celer (C) / (XI,63) *devia*: forveiabletés (D) formeyabletés (sic) (T) / (XI,71) *linthea*: gallice sigle, anglice mast (C) / (XI,72) *gracilem*: gallice greele (C) / (XI,73) *propungnacula*: gallice bretages (C) / (XI,79) *pomi*: poumeris (T) / (XI,80) *absconsa*: gallice muscés (C) / (XI,84) *domos* grece planum, latine doma .i. planities: anglice rof (D) / (XI,97) *vite*: gallice vine (C) / (XI,99) *furire*: gallice forsaner (C) / (XI,100) *carchesia*: gallice godeds (C) / (XI,115) *diaria*: gallice livresun (C) / (XI,120) *subtegmen*: gallice treyme (C) idem quod *trama*: anglice hof (D)[152] / (XI,122) *succus*: gallice jus (C) / (XI,128) *stropheum*: lisur (T) / (XI,131) *confraga*:

---

142 See MED sub *besm(e* n.
143 See OED sub *twibill, twybill*.
144 See MED sub *marl(e* n.
145 See OED sub *wreck sb.*[1]2. The second word is obscure.
146 This word, not attested in the dictionaries, is also found in MS Oxford, Bodl. Libr., Digby 172 f.143va (letters of Sidonius Apollinaris), see Hunt in *Zeitschrift für französische Sprache und Literatur* 89 (1979), 136 n.9. In a MS of the *Merarium* (see vol. 1, p.368) *chenaupé* glosses *ulva*.
147 = goldmine? See MED sub *bore n.(1)*.
148 See OED sub *tail-rope*.
149 See MED sub *cutte-purs* n.
150 Both glosses are written at the bottom of f.59v in a fourteenth-century hand. See MED sub *cover-chef* n.
151 Part of the commentary on f.60r written at the top of the page. An interlinear gloss reads 'ludus, branne, totir, brandoier'. See OED sub *totter sb.*[1] and A. Delbouille in *Romania* 17 (1888), 286–7.
152 See OED sub *woof sb.*[1].

fresis, berris (T) / *fragorum*: fresis (T) / (XI,133) *crinis*: chevelure (D) / (XI,136) *uvarum*: grapis (T) / (XI,137) *acinium*: mars, .i. anglice kirneles[153] (T) / *uva*: grape (T) / (XI,138) *gummi* distillat ab arbore: gallice sapp (T) / (XI,150) *vaccinia*: gallice violettes (D) primerole (T) / (XI,157) *pastorum caveas*: huléss (T) / (XI,167) *pulvinar*: quisine (T) / (XI,170) *stannum*: esteym (T) / (XI,178) *monumen*: garnisemen, remembrement (T) / (XI,182) *libre*: balaunce (D) balanse (T) / (XI,186) *glabella*: la greve de la testhe (T) / (XI,189) *psalterium*: sautre (D) / (XI,190) *bruti*: sawage (D) / *pabula*: pastures (D) / (XII,26) *colubris*: dragun (C) / (XII,31) *lutum*: gallice boue (C) boue (T) / (XII,26) *colubri(s)*: gallice dragun (C) / (XII,44) *lasciva*: gallice way (C) veyse (T) / (XII,46) *etatem*: age de homme (T) / (XII,50) *certum* (= *sertum*): karlaundesche (D) / (XII,53) *celsa*: paleys (C) / (XII,72) *fremit*: gallice ruter, croyt (C) / (XII,84) *saxum*: la pesauntime (A) / (XII,89) *fundus*: gallice mesnage (A) / *fundum*: grount (A) / (XII,90) *bubo*: huan (D) huhan (A) / *nictimene*: chaut sorice (C) gallice freseye (T) / (XII,91) *vespertilio*: chausoris (T) (XII,102) *spinter*: gallice broche (C) / (XII,104) *scapularum*: gallice espaudles (D) / *scrapulorum* [sic]: espaudles (T) / (XII,121) *vitrum*: glas (T) / *saphirus*: saphir (T) / (XII,123) *fornis* (= *fornix*): bordel (T) / *lenonis*: huler (T) / (XII,131) *insitio*: gallice entesun (A) / (XII,135) *olera*: cholet (A) / (XII,137) *scalam*: gallice echele (C) / *testa*: scale (D) / (XII,143) *sarchophagum*: gallice sarcue (T) / (XII,147) *feretri*: gallice bere (C) / (XII,151) *remex*: gallice [sic] ster (C)[154] / (XII,152) *remus*: anglice rochul(?) (A) envirunment (T) / (XII,154) *remorum*: viruns (T) / (XII,162) *lichnus*: gallice (sic) wehc (C) luminun, weke (D) gallice [sic] weke (A) ueche (T)[155] / (XII,161) *tegula*: un tule, tyl (A) / (XII,166) *statera*: gallice balance (C) balaunse (T) balannce (A) / (XII,164) *cingula*: sengle (A) / (XII,168) *cratis*: gallice cleye (T) anglice hudel (D) anglice hurdil (A) / (XII,172) *sinum*: gallice [sic] chesevet (C) chesefat (A) / (XII,174) *lactis*: gallice letense, roun (T) roune (D) / *intestinorum*: bouel (A) / (XII,174a) *lactes*: letenses (D)[156] / *lactis*: gallice eus, anglice roune (A) / MS T f.66r *catopesium*: gallice chipois[157] / (XII,185) *viciam*: fecchis (T) vesce (L) / (XII,187) *fibrum*: gallice tessun, broc (C) tesun, broc (D) bever (T) (dic fibram venam .s. in brachio sive in corpore) b[r]oche (T) / (XII,189) *incurius*, non curialis: curtays (A) / (XII,192) *sororius*: gallice sorour (A) / (XII,195) *libitinam*: bere (C) / (XII,202) *palus*: gallice (sic) stake (C) / (XII,208) *clavis* [= *sera*]: barre (C) cerure in lok (D) / *clavem*: nayl (A) / (XII,210) *plaga* [= *retis*]: reis (A) / (XII,213) *buxus*: gallice [sic] box (C) / (XII,215) *cultri*: de le cutel (A) / (XII,224) *malus*: gallice (sic) mast (C) / (XII,226) *aule*: cortine (T) / (XII,225) *faux*: gallice goue (C) / (XII,241) *affectus*: gallice le talent (C) / (XII,244) *cauterium*: gallice merche (C) / (XII,245) *cauteriam*: anglice barnet (C)[158] / (XII,248) *trapezata*: gallice changur (C) / (XII,260) *cirrus*, inde *cirritus*: gallice rechokilé (A) / (XII,269) *insuimus*: encusum (T) / *humandum*: a enterrer (T)

---

153 See DMLBS sub *acinus* and MED sub *kirnel* n.1(a).
154 See OED sub *star sb.*².
155 See OED sub *wick sb.*¹.
156 MS D also has 'letagis, pinguedo latens in intestinis'.
157 Both lemma and gloss are obscure.
158 See MED sub *bernet* n.

/ (XII,270) *sudaria*: gallice hose (C) / (XII,271) *sudore*: swot (C)[159] / *uda*: gallice moste (C) / (XII,273) *pelta*: talevas (C) gallice talevace (D) / (XII,277) *scaber*: gallice royne (C) roine (D) gallice eroiner (A) une runne de kyval (T) / *pes*: rune (T)[160] / (XII,278) *scabiosum*: escracheus (A) / (XII,288) *torrens*: gallice crecine (C) / (XII,286) *affeccio*: teinaunce, anglice liein (D)[161] / (XII,291) *turbida*: gallice trublé (C) trubelé (T) / (XII,294) *puteus*: gallice puce (C) / (XII,296) *nexum*: lacement (C) / (XII,301) *servitus*: servage (T) / (XII,304) hec *taxus*: broc [sic] (T) yf (CD) / (XII,305) *melota*: tesun (C) tesun, brok (D) un tesun (A) / MS C f.41r *clepsedra*: doysil gallice / (XII,308) *soleas*: semeles (A) / (XII,310) *vellis*: gallice araches (C) / (XII,315) *fucus*: gallice [sic] drone (C) / *asilus*: gallice burdun (C) taun (T) / (XII,319) *pomus* (arbor): gallice pomer (A) / (XII,324) *olea*: gallice olive (C) / (XII,331) *veternum*: gallice gaunis (C) gallice jauniz, anglice yelu sout (D) yeleu sot, gaunis (T)[162] / (XII,335) *sordidus*: gallice led (C) / (XII,338) *scortum*: gallice bordel (C) / (XII,342) *lacerti*: gallice [sic] fadme (D)[163] / MS C f.41v hec *tensa*: gallice [sic] vedme / (XII,355) *acus*: gallice aleyne (C) / (XII,364) *tribulus*: pestel (T) / *tribulum*: pestel (T) / *allea* [= *allia*]: aus (T) / *salsa*: sales [sic] (T) / (XII,365) *tribula*: gallice [sic] scovele (C) / *gleba*: blet (T) / (XII,366) *corus* (= *caurus*): gallice croye (C) / (XII,367) *corea*: gallice caroule (C) / (XII,374) *bruma*: gallice [sic] yekel (C)[164] / (XII,383) *multrale*: gallice boket (C) stoppe, fissele (T)[165] / *mulsum*: anglice wei (D)[166] / (XII,392) *cornus*: eglenter gallice, hope (C)[167] / (XII,394) *pila* (ludus): pelot (T) / *pila* (pes pontis): gallice peler (C) / (XII,395) *pila*: pestel (T) / (XII,401) hec *nurus*: gallice brue, anglice snore (T)[168] / (XII,402) *nurus*: gallice brus (C) / MS C f.43v *inescare*: gallice [sic] esen[169] / (XII,403) *soceri*: pere en ley (T) / (XII,415) *ostri*: gallice purpure (C) / (XII,417) *pilleus*: gallice hure vel coyfe (C) / *galerus*: gallice coyfe de quir (C) / (XII,421) *laqueus*: anglice snare (T) / (XII,422) *laquearia*: cuples (T) / (XII,427) *fultrum*: gallice [sic] velt, futre (C)[170] / (XII,429) *speculam*: woch (T) (?)[171] / *excubiarum*: de geyte (C) de vaytis (T) / *specula, -e*: gallice bretasche (D) / (XII,431) *lucar*: gallice paunage (C) / (XII,433) *ceparium*: gallice de hoynuns (C) / *ceparum*: oynun (D) ununs (T) / *ceparia*: gallice oynuné (D) gallice unu[n]é (T) / (XII,434) *cepulatum*: gallice sevé (C) gallice cyvé (D) / (XII,435) *scrobes*: fosce (C) / (XII,436) *fovee*: gallice fosce (C) / MS T f.70r *vectis*: anglice yryne barre, roude / MS T f.70v *arbuta*: botun de haye / (XII,442) *vectis*: gallice barris, gallice gunfes (C) /

---

159 See OED sub *swote*.
160 The full line runs 'Est scaber ferrum quo pes purgatur equinus'.
161 See TL 10,182 sub *tenance* and MED sub *lien n.*
162 See OED sub *yellow a. & sb.* C.1.d and *sought sb.*
163 See MED sub *fadme n.*
164 See MED sub *ikel n.*
165 See OED sub *stop sb.*[1].
166 See OED sub *whey sb.*
167 See MED sub *hepe n.(2).*
168 See Bosworth and Toller, An *Anglo-Saxon Dictionary* sub *snoru.*
169 The gloss appears to be English (see MED sub *essen v.*), but is difficult to connect with the lemma.
170 See MED sub *felt n.*
171 'ubi vinitor observat uvas'. Cf. OED sub *watch sb.II,14.*

(XII,444) *vertevellas*: gallice guns (D) / (XII,447) *cin[c]ta*: gallice averuné (C) / *ampnis*: gallice wé (C)[172] / (XII,448) *arbuta*: botun de hay, eglentere (C) / (XII,450) *inguine*: gallice penil (C) / (XII,451) *sura*: estrumele (C) estrumel (T) / (XII,455) *limus*: boue (C) / *lima*: gallice feyle (C) vile, anglice file (D) / MS C f.44r *calibs*: ascer / (XIII,11) *incuria*: nunchalerie (D) / *dustria*: conytise (C) / (XIII,33) *velox*: gallice ignel (C) / (XIII,60) *fissus*: clevé (T) / (XIII,61) *hyatum*: gallice crevese (C) / (XIII,69) *maculatus*: entechelé / (XIII,71) *pura*: gallice nette (C) / MS C f.46r *solicitare*: gallice [sic] souen[173] / (XIII,84) *strumam*: boze (D) bose (T) / (XIII,115) *facundus*: gallice renable (C) / (XIII,106) *rabidus*, faciens tumultum: noise (D) / (XIII,117) *superbus*: engrés (T) / (XIII,133) *ignavus*: persus (C) / (XIII,145) *inmemor*: gallice nent remenbrable (C) / (XIII,189) *furit*: gallice andevit (C)[174] / (XIII,210) *levigat*: gallice planez (C) / (XIII,226) *remeabit*: gallice repererce (C) / (XIII,234) *lubricus*: sliper (T)[175] / (XIII,237) *flavum*: gallice bloy (C) bloye (T) / *fluvum*: gallice bloy (C) bloye (T) / (XIII,251) *celas*: gallice muses (C) / (XIII,265) *spatiare*: enveyser (T) / (XV,4) *vela*: ciglis, seil (D) / (XV,45) *perfero*: percer (T) / (XV,62) *operam*: entente (A) / (XV,57) *minat* .i. ducit: guyit (T) / (XV,72) *omix*: feysaunt (A) / (XV,73) *excubies*: weytes (T) / (XV,75) *rixantur*: enchinunt (A) / (XV,89) *vadus*: wé (D) / (XV,101) *ructacio*: ruture, bolking (T)[176] / (XV,103) *ructacio*: bolkin (T) / (XV,104) *liba*: gastels (D) / (XV,108) *palmito*: barganer (D) bargauyner (T) / *subarro*: dare hernes, handfest (T)[177] / *aras*: gallice ernist (D) / (XV,120) *lugubrum*: anglice crusel (D)[178] / (XV,122) *titubat*: chaunselet (D) canselit (T) / *vacillat*: croulit (A) / (XV,123) *nutat*: chaunselit (A) / (XV,126) *ossitat*: balet (C) gaspin (T)[179] / (XV,128) *sculpo*: taler (T) / (XV,129) *celtis*: chisel (D) / (XV,162) *merenda*: russi(ci)n (A)[180] / (XV,162) *conspicor*: gallice glener (C) / *conspicamen*: anglice glene (D)[181] gallice gavele (T) / (XV,167) *ex[s]quamo*: eskerder (D) / *exentero*: enbueler (D) / (XV,173) *suscreo*: escracher (T) / (XV,181) *scrutor*: serche (A) / *ut sanem*: pusse saner (A) / (XV,183) *investigo*: encerche (D) / (XV,191) *rugo*: frunse (T) frunce (A) / (XV,217) *adlactat*: aletet (A) / (XV,218) *ablactat*: il enseviryt (A) (right-hand margin) .i. severit (A) / (XVI,14) *arconius*: mulun de feyn (A) / (XVI,58) *obsidet*: aseget (C) / (XVI,88) *scatere*, squam[a]s habere: hauler, hec *scama*, -me: anglice frekne (A)[182] / (XVI,112) *caneo*: enblanchir (T) / (XVII,10) *resilit*: resalyt (A) / (XVII,79) *conpellit*: aresunet (D) / (XVII,145) *sero*: henter (T) / (XVIII,4) *conpello*: aresuner (T) / (XVIII,60) *perio* (=*pereo*): peris (T) / (XVIII,70) *diruo*: batre (T) / (XIX,36) *vesperti-*

---

172 See DMLBS sub *1 amnis b* and FEW 17,438b *et seq.* (*wað*).
173 See OED sub *sue v.*
174 See TL 3,i,283 sub *endesver.*
175 See OED sub *slipper a.*
176 See MED sub *bolking ger.*
177 See MED sub *ernes n.* and *hond-festen v.*
178 See MED sub *crusel n.*
179 See MED sub *gaspen v.*
180 See Du Cange sub *recticinium.*
181 See MED sub *glene n.*
182 See MED sub *fraknes n.(pl.).* In the margin of MS A f.21v is the gloss 'scalprum . . . gallice grate'. For *scatere* = 'haler', see below p.34, MS T f.83v. See also below p.42 n.46.

lio: reremus (C) [183] / *yrundo*: swalewe (C) / (XIX,37) *gracilat*: clocket (C) [184] / (XIX,38) *aper*: sengler (C) / (XIX,39) *nisus*: esperver (D) / (XIX,57) *la[s]civit*: enveeyser (T) / (XIX,60) *adulamur*: losengum (T) / (XIX,74) *compello*: je hoche (D) anglice hosche (T) [185] / (XIX,84) *vado*: je way (A) / (XIX,97) *sepinus, sepes, -is*: haye (A) / (XIX,101) *vitem*: la vine (T) / *torris*: tisun (T) / (XIX,104) *stallat*: estalit (A) / (XIX,106) *pulmo*: anglice longe (D) / (XIX,114) *colo, -as*: gallice coler (A) / (XIX,115) *vado*: vayer (T) / (XIX,117) *redimo*: recater (T) / (XXI,41) *manuleatus*: manché (T) / (XXI,42) *caligatus*: chaucis (T) / (XXI,76) *anelatus*: travelé (A) / (XXIII,83) *trano*: suymme (A) / (XXIII,145) *crurum tenus*: dekes a le quisis (A) / (XXV,41) *faginus*: beche (T) / *abienus*: sap (T) / (XXV,190) *vectigal*: trouage (A) / (XXV,320) *cucumus*: gallice gourde (A) / (XXVI,87) *incubo*: cover (A) / (XXVI,155) *nideo*: odorer (D) / *strideo*: fere noyse (D) / (XXVI,162) *rausum*: enroyé (A) / (XXVI,205) *confiscare*: seysir / *conviscare*: engluer (A) / (XXVI,208) *prurio*: escaufer (T) / (XXVI,214) *cedo*: trenscher (T)

Vernacular glosses from the commentary in MS T:

[f.41v] *fel*: anglice galle / *git*: gallice get .i. lollium vel nigella alio nomine, anglice cockil / [f.43v] *beta*: alio nomine dicitur magudaris .s. illa *parva folia* que crescunt post evulsionem magnorum foliorum: gallice chiiuuns / [f.51r] *viratim*: anglice fro man to man / [f.53v] *calculus*: gallice poun / [f.55v] *strigilis*: gallice grate (dicitur strigilis cava vel dentata supellex .i. micatorium) / *cava*: crosse / [f.56r] *calcheteon*: anglice sindir / [f.56v] *acerra*: ensenser / [f.57r] *scobs*: scovele / *scoba*: bayleys / [f.57v] *subula*: alene / [f.58r] *instita*: anglice cradilbond [186] / [f.59r] *sagana*: hure / [f.60r] *coagulum*: gallice presure, anglice cheselep [187] / *epicausterium* (cathedra monachorum): gallice carole / [f.61v] *diaria* (que dantur bubulco per diem ad commedendum sicut unus panis vel dimidius): gallice liv[r]esun / [f.61r] hec *casma*: gallice escleyr / [f.62r] *columbar* (foramina currus per que trahunt equi): of þille [188] / *casma* (.i. fulgetra): escleyr / [f.63v] *certum* (= sertum): chapel de flories / [f.65r] (top of the page) . . .: gargue, anglice yker [189] / [f.66r] *ova*: heovys gallice, et dicuntur quod est in allece, anglice hard rouue [190] / *vicia*: vesce gallice, fecche anglice / *malo*: gowe / *mali*: pomer [191] / [f.67r] *zelotipus*: geluss / *zelotipia*: gelosie / *zelotipus*: geluss / *zelotipa*: gelusse / *zelotipia*: gelusse (sic) / [f.68v] *exactio* (.i. extorsio): gallice tort / *veternum*: gaunice / *traha*: herce gallice / [f.71r] *dealbatus*, unde bene dicitur in dealbatione murorum calce: gallice daubé / [f.79r] *capere*: gallice prendere (sic) par le gouhe / [f.80r] hec

---

183 See OED sub *rearmouse, reremouse*.
184 See MED sub *clokken v.(1)*.
185 See TL 4,1122 sub *hochier* and MED *hotchen v.*
186 See MED sub *cradel n.(b)*.
187 See MED sub *chese n.3(d)*.
188 See OED sub *thill*[1] and DMLBS sub *columbar e*. (= *arquillus*, 'ox-bow').
189 The page has been cropped and no trace of the lemma is now visible.
190 See OED sub *roe*[2] 1. (*hard roe*, spawn of a female fish) and also sub *rown 1*. It would be equally possible to read *rouue* or *roune*.
191 This and the preceding lemma occur in verses beginning 'Mala mali malo . . .', see B. Hauréau in *Notices et extraits de quelques manuscrits latins de la Bibliothèque Nationale* 4 (Paris, 1892), p.287.

lugubra: [192] gallice chex / *nuto*: chau[n]celer / [f.83r] *obsidium*: sege gallice / *obsidens*: ostage / [f.83v] *scatere* (.i. fervore solis): gallice haler vel escerder / [f.86v] *haustrum*: boket / [f.89v] *redimo*: gallice rechater / [f.102r] hic *panus*: gallice broche, anglice essprickel / *grandula*: anglice wenne [193] / [f.102v] *betha* (genus oleris): gallice bete / *molosus*: gallice chin de muloce(?) ou limer [194] / [f.104r] *vectigal*: gallice dicitur truage / *juger -ris*: gallice un arpent de terre (spacium quantum unus bos potest arare de die) / [f.106r] *cetus*: anglice wal, gallice baleyne / *suparus*: roket / [f.114r] (bottom of the page) mew and charne holt and hawe

---

[192] The commentary also has 'lugubrare est cum crucibolo vigilare ad librum de nocte'. The gloss 'lucubre: keus / kexis' is found in MSS of Adam of Petit Pont's *De utensilibus* (see below p.50 n.116) and confirms that what we really have here is ME *kex* and not a romance reflex of Latin *cos*, see MED sub *kex(e n.(a)*.

[193] See OED sub *wen*[1]. The commentary explains 'grandula quedam macula que quandoque aparet in facie quandoque in capite quandoque in manu ... et ita nuncupatur propter similitudinem quam habet ad glandem'.

[194] The commentary has 'Molosus est equivocum ad tria: est enim aliquis homo de Molosa regione et est idem quod magnus canis, gallice "chin de Muloce ou limer", vel molosus pes versificandi de quo patet supra in capitulo de pedibus metrorum'. The word 'Muloce' is something of a conjecture, for the third letter (which looks like 't') has been obscured by an ink blot and the 'o' is a superscript letter.

CHAPTER SEVEN

ADAM OF PETIT PONT'S *DE UTENSILIBUS*

THE MANUSCRIPTS FROM LONDON (A) CAMBRIDGE (CT), DUBLIN (D), LINCOLN (L) AND OXFORD (O) [1]

[76] *phale*: de une brethache (L) de brutache (O) / *tolum*: topet (A) tupet (LT) typet (O) [2] / *cillentibus*: movanz (L) / *radiis*: rais (L) / *perspicuum*: cler (D) / *prospicerem*: gardasse (D) / *ecce*: este vus (D) / *accelerantem*: hastaunt (C) astant (D) mey hastaunt (O) / *morabantur*: tarjeyent (C) / *tesqua*: wasceus (C) wasseus (D) waseus (LO) uassés (T) / *scabris*: aspres veis (L) / *dumeta*: busseneus (C) bussuns (D) bossunerus (L) busseners (O) / *quisquiliis*: ramayl (C) ramailis, scredingis (D) [3] ramalys (L) ramayles (O) ramillis (T) / *confraga*: lé pleses [4] (C) altesses de montans (T) / *rubetis*: bossoneus (C) bussuns (DL) bussuners (O) / *circumvallata*: environé (O) / *satietatem*: la saulesse (C) saulablieté (D) la saule (L) saule (O) [5] / *cotidiani*: de jurnable (D) [6] / *acido*: egrisans (D) egre (T) / *scriptuncule*: escrit (O)

[77] *adverte* .i. intellige: receyf, aperceyf (C) entendet (O) / *Gallia*: Fraunse (C) de France (D) / *adire*: visiter (L) entrer (C) / *adierim*: ey entré (C) / *invenerim*: ey trové (C) / *optabam*: require (D) requere (L) / *formam*: forme (D) / *evagationis*: de trepas (D) [7] de une trespas de curage (L) / *ymaginarie*: pensable (DL) semblable (O) / *ruralium*: uppelaund (D) opolande (A) [8] / *mansionum*: mises (O) / *ruralium mansionum*: de misis de chans (L) / *construendi*: fere (D) / *incomparate*: a comparisuner (D) / *venustatis*: curteysie (D) avenauntise (O) / *exemplar*: ensaplarie (L) ensaunplarie (O) / *argui*: estre pris (L) estre repris (O) / *licitum*: cunjable chose (D) [9] lue chose (O) [10] / *comprehensionem*: reprises (L) semble prise (O) / *planum*: plané (A) / *in yma*: dekis a funs (D) bassete (L) / *admittendi*: a reseyvre (O) / *comparabas*: tu compariez (D) / *tranquillitas*: peysebleté (D) pasibilité (A) peysibleté (O) / *rivulorum*: de russeus (D) / *incursione*: encurs (D) [11] / *lucidi*: lusable (D) / *serenitas*: clarté (D) / *nebulosa*: noyluse (D) / *densitate*: espesseté (D) / *obvolvi*: estre volupé (D) [12] / (*latine a*) *Latio*: Lumbardie (O) / *minui*: estre menusé (D) estre amenusé (O) / *querebaris*: pleynouis (D) tu compleynowes (O) / *usitatissimarum*: de usis (D) mout usysse (L) / *ignotissima*: tres mescunu (O) / *absoleta*: lesuseis [corr. desuseis] (D) / *eruditos*: aprisés (D) / *celebrari*: estre celebré (O) / *oportere*: convenir (DO) / *labinas*: waciaus, vaseus (A) mareiys (D) mareis (L) lé mareys (CO) / *recidiva*: lé recoupures (C) [13] recoupurus (D) plaisuz

---

1 For full details see vol.1, pp.166f.
2 See TL 10,316 sub *tipet*.
3 See OED sub *shredding vbl. sb.I,b*.
4 See TL 7,1056 sub *plaisse*.
5 See the forms in TL 9,166-7. *Saulé* for *saulee*? FEW 2,247a cites Judaeo-French *saule*.
6 Not in TL or Gfry.
7 For *trepas* = digression see TL 10,617.
8 See OED sub *upland sb.*[1] & *a.*[1]B.
9 See AND sub *cungeable*.
10 See Gfry 5,23b sub *loisir* and FEW 5,308.
11 See Gfry 3,120c sub *encours*.
12 See Gfry 8,297b sub *voloper*.
13 See Gfry 6,686a sub *recoupure*.

(A) [14] recoperes, lé copurus (L) la recoupure (O) / *arbusti*: arbirine,[15] bussuner (D) butunire (L) buttunere (O) / *flagella*: les sumés (T) escurge (O) lé batures (C) / *cime*: anglice crop (C) butuns (A) coumis (D) [16] botuns de verges (T) / *intuitum*: gart (D) men regard (C) / *vepricule*: runces (A) lé rounces (C) petites runses (L) petites runces (O) / *sirmata*: lé repliures (C) les emplés, les enpleys (D) les enpleys (L) emplet (O) / *oblitantes*: ravisauns (O) / *planete*: de mantel (D) de mantel plen (L) mauntel (O)

[78] *territorii*: terroal (D) terrail (L) torayl (O) del tarail (T) de terre waynable (C) / *circumspectio*: la viroun regard (C) virun gard (D) verun gar (L) la virun agard (O) / *sationales*: chans semables (L) semables (O) / *pascuos*: pe(n)sablis (D) pessables (LO)[17] / *consiti*: chauns entablis (D) / *consitos*: entablis (D) entablés (L) entés (O) / *floreos*: florisables (O) / *intemoscebam*: entrekoneysey (L) je entreconisowe (O) / *habundabant*: furent paremplés (O) / *pascui*: chaump pe(n)sables (D) / *apiculis*: de ez (C) de petites yez (L) / *sationales*: semables (LO) / *caulis*: faudes (DL) de faudes (CO) / *opilionum*: berchers (CD) de bercher (L) bercher (O) / *mapalibus sive magalibus*: holez (C) hulez (A) hulettis (D) de oletes (L) holet (O) / *consiti*: entés (A) / *surculis*: petit entis (D) de grafe (L) greffes (O) / *corticibus*: cors (D) de cores (L) / *intersertis*: entrelacez (C) entoys (D) entés (L) / *libro*: escors (C) / *ramusculos*: brancheries (L) / *translatis*: remuesz (A) utre porteys (L) / *sationalibus*: semablis (D) semables (LO) / *arcifinii*: les foreres (C) crufftis, finis, forreris (D) crufteyt (L) croftes (A) cruftes (O) crofs (T) [18] / *squalidi*: cotefeys, freges (D) [19] cotyfyez (L) ben cutifiez (O) / *novalia*: waresz (A) warez (C) warest (D) uaresz (L) warés (O) uuarés (T) / *cum succiniis*: hevedlaundes (A) purpreturis (C) purprestures (O) ov autre purpresturis (D) purpreturis, anglice sege (L) [20] / *uliginos*: grasses (T) / *acurate*: ententimen (D) cortese-

---

[14] See TL 7,1057 sub *plaissëiz* and *plaissié*. On f.12r of MS A there is the gloss 'rami qui scissi sunt ab arboribus et per umorem iterum reviviscentur'.

[15] MS O f.150v glosses with 'locus ubi crescunt arbores'. Cf. FEW 1,125a.

[16] MS O f.150v glosses *cima* with 'summitas virgarum' and *cime* with 'folia arborum'. See MED sub *crop* n.2(c) and TL 2,602 sub *come*.

[17] In D *pensables* is written out, but later recurs as *pēsables*. FEW 7,695a–696b does not give this adjective.

[18] See DMLBS sub *arcifinium* ('land at edge of field, headland (in open field), croft'). See also MED sub *croft* n.

[19] See TL 3,ii,2261 sub *friche*. Normally (see Isidore, *Etym.* XV,13,13) *squalidus* indicates waste or barren land, but Scheler's gloss (*art. cit.*, 78) *compotés* shows that the word might also be interpreted as 'covered with muck i.e. manure' and hence give rise to the glosses which give the sense 'cultivated'. In both D and L *squalidi* is also furnished with the Latin gloss *culti*.

[20] Scheler's text has *cum succiliis* and offers the gloss *pourpastures*. Hauréau's base MS (Paris, B.N. 14877) has *cum succidiis* and the gloss *succidium est forieres et est souch gallice*. Haupt's and von Fallersleben's reading, *cum subcisivis*, is the best and is quoted along with Isidore, *Etym.* XV,13,15 ('subcisiva, agri quos in pertica divisos recusant quasi steriles vel palustres') in the commentaries provided in MSS CDL. The form *succinium* is several times cited as an alternative to *subcisiva* and D also offers *subcidium* and *subcizimum*. MS L f.54vb continues the gloss 'Item subcisivum est generaliter sumptum quod a nemore vel a saltibus vel a loco diu vel nunquam preparato abcisum ad culturam faciendam'. The word *porpresture* is given only as a legal term in Gfry 6,304c and OED sub *purpresture*. For *hevedlaund* = *foriere* see TL 3,ii,2100. See also OED sub *sedge sb.*[1]a.

ment (T) / *sucidiis*: buces (T) [21] / *cardinibus*: de divisez (L) [22] / *decumanis*: de reale viz (L) de reale veis (T) [23] / *limitati*: merchés (CDOT) merchez (L) / *glebas*: bleystes (C) blestis (D) bletez (L) blestes (O) / *ante sationem*: devant semesun (L) semysun (O) la semeison (T) / *runcatione*: sarclure (D) par sarclure (L) par serclure, a *runco -as*, sarcler (O) pessure (T) [24] / *letamine*: composture (D) compoturre .s. marle vel fezniz (L) par composture (O) de fen (T) / *occatione*: par ersure (L) hersur (O) debrussure (T) / *occetacione*: par blesture, bature (D) par bleture (L) par blesture (O) [25] / *occacionem*: bature, ab occo -as, gallice hersure (D) / *veracta*: warés (CO) uarest (D) waressy (L) / *prohibebat*: defendoyz (L) / *frutecta*: bossuns (T) bussuneris (D) / *fructeta*: busuneres (L) / *fructecta*: bussuners (O) / *inter fructeta*: entre les bussoneus (C) / *equitio*: harases (L) haras (O) hars (T) / *vagantes*: wacerauns (D) wagerans (L) wacrauns (O) / *non tedebat*: il ne mey anuad pas (O) / *badios*: bayz (C) bais (A) bays (DLO) / *aureos*: orius (A) [26] sorz (C) / *mirrheos*: auke sorz, liarz (C) auke sors (DO) sors (A) acuy sors (L) / *cervinos*: meyneit sors, mey[n] sors (D) mens sors (L) / *a vulgo*: comunement (L) / *vocabantur*: astent apeleyz (L) / *garannes*: lyarz (C) liards (D) lylares (L) bayars (O) / *gilvos*: fauz (C) faunis (D) faves (LT) fauves (O) / *gillos*: favel (A) / *glaucos*: bloys (CD) / *scutulatos*: techelez, vergilez (C) virgilez (D) vergelés (LO) techilés (T) / *guttatos*: pomelés, techilez (C) pumelés (DO) pomeleys (L) pomelés (T) a gutta .s. pumel (A) / *gillivos*: a gutta .s. pumelee (A) [27] / *canos*: chanuz (C) / *candidos*: blanz (C) pure blancs (D) pur blanch (L) pur blans (O) / *albos*: aukis [blancs] (D) acuys blanch (L) meyns blans (O) / *glaucos*: ferant (A) / *nigros*: nerreyz (L) neirs (O) / *varios*: veyrous (C) veyrus (D)

[79] *dosinos*: faus (C) ferrauns, colur de ane (D) feranysz (L) / *dosios*: ferrans (O) / *cinereos*: bloy (A) / *equiferos*: afre (C) afris (D) averes (T) [28] havere (L) averis (O) / *quadripartitum*: parté en catre (D) party en catre (O) / *jocundabar*: delytoye (L) je delitowe (O) / *vestigatores*: traseours (C) schasurs (D) cha[s]urs (L) chasurs (O) / *indagatores*: enserchours (C) enserchurs (D) eserchurs (L) / *sallatores*: escorchours (C) eschorchurs (D) echorchrus (L) escochurs (O) / *pressores*: berseours (C) berssurs (D) bersurs (LO) / *venatorum*: de chasour (C) / *huiusmodi circumspectione*: de tel veruntgard (L) environ agard (O) de verun gart (D) / *nondum saciatus*: ne mie

---

21 *Buces* for *bouges*? Cf. Gfry 1,698a sub 5. *bouge* ('terrain inculte et couvert de petites brandes') and FEW 1,424a sub *bodica* (*brachfeld*). The Berlin MS has *bucces*.

22 See DMLBS sub 1 *cardo c* ('boundary') and Isidore *Etym*. XV,14,4. MS O glosses *cardinibus* with *limitibus, de veis*.

23 Several MSS gloss *viis regalibus* (e.g. CDL) and L explains 'quia .x. facit foras .i. spacia pedis', whilst C has '.i. spacium .x. pedum'.

24 See FEW 8,334a (*peceure* 'rupture, fraction') and 335a (*depeceure*).

25 See Isidore, *Etym*. XVII,2,4 and FEW 1,410a.

26 See TL 6,1285 sub *oriuel*.

27 This seems to be misplaced from the previous entry where the noun *pumel*, if it is not an error (it is not attested with the sense given there in FEW 9,151b et seq.), is probably a back formation from the adjective.

28 See FEW 4,363a for *avre* = 'jument'. In the right-hand margin of f.136r T has 'indago, encherchisun'. At the bottom of the same folio there is the entry 'ulva, jaupie'. In MS Oxford, Bodleian Library, Digby 172 f.143va we find 'ulva [= herba], chenapie' and in MS Oxford, Corpus Christi College 62 f.31r [*Graecismus* X,281] 'ulva paludis, gallice canne, chenaupie'. See above p.29 n.146. The word is not recorded in the dictionaries.

uncore asaulé (O) / *metatum*: une mote (CD) mote (D) chastel (A) / *tanta*, a quo *tantillum*: neym (O) / *vallum*: bayl (C) bayl, paliz (A) le bayl (O) bail (T) / *circumluvio*: un wassel (D) wasel (L) le wase[l] (O) fossa, ordure (A) / *mole*: purseynt (C) aparaylemen (D) aparalement (L) / *circumlinio*: le gort (T) / *extrinsecus*: par dehors (D) / *vallos*: les peuz (C) haye (L) hayes (O) / *sepes*: hirsuns (A) les hirsuns (T) [29] / *sudibus*: peus (DLO) par peus (C) / *lentatis*: turneys (L) / *intextos*: tyssuré (L) / *intervallis*: espacis (D) entre-espaces (O) / *angustis*: estreytes (O) / *distantes*: purloynant (D) / *munitionem*: garnisement (L) garnicement (O) / *munitiones*: garnicemens (D) / *porta*: porte (D) / *valvas*: wikés (C) wykeis (D) wyckés (L) wichés (A) wicas (O) / *complicabiles*: movables (C) pliables (O) / *conspicabiles* [sic]: plyabelis (D) pliables (L) / *cilleri*: estre . . . (L) / *celerimum introitum*: a l'ignel entré (L) / *celerimum*: ignel (D) / *introitum*: entreye (O) / *anno duodecimo*: du utym auns (sic) (D) / *nothi*: lé bastarz (D) bastard (D) bastars (AT) baistard (L) / *consobrini*: cosins (O) / *patrueles*: fis de mes huncles (T)

[80] *veneram*: je suve . . . (D) / *martertere*: de ma haunte (D) de une aunte (L) de ma aunte (O) antee (T) / *stematum*: genologie, de linnache (L) de lignage (O) de lyne (D) genologie (A) / *colloquendo*: en parlant (L) / *vestibulum*: porche (CD) pocche (L) une porche (O) / *amplum*: large (C) / *habitatoriis*: habitables (D) / *repositoriis*: wardorobas (A) wardrobes (C) varrobis (sic) (D) de warderobus (L) warderobes (O) de uuarderobis (T) / *operariis*: de mesuns a mester (D) de overus (L) uverurs (O) / *officiniis*: de brasines (C) metrez (L) [30] / *circumdatum*: verunturné (L) / *spatio quintane*: de veie de .v. pas (T) / *porticum*: porte vel porche (D) porche (L) / *forme*: furme (D) / *inbulis*: a les vousures (C) woutsurres (D) vosure (L) a vousure (O) wuosuris (T) / *comparandam*: a comparesoner (D) comparisunner (D) a o(l)yler (L) / *licostrata*: pavemen de per (D) pavemens (O) lé pavemens (T) / *tessellis*: de tyulez quarés (C) de per de marbre (D) de pere de mabre (L) de peres quartes (O) / *crustis*: de pesez de marbre (C) pecis de metal (D) de peces de metal (O) de pase de metal (L) / *ostracum*: pavement de terre (D) / *testaceum*: de tees, testaceus, -a -um . . . est gallice tees et alio nomine tyule de tere (O) tesogés (A) [31] / *calcari* a quo *calcatorium*: presur (O) pressur (D) / *colluvio*: wassel (D) wasel (L) de wasel (O) ordure (T) / *palacium*: paleys (D) / *edulio*: frese (A) compange (CT) gerunner (D) de chaylun (L) geruner (O) [32] / *terserat*: ut ters (D) avet sué (O) aveit ters (C) / *luxo*: aloché (C) losché (D)

---

[29] See TL 4,1086 sub *hericon*.

[30] Hauréau's text has *officiariis*, Scheler's *officinis*. MS C has *officinis vel officiniis* and in the commentary glosses with .*i. pandoxiniis*, which explains the vernacular *de brasines*. In D, following *operariis*, the Latin gloss is *idem est* and what must be regarded as 'ateliers' explain the use of the word *mester* in MSS DL and the Berlin copy. Scheler cites the gloss *u de quisines*.

[31] See FEW 13,i,286b *et seq.* and TL 10, 279 sub *tessoncel*. The gloss in O is written in the left-hand margin of f.151v.

[32] MS L f.56rb glosses 'edulium, numiculum quod cocus habet ante gremium dum tractat cibaria, ab edo -es, vel est pinguedo carnei cibi', as does D f.171v. MS C p.23 glosses *edulium* with 'pinguedine, companage' and O f.151v explains *edulio* '.i. panniculo quod cocus habet ante gremium'. MS A f.12v has 'edulium dicitur de edo -dis, quod dicitur gallice frese', see TL 3,ii,2221 sub *frase*. Cf. WW 661,9 'edulium: sowle' and see OED sub *sowl*. See also Du Cange sub *gremiali*.

eloché (LO) anuché (A) russché (T)[33] / *parasitastro*: jujeler (D) glutun (O) / *obgan-nienti*: rechinaunt (CO) eschinant (D) rechinant (L) / arridentem (corr. alliden-tem): ahurtant (O) / *in abacte*: veylesse (D) en veylye (O) / *glore*: la feme mun frere (L) / *matertera*: haunte (D) / *in pueritia*: en ma fance (D)

[81] *expostulant*: demandent (C) / *meniana*: solers (CDO) aus solers (T) / *lectisternia*: seges (L) de lectun (T)[34] / *discumbendum erat*: a ser a manger (C) a manger (O) l'on dust manger (L) / *simplis*: curtines, boncs (A) cuverturis (D) de cortines (L) de cuverturis (O) / *siplis*: de simpl[e]es chalouns (C)[35] / *amphitapis*: doubles chalouns (C) de tapys (L) de tapiz (O) / *siphis* [sic]: peti banchers (T)[36] / *amphitacis* (sic): grans banchers (T) / *coornata*: atifez (C) urné (O) / *cene*: del soper (C) / *apparatum*: le aparaylement, le atyr (C) le apparaylement (O) / *compellit*: aforcet (O) / *admiratio*: amerveylement (O) / *azimus*: aliz (ALO) levene (T) / *hirfungia*: coket (C) / *yfungia*: coket (D) / *hyffungia*: cocket (L) / *effungia*: koket (O) kochet (C) / *hiffungia*: kochet (A) pan cochet (T)[37] / *placenta*: simenel (CD) symenel (O) wastel (AL) uateus (T) / *celia*: cerveise (L) serveyse (O) cervece (T) / *mulsum*: mede (CDO) musti (L) bochet (A)[38] / *succinatum*: vin epurgé vel sisere (C)[39] espurgé (DO) vin purgé (L) / *passum*: vin de Aucernez (L) / *lorea*: de lorer (O) laurer (L) / *genera*: maneres (O) / *murina*: vin vermayl (C) muree (A) moree (L) / *succiduis*: de suse (C) suz (D) de suz (L) suz vel mirsaus (A)[40] de suz (O) / *taxea*: lardys (C) lardice (D) lard (AL) larduz (O) tripes (T) / (*taxea*) *taxum, -xi*: lard / *taxor, -ris*: bargayner / *taxum*: lard / *taxus*: tesun (O) / *cruda*: tripes (L) / *scruta*: tripes (CO) tripe (D) / *colustrum*: besting (C)[41] qualeboz (O) meg (T) / *quactum*: lait egre (A) let egre vel creme (C) surlet, creme (D) surlet (L) let egre (T) / *cimbiis*: bucheés, grand aquiel (L) / *genera*: la diversté (L) / *metodis*: de arts (D) / *iter agentium*: peuners (T) / *gentaculo*: deyner (DO) digner (A) mautinel (L)[42] / *viali*: fet en weye (D) / *merenda simplici*: simple meryene (C) / *merenda* vel *malimerenda*: rusy (A) russine (D) meriene (L) russie (O) ressie (T)[43] / *appetitum*: le appetit (C) / *represseram*: aveye estaunché (C) reprent (L) je avey estaunché (O) / *ad ultimum*: a dreynt (C) / *mala*: poumis (D) pumez (L) / *apoferetris*:

---

33   Corr. *lussché*? There seems little likelihood of a connection with *rocher* 'throw', see FEW 10,439. The form *anuché* in A is also problematic cf. Wace, *Roman de Rou* ed. A. J. Holden, 1.1772 (*noxer*). To the previous lemma, *terserat*, seems to belong the gloss *haveit terçs* in MS T f.137r which is apparently misplaced at *conquexerat* (see MS C p.23 'conquexerat .i. coinqui-naverat et tamen conquinisco -cis est inclinare caput ad dormiendum').
34   See Du Cange sub *lectisternium*. In Dief.[1] and [2] the majority of the German glosses give the sense of 'bed-cover', but Scheler cites the gloss *seges devant leitz*.
35   See Isidore, *Etym.* XIX,26,10 'Sipla tapeta ex una parte villosa, quasi simpla'. The forms *sipla* and *simpla* are constantly interchanged in our MSS. See TL 2,150 sub *chäalon*.
36   See TL 1,820 sub *banchier*.
37   See MED sub *coket* n.(2).
38   See TL 1,1018 sub *bochet*.
39   See TL 9,628 sub *sidre*.
40   See MED sub *mere-sauce* n.
41   See MED sub *besting* n.
42   See TL 5,1268 sub *matinel*, Du Cange sub *jantaculum* ('cibus quo solvitur jejunium ante prandium') and TL 2,1950 sub *disner* (where the form *digner* is frequently cited). Hauréau, *art. cit.* 48 prints the gloss *gentaculum: gallice matinés*.
43   See TL 8,421 sub *recie*.

paniers (C) petit paners vel corbuluns (D) paniers (A) corbiluns (O) haniers (sic)
(T) / *allata*: portez (C) aportez (L) partés (O) / *sufficerent*: suffeycent (O)

[82] *inter cenandum*: entre manger (D) al manger (L) / *colomen*: campanais (A)
chanpeneys (D) campeneis (L) champeneys (O) [44] / *apparitorem*: somenour (C)
bedel (ADLOT) / *calamistratum*: recokilé (C) [45] beu peyné (D) crespé, peniz, bey
pené (L) kokelé vel beu peyné (O) / *cesium* .i. nevosum: haudlé (C) tezchelé,
thechelé, .a. frekeneyt (D) [46] thechelé (L) techilé (O) / *atratum*: neir (L) de *atro*, -as:
enneyrer (O) / *gipsatum*: techilé de tere (C) halé (DO) teint de tele tere, ahalé (L)
bouié (T) / *giphatum*: arnement (A) / *cernebam*: je agardowe (O) / *plagiatorem*:
awertur (L) [47] / *scenium*: covert (D) culvard (A) culveret (L) culvert (O) / *intempto-
rem*: ginur (D) enchinur (L) engynur (O) / *bilosum*: irosue (D) irus (L) yrus (O) /
multatorem: turmentur (DL) murþrur (O) [48] / *gannionem*: enchinur (D) taverner (L)
tavenur (A) rechinur (O) / *oblectatorem*: desevur (D) decevur (L) / *femellarium*:
lechere (DL) / *buccum*: gabur (T) gangeler (D) janglur (L) / *balbut(i)um*: baube (D)
baubes, wlaffard (O) [49] / *balbarrum*: baubur (L) baubeur, fol losengur (A) / *babucio*:
losenger (T) / *lanistam*: pendur (D) bucher, pendur de larun (L) a *lanio*: depesser (T)
/ *susurronem*: groundilour (C) grundilur (DO) grundelur (L) / *ambigium*: de larunnis
(D) cuveitus larun pecorum (L) / *malis*: les joues (C) jowes (LO) / *inequalibus*:
disowilz (L) / *toxillis*: faces (DO) ces faces (L) anglice toskez (C) [50] / *ocillo* .i. parvo
ore: buche (L) / *oblongo*: auke long (C) beulonge (D) beslung (L) belung (O) /
columpna: le piler (C) piler (DO) / *obliquata*: esclenc (C) [51] esclem, returné (L) /
columpna narium: elung del nes (C) / *narium*: de nariz (C) narilis (D) de narrils (O) /
pirula: le bec (C) pirrun (A) bek de narit (D) beke (L) bec (O) / *obtusa*: rebuk (C)
rebuke, rebatu (L) rebuc (A) [52] rebatue (O) / *penulis*: espace de narice (D) narilles
(L)

[83] *interfinio*: l'ezpasz intre lé narilz (L) / *indecentiore*: en plus desavenant (L) /

---

[44] MS L f.57ra has 'colonis, chaumpenoys, a columpna vel quasi colentem comam .s.
copertum quia procedit erectus tanquam columpna . . .' and D f.172r 'colonus, chaumpeneys,
a columpna quia procedit erectus tanquam columpna . . . vel quasi colens comas'. MS C p.24
glosses *colomen* 'habentem longum collum'.

[45] See TL 8,464 sub *recoquiller*.

[46] See MED sub *frakned adj*. and for *haudlé* (= *haslé*) see TL 4,956 and FEW 1,162a. MS O
has *celium* ('in facie maculatum').

[47] i.e. *agaiteor*.

[48] See MED *mortherer* n.

[49] The normal form of the adjective is *balbutus*. See OED sub *wlaffe v*. and MED sub *blaffard*
n.(1).

[50] MS D f.172v has 'hic toxillus rotunditas est et diminutivum huius nominis .s. toxus .s.
face'. MS L f.57vb glosses *toxillus* with 'rotunditas gene' and the commentary on f.57rb has
'rotunditas gene et est diminutivum huius nominis toxus quod idem est quod fause'. MS C
p.24 has the interlinear gloss 'longis dentibus', whilst in the right-hand margin we find
'toxillus est locus ubi [dentes] infiguntur sive rotun[ditas] genarum'. Scheler, *art. cit.* 82 n.21
cites the gloss 'par rondesse de joues faelz'. For *face* = cheek see TL 3,ii,1547 and see, for the
gloss in C, OED sub *tusk sb*[1].

[51] See TL 3,i,924. Over *columpna* D has 'scim, chanil', see TL 2,216 sub *chanel* and AND sub
chanel[2]. See also OED sub *shin sb*.

[52] See TL 8,376 sub *rebois*.

indumento: par affublement (O) / *amiscuit*: meslat (L)[53] cuveri (O) / *liricines*: harpurs (DLO) / *tibicines*: estivors (C) estivurs (DLO) / *liticines*: cornurs (LO) / *cum lituo*: ruhet (A) ov grelez (C) ruet (DO) grele, ruet (L) / *in lectionum antiquarum commentariis*: ansy en estories (D) / *edificii*: herberjage (D) / *in conjectaneis*: en ses livvers (L)[54] / *admirari*: agarder (O) / *in menianis*: en les solers (C) solers (LO) / *egregie*: noblem[en]t (O) / *celii*: chicel (C) cisel (A) cicel (DLT) de cycel (O) / *pincelle*: pincel (ALO) pinsel (D) le pincel (C) pincele (T) / *licebat*: il me plust (C) / *phalarice*: berfrai (A) de befreis (C) berefrey (D) beferez (L) berefreys (O) berfrés (T) / *hastilia*: les launces (C) / *torno*: de vyse (C)[55] turnel (L) de tornel (O) / *phalam*: tor de fut (T) / *teutones*: les tyeys (C) teyés (D) tyez (L) tyés (O) / *pila*: darz (C) gaveloc (A) / *ca[t]aice*: haste (A) / *cateias*: haunstes (A) / *venabula*: espeie, lance a poy[nt] (L) espai (A) gleyves (O) / *amentate*: a coreyis (D) / *lancee*: birraus (A)[56] / *ferrate*, inde *ferrito*, -*tas*: ferrer un cheval (O) / *sudes*: peus (DLO) / *acuta cuspide*: par ague poynte (C) / *conti*: perchez (C) perches (DO) perches, peles (L) / *thecis*: foreus (C) fureus (D) furaus (L) furures (O) foris (T) / *pharetris*: en quyveres (C) quiveresz (L) quivres (O) / *coritis*: foreus (C) fureus (D) en furures de quir (O) fourés (T) furel de quir (L) / *a quorio*: de quir (D) / *scorpiones*: setes barbelees (L) / *spicula*: darz (C) / *spiculator*: flaelur (T) / *arcus*: arz (C) / *in vaginis*: en lur escauberd (C) echoubreis (A) wainus (L) waynes (O) / *mucrones*: espez (C) espey (D) espeyes (O) / *pugiones*: misericordes (ADLO) / *in dolonibus*: en burduns (A) furaus, haubercchez (L) .i. baculis vel en lur forrés (T)[57] / *genera*: maneris (D) / *frameas*: girsarmes (A) gysarms (C) gisarmis (D) gissarme (L) gwisarmes (O) / *macheras*: grant aspeis (T) / *semispatas*: fauchonz (C) / *semiplatas*: fauchuns (D) / *sicas*: gisarme (L) girsans (A) / *secures*: coyns (C) coynis (D) haches (L) / *spatas*: lees (A) / *propugnacula*: bretaches (C) bretagis (D) garnisement, bretache (L) brutaches (O) / *peditum*: de pouners (C) del pauners (A) pouners (D) de peoners (O) de poners (L)

[84] *clipeos*: escus (CDLO) / *loreas*: de quir (AL) / *peltas*: talevaz, bouclers (C) talevasis (D) talewaz (L) talavas (T) / *lunares*: rond (L) talevaz (O) / *parmas*: tarches vel targes (C) targis (D) tarche (L) targes (O) / *habiles*: legers (A) talavas (T) / *ancilia*: bouclers (C) targes (A) eskus (D) talevas (LO) / *ciliciis*: talevas, gall. forure de here (C) en foreus (D) forez de heyre (L) heres (A)[58] herris (T) en furés de here

---

53   L has confused *amicio* with *misceo*, although the Latin gloss correctly reads *tego -is -texit*. The text has *amiscivit*.

54   MS C p.24 glosses 'in illis libris probabilibus' and in the left-hand margin has 'conjectura est oratio probabilis et inde conjectaneus -a -um et conjectanei in numero plurali dicuntur libri loquentes de probabilitate'. MS D f.172v has 'liber quidam proverbiorum factus de conjecturis' and L f.57vb glosses 'in libris proverbiorum' and in the commentary, f.57va, explains *conjectaneum* as 'liber quidam proverbiorum factus de conjectanea vel a conjecturis'. MS O f.152v also has 'in libris proverbiorum' and in the left-hand margin has the entry 'consumare, echevir in bono'.

55   See Gfry 8,261a sub *vis*.

56   The word is obscure. Is there perhaps a connection with *beroyer*, TL 1,931?

57   The gloss *baculis* in T suggests the sense 'pilgrim's staff' which would accord with A's *burduns*, see FEW 1,632b et seq. The sense 'sheath' (see Scheler's gloss *gaines*) does not seem to be well attested.

58   A also has *hars, hen*. Cf. Scheler, *art. cit.*, 84 n.7 who cites the gloss 'cuverture de heuc (heut, hent?)'.

(O) / *politas*: forbies (L) furbés (O) armés, forbis (T) / *pelitas*: furbés (D) / *loricas*: haubercs (C) haubers (ADL) / *ciliciis*: gallice forure de here (C) / *textas*: tisues (D) tissues (O) mailes (L) / *ex circulis*: mayles (C) de mayles (DO) de malis (L) de mailes (T) / *circumsquamatas*:[59] gallice teus haubers, gallice emvirounés (C) environ regards (sic) (D) escardus, ferun veyz (L) / *ex laminis*: plates (C) platis (D) de plates de fere (L) plates de fer (A) de plates de fer (T) / *cassides*: heumes (C) heaumes (LO) / *lamina*: de plate de fer (O) de plate de ferz (L) plate de fer (O) / *galeas*: chapeaus (A) coyfis (D) heumes (L) / *ex corio*: de quir (DLO) / *tela*: darz (C) dars (DO) / *jacula*: kavelocs (C) gavelocis (D) gaveloc (L) gavelocs (O) dart (A) / *gladii*: espez (C) / *historiis*: estories (O) / *soliferrea*: tut de fer (L) sulement de fer (O) / *gesa*: gysarmz (C) / *mensacula*: quirees (L) quirez (T) hansax (A)[60] / *sibones*: armes sonans (T) / *verutenses*: espais (A) fusses (T)[61] / *clunacula*: hansers (AL)[62] / *lingulaverunt*: lancerunt (L) / *admirati*: agardés (O) / *ipogeum*: celers sos tere (T) / *edificia*: herbergagis (D) herbejages (O) / *vallo*: bayl (CDLO) / *in circuitu*: virun (D) en virun (O) / *spaciando*: enveysaunt (C) enjuaunt (O) / *bibliotecam*: livre (L) / *basilicam*: eglise (L) / *analogium*: lettrun de fest (D) letrun de feste (L) eglise (L) / *analogium*: lettrun de fest (D) letrun de feste (L) lectrun de feste (O)[63] lectrun (A) letrun (T) / *pulpito*: lettrun de semayne (O)

[85] *antica*: partie dewant (L) / *postica*: partie derere (L) / *parietinis*: lé mesirs (T) / *interaicentibus* (corr. *interiacentibus*): entir crevasses (D) (*interyantibus*): entre crevés (O) / *xenodochium*: hospital (DLOT) un hospital (C) herberch (A) / *planctibus*: waymicemens (O) / *misocomium*: une maladerie (C) maladerie (L) malederie (O) / *missoconium*: maladrie (DT) *misoconium*: maladri (A) / *apotecam*: un gerner (C) larder (D) garrner (L) le gerners (A) gerner (T) / *horrea*: grangez (C) grangis (D) grange (L) granges (O) / *entheca multiplici*: de viaunde, estu vel warnesture (C) mut maner de susten . . . (D) mute maner de vyanz (L) de estu (A)[64] / *chilindros*: icés pers (A) baleys (C) ramirs (T) / *in horreis*: en graunges (C) grangis (D) / *tribulas*: trubles (C) flayel (D) flael (A) flaels (T) / *tribulos*: flael (L) flaels (O) / *palas*: scovels (A) vanz (C) vans, venturs (D) ventor, ventorus (L) vans (O) ventoris (T)[65] / *pastinacas*: forche ferré (C) furchis de fer (D) furches de fere (L) furches od fer (O) / *forcillas*: furchis sant fer (D) restaus, forches sane fer (L) furches sant fer (O) furches (A) hars (T)[66] / *tessaras*: mesuris, bussel (D) mesures (L) mesuris (T) / *platea*: rue (O) /

---

59 See Isid., *Etym*. XVIII,13,2 'Squama est lorica ferrea ex lamminis ferreis aut aereis concatenata in modum squamae piscis et ex ipso splendore squamarum et similitudine nuncupata'. The text of C has *circumsquamatas vel squamas*.
60 See MED sub *hond(e* n.8(*b*).
61 Cf. Gfry 4,185b sub *fuse*.
62 See DMLBS sub *clunaculum* ('dagger') and TL 4,877 sub *hansac, hansart*.
63 The commentary in L has 'pulpitum festivum'.
64 MS C p.26 at the top of the left-hand margin has 'enteca . . . inpositio, gallice estu'. MS D f.173v has 'omne bonum positum et utile conservatum'. MS L f.58vb notes 'entheca vel ent(h)eca, utraque littera est bona'.
65 See Gfry 8,178b sub *ventoire*.
66 *Forcilla* usually denotes a wooden pitchfork or forked prop. It also comes to mean 'gallows', hence T's gloss *hars* (= *hart*). Blaise gives the meaning 'râteau à faner' which would explain *restaus* (= *rastoires*) in L. See also Du Cange sub *furcillare* and *furcilles*.

adjacenti: vesyne (O) / *vehiculorum*: karettis (D) de chareyt (L) / *redam*: carette (C) karettis (D) charette (O) / *plaustrum*: char, anglice wayn (C)[67] char (DO) chars (LAT) / *genera*: maneris (D) / *carpentum*: chareyt (L) / *pompaticum*: cars vel curur (S) / *carracutium*: charet (L) / *capsum*: carette (D) charet (L) chaar (T) / *contextum*: tysu (C) tysue (L) / *artecanistrata*: hoser (A) de l'art de vergerie (C) de art de osier (D) de artz de ocyr (L) de osier (O) de art de hosier (T) / *pilentum matronale*: char (C) une carette a dame (D) charet a dame (L) cur[ur] as dams (A) / *basternam*: anglice yledde, birie (C) une dreye (D) dreie (L) lede (A) une draye (O)[68] / *ruris fractii*: de arable (L) arrable (O) / *fracticii*: vanabel (A)[69] / *utensilia*: ustilemens (D) / *bures*: le manchoun (C) manz de la charue (L) / *dentalia*: dentauus (sic) (D) dentaus (O) cuins (A) herces (T) chep (L)[70] / *stive*: mauncheles (O) / *falcastra*: cutir (A) cutres (L) cotris (T) wedhoc (C)[71] / *runcones*: serclers (C) sercluris (D) sercles, hec (sic) (A) sarclers, wethoc (L) sarclers (O) cerculuris (T) / *scuticia*: bechez (C) bastuns (D) bastunis de fens (L) beche (O) / *seudicia*: beches (A)[72] / *epiredia*: siveres (C) civer ov roe (D) wolbarirue, civere a ré (L) civere (O) civere a roe (T) quelbarue (A)[73] / *occidentalem*: uest (D) de weyt (L) del wet (O) uesst (T) / *semicirculum*: dimesecle (L) demisercle (O)

[86] *parte alteri*: de la porte (C) / *in semicirculo*: virunment (D) / *orientali*: de est (D) de eyzt (L) del hest (A) del est (O) eest (T) / *appodentio*: a la lavenderie (C) pentiz (O) a la lavendrie (T)[74] / *haustra*: les buchés (A) les bokez (C) bokeis (D) buket (L) bukés (O) bochés (T) / *per vallem*: de val (D) de valey (L) / *phaleras*: herneys (CD) hernais a dame (A) harneys a houme, a dame (L) herneis a dame (O) / *saginas*: sambue a dame (C) herneys a damis (D) susseus, harneys a dame (L) sorcés (T)[75] / *saumas*: sarcibues (corr. sambues) (A) / *cauteria*: flemes (A) fleumes, anglice blodirnes (C) fleumes (L) chauferts (D, r-h marg. chaufreys a marchaus) flomis (T)[76] / *lupatos*: chanffreynz (C) chanfrey (D) chansfrenis (L) chanfreins (O) chanfrans (A)

---

67 See OED sub *wain sb.*[1]3.

68 Scheler, *art. cit.*, 85 n.23 quotes the gloss 'fled drae' which should no doubt be corrected to 'sled, drae', see OED sub *sled sb.*[1] and MED sub *draie n.* Cf. MS D f.145v (*Doctrinale*) 'truda, genus est veculi, anglice slede, dreye'. The commentary to the *Phale tolum* in D has (f.173v) 'gallice frode, anglice sclide'. In C the gloss *birie* is perhaps for *biere* (cf. MED sub *ber(e n.(8)1*). MSS A and O explain *basternam* with 'quasi vasterna' and O adds (f.153r) 'vehiculum sine rotis'.

69 Hauréau prints *rurisfractiva* whilst noting the variants *rurisfracticii*. Haupt has *ruri fracticii*, von Fallersleben *rurifracticii* and Scheler *ruris facticii*. See TL 4,5 sub *gäaignable*. MS T f.138v has 'fractia, howis, picoise'.

70 See MED sub *chippe n.1(c)*.

71 See OED sub *weedhook*.

72 MS T has a gloss 'scudia borduris', whilst in the left-hand margin of D (f.173v) we read 'scuticia, bastuns a carue, anglice a kir staf', see MED sub *kir-staf n.* MS C has *scucidia* in both text and commentary.

73 See MED sub *barwe n.1(b)*.

74 There is frequent confusion between *appendicium* (*apentiz*), *appodentium* (a sweep for raising water) and *apodyterium* (drying room).

75 See TL 9,969 sub *sossele*. The word is found as a gloss on *sagma* and *subsellium*. See also TL 9,923 sub *sorsele* and Du Cange sub *sagma*.

76 MS L f.59va has 'cauterium dicitur generaliter instrumentum ferreum quo utuntur marescalli vel aliter vero dicitur ferrum quo signantur latrones, inde versus: Quo latro signatur dic

/ *antellas*: arsounz devant (C) arçuns devant (D) arzuns devant (L) arsun devant (O) / *postellas*: derere (C) dere[re] (D) arsuns derere (L) / *deauratas*: suz orrés (O) / *nundiniis*: feyris (CD) a feyres (nundine Rome) (O) / *forum*: un pressour (C) pressur (OD) pre(n)sur (L) pressurs (T) / *iudiciis*: a jugemens (O) / *calcatorium*: un pressour (C) pressur (ADLOT) / *qualos*: paners (ALO) payners (D) paniers (T) lotez (C) / *quaxillos*: petyz paniers (C) petit paneris (D) peti paners (L) petiz paners (O) baschés (A) / *corbes*: corbales (A) corbayles (CLO) corbailuns (D) corbiluns (T) / *cola*: entoneours (C) colurs (D) saz, colur (L) sarz (O) sars (T) chalur (corr. cholur) de presur (A) / *prelorum*: de pressours (C) pressurs (D) pressur (LOT) / *acinii*: grein de grap (D) marc u drasche (A) de grein de grape (L) de drache de grape (O) de drache de oile (T) / *acervos*: musseler (D) muscesz, de *acervo* -as: munceler (L) munselemens (O) / *lacus*: un wé (C) uasel (D) / *trapetum*: mainmole (A) querne (L) trapel, querne (T) [77] / *fiscula*: sac (A) / *pinsentium*: de peytrisauns (C) pesturs (DO) de pestrizans (L) des pestrizans (T) / *ergastulo*: en un mesun traveyluse (D) / *cribra*: cribles (C) criveres (D) cribre (L) cribres (O) / *molas*: meles [sic] (O) / *clibanos*: forne de fer (C) petit furns (D) petit forns (L) petiz furns (O) furs (A) furnes (T) / *rotabula*: pele (C) brayheus .i. mensas super quas panes forantur .a. brake (D) brayes (L) sunt mense super quas panes forantur antequam ponantur in furno et secundum alios b[r]ayes, anglice b[r]aken (O) [78] / *popina*: quisine (LO) / *vercula*: espeyes (C) petit brochis (D) petit espeis, broches (L) broches (O) espais (A) peti apis (T) / *crates*: gridil (CD) greils (A) gredils (T) cleys (L) cleyes (O) / *creagras*: havez (AC) havets (D) havetiz (L) havet (O) / *fuscinas*: foynes (C) foynis, borissperis (D) [79] / *fiscinas*: fune, borsper (L) / *patinas*: paellis (D) / *coclearium*: de coylerz (L) de luches (O) / *patellas*: paelez (C) / *cacabos*: caudreuns (C) caudreuns (D) chadrun (L) caudruns (O) / *cacume*: chauderis (T) / *ollas*: poz (C) / *lebetes*: pots de arey[m] (D) pote de harem (L) poz de arrem (O) chaudruns (A) chaderuns (T) / *sartagines*: granz payles (C) grant paylis (D) grant chadrun (L) gra[n]t paels (A) / *mulgaria*: bukés (O) bochés (T) bokez (C) bouket (D) / *labra*: lavours (C) lavurs (DO) lavors (LT) / *pelwes*: basynz, gatez (C) bacinz (L) basins (O) gates (A) / *siciones*: grant basi[n]s (T) / *simphones*: basynz de arem (C) gatis (D) gatez (L) gates (O) bacines (A) / *angulo*: angle (O) / *girgullus*: un wyndaz (C) uindasse, turner (D) uindas (A) windas (OT) windanes (L) [80] / *funis*: corde (CLOT) cordis (D) la corde (A)

cauterium fore ferrum/ cauteriam proprie dices in carne foramen' (see, too, D f.174r). See MED sub *blod* n.(1)1b(d).

[77] See OED sub *quern*[1].

[78] MS L f.59vb has 'rotabulum, mensa super quam panis inforniatur' and on f.60ra 'mensas super quas panes forniantur'. MS C p. 55b (*Merarium*) has 'vibra est lignum ex quo pasta frangitur, anglice brake' and MS D f.144r (*Doctrinale*) 'vibra, tumberel vel bray, anglice brake'. See MED sub *brake* n.(1) and *brai* n. (2), TL 1,1162 sub *broie* and FEW 1,512b which cites the form *brayou* 'truelle à long manche, que l'on manie à deux mains, pour broyer le mortier'. Scheler, *art. cit.*, 86 misreads (presumably) *locabula* and cites the gloss *runde tables*, which fits the definition given in the commentaries, but does not explain our interlinear glosses. The latter are explained by Du Cange sub 2 *rotabulum* ('furca vel illud lignum cum quo ignis movetur in fornace causa coquendi') and by FEW 10,597b sub *rutabulum* ('Ofenkrücke'). See also Roques I, p.358 'rotabulum, -li: roables, c'est instrument a traire la brese du four'.

[79] See MED sub *bor* n.5.

[80] See TL 4,789–90 sub *guindas* and OED sub *windas*.

[87] *situla*: boket (C) seyll (D) buchet (A) buket, seolyz (L) buket (O) bochet (T) seyle vel buket (O f.153v l-h marg.) / *utres*: les boseuz (C) busseus (D) bucés (L) boteus de quir (O) buceaus (A) / *puteum*: puss (D) putyz (L) / *telon*: tumberel (ACDLO) / *ciconiam*: tumberel (D) ciconie (T)[81] / *pirgus*: fourn (C) furneys (D) petiz forn (L) forneys (T) / *opacorum*: de flaounz (C) flauns (LO) de rusçaus (A) flachuns (T) / *lagana*: turteus (D) flamiches, turteus en pale (L)[82] turteus en pain (O) pannechesles (A) fruture (T) anglice grampe kakes (C)[83] / *artocree*: russeus (C) rossolis (D) russoles (AL) russcholes (T) ruseus (O) / *ferreus arpax*: croc (COT) croc de fer, havés (D) croc de fere (L) croc de fer (A) / *nefrendes*: porceus (C) purceus (DLO) purcés (A) purcheus (T) / *cum sucula*: troye (D) truie (A) ov la true (L) une true (O) truette (T) / *arula*: petit porcherie (C) porcherie (DLOT) porcheri (A)[84] / *promptuaria*: gerners, selers (D) gheners (L) celers (O) / *arietina vasa*:[85] de terre (A) de tere (L) / *samia vasa*:[86] de arsile (D) de arzil (L) vasa facta de arsil (O) godez (A) / / *crisentica*: de horres (A) *crisendica*: hanaps de or (T) de or (L)[87] / *anaglipha*: entaylez (C) / *anagliffa*: entoilez (A) / *anaglipha*: vessuris taylis (D) / *mensoria*:[88] tablis (D) tabler (L) / *parapsides*: dublers (ALO) dubelers ou esquele (D) / *patenas*: paeles (C) plateneys (D) platenes (L) plateyns (O) / *lances*: esoles (A) / *gavatas*: salers (T) / *apoferetra*: corbaylunss (D) corbiluns (L) baskés, corbeus (O) paniers (A) paniers (C) / *discos*: esquelez (C) / *salina*: salers (ACDO) saler (L) sausers (T) / *acetabula*: saucers (CO) sauceris (D) sausers (L) sasuers (A) / *trisiles*: tresteus (CDO) trestés (LT) / *poculorum*: de hanaps (O) / *phialas*: vinagers (C)[89] violis (D) phyoles (L) phioles (O) / *pateras*: hanaps (CD) hanap (L) / *crates vel crateras*: godet (L) / *cratos*: hanap (L) / *cimbias*: beslunges (A) grosses aquieles (L) / *calathos*: paniers (C) paners (DLO) / *calices*: hanaps (CD) chaliz (L) / *scalas*: chals (A) anglice scole (C)[90] escolis (D) ascoles (L) eselles (O) / *ampullas*: ampule (C) / *onophora*: costreuz (C) costereus (D) costreus (O) / *enophora*: costreus (A) costrez (L) / *anaphora*: coterés (T) / *flascas*: costreus de quir (A) flaskez (C) hanap flat (DL) flakes (O) poteus (T) / *lagenas*: galouns (C) jaluns (D) galuns (ALO) / *situlas*: bokés (C) bochésç (A) seylis (D)

---

81   MS D f.174v has 'hic telo -onis, tumberel, a telon, longum, et alio nomine dicitur ciconia et est longum lignum quo aque hauriuntur et est ciconia lignum hispanicum, ut patet in litera' (see, too, L. f.60rb). MS C p.26 explains 'ciconia dicitur propter suam longitudinem ad similitudinem rostri cuiusdam avis que dicitur cigonia'. Cf. Gfry 2,133c sub *cigonille* ('mani-velle d'un puits'), *ibid.* 8,104a (*tumerel*, 'trébuchet, ressort') and *ibid.* 9,92b ('telo: cigugne, instrument à élever eau de puits comme font courtiliers'). See also DMLBS sub *ciconia* 2. and OED sub *tumbrel*[1] † 2.

82   The last word is difficult to read, but the entries in TL 10, 458 confirm the conjecture 'turteus en pale [= päele]'.

83   See MED sub *cram-cake.*. See also Bibbesworth 1.1125 'braoun, crispes e fruture (var. frutours)' and MS Cambridge U.L. Oo. 6. 110 f.50v 'hoc fructuarium, fruture' and MED sub *panne-cake n.*

84   MS C adds 'de ara, anglice coul, paroc', see MED sub *coule n.(2)*.

85   The texts and commentaries variously offer *arietina* and *aretina*, see Isidore, *Etym.* XX,4,5.

86   MS A has *semia*, see Isidore, *Etym.* XX,4,3.

87   MS T actually reads *de os*.

88   MS D f.174v has 'hoc mensorium a mensa; mensoria dicuntur vasa officio mense deputa-ta' (see, too, L f.60rb) and C p.27 glosses 'vasa pertinentia ad mensem [sic]'.

89   See Gfry 8,250a sub *vinagiere* ('vase à mettre le vin').

90   See OED sub *scale sb.*[1].

buket (L) bukés (O) bochés (T) / *cantaros*: hanaps (D) godermers (T) [91] justes (A) / *catinas*: gatez (C) gates vel poz (A) gatis (D) gate, granz poz (L) gates (O) / *orcas*: pois de speicer (D) poz (L) / *urceos*: poz (C) poss (D) / *urceolos*: possenez (C) posceneus (D) petis poz (L) petiz poz (O) / *sina*: anglice chesefad (C) [92] ficcelis, chesefas (D) ficel (L) buchés (A) / *seria*: buchez (T) / *seriolas*: corn de bugle (L) corns de bugle (O) / *dolia*: toneuz (C) toneus (D) tunel (L) cuves (A) / *cuppas*: coupe (C) cuvis (D) cuves (AOT) cuvey (L) / *semicadia*: gallice pipe (C) [93] petit barreylis (D) petit baril (L) petiz bariz (A) petit barils (O) peti baris (T) / *scorticas*: busseus de quir (D) buscel de quir (L) buceus a corio (A) bussés de quir (T) / *scortias*: boceus de quir (O)

[88] *perticis*: perches (LO) / *mappe*: napes (CLO) nape (A) napis (D) / *mantilia*: dubler (A) twayles (C) tuayles (D) tuallys (L) / *gausape*: grant nape (A) napes (C) tualis (D) / *manutergia*: tuuale a manz (L) twayles (O) / *facitergia*: curchevis (sic) (D) cuvechiés (L) kevrechefs (O) / *sarcitectoris*: de charpunter (L) / *cementarii*: mason (C) massun (D) maisun (A) de masun (L) masun (O) / *cindulis*: sendlez, lates (C) cendelis (D) cendles (LO) / *artificio*: engin (D) / *per succedines*: kevilis (D) chiveles (L) par le severunde (O) pans (A) / *epiros*: clowis (D) cheveruns (L) [94] / *compactum*: aseble fetez (L) / *patria*: par pays (O) / *Belvacensis*: de Beuvey (C) Beweys (D) de Beveys (L) de Beuvers (O) beauvaisin (A) / *mansione*: mise (L) / *diutiore*: plu loy[n]ss (D) / *Parisiensis*: parisien (O) / *ruralem edificium*: mise de champ (L) / *rurale*: de champ (C) / *edificium*: herberge (O) / *rure paterno*: paterne le champ (L) / *sallarii*: de sal (C) de sallaray (L) / *lucello*: gayn de leygistre (D) petit ganez de ly chigistre (L) / *addictum*: atitlé (A) atilé (C) teytelé (D) [95] baylé (LO) / *circumvolvendis*: a penser (DO) avirunturnés (L) / *pluscula*: par poye plus (C) / *presertim*: nomément (L) / *trapezete*: chaunjurs (D) chaungur (O) de cha[n]gur (L) / *circuitu*: inverunement (T) cumpaz (C) virun regart (D) / *pergirato*: environé (T) / *triviis*: carfucs (O) / *ab occidentali*: del west (DO) de wet (L) / *ad orientalem partem*: de ewyt (L) del est (O) / *meniana*: solers (D) en lé solers (O) / *de promptuariis*: gerners (D) de gernis (L) / *venimus*: nuz emes venuz (C) / *egredimur*: nouz yssums (C) issum (D) hissummis (L) nus yssums (O) / *a latere septentrionali*: cowte de norz (D) parte del norhit, dul choyt de norht (L) del nort (OT) del norte (A) partie de north (C)

[89] *meridiano*: ver le su (A) al su (L) al suz (O) en su (T) del su (D) / *oppositum*: acontre mise (C) cuntre mis (O) / *a latere dextro*: a destre coythz (L) / *virgultum*: verger (ACDLO) haie (T) / *geneceum*: mesun de sutre (L) / *adivimus*: nous entrames (C) / *telarum*: de teyles (O) / *stamina*: warp (C) [96] estayms (D) esteim (L) esteymes (O) / *tramas*: of (C) tremis .a. of (D) [97] treime (L) treymes (O) / *insubulos*:[98] eveldes

91   MS = *god'm's*. The word remains obscure. Cf. *godet* in FEW 16,340a et seq.
92   See MED sub *chese n.3(b)*.
93   See TL 7,962 sub *pipe*.
94   Scheler, *art. cit.*, 88 cites the gloss 'chevruns .i. clavos, bord nail'. (Cf. MED sub *bord n. 1(c)*).
95   MS O has *adductum* ('.i. deputatum'). See AND sub *atitler*.
96   See OED sub *warp sb.*[1].
97   See OED sub *woof sb.*[1].
98   MSS DLO have *subulos*. In the text MS C has *insubulos* ('spolus vel navicula') and in the

(A) essubles, navet (L) navez (O) navés (D) / *radios*: rays (DO) slays (C) / *licia*: hevelyredes (C)[99] filis, heldis (D) filiz (L) / *panulos*: navez (A) broches (CLO) perchis (D) / *globellos*: luceus (C) lusseus (D) lussel (L) petiz luceus (O) lussés (T) / *mataxas*: cerences (C) serencesz (A) serencis (D) serenze (L) serenses (O) / *alibra*: balaunces (C) / *alabra*: trauylis, rel (D) / *alibra*: peiz, trayus, vel *alabra*: trauls, rel (L) / *alabra*: trauls, rel (O)[100] / *celata*: chaylz (L) / *calathos*: paniers (D) banestuns, paners (L)[101] paners (O) / *pensis*: fusils (CO) fusilis (D) de fysil (L) / *quaxilla*: petiz paners (O) / *vopellis*: peysouns (C) pessuns (D) pessun, vertolye, anglice werve (L) vertoyls (O)[102] / *bissum*: cheycil (C) chesil (D) chaisil (A) cheysil (O) chaisil (T) / *canabum*: chamfre (C) chaubre, anglice henep (D) henep, cambre (L) chanver (A) chaunvre, henep (O) chanape, henep (T)[103] / *fibricium*: camelot (C) / *fibrum*: sclaveyn (L) / *sericum*: say (A) eseye (D) seye (LO) / *placium*: estoupe (C) estup (AD) astope (L) estupe (O) estupes (T) / *velo*: cuverture (O) / *auleis*: curtine de sale (D) curtineys (L) cuverture de sale (O) / *cortina*: surtine de chaumbre (D) fetiz de quir (L) / *cilicio*: de heyre (C) de here (DLO) hairer (A) / *cum primum intueremur*: cum nous agardames (C) gardasun (D) / *vestes expositas*: dubees (D) dublés (L)[104] / *vehementer*: durement (O) / *textura*: tissure (O) / *specie*: par manere (O) / *sericas*: de say (A) de seye (O) vestes de sey (T) / *olosericas*: tut de sey (D) tote de sey (L) / *tramosericas*: treme de sye (L) / *bissinas*: de cheycili (sic) (C) de chesil (D) cheysel (L) de cheysil (O) de chai[n]s (A) / *lineas*: fetes de lin (A) / *linosticas*: de lin et say (A) lin a steme (L)[105] / *melotinas*: de tessun (D) de tessun, broc (L) broc (O)[106] / *manuelas*:[107] velu (A)

[90] *trilices*: de trebble lyz (C) / *rallas* .i. raras: say (A) lincés de say (T) / *acupictas*: peynt aguel (D) pent des acules (L) peynt de agule (O) ataylés (T) / *jaculatas*: raés (CO) raees (D) rayés (L) / *acuatas*: fetez de acule (L) / *segmenta*: sage vestures (L) / *licina*: cleres vestures (A) / *interpole*: refelipes (C) refelepis (D) feblies (L)[108] / *pannucie*: clutez vel filieres (A) clotes (C) reclutes (D) recloytes (L)[109] / *polimitas*: pipelori (CDO) pipulori (L)[110] / *coccineas*: rug (A) de carlet (D) ascarlet (L) de escarlete (O) / *rosatas*: ruges (A) / *jacinctas*: colur de hinde (D) / *masticinas*: de blue

commentary there is a marginal addition 'hic subulus'. MS A has *insubulos*. MS C p.28 distinguishes *subulus* 'navicula textoris' and *insubulus* 'spola'. See FEW 4,727b sub *insubulum*.
[99] i.e. *hevelþredes*, see MED sub *heveld n.(a)* ('heveld-thred').
[100] MS A has *alibia*. See TL 7,2139 sub *poise*, FEW 13,ii,154 et seq. sub *traduculus*, and OED sub *reel sb[1]*.
[101] See TL 1,823 sub *baneton*. MSS CL have *calatha*.
[102] See TL 7,840 sub *peson*, Gfry 8,208c sub *verteil*, and OED sub *wharve sb*.
[103] See MED sub *hemp n*.
[104] See AND sub *dubber*.
[105] MS L f.61va has 'linosticus est vestis mixta cum lana et lino eo quod stamen est de lino.. . linosticus quasi habens lineum stamen' (see, too, D f.175v). Isidore, *Etym.* XIX,22,17 explains: 'linostema vestis est ex lana linoque contexta: et dicta linostema quia in stamine linum, in trama lanam habet'. See FEW 12,229a (*stamen*).
[106] See MED sub *brok n.(1)*.
[107] MSS CDL have *manellas*. Haupt prints *malvellas*, von Fallersleben *mavellas*. Hauréau, *art. cit.*, 52 notes a gloss 'a manu, quia manu debet teneri'.
[108] Cf. Du Cange sub *refibulare*. MS C glosses with 'vestes resarcite, gallice dobbé'.
[109] See TL 3,ii,1852 sub *filiere* and ibid. 8,435 sub *recluter*.
[110] See Du Cange sub 1. *Bursa* and TL 7,966-7 sub *pipoler*.

(L) waids (A)[111] / clofiolas (corr. oloforas): tot de poupre (L) / tunicas: cotes (O) / manubiatas: maunchés (O) / collobia:[112] frokis (D) froc (AL) frocs (O) / levitonaria: escapeloris (C) heykis (D) ekies (L) heykes (O) scapoloris (T) happruns (A)[113] / armilausas: espaulers (DO) apaulers (L) / lumbaria: wardecors (C) braylers ou uarde-cors (D) braeles (LT) b[r]ays (O) / tibialia: jenulers (L) genulers (O) / limos: manteus (O) / exotice: mut usé (O) usez (T) / sarabarra: esclaveyns (C) ces vestures qui usuntur Parthi (A) / Parthorum: de Torqueys (C) Turkés de Turké (L) de Turkés (O) / Gallorum: de francés (O) / lingue, vestes de lino: chemis (A) / Germanorum: des alemauns (C) de germayns (O) / renones: tabars (C) pelices (A) pelisuns (T) / plereque: les uns (T) / stringes: visers (T) / palliorum: de mantel (L) a pallio, -is: kuverer (O) / diploidem: mauntel furré (D) forye (L) furré (T) / antiquitus: aun-ceymen (D) / penulam: bife (L) / lacernam: blufe (sic)[114] (C) la çorcot (A) / mantum: mantel (CT) / pretextam: pal noble (T) / togam: gonele (D) / disploidem: mauntel furré (D)

[91] planetam: pleyn (D) pal (T) pal hairunner (A) / casulam: chape close (CO) cap et pal close (A) cape close (D) chap close (L) pal vel cape cloce (T) / birri: cherouns (C) geruns (T) / melotes: lutre (D) / pallia: manteus (D) / pepla: wy[m]ples (L) wimpel (A) wimplis (D) wymple (O) / richidiplum: pal suztrainaunt (A) / pallas: petiz man-teus (O) / libebat: il me plet (L) / anaboladia:[115] rochés (A) rockeyt a fem (D) rochés (LO) riverochés (T) / amiculum: coverture (T) / teristrum: rochet (C) rochet a point (D) rochés apicty (L) rochet a poynte, riveroket (O) / archa: huche (C) cofre (D) couefre (L) une wiche (O) / reculas: de beubelés (A) beubelés vel jueus (CO) beubeloss (sic) (D) bebielés (L) beubelés (T) / prenuntiante: awant nunciant (D) / lacunaria: chandelabres (C) chadelabres (T) chaundelabers (A) / lucubre: escorces, keus (O) kexis, eschors .g. (D) cresils (T)[116] / lanterne: launternes (C) lanterne (D) lanternes (LO) / cruciboli: crucel (C) crosel (D) crusel (L) crusil (O) / cerei: sirges (O) cirgis (T) / lichiniis:[117] de mecchez (C) liminuns (D) meches (LO) mechis (T) / preustis: awant ars (D) avant arces (L) avaunt ars (O) / cinduli: cospeus (DO) copés (L) / scincenduli: escorces (A)[118] / archa: huche (D) / aperuerant: overerint (L) / apices: garloundechis (D) garlandes (L) garlaundeches vel augmuces (O) / infula: chesubles (C) mitres (D) mitheres (L) chesubels (A) / pillea: hures (AC) heuris (D) ures (L) huris (T) / galearia: garland de or (C) chapeus de feutre (DT) chapeaus de feuter (A) chapeos de fetre (L) / cidares: round garlonds (D) garlaundeches (C)

---

111 See TL 4,721 sub guaide. MS C has '.i. habentes colorem masticis, anglice mader'.
112 MS A has colobaria.
113 See MED sub heuk(e n. and napron n.
114 See FEW 1,355b sub biff-. Bife and bifle are commonly interchanged forms.
115 MSS AO have anabolodia and D has anapolodia.
116 Isidore, Etym. XX,10,8 has 'lucubrum vocatum quod luceat in umbra; est enim modicus ignis qui solet ex tenui stuppa ceraque formari'. See MED sub kex(e n. and TL 2,1085 sub croisuel. Scheler, art. cit., 91 cites a gloss 'cortices' on the lemma cincenduli. See also Du Cange sub lucibrum.
117 The MSS variously offer lichinis, lichiniis or both. See TL 5, 474 sub limegnon.
118 MS C has cincenduli vel scicendeli. See DMLBS sub cicindela b ('lamp, wick'). See n.116 above.

runde garlande (L) / *ciclare*: gerlandesges (A) / *ciclades*:[119] gerlondeches (T) / *nimbos*: chapeus a plue (D) chapes a plu (L) chapes a plue (T) / *capitula*: chapeus de feutre (C) / *mitras*: coyfes (C) coyfis (D) coyfe (L) / *redimiculis*: les aurnemens (A) / *reculas*: chaufes (A) beubelés (L) veteles (T)[120] / *vittas*: bendes (C) bendis (DT) bend (L) / *teniis*: frenges (CLT) frengis (D) / *reticula*: crespines (C) britilis, kellis (D) kalles (L) chales (A) gallis (T)[121] / *discriminalia*: greve (A) anglice herbondes (C) grivurys (L) broches a greil (T)[122] / *acus*: guinoles (D) gwinoles, wyndre anglice (L) winre (T)[123] / *ancias*: tresures (C) tressuris (D) trasurus (L)[124] / *humerorum*: de spaulers (D) / *torques*: boos de or (?) (A) beyfis de or (D) beves do or (L) buis (T) / *bulle*: buttuns (A) botouns (C) botuns de or (D) botun (L) botons (T) / *monilia*: nuches (A) li fermaus de or (D) fermays, nuches (L) / *murenule*: cheyns (A) keynez (C) chonyes (L) / *catelle*: petit cheins (D) eschaeles (A)[125]

[92] *bubule*: botuns (T) / *fibule*: taches (CD) tache (L) / *bibule*: thasches (A) / *linule*: tassel vel layner de quir (D) / *lunule*: fermayles (C) taschez (A) layners (L) / *crurum*: quisse, de quis (L) de quises (T) / *perichelides*: bauis (A)[126] / *cinctorum*: de sentures (L) / *semicinctea*: seyntur demyparty (C) / *somotacia vel sem[otacia]*:[127] de taches (A) / *succintoria*: braels (T) / *baltheos*: baudrees (AL) bauderikis (D) badrés (T) / *strophea*: lisers (A) lisurs (CD) liser, lyseruns (L) / *catula*: chayn (A) / *brachilea*: braelis ou lisurs (D) brayles (L) / *odoramentis*: duz piemenz (C) de letuaries (L) / *olofactoria*: boystis (C) boistes (T) / *pixides*: boyste (L) / *inspectione*: en regart (D) / *saciati*: saulis (D) / *suppedaneis*: ecsameles devant le lit (C) / *subpeditaneis*: bauns (D) / *suppedita-neis*: banc (L) / *suppeditareis*: les desges (T) / *fulcra*: cultis (D) quisinez (C) chu[te] punte (A)[128] / *stragula*: vesture raé (C) chaluns (DL) dras raiis (T) / *lodices*: veluses (A) langeles (C) langeus (D) langés (L) veluz (T) / *pulvilli*: quissins (A) petites quisines (C) quisinis (D) quisun (L) quisins (T) / *culcitre*: cute punte (A) de plume (L) coltis (T) / *ex tomento*: de cotoun (C) de cotun (LO) purpre (T) / *lectice*: cheliz

---

119 There is a confusion of forms in the MSS. MS C has *cidaris* in the text and commentary, D has *siclades* in the text and *ciclaris* in the commentary, O has *ciclares* and A *cidare*. See DMLBS sub *cidaris*.

120 FEW 14,570b gives 1611 as the date of the first attestation of *vétilles*.

121 See MED sub *calle n.1(a)* and AND sub *cresspyne*.

122 MS L f.62va has 'hoc discrimen instrumentum separandi crines in vertice capitis; alio nomine dicitur glabella capitis'. The latter meaning is, of course, conveyed by *greve*. See also MED sub *her a.4(b)*, which cites examples of *herbonde* as a gloss on *discriminale*, and Gfry 4,342b sub *gravoire* ('sorte de peigne servant à séparer les cheveux') and FEW 16,48a (*graban*).

123 TL 4,791 gives only one example of *guinole* (glossing *forpex*). MS L f.62va has 'pectoris est proprie spinter, pariter est monile'. MD D f.127r (*Doctrinale*) has '*forpex*: gynole, uinnere', MS London, British Library, Arundel 394 f.59r (*Doctrinale*) has '*forpex*: guinole', and MS Cambridge, Peterhouse 215 f.38r (*Doctrinale*) has '*forpex*: wyndre'. See TL 4,790 sub *guinde*.

124 For *ancia = fibula* see MLW sub *1 ansa 1(b)*, DMLBS sub *2 anca* and cf. OED sub *tache*, *tach sb.²*. For *tresures* see Gfry 8,61b and TL 10,563.

125 See DMLBS sub *catella* ('ornamental chain') the vernacular reflex of which appears here to be a hapax.

126 *Periscelis* 'anklet, leg-band' is glossed in the commentaries here as 'ornamenta brachiorum' (MS L has *boez d'or*). See Gfry 2,753c sub *buie*.

127 MSS CD do not add the form *semotacia*, D having simply *semotracia*.

128 The MS has *chū pūte*.

(A) chasliz (C) chauleys (D) chalys (L) chaliz (T)[129] / *stratoria*: de estraim (A) leyt de streym (D) de stremt (L) lis a terre (T) / *came*: de jaume (A) de caume (L) champ (D) / *grabata*: leit de maladis (D) / *bajole*: portabels (A) lit portables (L) lis portablis (T) / *pernoctaturi*: demorir (D) / *calceis*: chausis (D) / *extractis*: de creyes (D) / *exutis*: de poylis (D) de spoleys (L) / *conscendi*: muntay (C) / *sponde*: furme (D) a une forme (L) a la spu[n]z (T)[130]

[93] *conieci*: je jetay (D) / *sedatus*: enpeysé (D) / *satis*: le saule (L) / *perspicuam*: cler (D) / *crepusculum*: oscurté (D) / *clarescentibus*: enclarissant (D) / *querebas*: tu demaundastes (C) / *obductam*: estopé (C) estupé (T) / *palpaturo*: tauster (C) taste (D) taster dé mayns (L) / *destinata*: aweyé (DL) / *efficaciam*: espleit (C) forsse (D) / *profitentur*: reieysinz (L) / *alliciendi*: detrere (L) treere (D) / *abducendi*: de aveie trere (C) / *videatur*: escreyw (D) / *intelligitur*: sseyt entendu (D) / *dissimula*: disseleyt (D) / *philologis*: prechurs (D)[131]

Glosses from the commentary in MS A

[76] *ocillo, -as*: pur branler / *rubetum*: englenter /

[77] *labina*: marais

[78] *squalidus*: . . . extra culturam positus .s. qui iacet fresche

[79] *equiferus*: aver / *metatum*: chastel / *clepsedra*: dusille / *wallum*: baille / *galaurium*: sors / *wallos*: sepes u irçuns

[81] *effungia*: coket et alio modo dicitur concavus lapis et fistulosus .s. pumice / *collustrum*: bestingue, anglice boisti[132] / *passum*: fort vin / *succiduum*: suz / *amphitapum*[133]

[82] *cessium*: tecchelé / *gentaculo*: digner / *apofare[tra]*: paniers / *multator*: bucher / *lanista*: bucher u pendur de laruns / *columpno, columpnas*: encaser[134] / *pirula*: puirrun del nes

[83] *liricines*: arpurs / *liticines*: cornurs / *penicille*: pincel / *celum*: cisel / *tornus*: turnel / *chateias*: haste / *cunacula*: hansax[135] / *dolones*: waines de fust

[84] *pilum*: gaveloc / *tecis*: fureus / *vagina*: gaine / *cassides*: haumes / *lingule*: lenge

[85] *pastinata*, instrumentum bifurcum: furche a estraim / *falcastra*: rest anglice[136]

[86] *haustra*: buchet / *saginas*: hernais vel hucel / *cauterie*: fleume / *excinis*: arche de vin, anglice drasche[137] / *forum*: pressur / *trapetum*: mainmole / *clivo*: pendant / *polentrudium*: buletel / *trubulum*: truble / [85] *epiredia*: kelbaru / *scudicia*: beche /

---

129 See FEW 2,i,488b sub *catalectus*.
130 See FEW 12,205a (*sponda*).
131 MS L f.64ra glosses *predicatoribus* and the commentary explains the lemma as meaning 'amator sermonum'. MS C p.30 has '*philologis* .i. predicatoribus et non ab omnibus sed ab hiis qui sola verba jactant et bene dicit sola quia non exsequuntur opere quod dicunt'.
132 See MED sub *best n*.
133 The word is explained thus: 'ab an, quod est circum, et tapetum -ti vel tapeta, tapete, de chaluns vel tapisce'.
134 See DMLBS sub *columnare* ('provide, support') and FEW 2,i,450a (*chaser*).
135 See MED sub *hond(e n.8(a)* and FEW 16,140a (*handsax*).
136 See OED sub *reest sb. Falcastrum* really means 'scythe'.
137 corr. *drache de vin*. See MED sub *drast n*.

[86] *cola*: culur vel tunnedur anglice [138] / *vercula*: petit espay / *creagros*: havet / *sartagines*: grands paels / *lebetas*: chaudruns / *alveum*: hauge / *labium*: lavur et pur lever / *girgillus*: windas

[87] *pirgus*, fur, et dicitur a pir, quod est ignis, et potest dici: escher [139] / *promtuaria*: sceler / *opacorum*: faluns / *scalas*: scales / *lagena*: galun / *apoforetra*: paner / *sina*: buket *sinus*, sinus, -nui: sain et pur sigle .s. pro tumore veli / *thelon*: tumberel / *cinofora*: costreaus

[88] *gasapa*: chape / *septentrionalis*: del nort

[89] *insubelino*: essubels u heveldes ab insubilo / *pencis*: .i. fisel et quandoque dicitur fusel / *bombicinium*: de say / *bombex* (corr. *bombus*?), media producta: winde / [90] *interpole*: redubés / *pannicie*: clutez / *levitonoria*: escapolori / [89] *mataxas*: sirences u tramois u char . . . a manu et terago . . . unde 'feves et pois sunt bon tramois' .s. lentensed [140] / *bissus*: chasil / [90] *limis*: ruchet a femme

[91] *pepla*: uinpel / *reticulas*: beablet / *reticula*: quaif / *lununar* (for *lacunar*): fester / *scindila flammantes*: sonses ardosz (?) [141] / *inculas* (corr. *infulas*): chesubeles u rochés / *galearum*: chapau de feuter / *ciclares*: garalandesches / *nimbos*: chapeaus contra nimbos / *acus*: winere / *catelle*: eschalers / *monile*: tache / *anabolodia*: cuvrechef / *licinis*: meches / *monilia*: nuges / *murena*: lamp[r]ei / *bulle*: butun

[92] *succinctoria*: baudree / *strophea*: lesere / *brachilia* (zona): anglice wachelode arcel [142] / *balteos*: baudré / *olofactoria*: buistes / *pixides*: buistes / *licticis*: chalit / *alabaustra*: bustes

Glosses from the commentary in MS C

[76] *inicia*: gallice agnyz [143] / *extemplo*: gallice meyntenaunt

[80] *officiniis* .i. pandoxiniis: gallice bracines / *terserat*: av[e]it (en)emflé [144]

[81] *taxea*: gallice lard / *taxea*: gallice lardun

[83] *sicarius*: gallice murdrisur

[85] *enteca*: gallice estu / *chilindrum*: anglice besme [145]

[86] *appodiencium* est tale longum lignum quod ponitur supra puteum a quo dependet catena vel corda . . .: gallice lavenderye / *colum* est id in quo calcantur vel primuntur uve; tamen colum proprie dicitur: entoneour / hic *acinus* vel hoc *acinum*: anglice hole .s. uve [146] / hic *girgillus* et hoc telon et hoc apodiencium idem sunt . . .: gallice tumberel / *puteum*: anglice welle

---

138   See OED sub *tunder¹*.
139   See TL 3,i,893 sub *eschier*.
140   See TL 10,578 sub *tremois* and MED sub *lent(en n.1*.
141   The first word of the gloss is uncertain, but behind it probably lies *sclises* (*esclices*) which the scribe miscopied.
142   I can offer no explanation of this gloss.
143   *Agnice, agnyz* etc. often gloss *cedula* or *appendix* in MSS of Nequam's *De nominibus utensilium*. In MS C p.76 (Adam Nutzarde's *Neutrale*) *agnyz* glosses *hec indula* and *agnicer* renders *indulat*. The link is provided by the gloss 'wickelschnur' in *Dief¹* p.299a (*inicia*). Cf. DMLBS sub *1 agnicium*.
144   The commentary confuses *tergo* with *turgeo*.
145   See MED sub *besm(e n*.
146   See MED sub *hol(e n.(1)1(a)*.

[87] *situlas*: boket

[89] *falcastra*: gallice serclers / *vopellum*: pesoun, anglice werve / *melos*: gallice tesun, anglice brocke

[90] *reptus* dicitur de repo, -pis, quod a quibusdam dicitur repta: anglice oversloppe[147]

[92] *semicinctum*: est zona ex diverso corio, gallice myparty

[93] *pluteum* equivocum est; est enim concavitas lecti, sicut hic, et pluteum dicitur tabulatum, gallice planchys, unde Lucanus 'sub pluteis cuius et tecta fronte latentes / moliri nunc yma parant' [III, 488–9] et pluteum dicitur gallice karole, cuiusmodi habent mona(r)chi cum libris et ad superpondendum incaustum, unde Persius 'Nec pluteum cedit, nec dimissos sapit ungues' [*Sat.* I, 106)

Glosses from the commentary in MS D

[76] *phalanga*: gallice tinel / *phalere*: herneys

[77] hec *cima*: leyveyn[148] / hec *sirma*: e[m]pleez

[78] hoc *territorium*: terrail / hoc *magale*: hulke[149] / *liber*: escorce / *arcifinius*: forere / hec *satio*: semissun / *runco*: sercler / *mirreus*: auke sor / *glaucus*: ferant / *guttatus*: pumelé / *candidus*: purblanc

[79] *dosius*: faune / *indago*: parc / *viaticum*: espense en chimin / *clepo*: embler / *vallum*: bayl / hic *vallus*: peus de paleys / *molior*: aparayler / hec *sudis*: peus / *intervallum*: espace / *ango*: destrendre

[80] *inbulus*: vousure / *licostratum*: pavement / *tessellum*: quarere / *crustum*: pece de metal / *luxus*: loché, par le lochure / *taxum*: lardiz

[81] *taxum*: lardiz / hoc *passum*: vin de Aucerne / *scrutum*: tripe / *merenda*: russin / *onocrocolum*: .i. butor, anglice rodrumbil[150] / hic *malus*: mast / hec *mala*: joue / *merenda*: russin

[82] *colomis*: chaumpeneys / *celium*: techilé vel lentilus, frecned / *scenium*: soulé / *gipsatum*: haulé / *scenius*: culverd / *intentor*: enchinur / *mala*: jowe / *toxus*: face / *naris*: li bec / *obtusus*: rebatu

[83] *consumare*: est echever / *celium*: chisel / *penicella* vel *pencella*: pincel / *phalerica*: berefrey / *cornum*: turnel / *lancea* (herba): gallice lanceleyt / *ferro*: ferrer un chival / *ferrus*: fer de chival / hec *sudis*: peuz / *contus*: perche / *teca*: furel / *coritum*: forel di quir / *pugio*: misericorde / *dolo*, -as: doler / *framea*: gishareme / *sicarius*: murresur / *propugnaculum*: bretage

[84] hec *pelta*, scutum amazonum: gallice talevace / *cilium*:[151] fureus de heyre / *circulus*: maile

[85] *xenodochium*: aumonorie sive hospital / *missocomium*: maladerie / *apotecha*: larder / hec *pasina* vel *patina*: furche a fer vel patina / *forcilla*: furche santz fer / *arundo*: osier / *basterna*: gallice frode, anglice sclide / hic *runco*: sarclur / *scudium*: becle (corr. *beche*), a kirstaf

---

147 See OED sub *overslop*. MED sub *overslop(pe* n. offers only one example, from Chaucer.
148 Confusion with *zima*.
149 See MED sub *hulk* n.1(a).
150 Cf. Bosworth and Toller, *An Anglo-Saxon Dictionary* (Oxford, 1898) p.786b sub *rare-dumla* and *Suppl.* (1921), p.684b and MED sub *mire* n.(1)4 (*mire-dromble*).
151 Corr. *cilicium*.

[86] *haustrum*: lavur, boket / hec *sagina*: herneys a dame / *saginarius*: pallefrey / *sagena*: rey / *ancillas*: arsunis dewant / *postella*: arsun derere / *colum*: sarz / *colo*: coler / *prelum*: pressur / *acinum*: drache / *acervus*, ab *acervo*, -*as*: musceler / *fiscina*: angle .i. angel[152] / *lebes*: caudrun, pot de arrem / *labrum*: lavur / hec *cimpho*: gate / *girgillus*: uindas a *giro*: turner / *funis*: corde / hic *funiculus*, hec *funicula*: boket

[87] *uter*: bussel / *telo*: tumberel / *opacum*: flaun / hoc *artocopum* vel hic *artocopus*: paste / *artocrea*: russel / hic *arpax*: croc de fer / hec *nefrendis*: porc, purcel / *sucula*: troye / *arula*: porcherie / *patena*: platel / *apoferetra*: corbilun / *accetabulum*: saucer / hec *trisilis*: trestel vel trepé / *gradus*: echele / *ydra*: tonnel / *catina*: gate / *sinum*: fessel / hec *cereola*, vas corneum: corin de bugle / *dolo*: doler / *semicadium*: baril / *scortica*: busseus de quier

[88] hoc *toral*: clalun (corr. chalun) / *sarcitector*: carpenter / *cementarius*: masun, a *cemento*: morter / *succedo*: cheverun / *Belvasensis*: beuveys

[89] *subulus*: navet / *panulus*: petit broche / hic *panus*: drap / *mataxa*: serence / *alabrum*: trauuls, anglice reil / *alibrum*: balance / *vopellum*: vertoyse,[153] anglice werve / *bissum*: cheisil / *canabium*: cambre / *fibrum*: sclaveyn / *placium*: estupe / *velum*: coverture

[90] *jaculatas*: raez / *interpola*: dras revoluté / *coccineus*: vesture de scarlet / *masticinus*: vestur blu / hoc *lu[m]bare*, a lumbo, *a[r]millare*: espauler, ab *armis*: espaules / *penula*: bifle / *palla*: petit mantel / hoc *tubrale* (sic) vel *tibratus*: genuler

[91] *regidignia*: cheinse / *regula*: beubelot / *cereus*: cirge / *lichinus*: mesche vel liminiun / *apex*: garlandeche / *infula*: mitre / *pileus*: hure / hoc *galiale*: eschapel de feutre / hec *ciclaris*: garlound / *capitulum* et hoc *capitulatum*: garland / hic *nimbus*: scapel a plue / hec *vitta*: bende / hec *tenia*: frenge / *reticulum*: kelle / hoc *humerale*: espauler / hic *torques*: bow de or / hec *bulla*: botun

[92] hec *linula*: tassel vel layner / *balteus*: baudric / hoc *brachile*: brael / *odoramentum*: letewarie / *alabaustrum*: boyte / *fultrum*: coylte / *stragulum*: chalun raé / hic *lodix*: langel / *pulvillus*: quisine / hoc *tomentum*: plume / *lectica*: loftbed[154] / hoc *stratum* vel *stratorium*: lit d'estrem

[93] *palpo*: taster dé meyns / *objurgor*: tenser / *reputo*: retter / *computo*: cunter / *deputo*: bayler[155]

Glosses from the commentary in MS L

[76] *phala*: bretache / *falanga*: tynel / *phalere*: herneys / *tolus*: tupet / *stola*: estole / *ocilleo*: braunduler / *ocillum*: brandelun / *tescum*: wasel / *scabo*: grater / *cibo*, -*as*: pestre

[77] *optamen*: desyr / *latino*, a *Latio*: Lumbardye / *absoletus* (sic) : desusé / *labinas*: mareys / hoc *residivum*: recoperun / *vepriculam*: peti runce / *flagellum*: escurge / *syrma*: empleyz

[78] *teritorium*: terrail / hic *sirculus*: ente / *liber*: escorce / *arciffinius*: forere / *squalidus*:

---

152 See MED sub *angel* n.1(a).
153 Corr. *vertoyle*.
154 Not recorded in MED. Cf. Scheler, *art. cit.*, 92 n.24.
155 At the bottom of f.177r there is a drawing of a plough with the gloss 'canti: stroc' (see MED sub *strake* sb.¹1a.).

freche / *abcisiva*: forerys / *succinium*: gallice purpresture, anglice juwoyngys (?) / *gleba*: bleyte / *satio*: semysun / *runcatio*: cerclure / *runco*: cercler / *letamen*: de creie, marle / *occasio*: hersure / *occetatio*: depessement / *veractum*: waret / *badius*: bay / *mirrheus*: auke sors / *gilvos*: fauvel / *scutilatus*, a *scuto*: escué / *canus*: un poi blanc .s. remisse / *guttatus*: pumelez / *candidus*: purblanc

[79] *dosius*: fauve / *indago*: palyz / *metatum*: mote / *tantillum*: neym / *viaticum*: despense / *clepo*: embler / *vallum*: bayl / *vallus*: haie / *sudis*: pel / *intervallum*: espace / *ango*: estreyndre / *munitio*: garnisement

[80] hic *imbulis* (sic): la vouysure / *crustum*: cruste vel pece / *morio*: fol / *luxus*: lochee / *luxu*: par le luchie / *genu*: de genuyl / *parasitastrus*: glutun

[81] *taxum*: lardyz / *amphitapum*: cuverture / *hufungia*: cokés / *placentum*: symenel / *passum*: vin de Auucerne / *succinatum*: espurgé / *scrutum*: tripes / *succiduum*: suz / *vo*, vis: moyster[156] / *colustrum*: caleboz / *quactum*: purled[157] / *merenda*: rusyne / *onocrodolon* (sic): butor, anglice dicitur rodrumbul / hic *malus*: mast / *apofe[re]trum*: panyr

[82] *colonis*: chaumpeneys / *apparitor*: bedel / *cesium*: techelé / *atro*: enneyrsir / *gipsatum*: haulé / *scenius*: kylvert / *intentor*: enginur / *gannio*: eschynur / *balburrum*: baubur .i. male loquens .i. wlastard [sic][158] / *lanista*: bucher / *mala*: jowe / *maxilla*: face / *oblongus*: beslung / *penula*: bifle / *obtusus*: rebatu / hec *pirula*: pinun del nes

[83] *interfinium*: espace / hic *liricon*: harpurs / hic *tibicon*: estivurs / hic *lituus*: ruet / *lituo*: corner / *menianum*: soler / *celium*: cisel / *pincella*: pincel / *phalerica*: berefrais / *tornum*: turnel / *teuton*: teys / *venablia* (sic): gleyve a sengler / *lancee*: gallice lanceley / *ferreto*, -as: ferrer / *ferrus*: fer de cheval / *sudis*: peus / *conthus*: perche / *techa*: furel / *pharetra*: quivere / *corium*: furel de quir / *pugio*: miserycorde / *siccarius*: murdrissur / *propugnaculum*: bretache / *pedes*: pouner

[84] *pelta*: talevaz gallice / *ancile*: talevaz / *ciliciis*: foreus de heyre / *politus*: planeys / *circulus*: mayle / *cassis*: heume / *analogium*: leytrun / *pulpitum*: leytrun

[85] *xenodocheum*: aumunerye / *misoconium*: maladerye / *apotheca*: larder vel gerner / *palas*: vente / *pastinata*: furche de feyr / *furca*: furca a fein / *forcilla*: furche saun fere / *reda*: charette / *carpentum*: chars / *canistra*: oseyr / *basterna*: dreie, freyde, anglice syide[159] / *falcastrum*: fauz vel faucile / *runcio*: sarclur / *scudia*: becche

[86] *haustram*: buket / *phaleras*: harneys a hume / *sagina*: harneys a femme vel a dame / *saginarius*: palefrey / *sagena*: deche[160] / *apodencium*: rode[161] / *postellas*: arçuns derere / *forum*: pre(n)sur / *colum*: sarz / *colo*: coler / *prelum*: pressur / *acinum*: raspe

---

[156] The full gloss is 'succiduum, suz, a succo et vo, vis, moyster'. The normal verb form is *uveo* or *uvesco*.

[157] Corr. *sur led*.

[158] Corr. *wlaffard*.

[159] Corr. *slide*. See note 68 above.

[160] The commentary has 'aliud est sagena .s. deche, unde 'simile est regnum celorum sagene etc.' [Matth. 13,47] et dicitur a sagis quia apud illos sunt huius ornamenta'. For *deche* = *tache* see Gfry 7,620b.

[161] See note 74 above. The Latin commentary here interprets 'drying-room', but *rode* is probably English 'rod' and connects with the correct meaning of the lemma, which is 'a sweep for raising water'.

de graps, anglice dref[162] / *acervo*: monceler / *trapetam*: mainmole, anglice querne / *pinsentium*: pestrisanz / *clibanus*: furneys / *popina*: quisine / *verculum*: broche / *fiscina*: ficine, anglice algar, borsper / *labrum*: lavur / *pelvis*: bacyn / *simpho*: gate / *ango*: estreyndre / *girgillus*: wymdase / *giro*: turner

[87] *situla*: boket / *utres*: bossés / *artocrea*: russole / *laganum*: turtel / *arpax*: croc de fer / hic *nefrendis*: porc / *sucula*: truye / *arula*: porcherie / *parapsis*: dublers / *apoferetrum*: paners / *salinum*: salers / *acetabulum*: sausers / *aceo*: enegryr / *trisiles*: trestel / *patera*: hanap / *pocula*: godés / *crateras*: hanap / *cimbia*: grosses equiles / *calathus*: panir / *scala*: escole anglice[163] / *scala*: escheyle / *lagena*: galuns / *situlas*: buket / *ydria*: cuvel anglice[164] / *catina*: gate / *sinum*: fessel / *sceriola*: corn de bugle / *semicadium*: peti baril vel estandard / *scortica*: buscel de quir

[88] *thoral*: chalun / *mappa*: nape / *sarcitector*: carpenter / *cementarius*: masun / *cindula*: cendle / *succedo*: cheverun / *epirus*: cloue / *Belvacenses, a Belvacio*: Beveys / *addictum*: baylé / *septentrionalis*: north

[89] *subulus*: navet / *panulus*: broche / *globellus*: petyt lussel / *mataxa*: serence / *alabrum*: traul, anglice rel / *calatha*: balestuns[165] / *pensum*: file, fusel / *vopellum*: vertoyle, anglice werve / *bissum*: chesyl / *canabum*: canbre / *fibrum*: sclaveyn / *placium*: estupes / *velum*: veil vel cuverture de lyt / *auleum*: cortine / *byssinas*: cheinse

[90] *coccineus*: vesture escarleyt / *masticinus*: bluys / *levitonaria*: scapelori / hoc *armillare*: espauler, ab *armis*: espaulis / hic *Parthus*: tu[r]keys / *pallium, a pallio*: cuveryr / *penula*: bifle

[91] *planeta*: mauntel / *casula*: chape close / *regillum*: mauntel regine / *anaboladia*: covrechef a dame / *recula*: beaublez / *crepida*: bote a moine / *noctilia*: anglice gloubert[166] / *lacunar*: lover / *apix*: garland / *infula*: mitre / *pileus*: hure / *galeare*: chapeus de feutre / *ciclaris*: garland round / *nimbus*: chapeus / *mitra*: coyfes / *vitta*: bende / hec *tenia*: frenge / *reticulum*: kalle / *acus*: guinole / *anca*: tressure / *humerale*: espauler / *torquis*: beu(de) de or / *bulla*: botun / *monilia*: nuches / *murena*: lampreye / *catella*: escheletes

[92] *perichelides*: boez d'or / *baltheus*: baudré / [s]*tropheum*: liser / *brachileum*: brayl / *odoramentum*: letuarye / *pixis*: buistis / *alabaustrum*: boyte / *fultrum*: coylte / *stragulum*: chalun rayé / *pulvillus*: quisins / *lectica*: chalet, lofdbed / *bajola*: lyt portable / *stratum* vel *stratorium*: lyt de estremy[167]

THE BERLIN MANUSCRIPT

Vernacular glosses from the text of Adam's *De utensilibus* in MS Berlin, Deutsche Staatsbibliothek, Preussischer Kulturbesitz lat. fol. 607 ff.13v–19v[168]

---

162 See FEW 16,671a and MED sub *draf* n.1(b).
163 See OED sub *scale* sb.[1].
164 See MED sub *covel* n.(a).
165 For *banetuns*.
166 See MED sub *glou-berd* n.
167 See FEW 12,285a (*stramen*).
168 This MS is extremely unreliable and its evidence must be looked at sceptically. All too often the scribe did not understand what he was copying and there are no doubt many errors above those that are clearly recognisable. There is an *accessus* which begins in a manner

[76] *tesqua*: vaseus / *dumeta*: busunetis / *confraga*: plesih / *rubetis* (.i. rubis): busunes / *delectat*: aucesme

[77] *venustatis* .i. nobilitas de cyr[t]: cor[t]isye / *perturbari*: etre trublé / *absoleta*: desusé / *labinas*: gallice mareys / *recidiva*: lé recopurus / *arbusti*: de l'arborie / *cime*: gallice cropis / *scirmata*: anglice ragys .s. plicas vel tenies gallice, vel burs, lé frengis [169]

[78] *territorii* .i. terre arabilis: ter wanabil [170] / *circumspectio*: la virun engat (sic) / *opilionum*: de berchers / *consiti*: chons enteis / *codicibus* .i. corticibus: a les escorchis / *libro*: a l'ecorche / *arcifinii*: forers gallice, anglice evitlondis / *squalidi*, asperi: ruch anglice [171] / *iuxta novalia*: jute lé wretis rabinés [172] / *cum subciniis*: o lé purreturus, buccis [173] / *cardinibus*: de merchis / *limitati*: merchés / *varecta*: varetus / *glebas*: bletis / *badios*: bays, bruns / *glaucos*: bloys / *aureos*: red, sorz / *guttatos*: pumelés, techelés

[79] *equiferos*: avris / *venatorum*: de chassur / *vestigatores*: trasçurs / *hylarius*: plus a . . . / *indagatores*: encerchurs / *satiatus*: asaulé / *metatum*: un mout / *conspicabiles*: agardablis / *clepsisse* [MS depsisse]: aver emblé

[80] *vestibulum*: un largy porche / *amplum edifficiis*: de mes vagis edifisys [174] / *habitatoriis*: de mesons habitables / *repossitoriis*: de warderobes / *operariis*: de meyso[n]s ovrables / *officinis*: de mesons de mester / *inbulis*: a voysurs, a voutis / *tessellis*: lapidibus picoys (sic) / *crustis*: de pecis de marbre / *colluvio*: de boy / *edulio* (.i. pinguedine edulii): de gres / *luxo*: loché / *conantem*: forsant / *parasitastro*: jugulur / *ogganienti*: arrechin(i)ont / *arridentem*: echinont

[81] *simplis*: de simple chauluns / *amphitapis*: de duple tapis / *cho[o]rnata*: athiphés / *apparatum*: le apparelement / *yffungia*: saminel / *placenta*: simeneus / *mulsum*: mede / *succinatum*: vin epurgé bloy / *barbara*: estrange pays / *taxea*: lard / *scruta*: (s)tripis / *succinduis*: de susis / *collustrum*: bustinc / *cactum*: creyme, sur lete / *mali et merenda simplici*: par un simple rusym / *represseram*: avey hetanché / *in apoferetris*: en paners

[82] *quesivi*: ge enquesy / *apparitorum*: bidelur / *calamistratum*: beu *cesium*: haulé, techelé / *gipsatum*: tachehilé de ter / *plagiatorem*: quchur [175] / *senium*: lechur / *bilosum*: cursus / *mulestatorem*: murdrissur / *ganneonem*: rechigneur / *oblactatorem*: decevur,

resembling that to the *Merarium* in MS C. The Berlin MS begins: 'Quamvis Moyses perceperat quo[modo] in carminibus verba falerata .i. ornata et exotica . . . eantur, tamen magister Adam de Parvo Ponte per verba alicuantulum inusitata proponit [MS proponere] se scribere . . . Intentio sua est illa vocabula in quamdam summulam compilare et omnibus scire volentibus publicare. Utilitas est ut, hoc libro audito, intellecto et retento, perspicasiores simus in vocabulorum significatione. . .' The instigator of the work is said to be 'Dominus Anselmus Contuaricensis (sic) archiepiscopus' and the author is identified as 'magister Adam Ballamum sive magister Adam de Parvo Ponte'.

[169] See OED sub *rag sb.*[1].I.1.
[170] See TL 4,5 sub *gäaignable*.
[171] See OED sub *rough a.*B.I,3.
[172] i.e. 'guérets rebinés'.
[173] Corr. *purpreturus* and see n.20 & 21 above.
[174] Corr. *largis*?
[175] A misreading of *cerchur*?

blandessur / *femellarium*: puters / *buccum*: janlur / *balburrum*: fol e mauveys / *susurronem*: grundilur, grunnur / *ambiguum*: decevabel / *lanista*: macecrers, macecrene / *notificas*: fet apeler / *toxillis*: gowis / *oblongo*: bellong / *columpna*: piler / *obliquata*: hlenqui / *pirula*: le bec du nes / *obtusa*: rebuc

[83] *liricines*: harpurs / *tibicines*: estivurs / *liticines*: curnurs / *lituo*: ruet / *edificii*: edefeys / *menianis*: solers / *celii*: chiscel / *pincelle*: pincel / *generum*: maneres / *licebat*: y me plut / *phalarice*: berfreys / *torno*: par vice / *cahyce*: gleyves / *teutones*: lé tyes / *pila*: dars / *lancee*: lances / *sudis*: des peus / *acuta cuspide*: de agu poig / *conti*: perchis / *in thecis*: en fureus / *scorpiones*: tales sagittas sed barbilé / *pharetris*: en quidvris (sic) / *in coritis*: en fureus / *in vaginis*: en lur escauberges / *pugiones*: misericordis / *macheras*: a gros espeys / *frameas*: gisarme / *secures*: escanis [176] / *propugnacula*: bretaschis

[84] *peltas*: talevas vel targis / *parmas*: targis / *in ciliciis*: en roulis / *politas*: furbés vel planiés / *loricas*: heuberquis / *circulis*: de maylis / *circumscamatas*: environ eskerdis / *laminis*: de platys / *cassides*: heumis / *ex corio*: de quyr / *tela*: dars / *jacula*: gavlokis / *gesa*: gisarmis / *sparrium*: fauchuns / *morem*: gallice maner / *sub vallo*: desus un val / *spaciando*: envesond / *armariolum*: almayre / *analogium*: un lectrun / *pulpito*: a le lectrum

[85] *patebat*: aperçut / *senodochium*: un hospital / *misocomium*: un fermerey, un maladrii / *apothecam*: un gerner / *entheca multiplici*: de mut maner de uarnisture / *apotheca*: un gerner / *entheca multiplici*: l'etyu de maigte manere / *orrea*: grongys / *chilindros*: baleys, besmis / *tribulas*: triblis vel flael / *palas*: vans / *pastinacas*: pikeis / *vehiculorum*: de caretis / *redam*: .s. caret / *plaustrum*: un charre, vehyn [177] / *carpentum*: caret / *carricutium*: chareta (sic) / *arte canistrata*: par har de verge(g)rie / *contextum*: tysu / *pilentum matronale*: un char a dame / *basternam*: (co)drey vel slite [178] / *dentilia*: chip / [s]*tive*: manchels, anls [179] / *falcastra*: serclers, weedhokis vel houes / *scudicia*: bechis, spadis [180] / *semicirculum*: demicercle

[86] *in semisirculo orientali*: en le demicercle del est / *appodentio*: par cumbl, a la lavandrii [181] / *haustra*: buchés / *valli*: d'un val / *per medium*: par mileu / *administrabant*: dunoent / *phaleras*: verneys (corr. herneys) / *saginas*: sambues a dame / *cauteria*: vlemis, blot-yrnis / *cellarum*: de sels / *antellas*: arsuns devant / *postellas*: arsuns darier / *forum*: un pressur / *calcatorium*: pressur gallice / *qualos*: paners vel ottis [182] / *quaxillos*: paners, petit ottis / *corbes*: corbals / *cola*: tunores, tunudors / *prelorum*: de pressurs de viz / *acinum*: du lye de vin vel cisere / *acervos*: musels, epis [183] / *lacum*: vasels / *pretereuntes*: passons nos / *pinsentium*: de pestrisun / *molas*: mules / *cribra*: cribris / *clibanos*: furneys / *vercula*: espeys, spitis / *crates*: grudals, greys / *creagras*: avés /

176 A form of *cuinies*? Cf. TL 2,534.
177 i.e. 'wain'.
178 Read *drey*.
179 See MED sub *hondel* n.
180 See OED sub *spade* sb[1].
181 The gloss *cumbl[e]* 'roof' suggests confusion with *appendicium*.
182 See TL 4,1186 sub *hote*.
183 Read *mu[n]sels* and see MED sub *hep* n.2(a).

fuscinas: a sper, crobas [184] / *ollas*: paels / *cacabos*: cauderuns / *gartagines* (corr. *sartagines*): paels a floer / *mulgaria*: buchés / *labra*: lavurs / *alvea*: grande lavurs / *pelves*: bacins / *ciphones*: bacings / *girgillus*: un windas

[87] *cum situla*: a un buket / *utres*: lé buseus a le quir / *in puteum*: en la pute / *siconia*: storc vel tumberel / *ferreus arpax*: un croc de fer / *pirgus*: un furneys / *opacorum*: de flauns / *laganas*: pancolas [185] / *a[r]tocree*: russeus / *cum succula*: o la truie / *in arula*: en un porrochc (sic), en la porcheryi / *promtuaria*: celers / *vasa*: de terre / *pathenas*: plateus / *lances*: esquelins / *apopheretra*: paners / *salina*: salers / *acetabula*: saucers / *trisiles*: trestels / *pateras*: hanapis / *crateres*: grant henapis / *calatos*: paniers, bakés / *onophora*: costrés / *flascas*: flakes / *lagenas*: gabins (corr. galuns) / *situlas*: bukés / *[c]antaros*: anaps / *urceolos*: peti pote / *dolea*: toneaus / *scorceas*: costrés / *semicadia*: pipis

[88] *mappa*: napis / *mantilia*: tualis, napis / *gausape*: un nap / *manutergia*: tualis / *facitergia*: keverchis / *sementarii*: de massun / *ex cindulis*: de cendlis, .i. hinglis [186] / *per succedines*: par cevrumdis, evesingis [187] / *Balsamensis*: Balsom / *Belwacensis*: Belvesin / *alicubi*: en aucun leu / *rurale*: champestre / *salari*: de salarie par gen(?) / *adictum*: atitlé

[89] *virgultum*: un verger / *stamina*: werp, esteyms / *patebat*: aparout / *oppositum*: encuntre mis / *tramas*: ... roes / *radio*: lé rays de [s]leybred / *panulos*: brochis / *mateaxas*: ceren[c]es, hechilis [188] / *calathos*: paners / *quaxilla*: petiz paners / *pensis*: pinelis de fusils / *vopellis*: weyrils, de poyssons [189] / *cannabum*: conwre, hemyp [190] / *sericum*: sey / *placium*: tonekun, estopes [191] / *velo*: de beu curtin / *in auleis*: de curtins de sal / *cortina*: de curtiy a muycer [192] / *cilicio*: de cenehle vel de here [193] / *vehementer*: grevment / *materia textura*: par tysur / *sericas*: de sey / *bombicinas*: vesture de coton / *bissinas*: de chesil / *linias*: de lin

[90] *tunicas*: cotis / *pannucie*: clute / *polimita*: pipilori / *manubiatas*: maun(b)chés / *collobia*: frocs, gulunis [194] / *levitonaria*: scapuleres / *armilausas* (vestes tegentes armos .i. scapulos): espalés / *lumbaria*: widicoloris (!) [195] / *Parthorum*: de Turkeys / *sarrabarre*: esclavi[n]s / *Germanorum*: de alamans / *renones*: anglice tabars [196] / *Hyspanorum*: de espagneus / *togam*: gunel / *diploydem*: mantel forré / *penula*: un pan / *lacernam*: un tenue biflor / *mantum*: un mantel

[91] *casula*: un chensel / *planetam*: un mantel / *biri*: vestur, gironet [197] / *pepla*: uinplis /

---

184 A misreading of *crokis*?
185 A miscopying? Cf. MED sub *panne-cake* n.
186 See MED sub *hengel* n.
187 See MED sub *evesing* n.
188 See MED sub *hechel(e* n.
189 See OED sub *whirl* sb. *I,1*.
190 i.e. 'chanvre, hemp'.
191 It looks as if the scribe has run together two English words, *tow* and *oakum*.
192 *muycer* for *mucier*.
193 I do not recognise the first gloss; corr. *crenehle*? (Cf. FEW 2,ii,1343b).
194 Corr. *gunulis*.
195 A typical miscopying of the scribe. Read *wadecors*.
196 See OED sub *tabard*.
197 Corr. *gironer*.

terristrum: unne roket / *archa*: un huche / *reculas*: bubelés / *lacunaria*: chondelabra / *crucibola*: cruseus / *lucrubra* (sic): petit lumeres / *lanterne*: caternis (corr. laternis) / *licinis*: meches / *piustis* (corr. preustis): avvant ardis / *cicenduli*: corcis de bule et (e) lé mechis [198] / *infulas*: chessiblis / *pillea*: huris / *galearia*: garlondeche de kuir / *cidares*: gerlandeche / *capitula*: chapeus a cheus / *nimbos*: chapeus de plum / *riculas*: croypnis, callys [199] / *vittas*: bendis / *teniis*: frengis / *reticula*: heyris, callis / *discriminalia*: grevurs / *ancias*: bendis, buris / *torques*: bues de hore / *monilia*: fermals

[92] *fibula*: taches / *lunule*: petit fermal(ut) / *crurum*: de quisis / *perichelides*: terçuur [200] / *cinctorium*: ceinturs / *semicintia*: miparti / *lingula*: ceinturs / *strophea*: lisere / *olfactoriola*: mugers, boytis [201] / *saturati*: saulés / *stragula*: chaluns rayés / *culcitre*: de plume o de coton / *bajule*: liz portablis

Vernacular glosses from the commentary:

[f.13v] *stola* -le: gallice estolis / *ocillum*: gallice brandil / *supercilium*: gallice surcil / *steca* (for tesca): woseus gallice / *rubeta*, idem est quod crassantum: gallice crapot / hic *vallus* -li: gallice hurdy / hoc *vallum*: gallice bays (sic) / [f.14v] *absoletum*: gallice desusé / inpedio, de in et *pedita*: gallice calke[t]rap / *labina*: gallice mareis / (recidiva, arborum superfluitas ab arboribus resecate in humore proiecte et iterum radicate) *flagella*: gallice escurge / *smigna* -tis: gallice sabun, .a. sep / *planeta*: gallice mantel / *magale*: gallice hulet / *palus*: gallice peel, .a. stake / *surculus*: gallice ente / *arcifinius*: gallice forreris / *squalidus* dicitur de *squaleo* -es: gallice hesquerdus / *novale*: gallice varet / *subcessivium* (also has subcivium, susvicinia): purpreturs / [f.15r] *gilvus*: gallice faun / *sollator* (sic): gallice escorchur / *indago*: gallice parc / *clepsedra*: gallice dusel / *nothus*: frere abast (sic) / [f.15v] *repositariis*: gallice guarderobe / *operariis*: mesinis (sic) uverablis / *officiniis*: gallice mesuns de mester / *porticus*: gallice pentise vel porche / *inbule* -arum: gallice woysur / *licostratum*: gallice pavement / *tessella*: per quarré / *tesera*: herssur / *ostrac[i]um*: gallice paviment de ceste de ostres / *calcatorium*: gallice passur / *colluvium*: gallice bow / *edulium*: gallice gresse / *oggannens* (sic): gallice eschiner / *penitius*: gallice plus privez / [f.16r] *meniana*:[202] gallice solers / *lectisternium*: gallice lege de fut [203] / *simplis*: gallice sinple chaluns, gallice larga (sic) curtyn / *succidium*: gallice suce / *colustrum*: gallice beht / *cactum*: let egre / *cenovectorium*: gallice civer / *cena*: gallice supper / *azimus*: gallice levayn, payn alis / *yffungia*: gallice coquet / *placentum*: gallice gastel / *mulsum*: gallice must / *morum*: gallice muris, a blakeberye [204] / *taxea*: gallice tripes / *taxo*: bargagner / hic *taxus* (arbor est): gallice tayssun, .a. yff [205] / hoc *mali*, hec *merenda*: gallice ruyssine / [f.16v] *apoferetrum*: gallice panyer / hic et hec *colonis* et hoc *colone*: gallice champneys / *apperitor*: bedel vel cachebol [206] / *cessium*: thceelus (sic) [207] / *senium*: gallice suhlé / *attratum*: neyr /

---

198 See note 118 above.
199 Cf. OF *crespine* and MED sub *crepin* n.
200 i.e. *treçur*.
201 See TL 6,460 sub *musgode* (cites the form *murgoire*).
202 MS = *memeniana*.
203 Corr. *seges*? Cf. Scheler, *art. cit.*, 81 n.5 'seges devant leitz'.
204 See MED sub *beri* n.2(a).
205 Clearly compounds an error of gender with one of sense.
206 See Gfry 2,30b sub *chacipol* and DMLBS sub *cachepollus*.
207 A misreading of *techilé*.

gipsetum: gallice tayns / *plagiator* (factor plagarum): cercheur / *bilosum*: janglur / *mulctator*: gallice murtrissur / *gannionem*: gallice echiniur / *babirrus*: gallice fol e maveys / *susurronem*: gallice grundilur / *lanista*: turmentur / *obliquor* -aris: gallice esclenqier / *obtusus*: gallice rebuché / *interfinium*: gallice espace / [f.17r] *liricen*: harrur (corr. harpur) / *liticen*: gallice cornur / *lituus*: ruet gallice / hoc *celium* -lii: gallice cise[l] / *speculum*: gallice mirur / *phala*: gallice berfreye / *venabulum*: anglice borsper / *scorpio*: gallice .s. hoc barbilé [208] / *dolo* -onis: gallice escarberke / [f.17v] *ancile*: talvas / *cilicium*: gallice heyre / *circulus* .i. macula: gallice mayle / *lamina*: gallice plates / *galea*: gallice galey / *perietina*: gallice meser / *scenodochium*: gallice hospital / *misicomium*: gallice fermerie / *horreum*: gallice grange / [f.18r] *chilindrus* (mesura): gallice bussel / *tribula*: gallice trible, a houil [209] / *tribulum*: gallice flael / *vimen*: gallice osier / *falcastrum*: gallice faucihle / *scudium* (eo quod terram excutit ab aratro): anglice paddil [210] / *epiredium*: civer / *sagenarius*: gallice palafrey a dame / *lupatus*: gallice chanfreyn / *confisco*: gallice sayser a la mayn le rey / *clibanus*: furneys / *pelvis*: bacyin / *uter*: bussel de quir / *opacus*: flaun / *artocrea*: peussenole (corr. reussole) / *arpax*: croket de fer / [f.18v] *succula*: a sue / *flasca*: henap / *scortea*: bussel de quir / *ceriola*: vesseus a rachal sem(?) / *alibra*: baloncis vel peys e reol / [f.19r] *semicinctum*: gallice miperti / *pluteum* (tabulatum): gallice planche / *pluteum*: carole

THE WORCESTER FRAGMENT

Vernacular glosses from the fragment of the *De utensilibus* in MS Worcester Cathedral Chapter Library Q.50 (s.xiii[1]) ff.28ra–29vb.

[78] [f.29va] *frutecta*: bussuns / *non tedebat*: ne vergoynout / *badios*: bays / *aurea*: sorrus / *mirtheos*: powis [211] / *glaucos*: ferauns / *gilvos*: fauves / *scutilatos*: techelés / *guttatos*: pomelés

[79] *varios*: veytrirus / *dosios*: doynus / *equiferos*: (n)averes / *venatorum*: de venurs / *vestigatores*: trasours / *sallatores*: escorchurs / [f.29vb] *indagatores*: enserchurs / *clepsisse*: aver emblé / *vallos*: hurdys / *sudibus vi lentatis*: curvis / *intervallis*: espaces / *angustis*: estreytes / *valvas*: wykés / *celerimum*: ignel / *introitum*: entré / *patere*: aparer

Commentary

[f.28ra] *tesqum*: gallice wasseu / [f.28vb] *absoletus*: gallice desusé / [f.29ra] *labina*: gallice marreys / *flagellum*: gallice escurge ... gallice flayele / [f.29rb] *magale*: gallice hulette / *surculus* .i. vimen: gallice graffe / *oculus*: gallice heehe, anglice hye / *squaleo*: gallice escherdir / *novale*: gallice waret / *renovo*: gallice rebiner / [f.29va] *gilvus*: gallice fauve / *sallator*: gallice escorchur / [f.29vb] *indago*: gallice parc.

---

[208] The MS has *ħ barbile*.
[209] Cf. *ħöel* in TL 4,1125. English *houel* is a quite different word, see MED sub *oul* n. The scribe's 'a', whether it should be expanded to *anglice* or not, is probably best ignored.
[210] See MED sub *padel* n.(1).
[211] Scheler, *art. cit.*, 78 n.27 cites a gloss on the next word, *cervinos*, which runs 'poubuis (?), spotted'.

CHAPTER 8

ALEXANDER NEQUAM'S
DE NOMINIBUS UTENSILIUM

THE CAMBRIDGE, DUBLIN AND LINCOLN[1] MANUSCRIPTS[2]

[60][3] *disponere:*[4] ordiner (C) / *domi sue*: a sa mesun (L) / *utensilibus*: ustilement (D) utillemens (L) / *in supellectilibus*: granz uteylem[en]s (C) en urnemens (L) / *minuatur*: mincé (D) seyt minsé (L) / *fabe frese*: feve frasé (L)[5] / *fabe silique*: o lles coss (D) en coses (L)[6] / *fabe esilique*: sanse cosse (L) / *milium*: mil (D) / *legumina*: potages (L) / *cepulatum*: cyvé (D) / *tripodes*: trepez (D) treves (L)[7] / *securis*: cuné (L) / *mortarium*: morter (L) / *pilus*: pestel (L) / *contus*: mowr (D) movus [sic][8] (L) / *uncus*: croc (CD) havet (L) / *cacabus*: caudroun (C) havet (D, misplaced) jadrunt (L) / *aenum*: pot de areym (D) jadret (L)[9] / *patella*: paele (D) peti quile (L) / *sartago*: palye a var (L)[10] / *craticula*: grediler (L) / *urceoli*: poss (D) posseney (L) / *discus*: plateu (L) / *creagra*: havet (L) / *scutella*: asculey (L) / *parapsis*: dubler (D) dopler(ir) (L) / *salsarium*: saucers (D) sauser (L) / *exenterari*: eystreir (C) / *artavi*: qniveys (L) / *gurgustio*: rei de gort (D) reys de grot (L)[11] / *fuscina*: anglice algere (C)[12] fone (L) / *funda*: fune (D) / *jaculo*: lancet (DL) / *hamite*: hamet (C)[13] croc (D) de une reys (L) / *nassa*: gallice bewet, anglice bellep (C) nase, fezlep (D) de nasse (L)[14] / *deprensi*: etre pris (L)

[61] *capanam*: petite chambre (L) / *coquina*: cusyneyt (L) / *aromaticas*: precio(s)use (L) / *amolum*: flour (D) flur de furment (L) / *cribro*: crivre (D) de cribre (L) / *sinceratum*: sacé, siftit (D)[15] sazé (L) / *contritum*: depescé, triblé (D) triblé (L) / *pisciculos, parvi pisces*: menus (D)[16] pessunnes (L) / *consolidandos*: friers (D) a frire (L) / *deponat*: estuez (D) / *reponat*: estuet (L)[17] / *in abditorio*: muset, loco privato (D)[18] / *allucia*: lavurs (D) lavrus (L) / *volatilis*: volables (L) / *anserum*: des oues (L) / *domesticarum*: priveys, damaches (L) / *exta*: bués (L) / *entera*: entrail (D) entralis (L) / *extremitates*: forentis (D)[19] a la dreinsté (L) / *crebro*: sovenerement (C) / *pulli*:

---

1   See vol.1, pp.178ff.
2   For a further selection of vernacular glosses, from Oxford MSS, see T. Hunt, 'Les gloses en langue vulgaire dans les MSS du *De nominibus utensilium* d'Alexandre Nequam', *Revue de linguistique romane* 43 (1979), 235–62.
3   Numbers in square brackets refer to the pages of Scheler's edition in *Jbch. f. rom. u. engl. Lit.* 7 (1866), 58–74.
4   The commentaries are excerpted separately, see below pp.82ff.
5   See FEW 3,777a (*fresum*).
6   See FEW 2,i,826a (*cochlea*).
7   See FEW 13,ii,292a (*tripes*).
8   See Gfry 5,436a and FEW 6,iii,165b (*movere*).
9   See Gfry 2,96b sub *chaudroite*.
10 Corr. *char* and also in [67] (*war de porc*).
11 See TL 4,457 sub *gort*.
12 See MED sub *alger n*.
13 See FEW 4,380b (*hamus*). (H)*ames* actually means 'pole' or 'fishing-rod'.
14 See MED sub *fish n.5(o)* and *lep n.(2)c* (also *ber(e)-lep(e)*. See also FEW 7,28b (*nassa*) and cf. OED sub *bow-net*.
15 See OED sub *sift v*.
16 See Tony Hunt, 'Les gloses en langue vulgaire dans les manuscrits de l'*Unum Omnium* de Jean de Garlande', *Revue de linguistique romane* 43 (1979), 168 'fundulus: piscis fundo aderens .s. menuse' and TL 5,1467 sub *menuise*.
17 See TL 3,ii,1497 sub *estuiier*.
18 See Gfry 5,438a and *infra* [67] sub *abditorio*.
19 See TL 3,ii,2054 sub *foraineté*.

posine (L) / *excaturizari*: escauder (D) / *scaturizari*: estre echaudé (L) / *mola piperalis*: petite mole (L) / *pisc[ic]uli*: pessunnes (L) / *coquendi*: a quire (L) / *spuma*: coum (D) / *ebulatio*: bulum (D) / *in salsa*: en sause (L) / *salsamentum*: sausse (D) sause, savurement (L) / *mugiles*: saumoun (C) samunt (L) / *amphinia*: anglice sole, porpeis (C) syole (D) soles (L)²⁰ / *congrus*: congre (CD) cungre (L) / *murena*: lampreie (C) laumpreye (D) lampré (L) / *musculus*: baleyn (C) baleeyn, wal (D) balene, wallay (L)²¹ / *ephimera*: esperling (CD) aperlinc (L) / *gobio*: gojoun (C) gugun (D) gujun (L) / *melanurus*: darz de mer (C) dars de mer (D) dars de mere (L) / *capito*: caboche (C) caboche vel gurnard (D) caboge (L)²² / *morus*: morue (D) morue, muluel (L) moru, keling (C)²³ / *ypotamus*: chival de mer, anglice sele (C)²⁴ / *pelamides*: playe (D) plais (L) / *mulus*: mulet (DL)

[62] *uranoscopus*: ray (C) rai (D) raye (L)²⁵ / *dentrix*: chevit de metir (L)²⁵ / *megarus*: makerel (CD) / *turtur*: turbot (LC) turbut (D) / *allecia*: aring (L) / *gomarus*: epinoche (C) / *confrictus*: frire (L) frié (D) / *ostria*: oystre (C) ostrei (D) hostre (L) / *bocca marina*: bar de mer (D) bars de meret (L) / *dentrix*: hocfiche (C)²⁶ / *micatorium*: une grate (L) grate (D) / *ruder*: guter (D) fose (L) / *gausape*: nape (DL) / *manitergium*: tuaile (D) / *manutergium*: tuale a man (L) / *mantile*: tuaile (CD) / *facitergium*: tuaile a face (D) kevertur (L) / *pertica*: perche (D) / *murium*: de rays (L) / *cultelli*: cuteus (D) peti kni[v]eyt (L) / *salsarium*: sauser (L) / *salinum*: saler (L) / *cultrum*: cutel (D) / *scultum*: taylé (D) / *scu[l]ptum*: cutel (D) / *teca caseorum*: casier (C) corbail, cheser (D) cheser (L)²⁷ / *candelabrum*: chandeler (D) chandelabre (L) / *absconsa*: escunse (D) asconse (L) / *onofora*: coustreuz (C) / *laterna*: lanterne (L) / *calathi*: baschez, paniers (D) / *promptuario*: gerner (L) / *in celario*: celer (DL) / *cadi*: bareilis (D) barill (L) / *utres*: busseus (D) bossués (L) / *dolea*: tonneus (D) / *ciphi*: hanaps (D) / *cophini*: hanapperis (D) hanipers (L) / *clepsedre*: dusilis (D) / *pelves*: bacinis (D) / *corbes*: baschés (D) / *claretum*: claré (D) clarey (L) / *ydromellum*: mede (C) bochet (D)²⁸ / *cervicia*: sicer (D) / *mustum*: must (D) / *nectar*: piement (L) / *medo*: mede (L) / *pingmentum*: piment (D) / *piretum*: peré (C) pereye (D) perey (L) / *rosatum*: rosé (L) / *ferratum*: ferré (L) / *falernum*: de Auserne, de tali monte (D) de Hauseney (L) / *vinum gariophilatum*: gilofré (D) vin gelofré (L) / *onophora*: picher²⁹ (D) / *lambris*: a lechours (C) lecheurs (D) a lechrus (L) / *ambubagis*: glutuns (D) al glutune (L) / *incompleta*: ne paremplie (L) / *perhendinaturus*: ly [hom] a sojurner (C) homme a surgurner (D) hom surgurnant (L) / *jupam*: jupe (C) surcote (D) surcot (L) / *penulatam*: furré (C) forré (L) / *manubiatam*: maunché (C) / *tunicam*: cote (CL) / *manubiis*: mauncez (C) manchis (D) de macheys (L) / *birris*: gerouns, anglice scurtez (C)

²⁰ See OED sub *sole sb.*².
²¹ See OED sub *whale sb.*
²² These forms are not given in FEW 2,i,334b–35a nor in TL 2,151a (*chabot*, but see *chaboce* = *caput*).
²³ See OED sub *keeling sb.*².
²⁴ See OED sub *seal sb.*¹.
²⁵ The scribe appears to have miscopied *chien de mer*.
²⁶ See OED sub *hogfish*.
²⁷ In MED *cheser* has a different meaning.
²⁸ See MED sub *med(e n.(1)*.
²⁹ See TL 7,874 sub *pichier*.

geruns (D) giruns (L)[30] / *munitam*: garni (L) / *laciniis*: des espauns, anglice gores (C)[31] / *femoralibus*: de brayz (C) brays (D) de brasy (L) / *pudibunda*: huntuse choses (D)

[63] *lumbaribus*: braylers (C) de braelleys (L) / *caligis*: chausces (C) chaucis (D) / *tibie*: jaumbez (C) jambis (D) jambe (L) / *estivalibus*: des estiveuz (C) estyvaus (D) de estiveys, de esté (L) / *calceis laqueatis*: a laz (C) solers a lace (D) de soluris (L) / *consutilibus*: soulers a curei (D) a coreys (L) / *camisia*: chemise (C) / *sindonis*: de sendel (C) cendele (D) sendel (L) / *serici*: de seye (C) seie (D) de sey (L) / *bissi*: cheycyl (C) chesil (D) de chesil (L) / *lini*: de lenis (D) / *saltem*: soveuz (C) / *sortiatur*: prenget (L) / *penula*: la pane (C) furure (D) pane (L) / *ex cisimis*: de ver et gris (C) de gris (D) de ver e di gris (L) / *experiolis*: esquireus (CD) de escirelys (L) / *laeronibus*: de lerouns (C) laeruns (D) de leoruns (L) / *cuniculis*: conyz (C) cunis (D) / *sabelino*: de sablyn (C) de sabilint (L) / *matrice*: putoys (C) de matrise (L) martrice (D) / *fibro*: bevere, lutre (C) bivere, lutre (D) lotre, otre (D)[32] / *castore*: chatrise (L)[33] / *vulpecula*: gupil (CD) de cupil (L) / *roserella*: roserel (CL) / *equitaturus*: le hom a chyval (C) echivachure (L) / *manubiatam*: mauncé (C) manché (L) / *capucium*: chaperon (C) / *minas*: manaces (C) / *ocreas*: hesez (C) hosis (D) / *calcaria*: esperouns (C) esperuns (D) / *stimulos*: agulouns (C) agulun (L) / *hortatorios*: amonestables (C) monestabelis (D) amo[nes]tables (L) / *succusanti*: trottant (C) trotant (DL) / *cespitanti*: cestaunt, stumbland (C) cestant, anglice stumbelant (D) cestant (L)[34] / *recalcitranti*: regibbaunt, wynsand (C)[35] regibant (D) regiebant (L) / *reculanti*: reculant, ararand (C)[36] reculant (L) / *recursanti*: rec[r]eaunt (L) / *neganti*: nediant (corr. deniant) (L) / *repedanti*: arere alaunt (C) realant (L) / *antepedanti*: ne trop avant alant (D) *antipedanti*: a trop avant (L) / *ambulanti*: amblaunt (C) / *ad mittendum*: a lacher (D) a lagir (L) / *habili*: avenable (C) avabele (D) / *ferri*: lé fers (C) ferré (L) / *clavis*: de clous (C) clouis (D) clou (L) / *fermati*: fermez (C) / *carentivillo*: canevas (C) canevace (D) de canevas (L) / *tergum*: dos (D) / *sudario*: suere, house (C) huce (D) de une osue (L) / *panello*: panel (D) / *cella*: sele (D) / *sudarii*: de la use (L) / *clunes*: croupes (C) crupis (D) cropus (L) / *pendentibus*: pendans (D) / *strepe*: estruis (D) / *sella*: cele (D) / *arculi*: arsun (L) / *teniis*: frengez (C) frengis (D) / *antela*: arçun devant (D) (s)arsu[n] devant (L) / *postela*: arsun de ... (L) derere (D) / *antelas*: trucis (D) coreyes (C) / *postellas*: trucis de[re]re (D)

[64] *involucro*: enplyure (C) enplet (D) enplet (L) / *mantica*: truce (D) la tru (L) / *pectoral*: le peyterel (C) / *phalere*: harneys (C) / *chamum*: bernakle (C) bernacle (L) / *lupatum*: chanfren (D) chanefren (L) / *capistrum*: chevestre (D) cheveystre (C) /

30   See OED sub *skirt sb.*
31   See MED sub *gor(e n.(2)2(a).*
32   See MED sub *oter n.*
33   There seems to be an association with the etymological play on *castor* and *castus* (see Ph. de Thäun, *Bestiaire* 1137).
34   See OED sub *stumble v.*
35   See OED sub *wince v.*[1].
36   See MED sub *areren.*

spumis sanguineis: spume de sa[n]g (D) de spume de san (L)[37] / *habenas*: reyns (CD) la renys (L) / *lingulam*: hardiloun (C) hardilun (D) ardilun (L) / *pusculam*: bucle (C) bukelis (D) la bocle (L) / *pulvillum*: baz (C) bace (D) la bas (L) / *trussulam*: trosel (C) la truse (L) / *strigilem*: estril (C) stril (D) / *pedes*: pouner (D) poner (L) / in *thalamo*: cha[m]bre de pere (L) / *curtina*: cortine (C) curtine (D) curtinir (L) / *canopeum*: cuverture (D) une cuveture (L) / *scenicum*: de thueatre (L) / *muscarum*: de muches (L) / *aranearum*: hiraynis (D) de yrenes (L) / *stilis*: de muluel (D) de milu (L)[38] / *epistilis*: chapetel (D) de chapetés (L) / *tapetum*: cape vel chaluns (D) cape (L) / *scabellum*: forme (L) / *tapete*: chaluns (D) / *lectica*: chautlit (C)[39] cherie a dame (L) / *culcitra plumalis*: coylte de plume, (later hand) bolstu (C)[40] culte de plume (D) de plume (L) / *cervical*: oriler (CDL) / *punctata*: pointe (D) puncte (L) / *vestis stragulata*: vesture rayé (L) / *pulvinar*: quisine (C) quicer, quicine (D) quisint (L) / *lintheamina*: lincheus (C) lincés (L) / *lodices*: laungel, witel (C)[41] langeus, weytil, gallice langers (D) langes (L) / ex *sindone*: sendel (C) ce[n]del (D) / *sagio*: saye (C) sarge (DL) / *viridi*: de vert (C) / *bisso*: cheysil (C) chesil (D) / *coopertorium*: cuverture (D) / *penula taxea*: pane tesoun (C) pane de texun (D) de pane de tessun, broc (L)[42] / *saltem*: sovez (C) / *catina*: de chat (C) chat (D) de chate (L) / *beverina*: de bevere (C) lutre (D) / *muniatur*: seit garni (D) / *deest*: defaut (D)

[65] *catum volatile*: une cour[tine] de quir (L) / *capus*: muschet (CDL) / *cirrus*: aloue, (left-hand margin) alou (D) / *nisus*: esperver (C) perver (D) espervir (L) / *alietus*: hoby (C)[43] / *herodius*: oustour (C) mereylun (D) merilun (L) / *tercellus*: gerfacun (C) tercel (D) tercel, faucun (L) / *falco peregrinus*: facoun ramayl (C) ramage (D) a peregre, facun ramage (L)[44] / *ascensorius*: facoun hauteyn (C) hauten (D) facun auteyn (L) / *ardearius*: herouner (C) hayrunir (D) erunnir (L) / *tardarius*: laner (CD) facun lanier (L) / *grua*: gyrfauc (C) a grue (L)[45] / *ancipiter*: oustour (C) hostilur (D) ostur (L) / *supara*: cheynces, roches (C) rochetis (D) chonsus, suttanye (L)[46] / *flammea*: volettis (D)[47] coverechefs (C) cuvrechis (L) / *flammeola*: peti cuver (L) / *perizoma*: brays (C) rochet (L) / *perizona*: rochetis (D) / *capa*: cape (D) jape (L) / *pallium*: mantel (DL) mauntel (C) / *tunica*: gonele (C) cote (L) / *collobium*: froc (DL) / *instita matronalis*: rochet a damis (D) rochet a dame (L) / *lumbare*: brayel (C) uardecors (D) vesture de reyns (L) / *ventrale*, de ventre: wardecors (C) wardecors (L) / *limata* (= *vestes coquorum*, D): vesture suylé (C) girunner (L)[48] / *cirrnata*: vestur

---

[37] A later hand has added in C the gloss *fome* (see MED sub *fom* n.) and over *lupatum* there is added *bridil of a rest* (see OED sub *rest* sb.[3]1.)

[38] The commentary in L f.40ra takes *columna* as the inclusive term which is made up of *basis*, *stilus* and *epistilus*.

[39] See TL 2,149 sub *chäalit* and FEW 2,i,488b (*catalectus*).

[40] See MED sub *bolster* n.

[41] See OED sub *whittle* sb.[1].

[42] See MED sub *brok* n.(1).

[43] See MED sub *hobi* n.(1).

[44] See OED sub *peregrine*.

[45] See MED sub *grue* n.(2).

[46] In FEW 12,372b *sottane* is cited only from the 16th C.

[47] See Gfry 8,283c sub *voilet*.

[48] This form does not appear in the dictionaries (cf. FEW 16,32 et seq.). In the margin of C is the gloss 'anglice barmclot', see MED sub *barm* n.2.

curtes (L) / *aspergines*: cheynces (C) longe cheins, (left-hand margin) suzchaneis, suzchanies (D)[49] / *cirophea*: longe cheynse (C) longe dras de purpe (D) draps de purpre (L) / *lodices*: laungels (C) langis (D) dras veliz, langesyz (L) / *teristrum*: rochet ridé (C) rochet a point (D) rochet a punte (L) / *amenet*: delitet (C) belit (D) beleyt (L) / *serenet*: enclareit (D) / *mataxa*: serence (CD) serennes (L) / *aufrigium*: orefrey (C) orfri (D) de orrefé (L) / *consuat*: ensemble couuset (C) cuset (L) / *tricaturas*: tressures (C) trisçuris (D) / *explicet*: despliet (C) despleit (D) / *sarciat*: refeytet (C) refeti (L) / *resarciat*: amendat (D) / *vestes laneas*: vestures de lyn (C) / *tecam*: deeyl (C) deel (D) delley (L) / *cirothecas*: wauns (C) / *amputatis*: coupés (D) trenchez (C) / *acui*: aguel (D) / *corigialem*: de quir (D)

[66] *pollicium*: deel (D) pocir (L) / *digitale*: deel (D) / *apellatur*: est apellé (D) / *forficem*: force (CD) forse (L) / *philarium*: filer (CD) philir (L) / *glomos*: luceuz (C) lusseus (D) lussel (L) / *extricet*: depliet (D) depley (L) / *ad opus anaglapharium*: burdure (D) a sutil evere a fere (L) / *ad birritricas*: gerunnis (D) a girrunnir (L)[50] / *acus grossissimas*: ginolis (D) guinoleys (L) / *illicebris*: enveysurs (C) / *poliendas*: planers (D) / *laqueos*: lacis (D) / *inducendos*: entrere (D) / *coralla*: garlaun de quir (C) garland (D) garlant (L) / *corocalla*: peti curchef (D) de veley (L) / *peplo*: gymple (C) / *crinali*: bende (C) petit bende (D) de bende (L) / *reticulo*: kelle (C) chelle, brile (left-hand margin, gallice brilye) (D)[51] de calle (L) / *comarum*: chevus (D) / *monile*: nuche (CL) mayle (D) / *spinter*: efficayl (C) ficale (D) afical (L) / *fuscotincti*: fustyan (C) de fosteon (D) / *colaria*: colereys (L) / *torques*: beydis [sic] de or (D) beue de orre (L) / *androgea*: deye (CD) daye (L)[52] / *gallinis*: gelins (C) / *pullificancia*: feçant puncis [sic] (D) fesant pusinz (L) / *anseribus*: ouez (C) gars (D) aus oys (L) / *acera*: escurayl (C) eschorayl (D) paylles (L) / *substernat*: aparaylit (D) agraventet, strayt (L)[53] / *vitulos*: les velz (C) / *subrumos*: letauns (C) feblis, endentés (D) sens dente (L) / *ablactatos*: severés, deletez (C) enseverés (D) severés (L) / *pergulo*: parrok (C)[54] enclos (D) closse (L) / *iuxta fenile*: juste le moyloyn de feyn (C) feniere (D) fanerie (L) / *indumenta*: fulemens (D) / *matronales*: cheynces (C) / *serapelline*: bel pelisoun a dame (C) pelesuns a dame (D) pellysun (L) / *terristrum*: roket ridé (C) rochet a poi[n]t (D) roche a punt (L) / *recinium*: cheynse ridé, bifle (C) chemés redelé (D) suttany (L)[55] / *subulcis*: a porchers (C) porchers (D) a porges (L) / *bubulcis*: bovers (C) a boveres (L) / *colustrum*: mek, bestink (C)[56] mec (D) meg (L) / *armentariis*: a vachers (C) vacers (D) a vagers (L)

[67] *oxigalla*: let egre (C) sur mec (D) sure let (L) / *obsoniis*: sopers (D) / *quactum*: idem (= let egre) vel creme (C) creme (DL) / *in cimbiis*: granz hanaps (C) en grant esquelis (D) / *pingue serum*: wryngwey, graz mek (C)[57] gras mec (D) grase mec (L) /

---

49 See TL 9,940f sub *soscanie*.
50 See note 48 above.
51 See Gfry 1,727a sub *breil*.
52 See MED sub *daie n*.
53 See OED sub *stray v.*[1].
54 See MED sub *par(r)ok n*.
55 See note 46 above.
56 See MED sub *besting n*.
57 See OED sub *wring sb.*[1] and *whey sb*.

furfureo: de brent (L) / *porrigere*: estendre (C) / *in abditorio*: en estu (C) musset (D) /
catulis: caelz (C) / *assa*: haste (DL) / *suille*: de porc (C) porc (D) de war [corr. char] de
porc (L) / *tractu*: tret (L) / *assata*: rostie (L) / *versata*: trové (L) / *craticulam*: grideil (L)
/ *prurio*: froter (L) / *furno*: furne (D) / *flamma*: flaume (D) / *condimentum*: savurment
(D) savurement (L) / *alleatam*: ail (D) alliyé (L) / *altilis*: chapun, jeline (D) geline (L)
/ *veru longo*: longe broche (L) / in *consiso*: consyz (C) consis (D) / *piperis*: peyver (D) /
circumvoluta: envirunturné (D) verunturné (L) / *domestica*: privé (D) / *alleatam*: al-
leyé (L) / *succo virido*: vergus (D) verjuz (C) / *racemorum*: reisinis (D) de reysins (L) /
pomorum silvestrium: pome dé boys (D) pumes dé bos, anglice crebbes (L) [58] / *scaturizata*: escaudé (D) eschadié (L) / *condiatur*: sey savueré (L) / *cumino*: comin (D) / *elixa*:
quit (L) quit en ewe (C) / *guticulis*: guteris (D) / *guttulis*: d'espés guut (L) / *alleate*: de
allye (L) / *postmodum*: emprés (L) / *sapidissima*: tre savuré (L) / *exenterati*: enbuylez,
eskerdez (C) defez, overs (D) abolyt, overt (L) / *petrosillum*: persyl (C) percil (D)
persil, anglice petir (L) [59] / *viridi sapore*: verte saus (D) / *costus*: coste (CDL) / *salgia*:
sauge (CD) / *ditanium*: ditayne (C) ditane (D) ditan (L) / *serpellum*: peleystre (C)
pelestre (D) pelletre (L) / *exillarat*: heytit (D) / *vinum ferratum*: ferré (C)

[68] *perspicuitate*: par clerté (C) par clereté (L) / *admirari*: amirer (C) / *conformetur*:
seyt conformé (L) / *fundum*: funz (C) / *bubali*: bugle (D) de bugle (L) / *impetuose*:
hastivement (L) / *nux phillidis*: alemander (D) alamander (L) / *repens*: ranpant (D)
rampant (L) / *experioli*: esquirel (D) de escurel (L) / *gesticulans*: enveisant (D) salant
(L) / *caprioli*: cheveryz (C) / *cintille*: centel (D) sentelle (L) / *grisorum monachorum*:
de grey moynis (D) / *emicans*: estenselaunt (D) / *delicatum*: delycious (C) leyé (D) /
bissus: cheycil (C) cheisil (D) / *excedat*: passit (D) / *construi*: estre aparylé (L) / *situm*:
scé (L) / *mota*: la mote (C) mote de castel (D) mote (L) / *castrum*: chastel (C) /
nativam: nayve (C) / *rupem*: roche (DL) / *sortiatur*: pergit (D) [60] / *moles*: aparilement
de mur (D) aparayllement(ent) (L) / *ex cemento*: morter (C) cement (D) de ciment
(L) / *exurgat*: s'adresyt (L) / *sepes horrida*: haye (CDL) / *palis*: de pus (D) peus (L) /
quadrangulis: quarris (D) quarrés (L) / *vepribus*: rouncez (C) runcis (D) de runces (L)
/ *pungentibus*: pungnans (D) / *vallum*: le bayl (CL) bail (D) / *amplis*: largez (C) largis
(DL) / *interstitiis*: largez espacez (C) espacis (D) aspacis (L) / *venis*: veynis (D) /
maritetur: seyt baylé (D) / *supereminentes*: suraperisant (D) aparisant (L) / *exterius*:
dehors (D) / *apodientur*: seit suz poués (D) seyt apuyt (L) / *superficies*: autesse (L)

[69] *muri*: del mur (L) / *trulle*: truel (D) de truel (L) / *equalitate*: a l'uleyté (L) /
cementarii: masçun (D) de masun (L) / *operam*: entente (D) a l'atent (L) / *cancelli*: lé
kerneus (C) carneus (D) kernerus (L) / *distinguantur*: devisés (D) seynt departiés (L)
/ *debitis portionibus*: duble aspaces (corr. due) (L) / *desint*: faylint (D) / *propugnacula*:
les bretaches (C) barbakanes vel brutaches (L) / *pinne*: sumet, ongles (L) / *crates*:
cleyes (C) cleis (D) cleys (L) / *eiciendes*: ors gutteris (D) / *molares*: granz perez (C) /
obsidiatur: ensegé (C) seyt ensigé (L) / *deditionem*: abandoun (D) abandun (L) / *farre*:
de blé (D) / *mero*: de pur vin (L) / *pernis*: pernis (D) de un bacun (L) / in *succiduo*:
suce (D) en suz (L) / *salsuciis*: sausugez (C) saucechis (D) sausiches (L) / *carne suilla*:

58   See MED sub *crab(be* n.(2).
59   See OED sub *peter sb.†3*.
60   Corr. *prengit*.

de porc (C) de por (D) charne de porc (L) / *tu(n)cetis*: bodeyns (C) puddingis (D) de puudincques (L) / *carne arietina*: de moton (C) de motun (D) char de mutunt (L) / *hyllis*: andulez (C) handuls (C) handuylles (L) / *bovina*: de bof (C) / *ex carne ovina*: char de ouales (L) / *jugiter*: pardurablement (L) / *caseis*: formagez (C) / *scaturiente*: sourdaun (C) surdant (L) / *alaturi*: a porters (D) / *posticis*: posterns (L) / *catharacteribus*: de lunges vehes suz terre (L) / *latenter*: atapisament (L) / *cathapulte*: setis barbis (D) seyt barbelés (L) / *lancea*: lanse (L) / *lancee*: lancis (D) / *ancilia*: bouclers (C) run escu (D) acue runt (L) / *pelte*: talevas (CD) / *peltes*: peti acues (L) / *baliste*: alebaste (C) alebrastis (D) arblas (L) / *fustibula*: mangoneuz (C) mangenell (D) mangunés (L) / *funde*: lengez (C) lingis (D) fundes (L) / *sudes ferrei*: peuz (C) peus (D) peys de fer (L) / *baleares*: perers (C) / *clave*: macez (C) massuis (D) massues (L) / *nodose*: nousse (L) / *fustes*: bastonz (C) bastuns (D) bastun (L) / *torres*: tisounz (C) tisuns (D) tysun (L) / *assultus*: les esausse (L) / *assultes*: les saus (D) / *elidantur*: seyn ostees (L) / *obsidentium*: segans (D) / *enerventur*: sen fibliys (L) / *propositum*: porposse (L) / *arietes*: berefreyz, gallice berfreyz (C) [61] berfreyis (D) befuers (L) / *vinee*: perreres (D) perees (L) / *vites*: garyz (C) garitis (D) garritis (L) / *crates*: cleis (D) cleys (L) / *cetere machine*: autre engynz (C) autre manere de gin (L) / *palefridi*: palefrey (C) palefreys (L) / *manni*: palefreis (D) runciny (L) / *gradarii*: chasour (C) chasurs (D) chasur (L) / *dextrarii*: deystrer (C) destrer (L) / *exeuntibus*: ors yssant (L) / *exanimentur*: que il seyt ahardiés (D) seint ardis (L)

[70] *tube*: businez (C) busine (L) / *tibie*: astive (L) / *buxus*: freytel (C) fleggars (D) buse (L) [62] / *litui*: grelez (C) greiles (L) greles (L) / *cornu*: grant cors (D) / *acies*: la eschele (L) escheles (L) / *tribunis*: conestablez (C) cunetable (L) / *tornamentum*: turnemen (D) / *troianum*: tornement (L) / *tirocinium*: bourdiz (C) burdis (D) bordys (L) / *girum*: runde table (D) / *hastiludium*: justez (C) / *hastiledium*: torneyment (C) / *succussorii*: chasurs (C) chevas sucurabelis (D) succurable (L) / *vernis*: sergauns (D) a chersans, a servant (L) / *vispilionibus*: robberis (D) robburs (L) / *coterellis*: corellis (D) sergauns a pé (C) a garsun a pé (L) / *viri*: hommes (L) / *clangatores*: defeyurs (D) defiorus (L) / *caduciatores*: afiurs fesant pes (D) afiorus (L) / *moles*: aparliament (L) / *summa*: la soverenté (L) / *mitius*: plus debonerement (L) / cum *supplicibus*: boneré (D) o deboners (L) / *degressatores*: avayurs (D) avayorus (L) / *rigore*: par reddur (D) / *plebicitorum*: commune de puple (D) comune de peble (L) / *plebis statuorum*: gallice de estabelemen de puple (D) / *abusores*: desusours (C) / *sicariis*: murdrisours (C) / *legerumpi*: pessant ley (D) / *clepi*: laruns (L) / *multatores*: mursesurs [sic] (D) murdrus (L) / *enectores*: occeurs (D) occisurs (L) / *antropossedi*: occisurs (D) / *fustigentur*: seynt batuz (D) seynt batues (L) / *puniantur*: seynt oniys (L) / *frugalitatem*: esperniable (D) esparniableté (L) / in *habundantia*: plenté (D) in plenté (L) / *parcitas*: escarcerie (D) / *dehortans*: deamonestauns (D) desemonetant (L) / sine *conjectura*: quidaunce (D) san quidasse (L) / *clangatores*: defiours (C) defeyurs (D) defiorus (L) / *sensibili*: sentable (D) / *caduciatores*: apesours [qui confirmant pacem] (C) feyurs (D) afiorus (L)

[71] *statelum*: standart (D) standar (L) / *stratilates*: conestabeles (D) / *animet*: ardiset (D) anardiyt (L) / *optinentis*: avant (D) / *telorum*: dars (D) / *stipendia*: luerz (C)

---

61 See MED sub *berfei* and FEW 1,332a.
62 Cf. MED sub *fleget* n. and *flagel* n.

gruerdurs [sic] (D) / *stupendium* [sic]: werdun (L) / *carceres*: presouns (C) presuns (D) pressun (L) / *nichiteria*: frunt de victorie (D) / *detrudantur*: seynt debuté (L) / *milites evocati*: soudeours (C) soudés (D) / *compediti*: les firgez (C) enfergis (D) enfirgis (L) / *distincti*: visés (D) / *manicis ferreis*: en maniclis de fer (C) maniclis de fer (D) manicle de fere (L) / *cippi*: cepz (C) ceps (D) cepses (L) / *columbaria*: piloryz (C) pilloris (D) pellory (L) / *excubie*: wey(n)tez (C) ueytis (D) wates (L) / *strepitum*: noyse (CD) nose (L) / *clangorem*: cry (C) crey (D) cri (L) / *granario*: gerner (CD) guernir (L) / *vannus*: van (CDL) / *hostorium*: striclez, radure (C) radur (D) [63] / *chorus*: mesur (D) / *batus*: buscel (C) bussel (D) besul (L) / *diverse tece*: estuz (C) diverse repostaylis (D) diverse repostaylles (L) / *sigali*: segle (CD) seggle (L) / *ordei*: orge (C) / *avene*: aveyne (C) avene (L) / *lollii*: nel, cockel (D) [64] neelle (L) / *cortis*: de la cort (C) / *palee*: payle (D) palys (L) / *acus*: escurayl (C) escorael (D) / *silique*: escorayle (D) curaylle (L) / *avena sterilis*: wyld-hote (C) [65] haverun (D) avarunt, wild (L) / *pulli*: poucyns (C) puçsine (L) / *galli*: coc (L) / *galline*: gelines (L) / *gallinacii*: chapouns (C) coquerés (L) / *gallinarii*: cokereuz (C) cokereus (D) / *altiles*: gelines (CD) capuns, gelinis (L) / *altilia*: chapouns (C) chapun (D) capuns (L) / *anseres*: chars (C) houes (D) aues (L) / *antes*: anez (C) anis, henedis (D) [66] anes (L)

[72] *cigonie*: cigoyne (C) cygeonis (?) (L) / *ardee*: herouns (C) heydrunis [sic] (D) heyruns (L) / *phasadee*: fesauns (CD) phesans (L) / *fulice*: cotez (C) [67] mauvis (D) maviz (L) / *Libie*: de Grece (D) / *volucres*: grues (D) / *grues*: grues (C) / *alunbes*: popel (C) popul (L) [68] / *mergites*: plungouns (C) plungunnis (D) plunguns (L) / *mergi*: dovedoppe (C) motis, anglice mouis (D) moytes (L) [69] / *alciones*: su-meote, moues (C) mootes, meys (L) [70] / *galli palustres*: witecoks (C) moriluns [sic] (D) meriluns (L) [71] / *pavones*: poouns (C) pouns (DL) / *Junonius ales*: le oysel de dame Juneyne (D) / *bostar*: boverei (C) boverie (DL) / *presepe*: crecche (C) / *are*: porcherie (CD) porche-riis (L) / *alvei*: augez (C) augis (D) auges (L) / *alveoli*: peti augis (L) / *strigilis*: estril (C) strile (L) / *camus*: bernac (D) bernacal (L) / *salivare*: chanfreyn (D) chanefre[n] (L) / *cenovectorium*: cyvere (C) civere, barue (D) civire a reus (L) [72] / *epiredium*: civer ov roe (D) / *capistrum*: cheveystre (C) chevestre (L) / *fallere*: herneys (D) / *textor*: tystour (C) tistur (L) / *terrestris eques*: chivaler (C) chival a tere (L) / *adnitens*: pouant (D) apuant (L) / *streparum*: estruz (C) / *apodiamento*: apouement (D) de apual (L) / *admittit*: let coure (C) alachit (L) / *contemptum* (= contentum!): apayé (C) / *dieta*: jurney (D) jornee (L) / *scansilia*: estruz (C) estruis (D) estris (L) / *exili*: petite (C) / *mutua*: entrechaunjable (C) entrechanchable (L) / *vicissitudine*: entre-chanableté (D) feeze (C) / *evehitur*: sus porté (L) / *deprimatur*: set bessé (D) sey bessé

---

63   See OED sub *strickle* sb. and Gfry 6,546c sub *radouere*.
64   See MED sub *cokkel* n. and FEW 7,127a (*nigella*).
65   See OED sub *oat* sb. 3.
66   See MED sub *end(e* n.(2).
67   See MED sub *cote* n.(4).
68   It is not known exactly what sort of water-bird *alunbes* denotes, see OED sub *poppel* with only two examples (= 'spoonbill'?) and MED sub *popeler(e* n. ('European Spoonbill').
69   See MED sub *dive-dap* n. and below n.70.
70   See FEW 16,495b and Gfry 5,207c. See also OED sub *mew* and *sea-mew*.
71   See OED sub *woodcock* sb.
72   See MED sub *barwe* n.

(L) / *trocleam*: windaz (C) vindeyse (D) windeche (L) [73] / *circumvolubilem*: turnable
(L) / *pannus*: drap (L) / *maritari*: estre bally (L) / *cidulas*: cendlez, stodles [74] (C) latis
(D) latte (L) / *columbaribus*: pertuz (C) pertuse (D) / *distinctas*: visés (D) departies
(L) / *cavillis*: chevilis (D) / *pedorum curvatis*: camboc (D) [75] bastun de bercher (L) /
licia: hevelyredes (C) filys, anglice evedles (L) [76] / *tele*: teyle (D) / *teniis*: frenges (C)
frengis (D) a frenges ragues (L) / *fimbriis*: urlis (D) urles (L) / *interstitiis*: espaces (L) /
stamen: warp (C) [77] esteym (D) la tem (L) / *superponendum*: ke a surmettre (D) a
metre desus (L) / *trama*: of, la treme (C) treym (D) ove, treme (L) [78] / *navicule*: shitel,
del navet (C) navet (D) de navete, anglice scutel (L) [79] / *transmissa*: aveyé (L) /
consolidet: afermet (L)

[73] *pano ferreo*: broche (C) proche de fer (D) de broche de fer (L) / *pannus*: proche
(D) broche (L) / *muniatur*: garnit (D) / *spola*: espole (CL) / *glomeris*: lucel (C) lussel
(DL) / *trame*: of (C) treym (D) treme, anglice weht (L) [80] / *remissuram*: derere weyer
(D) rere feyr (L) / *iaculetur*: juttit (D) / *habilior*: avable (D) plus hable (L) / *ordietur*:
warpet (D) urdira (D) [81] / *pectines*: penes (C) / *moliendam*: moler (D) / *educta*: ors
mené (D) ors menee (L) / *staminis*: de esteym (C) de staym (L) / *certamine*: estrif (C)
/ *reciproco*: entrechan[j]able (D) / *floccis laneis*: bort de lane (D) flocsounz de leyne
(C) borun de lane, burres (L) [82] / *stuparum*: estoupez (C) estupis (D) estupes (L) /
sandicis: warence, mader (C) uarence, madir (D) warance (L) / *sindicis*: wayd (C) wot
(L) / *Belvacensis*: Beuveys (C) de Beuveys (D) Beveys (L) / *granee*: de greyn (C) greyn
(D) de grene (L) / *cribro condimento*: d'epés savurment (L) / *prorumpat*: for saylet (L) /
fullonis: folour (C) fullur (D) del fulun (L) / *indulgientie*: perdunanse (L) / *diligentie*:
amité (D) / *frequentem*: sover (D) suveurre (L) / *perduellio*: batayle (DL) / *ablutionem*:
lavur (D) / *exposcens*: mandant (D) / *maculas*: teches (L) / *abluere*: laver (D)

[155] *veredus*: chareter (C) caretter (D) le chareter (L) / *veredarium*: chival de la
charette (C) cheval de carette (D) echival de la chare (L) / *cuculam*: coule (C) cuuil
(D) quolun (L) / *collobium*: frogge (C) froc (L) / *caputio*: chaperoun (C) / *manubiatum*: maunché (C) manché (L) / *grisio*: grey (C) / *agasonis*: aner (D) de anetier (L) /
mulionis: moyler (D) de muler (L) / *explere*: parempler (L) / *fruatur*: uset (L) / *aculeo*:
aguloun (C) gode, agulun (D) agulun (L) [83] / *flagello*: escorge (C) securge [sic] (D)
scureg [sic], ekurge (L) / *scorpione*: escurge (D) / *lenta*: fligesable (L) / *auriga*: chareter
(C) carett (D) charegir (L) / *ocreas*: hesez (C) heses (L) / *aurem*: horail (D) / *tesqua*:
waseus (C) uasseus (D) de waseys (L) / *lutosas plateas*: tayous (C) bouuses, tazus
rue(?) (L) / *cenosas plateas*: rue bouuse (D) / *latus*: coute (D) coste (L) / *accendunt*:

73 See OED sub *windas* and TL 4,789 sub *guindas*.
74 See OED sub *studdle sb*.
75 See MED sub *cambok(e n*.
76 See MED sub *heveld n.(a)*.
77 See OED sub *warp sb.*[1].
78 See OED sub *woof sb.*[1].
79 See OED sub *shuttle sb.*[1] and sub *wethe v*.
80 See preceding note.
81 See OED sub *warp v*.
82 See TL 1,1075 sub *borre*. The gloss 'bort de lane' is found in MS Dublin, Trinity College
270 and 'borts' glosses *floccis* in MS Oxford, Bodleian Library, Rawlinson G 99.
83 See MED sub *gode n*.

muntunt (L) / *aptetur*: seyt afarie (L)[84] / *onus*: la charge (C) / *carri*: char (C) char (D)
vane del char (L)[85] / *declives*: pendans (D) pendauns (L) / *legere*: passer (L) / *capistro*:
chevestre (D) / *siniugi*: decouplés (D) cuplé (L) / *impetum*: fole haste (L) / *sinuato*:
turné (DL) / *poplite*: garet, hamme (D)[86] garret (L) / *atestetur*: temptet (L) / *temonis*:
temoun (C) temun (D) de timun (L) / *iuxta restim*: corde, trays (C) hart, veythe (D)
juste corde (L)[87] / *veredus*: chareter (CL) charetter (D) / *anteriorem*: devant (D) /
epiphia: herneys (CD) harnés (L) / *centone*: feutre (CDL) / *falleras*: herneys (D) /
saciata: saulé (C) / *suarium*: suere (C) huce (D) la usse (L) / *subcellium*: panel (C)
suzsegle (D) sucengle (L) / *carentivillum*: canevas (CL) canevace (D) / *omitto*: jo pase
(C) passe (D)

[156] *scutarium*: esquiers (C) esquier (D) la quier (L) / *armigerium*: esquier (L) quiser
(D) / *equitem*: chivachaunt (C) / *circumstantiis*: de environnances (L) / *non operis
executione*: por la sute (L) / *rota*: ré (C) de ruoes (D) rowe (L) / *axis*: esseyl (C) essel
(L) / *timpano*: mouel (CD) moel (L) / *cavilla*: chevil (D) pin (L) / *modiolo*: mouel (D)
/ *intrusa*: boté (D) / *radii*: les rays, spokes (C) rais (D)[88] / *modiolo*: mouel (CD) /
cantos: jauntes, phelewes (C) jauntis (D)[89] / *transmittendi*: utreveyés (D) / *stelliones*:
dreynereytis (D) / *examinatus*: examiné (D) aprové (L) / *orbite*: sente (C) / *circumferentia*: la roundesse (C) veruntume (D) / *scrupulorum*: de petite peres (C) peti
peres (L) / *asseres*: les es (C) es, bordis (D) lé esses (L) / *area*: plase (L) place (D) / *sub
cratibus*: cleyes (C) desuz lé cleyis (D) / *limonibus*: lymouns (C) batun de la charete
(L) / *cidularum*: cedles (C) de latis (D) de lathe (L) / *columbaria*: perteus (C) /
limonibus: boye (L)[90]

[157] *vestibulo*: porche (C) vestiarie (L) / *plateas*: rues (C) ruis (D) / *porticus*: porche
(C) une porche (L) / *transeuntes*: passauns (D) / *disposita*: ordiné (L) / *nidorem*: flavur
(D) / *atrium*: une place (C) place (L) / *iuxta plateas*: pré du rue (L) / *debitis intersticiis*:
duis espacis (D) deu spaces (L) / *asseribus*: es (C) ess (D) / *trabibus*: trefs (C) trifs (D)
/ *tignis*: cheveruns (D) geveruns (L) / *latis*: latis (CD) / *cidulis*: cendles (C) / *sindulis*:
latis (D) / *clavis*: clous (C) / *tigillis*: tiwels (C) / *doma*: autesse (L) / *edificii*: herberga-
geis (D) / *commissuram*: severendure, anglice evesing (C) ceverruner, hevesingis (D)
severrundere (L)[91] / *porrectis*: estendus (C) atenduesse (L) / *specularia*: fenestres (C)
fenestre (DL) / *succina*: bustice (D) buste (L) / *distent*: desseyverent (C) / *pixides*:
bustes (L) boytes (C) / *tortiles*: tournables (C) turnables (L) / *sigia*: la ley (D) lye (L)
/ *sigie*: de leye (D) / *corrimbrum vel -bum*: base lie (C) / *corimbrum*: basse leye (D) /
corimbum: base lie (L) / *contineatur*: seyt cont[e]nu (L) / *laurinum*: eule de lorere (C)
eule de lore (L)

84 See Gfry 1,131b sub *aferir*.
85 Scheler, *Jbch. f. rom. u. engl. Lit.* 7 (1866), 155 cites *vayn* as a gloss on *currus*. See OED
sub *wain sb.*[1].
86 See MED sub *hamme n.(1)*.
87 See TL 10,510 sub *trait*, Gfry 8,220c sub *vette* and FEW 14,569a (*vitta*).
88 See OED sub *spoke sb.*
89 See MED sub *felwes n.pl.*
90 See MED sub *boue n.7(d)*.
91 See MED sub *evesing n.* and TL 9,603 sub *severonde*.

[158] *crates*: clayis (D) cleyes (L) / *culmo*: chalemel, stoubel (C) chaum(p) (D) chamme (L) [92] / *calamo palustri*: de ros de mareys, anglice star (C) [93] ros de mareys (D) ros de marés (L) / *arundine*: rosel (C) franc ros (D) de franc rose (L) / *cidulis*: latez (C) latis (D) lathes (L) / *lateres*: tywel (C) teulis (D) / *laquearia*: lé laz (C) couplis de mesun (D) cuples (L) / *stipibus*: estoks (C) estokis (D) de stocs (L) / *insidias*: les enges (C) / *hostium*: le us (C) / *seram*: serure (C) serure, loc (D) loc, serrure (L) / *expellant*: deboutent (C) / *pessulam*: barre (C) pele, lache vel loc pendant (D) pele, cliketiti (L) / *vectes*: verteveles (C) verolis (D) verul (L) / *gumphos*: gonfs (C) guns, hockis (D) [94] guns (L) / *repagula*: barrez (C) baris (D) bares (L) / *valve*: wikés (C) pertis, ueykis (D) [95] / *bifores*: double portez (C) duble portes (L) / *porticum*: la porche (C) porche (D) / *collocentur*: seint mis (L) / *cardinibus*: chardinz, herres (C) [96] vertivelis (D) vertefelles (L) / *rure*: champ (C) / *senecte*: sofreytuse (D) / *inopi senecte*: a soffreitus veylés (L) / *corbibus*: corbayles (C) corbaylis (D) de corbi-luns (L) / *cumeris*: ruches (C) rusches (L) ruche (D) / hec *cumera*: gallice gerner (D) / *calathis*: panieres (C) paners (D) / *vimineis*: de osier (D) de osiere (C) de osirs (L) / *sportis*: corbayles (C) corbayluns (D) petit corbaluns (L) / *cophinis*: hanapers (C) cofins (D) hanaper (L) / *fuscinam*: une foyn (C) foyne (D) une fune (L) / *hamatam*: croké (C) crocé, heymé (D) croké (L) / *piscibus*: de pessuns (L) / *reficere*: resauler (C) refere (L) / *fiscina*: de une fesele, chesefat (C) fissele, chesevat (L) / *fuscina*: chesefat, une fesele (D) [97] / *multra*: bouket (D) buchet (L) / *lac*: let (C) / *expressum*: enpressé (C) forprent (L) / *coagulatione*: pressure (D) prensure, par apressementture (L) / *sero*: le mek (C) mec (D) megue (L) / *casei*: formage (D) / *eliquato*: hors tret (L) / *colustrum*: gallice beht, besting anglice (C) grose mec (D) creme (L) [98] / *propinan-dum*: bevre (D) a bevere (L)

[159] *caseus*: le formage (C) furmage (D) / *teca casea*: casiere (C) en un casyer (D) casire (L) / *teneritudine*: tendre (D) / *ex juncis palustribus*: juncs de mareys (C) junkis de mareys (D) juncs de maris (L) / *cinifum*: mouche de chen (C) de vibés (D) wibés (L) [99] / *papiro*: gunc grant (D) / *muscarum*: mouchez (C) / ex *cirpis*: juncs (C) de meyne juncke (D) / *locustarum*: de taoun, brese (C) landgutres (D) langoutris (left-hand margin, D) [100] / *brucorum*: burduns (DL) anglice dranis (left-hand margin, D) anglice catepeluz (C) [101] / *culex*: wibet (C) / *fucorum*: dranes (C) / *vesparum*: wepes (C) / *culicum*: wibez (right-hand margin, C) / *crabrorum*: charbot (right-hand margin, C) / *paleam*: pale (C) / *paleas*: paylis (D) / *acera*: escurayle (C) escurayles (D) curaylle (L) / *furfur*: bren (CL) / *furfuri*: brenis (D) / *gallinis*: gelines (C) / *anatibus*: anes (CL) anis (D) / *pabula*: pastures (D) / *anseribus*: chars (C) gars vel houis (D) gars (L) / *aucis*: houes (C) oysuns (L) / *auculis*: oysiluns petit (D) petit oyseus (D)

---

92 See OED sub *stubble sb*.
93 See OED sub *star sb*.²
94 See MED sub *hok n.6(b)*.
95 See OED sub *wicket*.
96 See MED sub *herre n.(1)*.
97 See MED sub *chese n.3(b)*.
98 See MED sub *best n*. and *besting n*.
99 See FEW 17,575b and TL 4,764 (sub *guibet*).
100 See MED sub *brese n*. and TL 5,144 (sub *langoste*).
101 See MED sub *drane n*., FEW 2,i,518 and Gfry 2,90c (*chatepelose*).

oysiluns (L) / *polentrudium*: boletel (C) bolter (D) buletel (L) / *taratantarum*: une sarce, anglice er-sive (C) [102] sarce (D) sars (L) / *pollen*: le flur (C) flur, farrine (L) / *eliquatur*: courit (D) seyt or tret (L) / *specificetur*: specefié (D) seyt lyé (L) / *cervisia*: serveyse (D) / *coletur*: set colu (D) / *frameam*: gisarm (C) gisarme, gleyve (D) gleve (L) / *vangam*: beyche (C) besche (DL) / *spatam*: fauchoun (C) / *tribulum*: flael (CL) flayele (D) / *tribulam*: pele (DL) truble (C) / *tribulos*: rounces (C) runcis (D) carduns (L) / *saticulum*: semecere (C) corbilun (D) / *sarticulum*: corbaylun, anglice hopere (top of f.164v, D) [103] corbilunt (L) / *sationis*: de semesun (L) / *qualum*: panier (D) panir (L) / *quaxillum*: petit panier (D) / *cribrum*: cribre (L) / *muscipulam*: rater (D) rature (L) [104] / *cenovectorium*: civere (CD) civire a res (L) / *pedicam*: calketrappe (C) pege (D) kalketrape (L) [105] / *rastros*: rasteus (C) / *fustes*: bastuns (L) / *capiantur*: seynt pris (D) / *palos*: peus (DL) / *qualus*: hote, hotte (C) / *exploratos* (= duratos): durciz (D) serchés (L) / *bisacuta*: bisacu (C) bisagu, bil (D) besuage, twibil (L) [106] / *eradicandum*: hors rasere (C) rater (D) / *tribulos*: rounces (C) carduns (D) espines (L) / *sentes*: espines (C) spy (L) / *vepres*: rounces (C) runcis (D) / *spuria*: bastards (L) / *vitulamina spuria*: branches baustars (C) branchis bastars (D) verges bastardes (L) / *ruscum*: jauns (C) pele (D) [107] / *sepes*: hayis (D) / *firmandas*: firmers (D) / *renovandas*: novelers (D) / *incuriam*: nounchalie (C) nunshalerie (D) [108] / *sopitis*: endormys (C) dormis (D) / *tempore furve*: larsinousement (C) / *subulcis*: porchers (C) porcheris (D) porcher (L) / *bubulcis*: bovers (C) boveris (D) bover (L)

[160] *artavum*: cotayl (C) knivez (D) / *surculos*: les entes (C) petitis entes (L) / *exsecet*: trenchet (C) trenche (D) / *inserat*: entet (C) entit (D) ente (L) / *arboribus*: en arbres (C) / *oculandos*: a mussers (C) / *opus*: mester (D) / *ligones*: de picoys (C) picoyis (D) pigosis (L) / *tirsos*: banestons (C) [109] / *extirpet*: hors rachet (C) rachit (D) / *intubas*: herbe benet (C) herbe benés (D) herbes benete (L) / *urticas*: orties (C) urties (D) / *ervos*: ternues, hery note (C) quichil, sternys (D) gallice ter[n]usse, quichil (left-hand margin D) esternurus (L) [110] / *lolia*: nel, kokel (C) [111] nel (D) / *carduos*: carduns (D) charduns (L) / *cardones*: en lez chardouns (C) / *perforandis*: a perser (C) / *avenas steriles*: wil-hotes (C) haveruns (DL) / *unco*: de crok (C) faucille (L) / *habilius*: plus demenablement (D) / *extirpantur*: sunt arachis (D) / *ligone*: picoyse (D) / *bubulcis*: bover (CDL) / *subulcum*: porcher (CDL) / *opilionem*: bercher (DL) / *letiorem*: plu lé (DL) / *caulam*: faude (CD) / *opulentia*: par la plenté (CL) plenté (D) /

---

102 See MED sub *her(e-sive n.*
103 See MED sub *hopper(e n.(a)*.
104 See TL 8,335 sub *ratier* and 336 sub *ratoire*.
105 See TL 2,320–1 sub *chauchetrape* and *chauchetrepe* and MED sub *calketrappe*.
106 See MED sub *bil n.* and OED sub *twibill*.
107 MSS C and D also have the gloss '.i. magnum palum', of which 'pele' (D) is presumably a rendering.
108 These forms seem unattested elsewhere. FEW 2,i,83b cites a form *anonchalie*. In MS C there is a nasal bar over the final *i*.
109 See Gfry 8,285b sub *banneton*?
110 The *sternuys* of D is not entirely certain, as the word is badly written. The texts of Nequam in MS Harley 683 have *esternues* (f.16r) and *ternues* (f.47v). See FEW 12,262b. The English gloss in C should be corrected to *hery hote* (see OED sub *oat sb.³*). See OED sub *quitch*.
111 See MED sub *cokkel n.*

pinguiorem: plu gras (D) / *tigurium:* holet (C) houlet (D) ole(le)t (L) / *mincture:* pissure (C) pissase (D) de pyssase (L) / *stercorationis:* de fens (C) / *stercorum:* de fens (C) fens (D) / *presepe:* crecche (L) / *transferatur:* seit outre porté (D) / *ovile:* faude (D) / *area:* place (D) / *stercora:* de fens (D) / *sentiat:* sentit (D) / *bostar:* boverie (CD) une boveri (L) / *rusticus noster:* nostre veyleyn (D) / *blandientis:* blandisant (D) debonere (L) / *agasonem:* un haner (D) aner (L) / *aliquantulum:* poy (D) / *in equitio:* en le haras (C) harace (D) arasse (L) / *mulionem:* gardeyn de mulis (D) / *emissarium:* estalun (CD) / *admissarium:* astalun (L) / *juvencas:* jenices (C) jenicis (D) / *tauros:* torz (C) / *buculos:* petit bovis (D) boves (L) / *buculas:* bovez (C) geniz (D) / *bubulos:* bugles (C) buglis (D) / *verveces:* moutouns (C) mutuns (L) / *hinnulos:* founs (DL) / *burdones:* burduns (D) / *casses:* reys (C) reyis (D) resse (L) / *laqueos:* las (C) las, scnares (D)[112] lasse (L) / *extensos:* estenduz (C)

[161] *ad circumvolvendum:* environtorner (C) / *lepores:* levere (C) leveris (D) / *cervas:* bises (CL) bisis (D) / *capreolos:* chiveryz (C) chevereus (L) / *damas:* deyms (C) deymis (D) / *cervos:* cerfs (C) / *arma:* armes (D) / *hinnulos:* fououns (C) founs (DL) / *odorinseci:* brachez (CL) brachéss (D) / *necessarium:* covenable (L) / *leporarii:* levrrers (CD) / *grande robur:* grant trif (D) pesant tref (L) / *aratrum:* carue (D) / *usualiter:* communement (L) / *sortiatur:* prengit (D) / *trabem:* tref (CD) trefe (L) / *medium:* meluel (D) / *temone:* temoun (C) temun (L) / *bifurcando:* enforchaunt (C) duble furchant (D) de deu furkes (L) / *lira:* reoun (C) reun (DL) / *binas aures:* deuz aunsis (D) / *in unica aure* (sive ansa): de une orayle, aunse (D) / *ansa:* anglice andle (L)[113] / *sulcus:* re(m)un (D) / *in obliquo:* en esclés (D) enn eclenc (L) / *efficiatur:* seyt fet (D) / *aratrum:* carue (D) / *burim:* cue (D) / *cauda:* coue (D) / *levetur:* haucé (D) / *stiva:* le estive, la manche (C) maunche (D) manche (L) / *capulus:* capel (C) broche (D) / *arator:* arrur (D) / *dentale:* gyp (C) chippe (D) carwure, anglice gip (L)[114] / *manu:* .s. manchel (L) manchet (D) / *difficilis regiminis:* strit governemen (D) grefe (L) / *extremitas:* pomel, hulte (D) pumel (L)[115] / *libitina:* ber (D) bere (C)[116] / *obliquando:* en eclenkaunt (C) / *gipsea:* arsilusse (D) arsiluse (L) / *retinacula saligna:* hart de sauz (D)

[162] *saligna:* de sauz (CL) / *vomes:* le sok (C) soc (DL) / *infigitur:* enficchi (C) / *sepem:* haye (DL) / *cratem:* clye (D) cley (L) / *traham:* herce (DL) / *clavos:* clouis (D) clou (L) / *cavillas:* kevillis (D) kivilles (L) / *restim:* hard (D) corde (L) / *cultrum:* cutre (D) cwtre (L) / *stercorare:* compouster (C) composter, grasser (D) compoter (L) / *fimo:* par fens (C) fens (D) de fins (L) / *sarcire:* sarcler (L) / *resarcire:* sarcler (C) amender (D) / *novalia:* lé warez, gayerz, falwew (C) uarés (D) warets (L)[117] / *rebinare:* rebiner (DL) / *veracta:* warez (C) uarés (D) waret (L) / *creta:* marle (C) creye (D) / *renovare:* renoveler (L) / *chilindro:* herce (D) / *letificare:* fere lé (DL) / *stipulis:* chaumes (L) / *incensis:* bracés (D) bracé (L) / *equare:* erser (L) / *quadratus:* quarré (L) / *cratis:* cleies (C) cleys, herce (D) de cley (L) / *munire:* garnir (L) / *cererem:* blé (D) /

---

112 See OED sub *snare sb.*
113 See MED sub *hondel n.*
114 See MED sub *chippe n.1(c).*
115 See MED sub *hilt(e n.*
116 See MED sub *ber(e n.(8).*
117 See MED sub *falwe n.*

grana: greins (D) / *terere*: tribler (L) / *trahe*: herse (L) / *commissam*: baylé (C) / *cooperire*: coverer (C) coverir (L) / *fissum*: fendu (CDL) / *prorumpat*: depeset (C) for saylet (L) / *calamum*: chalamel (D) chalemel, anglice red (L)[118] / *solidetur*: seit endursi (C) seyt fermé (D) seyt afermé (L) / *spicis*: espies (C) / *thecis*: de ecoles (C) hosis, cotellis (D) chocheles (L)[119] / *honeretur*: seyt largé (D) seyt chargé (L) / *calamus*: chalamel (D) / *metere*: sier (CL) / *spicis*: d'espiis (D) picis, erhey (left-hand margin D)[120] / *in area*: in une plase (L) / *triturare*: batre (CL) batere (D) / *manipulos*: gaveles (CL) gavelis (D) / *rastro*: rastel (CDL) / *gelimas*: garbes (C) / *mundificare*: fere nette (L) / *vanno*: van (CD) / *a mola*: meule (D) de mulin (L) / *confringi*: estre depeci (L) / *dissolui*: delyé (L) / *sinceratum*: sarcé (CD) sacé (L) / *cribri*: cribré (CL) criveré (D) / *eliquari*: estre hor tret (L) / *foraminibus*: pertuz (D) / *pinsendi*: de peyster (C) pester (D) de pestrur (L) / *enucleari*: a demoster (L) / *enuclianda*: mustrers (D) / *aculeum*: aguloun (C) agulun (DL) / *traham*: herse (CL) herce (D)

[163] *larvam*: visere (C) visure (DL) / *larvaticam imaginem*: ymage babywene (D) baboen (L)[121] / *omitto*: jo lez (C) / *priapi*: vit (C) / *palinodia*: yohie (D) / *navis*: nef (D) / *linter*: batel (D) / *cimba*: batel (CDL) / *rostrum*: bec (DL) / *chelox*: nef (D) / *in transferatione*: en passant (D) / *lolligine*: henke (D) tenche (L)[122] / *naulum*: quod in gallico dicitur fret (C) fret (D)[123] / *ve[h]iculo*: portage, porture (D)[124]

[164] *prora*: bec de nef (D) / *putredo*: pureture (D) / *classis*: navire (D) / *tubarum*: bosinis (D) / *lituorum*: greyles (D) de greiles (L) / *rotabitur*: roué vel sera rundé (D) sera turné (L) / *circumvolvetur*: virunturné (D) / *cuspis*: poynt (D) / *orientem*: este (D) / *comprehendunt*: aperseivent (C) / *turbatione*: trubelemen (D) / *occasum*: chesun (D)

[165] *farre*: blé (D) / *cibo*: viande (D) / *opus*: mester (D) mestir (L) / *securi*: coyné (C) coynié (D) de cuné (L) / *malus*: le maust (C) mast (D) / *abscidi*: estre trenché (L) / *emergente*: sordaunt (C) surdant (L) / *cumulus*: muncel (L) / *piratarum*: robeours de mer (C) galioss (D) galiots (L)[125] / *malleolis*: marteus (DL) / *asseres*: hes (D) / *fidis clavis*: leuz clous (C) / *pice*: peyz (C) poste (D) poys (L) / *cera*: sire (D) / *picata*: pyz (C) poee (L) / *liniantur*: seeynt hoynt (C) glués (D) sent e[n]glué (L) / *exterius levigentur*: dehors sente planiés (L) planeis (D) / *trabibus*: de glees (L) / *haustum*: espunchment (D) / *asseribus*: des ez (C) de es (L) hes (D) / *cratibus*: cleyes (C) cleyis (D) / *craticulis*: petit cleyis (D) / *maritetur*: seyt adjutét (L) / *velum*: sigle (DL) / *dissociet*: dispartit (D) / *modium*: mouel (C) / *malus*: le maust (C) mast (D) / *rudentes*: les cordes (C) / *inferior*: bas (L) / *malo*: maust (C) mast (D) / *veli*: le sigle (C) sigle

---

118 See OED sub *reed sb.*[1]I.1.
119 See FEW 2,i,826–7.
120 See MED sub *er(e n.(2)*.
121 See Gfry 1,544c and 8,265a/b (sub *baboe* & *babouin*), MED sub *babewin* n. and DMLBS sub *babuinus*. MS D f.166r has the further gloss 'ymaginem Priapi'.
122 Cf. OED sub *ink sb.*[1]I.b and II.4(b) (*ink-fish*). In the right-hand margin of f.48r L also has 'herba gallice neele'.
123 See FEW 17,435 and TL 3,ii,2255.
124 There are no clear attestations in FEW 9,206b.
125 See TL 4,73 and MED sub *galiot n.(2)*.

(D) / *tumor veli*: enflesurs (D) / *antennis*: cordis (D) / *sinus*: seyn (C) enflurs (D) anglice bosimhing (top of f.167r D)[126]

[166] *superiores extremitates*: sovereyns etremetés (C) sovereyne dreynereytis (D) / *foratoria*: pertuz de terere (C) terires gallice, navegas (L) navgeres, terereis (D)[127] / *fori*: pertuz (C) / *cornua*: cornis (D) / *mali*: mast (D) / *funes*: cordis (D) corde (L) / *ventilogium*: gallice cochez (C) / *stipites*: estokis (D) estoys (L)[128] / *in gallico ydioma*: en franceys (D) / *suppodientes*: apouauns (D) apuans (L) / *podium*: pouhayl (D) apual (L) / *navigio*: navie, rouyk (C)[129] navire (D) / *columbar*: pillori (C) / *procedantur*: entenduz (D) / *troclea*: wyndas (C) uindass (D) windés, windesses (L) / *remi*: del enviroun, anglice hore (C)[130] de le avirun (D) / *paume*: paume (D) / *transtrum*: sege (D) / *circumligati*: envirun ... (D) / *velum*: sigle (D) / *variationem*: diverseté (D) / *rudentes*: cordes (C) grosse cordis (D) / *aure*: del vent (C) / *anchora*: ancre (C) aunkere (D) / *chorum*: vent (C) /

[167] *porticulum*: le martel (C) maylet (L) maylet (D) teu maner de maylet (right-hand margin, D) / *applicetur*: set arivé, ke ele syt arivé (D) seit arivé (C) seyt arivee (L) / *rasorium*: rasour (C) / *novaculum*: id (= rasour) vel coureour (C) novacle, rasur (D) novacle (L) / *pumice*: pomiz (C) une pumice (D) punce (L) / *ad abradendum*: awey rere (D) / *planulam*: plane (CL) une plane (D) / *membrane*: parchemeyn (C) pel (D) / *superficiem*: la autesse (L) / *plumbum*: plum (D) / *quaternus*: quaer (C) quayer (D)[131] / *linietur*: seyt rulé (D) seyt riulee (L) / *tergi*: del dos (L) / *existente*: parmeynant (D) seant (L) / *exercitus*: del oust (L) / *cedula*: angniz (D) agnice (L) / *sedula*: croue, vel *apendice*: agniz (C)[132] / *apendice*: englu (DL) / *inferiori parte*: bas partie (L) / *registrum*: cordam libri vel clavun (D) / *punctorium*: poyntur, poynterole (C)[133] / *resideat*: se syt (L) / *ansis*: lé braces (C) bracis (D) bras (L) / *pluteum*: dese [sic] (C) deske (DL)[134] / *asserem*: hes (DL) / *scabello*: une furm(ur)e (D)

[168] *epicaustorium*: ez (C) une carole (D) une karole (L) / *centone*: feutre (C) de feutre (DL) / *artavum*: knyvet (C) cneyvet (D) cynevet (L) / *ylo*: la muele (C) meule (D) la meule (L) / *liquescat*: decuret (L) / *formet*: taylit (D) / *habilis*: havable (D) / *litura*: esquachure (D) equacheure (L) / *clavillum*: clavun (L) clawn (D) / *spectaculum*: espectacle, sive *cavillam* vel calvillam [sic]: spectacle (C) / *errorem*: foleur (L) / *dispendiosam*: damajuse (D) / *prunas*: breces (C) bresis (D) bresse (L) / *in epicausterio*: en chimené (C) chimenee (L) / *incaustum*: la enke (C) henke (D) enke (L) / *atramentum*: arnement (CD) arrement (L) / *lodium*: lover (C) lovere (D) luvere (L) / *insultus*: la noyse (D) la nosye (L) / *intrare*: entrer (D) / *aquilonaris*: de nort (D) / *aquilonari*: de norht (C) / *aquilonalis*: del norht (L) / *inpugnet*: cumbatyt (D) /

---

126 See MED sub *bosom* n.3(*a*) and *bosoming* ger.
127 See MED sub *nauger* n.
128 The form *estuye* is found in other MSS.
129 Cf. Scheler, *Jbch. f. rom. u. engl. Lit.* 7 (1866), 166. *Navigium* is given the sense *remigium*; *rouyk* = 'rowing' (see OED sub *rowing* vbl. sb.¹).
130 See MED sub *or(e* n.(*1*).
131 See TL 2,10 sub *caier* and FEW 2,ii,1437.
132 See TL 3,i,1010 sub *escröe* and AND sub *agnice* (cf. DMLBS sub *agnicium*).
133 Appears to be a hapax. OED sub *pointel* notes erroneous spelling *pointrell*.
134 See MED sub *deske* n.

fenestrella: fenestral (D) fenestrele (L) / *panniculo*: clotet (C) drap (D) drapelet (L) / *membrana*: de une pel (L) / *solatia*: confortz (D) / *albedo*: blanchisure (D) / *distincta*: departie (L) / *disgregat*: deseyveret (C) departit (D) departet (L) / *intensa*: espés (C) / *obtenebrat*: escurit [sic] (D) / *minium*: vermiloun (C) vermilun (DL)

[169] *puniceas*: vermailles (L) / *capitales*: chapiteus (L) / *fuscum*: bloye (CDL) / *pulverem*: poudre (D) podre (L) / *asuram* (= azuram): asure (CL) / *repertam*: contrové (D) / *notarius*: notarie (DL) / *Salomone*: Salomoun (C) / *sortiatur*: prengit (D) / *apices*: tytelis (D) titles (L) [135] / *aurifaber*: orfevere (D) orfere (L) / *caminum*: chemené (C) chimené (L) / *perforatum*: persé (CL) percé (D) / *pulsu*: debwtement (L) / *fumus*: le fume (C) / *folles*: les fouz (C) soflez (D) suflés (L) [136] / *diligentia*: amiableté (L) / *fistulas*: pipe, tuelys (D) tueles (L) / *prunas*: breses (CL)

[170] *accendat*: abrasit (D) / *crebra aspercio*: aspés (?) sovener apar[pi]liment (L) / *incus*: enclume (C) enc[l]ume (D) enclune (L) / *duricie*: de duresce (D) / *forcipis*: tenails (C) de le tenayl (D) tanaylle (L) / *molliatur*: seyt enmolly (D) / *mallei*: martel (D) del mayl (L) / *inexhauste*: nent espuché (C) / *extendi*: avan tendu (D) / *malleolum*: martel (C) maylet (D) mayllet (L) / *bracteas*: peces de hor (C) pecis (D) / *criseas*: pecis (D) / *laminas*: de plates (C) plates (L) / *auricalceas*: de latun (C) de orchaut, coper (L) [137] / *stangneas*: de esteym (C) de steyme (L) / *cupreas*: de quivere (C) de quivure (L) / *celtem*: chicel (C) un chiel (D) cicel (L) / *smaragdo*: emeraude (C) enmiraude (D) emiraude (L) / *adamentem*: adamant (C) / *marmore*: marbre (C) / *iacincto*: jagunsce (D) / *carbunculo*: carboucle (C) charbuncle (D) / *saphiro*: savire (C) saphir (D) / *jaspide*: jap (C) / *sculpere*: entayler (CD) / *margarita*: perle, margarite (C) / *cotim*: un coues (D) [138] / *molem*: pere mule (D) / *levigare*: planyer (D) / *extergere*: terdre (D) / *exploret*: enserchit (L) / *superficiem*: hautesce (D) autesse (L) / *granula*: la greins (L) / *corio gremiali*: gerun de quyr (C) gerunner (D) de quir(ir) (L) / *aceras*: boystis (D) boyt (L) / *ampullas*: ampules (C) ampoyl (D) ampuylles (L) / *minuta*: petit (L) / *figuli*: poter (CL) de poter (D) / *serram*: sey, anglice saue (D) [139] syee, saye (L) / *limam*: une lime (D) file (C) lime, anglice file (L) [140] / *aurifrigium*: orfreys (C) orferey (D) orefray (L) / *filum argenteum*: fil de argent (D)

[171] *consui*: estre cosu (D) [e]tre cusu (L) / *construi*: aparuliié (L) / *anaglaphario*: bordure (L) / *fusili*: espaundable (C) fundable (DL) / *ductili*: amenable (C) menable (L) / *tabellam*: table (D) / *ceratam*: en cyre (D) aceré (L) / *oblitam*: englué (D) engluee (L) / *protrahendos*: purtrere (D) / *argillam*: arsil (L) / *pingendos*: depey[n]dre (D) / *eliquatam*: degwtuz (L) / *obrisum*, purum: myré (D) / *inoffense*: san curusse (L) / *auricalcum*: latoun (C) orchaut (DL) / *a cupro*: de quivere (D) / *institoris*: de markant (L) / *pellacis*: decewable (L) / *lavacrum*: founs (C) une founs (D) / *tabateriam*: forge (L) / *mariolum*: mariole (C) / *pulpitum*: lectrun (D) leytrun (L) / *sciestrum*: leitroun

---

135　See FEW 13,i,359a (*titulus*).
136　See FEW 3, 688a (*follis*).
137　See MED sub *coper* n.
138　See FEW 2,ii,1242b.
139　See OED sub *saw sb.*[1].
140　See MED sub *file n.(1)*.

(C) / *pelves*: basin (C) bacins (L) / *urceus*: pot (C) poscenet (D) / *cathedra*: cheere (C) / *tribunal*: sege (D) / *tronus*: trone (CD)

[172] *absconsa*: esconz (C) une descunse (D)[141] / *sacrarium*: sacrarie (CD) / *vestibulum*: porche (C) une porche (D) porchiz (L) / *urceus*: possenet (D) / *vestiarium*: veystiarie (C) vestiarie (D) / *altare*: auter (C) / *scannum*: bank (C) / *loculus*: bere (CDL) / *phiole*: cruez (C) violis (D) / *pixides*: boytes (C) boystis (D) / *manutergium*: tuayle (D) / *facitergium*: coverchef (D) keverchef (L) / *examitum*: samite (D) [s]amite (C) samyt (L) / *libitina*: bere (D) / *columpne aenee*: pilers de arem (C) pilerres de areyme (L) de areyme (D) / *missale*: messel (L) / *gradale*: grael (L) / *antiphonarium*: antifiner (D) / *manuale*: manuel (D) / *superpelicium*: surpliz (C) surplis (D) surplus (L) / *amictum*: amuse (C) amyt (L) / *capitesium*: amite (D) / *alba*: aube (D) aubey (L) / *cingulum*: centure (D) curye (L) / *stropheum*: seynture (L) / *strophea*: lisur (D) / *casula*: chesuble (C) chesube (D) chesubele (left-hand margin, D) chesible (L) / *balteus*: bauder (D) / *phanum*: phanoun (C) fanun (D) / *acerne*: de arable (CD) arable (L) / *quercule*: de cheyne (CD) de keynne (L) / *trabes*: tref / *stola*: estole / *tigni*: cheverouns (C) cheveruns (DL) / *succedines*: severoundes (C) severunderes (D) severundires (L) / *tegule*: tiules (L) / *lignum*: fust (D) / *cindulis*: latis (D) / *lateres*: teules (D) / *suspendeantur*: seint pendues (L) / *nole*: cheles (D)[142]

[173] *campane*: camper[n]oleys (L)[143] / *tintinnabula*: chelettis (D)[144] seyns a mayns (L) / *campanarium*: clocher (C) chlocher (D) clochir (L) / *tolus*: tupet (C) topet (D) / *pinnaculum*: torele (C) / *ventilogium*: cochet (CL) chochet (L) / *limina*: esseul (C) / *additum*: entré (C) / *filatorium*: une boyste (C) / *vectes*: vertevelis, barris (D) veruyls (L) / *gumphi*: guns (DL) / *repagula*: barres (L) barris (D) / *pensule*: loc pendant (D) loc pendable (L) / *sere*: loc (D) serures (L) / *cardines*: verteveles (L) / *limina*: lintres (D)[145]

Vernacular Glosses in MS Cambridge, Gonville and Caius Coll. 385

[60] *gurgustio*, quasi gurgitem gustans: hedwile[146] / *hamite*: croc / *nassa*: bercel, lep[147] / [61] *capanam*: almarie / *alutia*: lavurs / *conpetere*: acorder / *mugiles*: saumuns / *amphinia*: raye vel sperlinges / *murena*: lampreie / *ep[h]imera*: baleine / *gobio*: menuse / *capito*: gaboche / *morus*: menuse (left-hand margin = muluel) / *pelamides*: plaiz / *mulus*: mulet / *gobio*: gujun (left-hand margin) / *melanurus*: darz de mer (left-hand margin) / [62] *dentrix*: luz / *megarus*: makerel / *gamarus*: espinoche / *ambubagis*: a ribauz / *lambrus*: lechere (right-hand margin) / *garifilatum*: gilofré / *appetibile*: desirable / [65] *instita matronalis*: cheinse a dame / *sirmata*: vestures trainans / *aspergines*: longe cheinses / *ludices treacles* (corr. lodices teatrales): a carole kemese / *teristrum*:

141 See TL 3,i,960 sub *esconse* and FEW 1,9a. *Desconse* is a hapax.
142 See TL 3,i,880 sub *eschele*.
143 See TL 2,202 sub *champenele* and *champenole*. Cf. MED sub *campernole* n.
144 See FEW 17,109b (*skilla*).
145 i.e. *linters*.
146 See MED sub *hed* n.(1)6(d) (*hed-wel* 'source of a stream').
147 See FEW 1,337b which gives very late dates for *berceau* = 'basket', whereas TL 1,923 cites *bercelet* ('kleine Wiege, Korb') from Philippe de Thäun.

riveroketh / [66] *recinium*: cheinse ridé / *abditorio*: parroc [148] / [70] *degrassatores*: envaisurs / *prevaricatores*: depessurs / *multatores*: penurs / *antropocedi*: homicide / *siccarius*: murdrisur (left-hand margin) / *clangatores*: afiurs / *caduciatores*: acordurs / [71] *stratilatis*: espie / *statelum*: standard [157] *specularia*: fenestre / *discernet*: remettre / [171] *tergiversationem*: terserie / [172] *succedines*: severundes

Vernacular Glosses in the commentary in MS C

[61] *lixa*: gallice quistroun / [62] *sculpator*: entaylour / [66] *birritrica*: gallice geroun / [67] *assa*: gallice haste / *pruna*: gallice brese / *pruina*: gallice gelé / *prunus*: gallice pruner / [68] *vallum*: gallice bayl / *eminere*: gallice aperer de loyn / *iminere*: aperer de pres / *podium*: gallice apuayl / *vas*: anglice fat [149] / [71] *stratilates*: gallice conestable / *hastiludium*: gallice bourdyz / *hastiledium*: gallice torneyment / *verna*: serjaunt / *vispilio*: gallice robeour / *coterellus*: serjaunt a pé / cultellus autem habet tres partes .s. manubrium .s. 'manche', scindula, et hoc pirasmium 'le assay del cotel' [150] / [159] *culex*: gallice wibet / [160] *equum admissarium*: gallice estalun / *ervus*: gallice ternue, anglice quycheen [151]

Vernacular Glosses in the commentary in MS D [152]

[60] *pisa*: peys gallice / *puls*: gallice gurel [153] / *moles*: pesentym / *faba fresa*: gallice feves molues / *fabe selique*: gallice feves od cose / *cepe*: oynuns gallice / *tripes*: gallice tripé / *contus*: gallice rabot [154] / *uncus*: gallice croc / *aqualicium*: lavur gallice

[61] *pullus*: gallice puleyn / *ruder*: guter

[62] *sculpo*: gallice entayler / *techa*: caser / *sera*: serure, loc / *cadus*: baril / *quisquilium*: gallice ramil / *dolabrum*: anglice bradax [155] / *uter*: bocel de quir / *clissedra*: dusil / *pelvis*: bacin / *mustum*: must / *ydromellum*: boket / *epitogium*: surcote / *penula*: furrure / *manubium*: manche / *birrus*: gerurs (corr. geruns)

[63] *opus*: overayne / *estivale*: estivur / *sindo*: sendel / *sericum*: seye / *bissus*: cheysel / *linum*: checes de flax [156] / *experiolus*: esquirel / *cuniculus*: coniz / *laero*: leyrun / *equicium*: haraz / *succusso*: troter / *clavis*: clou / *clava*: maçue / *clavis*: clef / *munio*: gallice garner vel estorer / *clunis*: croup de cheval / *strepe*: estru

[64] *antela*: truse devant / *postela*: arçun derere / *involucrem*: trusel / *mantica*: trusel vel sasel [157] / *camus*: bernacle / *lupatum*: fereyn a chival tirant / *habene*: rey[n]is / *puscula*:

---

[148] See MED sub *par(r)ok* n.

[149] See MED sub *fat* n.

[150] I do not know what is meant here ('dicitur a pirasmon grece quod est temptare latine').

[151] See OED sub *quicken* sb.[2].

[152] In general I omit *gallice* where there is no possibility of confusion.

[153] i.e. *gruel*.

[154] The meaning is uncertain. Cf. DMLBS sub *contus c* ('mundle, pot stirrer') which is usually rendered by *movur* (FEW 6,iii,165b 'long bâton, perche, dont on se sert pour diriger un bateau, une barque'). This may lead us to *rabot* 'instrument des pêcheurs pour troubler l'eau' (FEW 16,730b).

[155] See MED sub *brod adj.4(d)*.

[156] See MED sub *flex* n. Read *che[n]ces*?

[157] See TL 9,19 sub *sachel*.

boclil [sic] / *stilus*: pestel / *epistilum*: capital / *columpna*: piler / *thoral*: chalun / *cervical*: orirel [sic] / *bissus*: cheysil / *lodex*: veluse / *sargium*: sarge / *taxus*: tesun / *taxum*: lart / *taxo*: bargayn

[65] *capus*: muschet / *nisus*: esperver / *herodius*: girfauc / *tercellus*: tercel / *tardarius*: faucun laner / *gruarius*: faucun gruer / *an(ti)cipiter*: ostur / *jupa*, vestis nuptialis: kemese / *colobium*: froc a moyne / *facia*: bende / *falx*: brandun / *faus*: jowe / *mataxa*: serence / *aurifrigium*: orfreys / *tricatura*: enpliure / *trica*: trese de femme / *complicet*: empleer / *explico*: depleyer / *digitus*: deel vel dey

[66] *agulus*: agule / *acus*: escurel / *filarium*: filer / *glomus*: lusel de fil / *extrico*: ho[r]s plier / *opus anaglafarium*: overaine levé / *opus vulgare*: comun overayne / *peplum*: wemple / *corocalla*: cofie de linge / *crinale*: garlanddeheche / *reticulum*: buchet, calle / *monile*: nuche / *spinter*: ficalye / *fuscotinctum*: fustion

[67] *asso*: roster / *assatus* quod est: rosté(r) / *pruna*: bresse / *pruina*: geley(n)e / *condimentum*: savur / *altilis*, altile: chapun / *veru*: espey / *membranarius*: parcheminer / *admirari* equivocum est ad 'mirer' et ad 'merveyler' / *fundus*: funz

[68] *gesticulo*: enveyser / *cristallus*: cristal / *cementarius*: macyn / *lapidarium*: quarere de pere / *vepris*: runce / *interstitium*: espace / *fundum*: kernel vel cancel[158]

[69] *propugnacula*: bretage / *dedo*: abbandoner / *succidium*: suz / *hilla*: andule / *salsucrum* [sic]: salsucre [sic] / *catapulta*: sete barbé / *pelta*: targe / *ballista*: alblast / *sudes*: peuz / *fustis*: bleuturis[159] / *torres*: brandun / *elido*: enfebler / *mannus*: palfrey / *gradarius*: scasur

[70] *tuba*: busine / *lituus*: gleyve[160] / *buxus*: fregel de buz / *runco*: runfler / *vispilio*: hutlage / hec *preta*: utlage mans[161] / *clarigator*: defiur / *clarigo*: defier

[71] *fundus*: fu[n]z / *columbar*: pertuz de pillori / *excubie*: waites / *corus* est equivocum: pur quer et pur vent et mesure / *vannus*: van / *batus*: bussel / *palea*: chaf[162] / *anser*: jars / *anas*: ane

[72] *ciconia*: cigoyne / *merges*: plu[n]gun / *gallus palustris*: morilun[163] / *pavo*: poun / *ara*: porcherie / *cavilla*: cevile / *tenua*: frenge dehors / *fimbra*: fre[n]ge dedent / *pensum*: fusil / *pecten*: rake, rastel[164] / *scandex*: wesde[165]

[155] *veredarius*: cheval carter gallice / *cuculla*: cowel / *cucullus*: cowel / *aculeus*: agulun / *flagellum*: escurge / *auriga*: caret / *ocree*: hosis / *cenum*: bowe / *biga*: charette / *declivis*: dependant / *sinuo*: turner / *poples*: garet / *cento*: feutre / *centonarius*: feutrer / *fallere*: herneys / *subcellium*: sucele / *fallera*: herneis

[156] *scutarius*: esquier / *timpanus et modiolus*: moel, nave[166] / *cantus*: chant / *cantus*: jante / *cancello*: defacer

[157] *aula*: sale / *aulatus*: mesere .i. evesinge

[158] *latus*: coste / *arundo*: rosel / *irundo*: arunde / *irudo*: sancsue / *culmus*: chaume /

---

[158] The gloss is presumably misplaced (see *cancelli* [69])
[159] Cf. AND sub *bleterun*.
[160] An error for *greyle*.
[161] See Bosworth & Toller, *An Anglo-Saxon Dictionary* sub *út-laga* and *mán*.
[162] See MED sub *chaf* n.
[163] See note 71 above. The error is very common. Cf. MED sub *merlioun* n.
[164] See OED sub *rake* sb.[1].
[165] See FEW 17,471b (*waizda*).
[166] See MED sub *nave* n.

lacunar: fenestre / *pessulum*: keville / *vestes*: vertevele / *gumfus*: guns / *valla* (corr.
valva): wiket / *biferes* (corr. bifores): duble yssuys / *cardo*: char[n]ere de l'us / *cardo*:
cardun / *domicilium*: severunde / *domiciliarium*: severunder / *corbes*: corbaylun / *cala-
tus*: panier / *multra*: stope [167] / *coagulum*: cheselip [168] / *serum*: meg / *colustrum*: colustre,
bestinc

[159] *papirus*: papir, flagge [169] / *cinifus*: grosse muche / *locusta*: scarbot / *brucus*: hanet /
pollitrudium: boleter / *tarantarum*: sars / *colo*: coutefier / *colo*: coler / *speciamen*:
spicerie / *framea*: gisarme / *sicarius*: murdesur / *spata*: beche / *tribulus*: runse / *tribula*:
flael / *tribulum*: trubile / *pedica*: calketrap / *bissacuta*: besagu / *vitulamina spuria*: verges
bastars

[160] *surculus*: ente / *intuba*: herbe benet / *ervus*: ternue / *lolium*: nel / *cardus*: cardun /
bubulcus: bover / *subulcus*: po[r]cher / *lupanar*: bordel

[161] *hinnulus*: foun / *burdo*: burdun / *cassis*: heaume / *odorrinsecus*: brachet / *lira*:
harpe / *ansa*: andle de pot et brache de chaer et chapel de charue [170] / *stiva*: stapel [171] /
libitina: bere

[162] *dentale*: chip [172] / *instrumentum dentatum*: herce / *vomis vel* comeris: soc /
stercoro: enfencer / *fimus*: feince / *novale*: varette / *rebino*: rebiner / *triturare*: batere
blez / *manipulus*: poinellis [173] / [h]oreum: grange / *pinso*: peitir / *pincentium*: pestrin /
pandocino: bracer / *pandocinium*: bres / *larva*: visere / *larvaticus*: viseré

[163] *loligo* equivocum pro 'tenche' et pro quadam herba / *aper*: bor, sengl(el)er

[169] *fistulas*: gallice tuelis de fos / *celtem*: chi[s]el / *fi(n)guli*: gallice po[t]er

[170] *anaglaphario*: bordure / *ceromate*: blanchet

Vernacular Glosses in the commentary in MS L

[60] *pultes*: grueus / *sincopis*: gallice pamuesun / *securis* equivocum est: 'estru'(?),
instrumentum Hispanorum, gallice 'gisharme' / *contus*: muvur / *sartio*: gallice frire /
facio: espandre gallice / *amolum*: flur de furment

[61] *coclea*: gallice coquile / *mango*, emptor vel venditor equorum: gallice chossun /
amphinia: quarel de mer, anglice sale / *murena*: lampree / *musculus*: balene /
ep[h]imera: gallice esperling / *gobio*: gallice gujun / *melanurus*: gallice dras de mer [174] /
captio: gallice caboze / *morus*: gallice morue / *pelamides*: gallice plays / *mulus*: mulet
gallice / *megarus*: gallice makerel

[62] *pedes*: gallice poynir / *fibro*: lutre, bever

[63] *manubia*: manche / *ocreas*: hese gallice et chause de fer / *phalanga*: gallice tinel

[64] *stragulata*: gallice raee / *lodices*: langnés gallice / *catha*: anglice mote

[65] *ardea*: gallice hayrun / *perizoma*: gallice rochete

[66] *in pergulo*: en un clos gallice

---

167   See OED sub *stop sb.*[1].
168   See MED sub *chese n.3(d)* (*cheslip* 'rennet').
169   See MED sub *flagge n.(1)(a)*.
170   Cf. note 113 above.
171   See OED sub *staple sb.*[1].
172   See MED sub *chippe n.1(c)*.
173   See Gfry 6,247b sub *poignel.*
174   i.e. *dars de mer.*

[67] *cimba*: gallice batel

[70] *girum*: cembel / *clarigator*: criur gallice

[72] *fulice*: gallice mauviz / *alunbis*: anglice popel / *altiones*: wudekoces / *galli palustres*: gallice meriluns, anglice morkockes [175]

[73] *sandix*: gallice warence, anglice mader / *sindix*: gallice wede / *Belvacensis*: beuveyz

[158] *colustrum*: creme

[159] *ciniphum*: wybet / *locusta*, quasi longa hasta: dore anglice [176] / *brucus*: gallice hornet

[160] *ervus*: gallice esterrurire,[177] anglice quiche / *equus admissarius*: gallice estalun

[163] *loligo*, herba: gallice neele

[169] *fistulas*: gallice tueles

[170] *sculpo*: entayller / *figuli*: gallice poter

[171] *anaglapharia*: gallice bordure / *obrisum*: emiré gallice / *obrizo*: remettre

[173] *campane*: gallice campernoles / *tintinnabula*: seyns / *vectes*: veruyls / *repagula*: bares / *pessule*: loc pendables

MS EDINBURGH, ADVOCATES' LIBRARY 18.4.13

[f.iiir] [60] *familie sue*: a sa meynee / *in coquina*: en la cusine / *olus*: cholet / *minuatur*: seit mincé, anglice scherdent [178] / *pise*: peys / *pultes*: gruel / *fabe frese*: feves molues, novels / *fabe silique*: feves en escoce / *fabe essilique*: feves sanz escoce / *milium*: mil / *sepe*: hoynons / *tripodes*: trepes / *securis*: une coiné, hache / *morterium*: morter / *contus*: une perche / *uncus*: un cros / *creagra*: un caudrun [179] / *aenum*: une paele ou caudrun / *craticula*: un gredil / *urceoli*: poscenés / *parabsis*: dubler / *salsarium*: sauser / *salarium*: saler / *artavi*: cnivés / *exenterari*: estre abuelés / *gurgustio*: pro gard (?) [180]

[61] *consolidandos*: a frires / *allutia*: lavurs u goturs u condus / [f.iiiv] *entera*: boueus / a *lixa*: de le cuistron / *coclear*: graunt . . . / *spuma*: l'escume / *ebulicio*: le bulion / *mola manualis*: querne / *salsamentum*: saus / *murena*: lampreie / *efphimera*: sperling / *melanurus*: bars de mer / *capito*: caboche / *morus*: morue / *pelamides*: plaies / *mulus*: mulet

[62] *megarus*: makerel / *turtur*: turbud / *mantile*: une tuayle / *manitergium*: toayle . . .

[f.ivr] [168] *verris*: sengler / *cancellaverit*: esquache / *in epicausterio*: en la chim[en]eie / *lodium*: lover / *minium*: vermilun / *caminum*: chimeneie

[f.ivv] [169] *fistulas*: fresteles / *prunas*: breses / *folles*: lé fous, belies [181]

---

175 See MED sub *mor(e-cok n.*

176 See MED sub *dore n.(2)*.

177 The scribe may have intended to write *estermurie*; he writes *esternurus* in the interlinear gloss. The word is unstable in nearly all the MSS in which it appears. The form *esternue* appears in a receipt in MS Cambridge, Trinity College 0.1.20 f.36r.

178 i.e. French *escharder*.

179 Misplaced from *cacabus* (preceding).

180 The MS reading looks like *gard*, but read *gord* and see TL 4,457.

181 See MED sub *beli n.3*.

[170] *aspersio*: huevere rosure[182] / *incus*: enclume, anvelt[183] / *malleoli*: de martel / *laminas*: plates / *cuperas*: de quivre / *auricalceas*: de latun d'Espanie / *celtem*: un ch[i]sel / *carbunculo*: charbuncle / *cotim*: keus / *acutiem*: aguesce / *leporinum*: de levere / *levigare*: furber / *polire*: planie[r] / *extergere*: suer / *ampullas*: ampoiles / *serram*: une sie / *limam*: vele vel vile[184] / *filum argenteum*: fil de argent

[171] *fusili*: fundable / *ceromate*: de blanchet / *inoffense*: ne[n]t cursablement / *saditiam*: vif argent / *auricalco*: orpeter / a *cupro*: q[ui]vre, coper[185] / *auricalcum*: orpeter / *institoris*: de bargainur / *fabriteriam*: la forge

MS CAMBRIDGE, TRINITY COLLEGE 0.7.9 [186]

[f.122r] [60] *mensula*: eschamel / *minuatur*: seit mi[n]cé / *lenticule*: lentil / *pise*: pais / *pultes*: gruel / *milium*: mil / *cepe*: oinun / *cepe:[187] ongnun / *legumina*: leumes / *yo*, yas: abaier / *cacaber*: caudrun / *sartago*: grant paile / *creagra*: paele / *urcioli*: possoneit / *parapsis: dubler / *lixivum: lissue (corr. lissive?)

[61] *lixa*: quistrun / *pila: peil e pestel / *cuncta* -te: .i. demure vel encerche / *uncus: croc / *crata: cleie

[62] *micatorium*: mior / *ruder*: goter / *stillicid[i]um*: goter u iscer[188] / *gausape*: nape / *mantile*: touaile / [f.122v] *murium*: de soris / *sculptum*: taluré / *teca*: husce / *cadi*: barils / *ciphi*: anape / *clepsedre*: doseus / *pelves*: passins [sic] / *corbes*: corbiluns / *cisera*: cisre / *mustum*: must / *claretum*: clarei / *piretum*: porei / *rosetum*: rosei / *vinum ferratum*: vin ferré / *penulatam*: forré / *buris*: od geruns / *laciniis*: de panis / *femoralibus*: de brais

[63] *estivalibus*: de esteveus / *sindo*: cendel / *cerici*: saie / *bissi*: chesil / *penula*: la pane / *eximiis*: de gris / *experiolis*: esquireus / *cuniculis*: conigs / *laeronibus*: laruns / *matrice*: matris / *roserella*: roserel / *equitaturus*: le chevaucheur / *manubiatam*: od mances / **(ha)stibium*: blanchet / [f.123r] *ocreas*: hoses / *calcaria*: esporuns / *succursanti*: trotaunt / *recusanti*: reculant / *ad mittendum*: a cure / *carentivillo*: canevel / *panello*: panel / *tenuis*: lé frengus / *villus: floket / *villa: vile / *sudarii*: del suari / *sudarium: suere / *strepe*: estreus / [s]*cansilia*: estrus / *arculi*: arsuns / *arculus: arsun / *antella*: arsuns devant / *postella*: [arsuns] derere

[64] *antelas*: lur coreis devant / *postelas*: lur coreis derere / *involucro*: pliure / *mantica*: trouse / *mantico* -as: trosser / *camum*: bornack / *capistrum*: chevetre / *lupatum*: chaunfren / *cingulam*: cengle / *lingulam*: ardulun / *p[l]usculam*: bocle / *trusculam*: trouse / *strigilis: estreil / *libum: uastel / a *stilis*: degreis / *epistilis*: de cheveces[189] / [f.123v]

---

[182] The first word (= 'oeuvre'?) may have arisen from a misreading of *sovenere* (= *crebra*, preceding). For *rouseur* see FEW 10, 474b (1374) and Gfry 7,249b.

[183] See MED sub *anvelt* n.

[184] See MED sub *file* n.

[185] See MED sub *coper* n.

[186] See Ch. 7, pp.37ff for the glosses to Adam of Petit Pont's *De utensilibus*.

[187] Starred items are drawn from marginal commentary.

[188] The MS reading looks like *viscer*. See Gfry 4,618a (*issoir/issor*).

[189] The MS has *cheveces* and on f.140v (*Phale tolum*) has 'capitula: cheveces', but there is

tapetum: tapis / *lectica*: pro cheere a dame, chalun / *cervical*: oriler / *culcitra*: colte / *stragulata*: raié / *lintheamina*: linchés / *sindone*: cendel / *bisso*: chesil / *coopertorium*: covertor / *de sagio*: de say / *penula taxea*: pan de tesun / *hic *taxus*: tesun / *hec *taxus*: if / *beverina*: de beverine

[65] *capus*: muschet / *nisus*: asperver / *herodius*: merilon / *falco ancessorius* (= ascensorius): facun hautein / *falco tardarius*: [l]aner / *falco peregrinus*: facun pelerin / *ardearius*: herruner / *gruarius*: gruer / *ancipiter*: ostour / *supera*: choverchef / *flameola*: peti choverchef / *perizoma*: chemise vel bracce, chemise a femme / *flameola*: choverchef / *perizoma*: braez / *collobium*: froc / *mataxa*: serence / *aufrigium*: orfrei / *tricaturas*: trasuris / *complicet*: ensen pleit [190] / *explicet*: displiet / [f.124r] *consuat*: cousit / *sarciat*: amender / *cirotecas*: gauns / *tecam*: del / *corigialem*: de quir

[66] *pollicium*: polluz / *forficem*: forsis / *forfex*: forces / *forpex*: uinre [191] / *forceps*: tenailis / *filarium*: filerie / *glomos*: lusés / *extricet*: hors treit / *anaglafarium*: sul levé / *biratricas*: geruns / *illecebris*: a fol delises / *peplo*: de sun uinple / *corocalla*: gerlundeche / *reticulo*: bricun / *monile*: nuche / *spinter*: broche vel efficail / *fuscus*: blanket / *fuscotincti*: fustian

[67] *assa*: aste / *suille*: porc / *tractatu*: tret / *assata*: rosté / *craticulam*: gredil / [f.124v] *aliatam*: alee / *altilis*: capun / *consiso*: consise / *asperiolum*: wuçpilon (sic) [192] / *caupo*: taverner / *auca*: houue / *domestica*: domesche / *in veru*: en espei / *succo*: sus / *scaturizata*: acaudé / *cimino*: de comin / *condiatur*: seit savurét / *aliate*: de aile / *cum viridi sapore*: od verte sause / *salgia*: sauge / *petrocillium*: percil / *costa*: cote / *ditanium*: ditane

[68] *cornu*: de corn / *bubali*: bugle / [f.125r] *philidis*: alemande / *experioli*: escurer (sic) / *gesticulans*: sailant / *caprioli*: cheverer / *emicans*: hor salant / *Parvipontane*: de Peti Pont / *delicatum*: delié / *cristalli*: cristal / *excedatus*: passeit / *construi*: estre aparilé / *situm*: le sé / *mota*: mote / *nativam*: neive / *sepes*: haie / *palis*: peus / *quaderatis*: quarrés / *vepribus*: bussuns / *vallum*: ballie, idem quod betaile, fossa circuens castellum [193] / *interstitiis*: epaces / *appodientur*: apual

[69] *trulle*: del truele / *cementari*: del masun / *cancelli*: lé kerneus / *cancellus*: kernel, chancel / [f.125v] *propignacula*: breteche / *pinne*: sumet / *crates*: cleis / *molares*: peres / *eiciendos*: a or juttre (sic) / *farre*: forment, de blé / *yllis*: de andulis / *salsugiis*: sausuchiis / *arietina*: moton / *subterreneis*: su tere / *incedant*: voicent / *catapulte*: sette barbulé / *baliste*: alblaste / *fistibula*: mangunel / *pelte*: talavas / *fistibula*: manguneus / *sudes ferree*: peus de fer / *fustes*: peus / *torres*: tisuns / *elidentur*: seint otés / *arietes*: motuns de fer /

evidence that the scribe sometimes inserts a supernumerary nasal bar. The word *chevece* normally bears the meaning 'horse's headstall' and renders the lemma *capitium*. On f.126v we have the gloss 'in caputio: en le sumét' which may have a connection with *chevet* which FEW 2,i,262b attests (in dialect) with the meaning 'partie du pied-droit qui reçoit la retombée d'une voûte'.

190 i.e. 'ensemble plie'.
191 See TL 4,790 sub *guinde*.
192 See FEW 17,599b (**wisp*).
193 See AND sub *batailler* and TL 1,870 sub *batailles*.

vinee: vines / *crates*: cleies / *ballearia*: peris / *manni*: palefreis / *gradarii*: chasurs / *annuentur*: seient enardiz [f.126r]

[70] *tibie*: estivis / *buxus*: corn de bois / *acies*: achele de batale / *cunei*: companie de bataile / *cornu*: corn / *excercitus*: le hot / **scobs*: balei(n)e / *troiambitum*: bordis / *hastiludium*: bordis / *vispilionibus*: robors / *coterellis*: ribaus / *caduciatores*: gens fesans pes / *clangatores*: defiurs / *clarigo*: defier / *clarigatio*: defiement

[71] *compediti*: lé anbués / *compes*: bue / **columbar*: pillori / **manica*: manicle de fer / *cippi*: ceps / *columbaria*: pillori / *in granario*: en le gerner / *ostorium*: estric / *batus*: bussel / *tece*: hukes / *ordei*: orge / *siligindis*: de segle / *choortis*: curie / *silique*: acorses / *lollium*: nel / *gallini*: cocs / *galline*: gelins / *altiles*: chapons / *auceres*: houis / *anates*: anes

[72] *cigonee*: cigonies / *ardee*: heruns / *phasidi*: fesauns / **hic corus*: qur de eglise / **corea*: caroule / [f.126v] *mergites*: plungons / *palustres*: witecocs [194] / *bostar*: boveri / *are*: porgeries / *alvei*: auges / *cenovectorium*: civere / [t]*extor*: teser [195] / *terestris*: teru / *admitat*: broget [196] / *dieta*: jornei / *scansilia*: astrus / *cidulas*: fenestres (sic) / *trabales*: de tref / *cavillis*: kevilis / *pedorum*: de batons de pastors / *licia*: filturs, efel [197] / *teniis*: a frenges / *fimbribus*: a gerauns / *in caputio*: en le sumet / *suponendum*: a su metre / *superponendum*: sor metre

[73] *navicule*: espoule / *pano*: broge / [f.127r] *navicula*: espoule vel navet / *pectines*: peines / *floccis laneis*: flockis de laine / *stupa*: de attupis / *superstitibus*: remenans / *sandicis*: de uuaide / *sandex*: warence .s. mader (media producta), wede .s. uuode (media correpta) / *fullonis*: del folor

[f.127v] [155] *cucullam*: cuveele / vel *flagellum*: u ascorge / *scorpione*: ascorge / *cedat*: batet / *plateas*: veis / *carri*: charete / *vias legere*: passer / *subiungi*: ansemble juns / *poplice*: sun garet / *cavillam*: chavil / *epifia*: harneis de chevail / *centone*: foutre / *subcellum*: suscel

[f.128r] [156] *scuarium*: le quier / *timpano*: muel / *cavilla*: chevil / *cantos*: gauntes / *inscribant*: enstrent / *cratibus*: cleis / *limonibus*: limons / *cidularia*: cercles vel de hes [see Scheler's reading *cidularum*] [198]

[f.128v] [157] *vestibulo*: porge / *porticus*: portice / *atrium*: place / *plateas*: lé rues / *interstitiis*: epacis / *asseribus*: hes [198] / *cindulis*: cenglis / *lathis*: lais / *tignis*: ceverundis

[158] *crates*: cleis / *culmo*: chalemel / **hec calamaris*: penner [199] / *calamo palustri*: chalemel de palus / *arundine*: roseil / *cindulis*: cinglis / *lateres*: tiyles / *laquearia*: lé lais / *atrium*: porche vel place vel domus / *pessulum*: hasp / *vectes*: vertevelis / *gunfos*: guns / *repagula*: baris / *valve*: portes / *bifores*: duple porstes (sic) / *corbibus*: corbiluns / *calathis*: banastuns vel paners [200] / **domicilium*: severunde / **domicillator*: severunder /

[194] See OED sub *woodcock sb*.
[195] MS reading looks like *teler*.
[196] i.e. *broche* ('to spur'). The scribe regularly writes g for *ch*.
[197] See MED sub *heveld n*. The expected rendering is *files*.
[198] See TL 1,255 sub *ais* and 4,840 sub *hais*.
[199] See MED sub *penner n*. and DMLBS sub *calamare*.
[200] See DMLBS sub *banastrum* and FEW 1,328a.

*occilleo: braundoner / occillum: braundun / [f.129r] fiscinam: crohc / fuscina:[201] fessel, chesevat / multra: bochet / expressum: eperus (? for eprens) / coagulatione: coagulaciun / sero: le mec / eliquato: ors core / colustrum: bestig

[159] ex papiris: de juncs / techa: caser vel heke [202] / muscarum: mouches / palustribus: de palu / cirpis: juncs / locustorum: crapous(!) / bricorum: de borduns / paleas: pales / acera: acurailis / furfur: bran / anatibus: a anis / anceribus: a gars / aucis: a oys / pollentridium: bolenter / taratantarum: sarge (sic) / polen: le flur / eliquatur: seit ors colé / coletur: seit colé / specificetur: clerci / spatam: bege / frameam: gisarme / tribula: flaele / tribulum: truble / tribulos: runcis / cenovectorium: civere / quaxillum: paner / muscipulam: rater [203] / pedicam: calcatrape / fustes: bastuns / palos: peus / exploratos: endurcis / bisacutum: bisagu / vepres: runcis / sentes: espines / spuria: branges bastars / *spurius: bastard / *vitulamen: branche

[160] arthavum: cotel od punt / surculos: entes / [f.129v] excecet: trengit / oculandis:[204] a enters / inserat: entet / ligones: pichois / ervos: ache / cardos: carduns / unco: croc / ligone: pigois / bubulcum: bover / sub(bub)ulcum: porger / opilionem: berger / caulam: faude / tigurium: hute a berger / pernoctet: sojurnet vel parnutet / bostar: boverie / presepe: creche / in equitio: en le haras / equm admissarium: stalun, ab ad et mitto -is .i. eleser / buculos: bucles / onagros: anis sawagis / arietes: motons / burdones: bordunz / casses: reis / laqueos: las

[161] circumvolvendos: avoluper / damas: deims / [f.130r] capriolos: cheveres / cervos: cerves / cervas: bises / hinnulos: founs / odorinseca: brachés / leporarii: leverers / robur: tref / trabem: tref / temonem: temun / binas: deus / aures: orales, .s. ausa et werist, estopeus [205] / lira: reun / ausa: manicle / stiva: l'estapel

[162] dentale: herce / sepem: bordure / clavos: clouis / restim: corde / fimo: fen / resarcire: remander / rebinare: rebiner / creta: marle / [f.130v] thecis: cosis / manipulos: gaveles / rastro: ratel / cinceratum: seit pur / eliquare: hors coiler / pincendi: depestrir / aculeum: agulun / *pandoxator: brasur / *granatorium: gerner / *messator: hai-uard [206] / *nemoricolus: forster / cnipulus: knivet / coturnix: quaile / pertrix: pertris

[163] cimba: batel / liburna: batel

[f.131v] [164] jaculo: fuscilett

[165] malus: mat / piratorum: de ula de mer (?) [207] / malleolis: martilest / liniantur: seint englués / levigentur: seint planiés / [f.132r] clavum: kevil

[f.132v] [167] malleolus: martelet / aplicetur: seit arevé [208] / novacula: novacles / lineam:

---

201 MS = fiscina. The two words are frequently confused.
202 See MED sub hacche n.3(b).
203 See TL 8,335 sub ratiere.
204 MS = oculaneis.
205 Auris means 'plough ear'. Read ausa ('stilt of a plough') and see OED sub wrest sb.² and Gfry 3,601c sub estaple and estaplel (and see stiva below).
206 See MED sub hei-ward n.
207 One expects larun de mer.
208 i.e. arivé.

riulor / *linietur*: seit riulé / *quaternus*: quaer / *cedula*: de un hangnis [209] / *registrum*: un clavun / *punxi*: je ai punte / *pluteum*: charoule

[168] *epicaustorium*: hes [210] / *centone*: feutre / [f.133r] **rasor*: rasur / **auriculare*: oriler / **fugarius*: chasur / **vantipelum*: vuape [211] / **gantes*: howis / **hec privata*: champe privé / *vermis* (corr. verris): de sengler / *litura*: equasure / *cancellaverit*: il heit defacé / *clavillam*: spectacle / *prunas*: bres / *epicaustorio*: chimenei / *lodium*: lover

[169] *glosa*: boglossa . . .nche (?)

[170] *incus*: enclume / *bracteas criseas*: playtes de hor / *lameas*: plates / *stangneas*: de stan / *auricalceas*: scaces de hor / *cupreas*: de quivre / *in electro*: en elect / *exploret*: endurcit [212] / *levigare*: forber / *acceras*: posenés de ter / *ampullas*: ampules / *serram*: sie

[f.134r] [171] *anaglaphario*: sus levé

[f.135r] EXPLICIT LIBER MAGISTRI ALEXANDRI NEQUAM

MS LONDON, BRITISH LIBRARY, HARLEY 683
First Copy (ff.12r–19r)

[f.12r] [60] in *utensilibus*: grans ustilismens / *olus*: cholet / *minuatur*: seyt menusé / *lenticula*: lentil / *pultes*: grueus / *fabe frese*: feves mulues / *fabe silique*: feves en chosse / *exsilique*: saun cosse / *milium*: mil / *cepe*: uniun / *tripodes*: trepeis / *securis*: cuyn / *pilus*: pestel / *contus*: havet / *uncus*: crok / *cacabus*: chaudrun / *creagra*: paele / *aenum*: pot de areym / *patella*: paele / *sartago*: paele a char / *craticula*: gridil / *urceoli*: poscenés / *discus*: esquele / *scutella*: esquele / *parapsis*: dubler / *salsaria*: sausers / *artavi*: cuteus / *gurgustio*: de icel rei / *funda*: idem / *fuscina*: funie / *hamite levi*: de leger heym / de *nassa*: de bercel / *vivario*: viver / in *stagno*: estang

[61] *antimacherus*: mestre cu / *capanam*: chaumbre / *alucia*: guters / *volatilium*: de volatils / *anserum*: de jarces / *avium domesticarum*: de oyseus damesche / *entera*: entralies / *exta*: bueus / *extremitates*: extremités / *crebro*: suvenerement / a *lixa*: del quistron / *proiciantur*: seynt hors jetez / *purgentur*: seynt purgez / *coclear*: culier / *cocular*: idem / *spuma*: escume / *ebulicio*: ebuliciun / *pulli*: pucins / *exscaturizari*: estre escaudez / *mola*: mole / *piperalis*: a peyvere / *mola manualis*: mole a meyn / *castigari*: estre chastié / *lixa*: quistroun / *aquam*: ewe / *saporem*: savur / *sapit*: savuret / *exprimit*: demoustrat / *competere*: acorder / *mugiles*: samuns / *amphivia*: soles / *congrus*: cungir / *murena*: lamprei / *musculus*: baleyne / *gobio*: gujun / *melanurus*: bar de la mer / *capito*: caboche / *ypotamus*: chival de mer / *morus*: muluel, murue / *pelamites*: playz / *epimera*: esperling / *uranuscopus*: raye / *dentrix*: idem

---

209 See AND sub *agnice*.
210 Cf. MS Harley 683 f.18r which glosses *epicaustorium* with *asserem*, which is earlier glossed with *es*.
211 Read *vantipedum* and *vaumpe*? See OED sub *vamp sb.*[1].
212 There is a superscript *e* over the final *i* (i.e. <*endurcier*). MS Harley 683 f.16r glosses *exploratos* with *endurcis*.

[62] *megarus*: makerel / *turtur*: turbut / *allec*: hareng / *gamarus*: epinoche / *ovo*: of / *confrictus*: frié / *bocca marina*: bof de mer / *ostrea*: oystris / *micatorium*: miur / *ruder*: guter / *defluent*: decurent / [f.12v] in *promptuario*: en le celer / *cadi*: barils / *utres*: costerés / *onophorum*: idem / *ciphi*: hanaps / *cophini*: idem / *dolea*: tunels / *coclearia*: culiers / *clepsedre*: dusils / *pelves*: bacins / *corbes*: cobails / *mera*: vins / *vina*: idem / *cisera*: cisre / *cervisia*: cerveyse / *celea*: idem / *mustum*: must / *mulsum*: idem / *claretum*: claré / *nectar*: piment / *pigmentum*: idem / *medo*: mede / *medus*: idem / *ydromellum*: idem / *vinum rosetum*: vin vermeyl / *piretum*: peré / *phalernum*: de icel lu / *vinum ferrum*: vin ferré / *gariophilatum*: gilofré / *lambris*: a glutuns / *ambubagis*: a hulers²¹³ / *sitis*: seif / *lavernam*: dame de larcin / *perhendinaturus*: li asugurnau[n]t / *jupam*: surcot / *penula[tam]*: furré / *manubeatam*: manché / *tunicam*: cote / *manubiis*: de manches / *birris*: de geruns / *laciniis*: de pauns / *munitam*: garni / *femoralibus*: brais

[63] *lumbaribus*: brailers / *caligis*: chauces / *tibie*: jaumbes / *muniantur*: seient garni / *estivalibus*: estiveus / *consutilibus*: curues / *sindonis*: de sendel / *serici*: seye / *bissi*: de cheisil / *sortiatur*: prenget / *ex cisimus*: de veir e gris / *experiolis*: escurels / *cuniculis*: de cunilis / *laeronibus*: leeruns / *sabelino*: de sabelin / *matre*: matriz / *bivere*: bivere / *fibro*: lutre / *vulpecula*: de gupil / *roserella*: de roserel / *equitaturus*: le chevachur / *manubeatam*: maunché / *ocreas*: huses / *stimulos*: agulunis / *ortatores*: amonestables / *succussanti*: trotaunt / *cespitanti*: cestaunt / *recussanti*: reculaunt / *calcitranti*: regibbaunt / *repedanti*: referaunt / *antepedanti*: feraunt devaunt / *ambulanti*: amblant / *habili*: avable / *clavis*: clous / *muniti*: garni / *firmati*: fermé / *carentivillo*: de canevas / *tergum*: le bas / *sudario*: huuce / *panello*: de un panel / *teniis*: lé frenges / *sudarii*: de huuce / *clunes*: les crupes / *strepe*: estrus / *scansilia*: idem / *sella*: de la sele / *arculi*: arçuns / *antela*: arçun devaunt / *postela*: arçun derere

[64] *antelas*: trusses devant / *postelas*: trusse derere / sub *involucro*: en plet / in *mantica*: en truse / *pectorale*: peyterel / *non omittantur*: ne seynt pas lessé / *camum*: bernak / *capistrum*: chevestre / *frenum*: freyn / *salivare*: idem / *lupatum*: chanfreyn / *spumis*: escumis / *sanguineas*: de saunc / *habenas*: reyns / *cingulam*: cengle / *lingulam*: hardiliun / [f.13r] *pusculam*: buclus / *pulvillum*: et la base / *trussulam*: trosun / *pedes*: pounere / *strigilem*: estril / *camera*: la chanbre de celer / *ambiat*: environet²¹⁴ / *cortina*: curtine / *sanopeum* (= canopeum): une cuverture de quir / *muscarum*: de musche / *aranearum*: iraines / *columpne*: peler / *tapetum*: tapit, chalun / *bases*: fundemen / *scabellum*: une forme / *lectica*: chaulit / *culcitra*: quilte / *thorum*: lit / *plumalis*: de plume / *cervical*: oreyler / *punctata*: poynte / *stragulata*: raé, chalun de Reins²¹⁵ / *sindone*: cendel / *bisso*: cheysel / *sagio*: say / *panula taxea*: de un pane de teysun, broc / *vel catina*: u de scat / *beverina*: de bevere / *munitum*: garni

[65] *capus*: muchet / *nisus*: esperver / *alietus*: hobel²¹⁶ / *infestus*: hainus / *herodius*: gerfacun / *tercellus*: tercel / *ascensorius*: hauteyn / *falco peregrinus*: facun ramage / *tardarius*: laner / *ardearius*: heyruner / *ancipiter*: hostur / *gruarius*: gruer / *supara*: rochés / *flaminea*: cuverchefs / *flammeola*: petit cuverchefs / *perizoma*: chenese / *capa*: chape /

---

²¹³ See Gfry 4,486b sub *holier* and cf. MED sub *holour n.*
²¹⁴ The MS reading is a minim short.
²¹⁵ See OED sub *shalloon*¹ 1. which cites 'chalonibus de Reyns' (1270–71).
²¹⁶ See TL 4,1115 sub *hobel.*

pallium: mantel / *toga*: gunel / *collobium*: frog / *aspergines*: lunge cheneses / *circophea*: lunge cheneses / *terestrum*: rochet ridlé / *nimphula*: une damoysele / *serenet*: enclarzit / *mataxa*: serence / *nexus*: lacemen / *tricaturas*: tresçuris / *complicet*: complier / *consueat*: cuset / *sarceat*: refetet / *thecam*: dael / *corigialem*: de quir

[66] *vulgariter*: comunemen / *pollicium*: dael / *digitale*: idem / *forficem*: force / *filatorium*: boyste / *glomus*: lusseus / *anaglapharum*: triphure / *vulgare*: general / *birri*: gerun / *polliendas*: encreys[217] / *inducendos*: entrers / *illicebris*: a les foles enveysures / *excipiat*: hor met / *peplo*: gymple / [f.13v] . . .: beue de or / *carocalla*: de un veil, kelle / *criniali*: par large kele, garlonde, de un bende de chef[218] / *monile*: nuche / *spinter*: ficail / *fuscotincti*: fustanie / *torques*: u[r]nemenz / *androchia*: deye, baesse[219] / *pullificantia*: fesant pucines / *anseribus*: jarces / *substernat*: esparpilet, junchet / *foveat*: nuriset / *subrumos*: [e]denté / *ablactatos*: severez / *inclusorum*: enclos / *pergulo*: parrok / *fenile*: muliun de fein / *matronales*: rochet / *teristrum*: rochet / *subulcis*: porchers / *collustrum*: bene best,[220] mege / *bubulcis*: buveres / *armentariis*: vachers

[67] *obsoniis*: supers / *oxigallam*: let egre / *quactum*: creme / *abditorio*: cuche / *serum*: mege / *furfureo*: de bren / *carnis suille*: de char de pork / *condimentum*: aun sav[ur]me[n]t / *dedignatur*: deniet / *simplicem*: simple / *aliatum*: alié / *altilis*: geline / *conciso*: concis / *auca domestica*: un houue dameche / *circumvoluta*: tornés / *viridi succo*: vergus / *racemorum*: de reinsin (sic) / *cimino*: cymin[221] / *condiatur*: savuré / *crebris*: sovenner / *guticulis*: gutis / *reficiatur*: refeté / *condimentum*: savorremen / *sapidissima*: savurable / *exenterati*: debuelez, echerdés / cum *viridi sapore*: en vergus / *petrosillum*: persil / *serpillum*: pelestre / *costus*: coste / *ditanum*: ditalee[222] / *alea*: auz / *reficiat*: refetet / *vinum passum*: fort

[68] *virorem*: verdisur / *bubali*: de bugle / *impetuose*: hastivement / *nux phillidis*: del alemaunder / *repens*: raumpisaunt / *esperioli*: curel / *caprioli*: de cheverun / *emicans*: resplendisaunt / *delicatum*: delié / *bissum*: cheysil / [f.14r] *situm*: le sé / *mota*: la mote / *moles*: pesentune / *muralis*: de mur / *cemento*: ciment / *erigatur*: seyt adrescé / *sepes*: haye / *horida*: hyduse / *palis*: peus / *quadrangulis*: quarrez / *vepribus*: runces / *pungentibus*: puinaunt / *vallum*: le bail / *supereminentes*: hauz / *columpnis*: par pilers / *apodientur*: sein appoyez

[69] *trulle*: truele / *cementarii*: maçun / *cancelli*: kerneus / *propugnacula*: bretasches / *pinne*: turris / *crates*: cliis, herdles[223] / *molares*: peres / *obsidiatur*: seyt ensegi / ad *deditionem*: a rendre / *pernis*: pernis / *baconibus*: de bacuns / *succiduo*: suce / *hillis*: andulis / *salsuciis*: de saucis / *suilla*: de porc / *arietina*: de mutun / *bovina*: de bof / *leguminibus*: potage / *scaturiente*: surdaunt / *posticis*: posternes / *cathapulte*: setes barbeliez / *ancilia*: talevas / *pelte*: braceroles[224] / *baliste*: arblast / *fustibula*: mangeneus /

---

217 See FEW 2,ii,1330a (*creta*) and Foerster's note to l. 1885 of his edition of *Yvain* (1887).
218 See MED sub *calle* n. and TL 2,16 sub *cale*.
219 See MED sub *daie* n. and TL 1,795 sub *baiasse*.
220 See MED sub *best* n. I do not know what *bene* stands for.
221 See MED sub *comin* n.
222 This form with *l* is not recorded in the dictionaries.
223 See MED sub *hirdel* n.
224 Not recorded in the dictionaries with this meaning.

funde: lenges / *sudes ferree*: peus de fer / *clave*: masues / *fustes*: bastuns / *torres*: tisuns / *assultus*: les assaus / *obsidentium*: des assegauns / *elidantur*: seint blessés / *enerventur*: seyent enfeblés / *arietes*: engins, berefrés / *vinee*: garites / *crates*: clis / *manni*: palefreis / *palefridi*: palefreys / *dextrarii*: destrers

[70] *tube*: busins / *tibie*: estives / *litui*: greyles / *buxus*: flegol / *cornu*: corn / *acies*: cumpanie / *coortes*: compaynies / *exercitus*: host / *tribunis*: cunestables / *troiapium*: tornament / *tirocinium*: burdiz / *siccussorii*: chaçurs / *vernis*: a serjauns / *vispilionibus*: a robeurs / *moles*: la pesentune / *mitius*: bonurment / *cum supplicibus*: debuneyres / *censure*: de le jugement / *rigore*: redur / [f.14v] *digressatores*: wereurs / *legirumpi*: pesçures de ley[225] / *plebicitorum*: de status de peple, de le commun / *abusores*: desures[226] / *plebi statutorum*: de status de poples / *clepi*: laruns, simple laruns / *abactores*: laruns de bestes / *sicarii*: murdrisurs / *multatores*: penurs / *antropocedi*: homicidis / *fustigantur*: seint batuz / *puniantur*: seint puynz [sic] / *frugalitatem*: curteysie .i. perniableté / *clangatores*: criurs / *caduciatores*: peysurs, fesauns pes

[71] *stratilates*: espies, fors chevalers / *stantelum*: le staundard / *nichiteria*: cholers .i. chaumpiuns / *evocati*: souders / *tumultuarii*: fesauns noyses / *animet*: hardiet / *tuba*: busine / *decertantis*: estrivant / *donativa*: dons / *stipendia*: luers / *carceres*: chartres / *mansionibus*: espaces / *fundum*: funt / *detrudantur*: seint butez / *compediti*: fergis / *manicis*: espaces, maniclis / *cippi*: ceps / *collumbaria*: pilloris / *excubie*: enwez / *clangorem*: noyse / *granario*: gerner / *ostorium*: estric / *chorus*: cumbe[227] / *modius*: cumbe / *tece*: gerners / *cortis*: de la curt / *gallinarii*: cokereus / *pulli*: pucins / *anates*: malars / *anseres*: jarces

[72] *cigonie*: storkes / *grues*: grues / *fulice*: fulie / *alumbes*: popillis / *mergites*: plunguns / *altiones*: motes / *galli palustres*: coks de palyz, mor cok / *bostar*: boverie / *presepe*: creche / *are*: porcherie / *alvei*: auges / *st[r]igilis*: triles / *camus*: barnak / *cenovectorium*: civere / *epiredium*: civere / *dieta*: viande, jurneye / *scansilia*: les etrus / *deprimatur*: est avalé / *trocleam*: windas, trendel[228] / [bottom of f.14v] *circumvolubilem*: verunturble (sic) / *epirerodium* (sic): civer / [f.15r] *cidulas*: cedles, une lattes[229] / *trabales*: de tref / *collumbaribus*: de pertuz / *distinctas*: partis / *cavilli*: kevilles / *teniis*: par frengis / *fimbriis*: par lurlures[230] / *debitis interstitiis*: par dues epaces / *stamen*: esteym

[73] *trama*: la treyme / *navicule*: navette / *navicula*: navie / *pano*: broche / *naviculam*: navie / *ordietur*: urdirat / *pectines*: penies / *reciproco*: enterjaunchable / *educta*: hor mené / *sandicis*: warence / *condimento*: savurement / *frequentem*: suvenere / *ablutionem*: lavure / *perduellio*: estrif

[74] *sicomachia*: batalie de l'ame / *solicitudo*: curiuseté / *epicaris*: pleyn de grace

[155] *cucullam*: cuuele / *manubiatum*: maunché / *aculeo*: de un aguliun / *flagello*: escurge / *scorpioni*: escurge / *lutosas vias*: lé tayuse veis / [f.15v] *vias declives*: veies

---

225 Gfry 6,56a gives one example of *peceor*; FEW 8,335a cites only the form *depecheur*.
226 In the MS *sus* is written above the last three letters: corr. *desusures*.
227 See DMLBS sub *cumba, -us* and MED sub *coumb n.(1)*.
228 See OED sub *trindle sb.*
229 See Du Cange sub *scindula*. Some MSS have *cendula* and *cendles*.
230 Corr. *par les urles*.

pendanz / *legere*: passer / *dissociantur*: seyent desjoynz / *currum*: le char / *capistro*: del chevestre / *retardare*: targer / *poplice*: garret / *temonis*: temun / *epiphicia*: paruns, harneys / *centone*: feutre / *jugum*: jug / *phalera*: harneys / *sudarium*: huse / *carentivillum*: canevas

[156] *scutarium*: le quier / *circumstantiis*: par enverunnantis / *executione*: le pursute / *positione*: mise / *tenacissimi avari*: tro chinchis / *ipsam*: meme / *quadrigam*: char / *de cetero*: ore mes / *axis*: assel / *in tympano*: en le muele / *cavillam*: keville / *in modiolo*: en le muel / *sit intrusa*: sit debuté / *radii*: raes / *in cantos*: en lé gauntes / *inscribant*: entrent / *extremitates*: extremités / *stelliones*: estellunis, paumes [231] / *circumferentia*: le virunnaunce / *collocentur*: seynt mis / *cidularum*: cedles / *cavillas*: kivils

[157] *vestibulo*: porche / *porticus*: une curt / *atrium*: curt devaunt / *postes*: post / *asseribus*: des es / *cidularum*: cendels / *latis*: lates / *trabibus*: trefs / *tignis*: che[ve]runs / *tigillis*: petit cheveruns / *commissuram*: la severunde / *porrectis*: estendus / [f.16r] *eoas partes*: lé parties del het [232] / *sulcina*: boytes [233] / *pixides*: boytes / *calamita*: calamite / *corimborum*: corimbir / *sarcocalla*: sarcocal / *oleum laurinum*: oyle de lorer

[158] *culmo*: caume / *calamo palustri*: ros dé mareys / *arundine*: rosele / *cidulis*: lattis / *lateres*: teules / *laquearia*: lé cu[m]bles de .i. m. / *stipitibus*: truncs / *seram*: serure / *pensulam*: barre, loc pendable / *vectes*: verules / *gumphos*: guns / *repagula*: barres / *valve*: uickés / *bifores*: duble portes / *porticum*: porche / *cardinibus*: carreres [234] / *corbibus*: corbayls / *calatis*: bachés / *cophinis*: hanap[e]rs / *cumeris*: gerners / *vimineis*: de osers / *sportis*: petis corbilluns / *fuscinam*: fune / *harmatam*: crocké / *fiscina*: fiscele / *expressum*: formen preint / *a multra*: de un buket / *coagulatione*: priccure [235] (?)

[159] *pollentrudium*: buletel / *taratantarum*: sarce / *pollen*: flur de furment / *specificetur*: seyt enbelli u ennobli / *purgeatur*: e seyt purgé / *frameam*: gleyve / *spatam*: besche / *vangam*: idem / *tribulum*: flael / *tribulam*: truble / *tribulorum*: runces / *satilicum* (sic):[236] semençur / *sationis*: de semisun / *qualum*: panier / *quaxillum*: petit panier / *muscipulum*: ratuere / *pedicam*: kalketrappe / *fustes*: bastuns / *palos*: peus / *exploratos*: endurcis / (left-hand margin) *exploratos*: esprovez / *bisacutas*: besagues / *vepres*: runces / *sentes*: espines, spicus [237] / *vitulamina*: greffes / *spuria*: bastards / *abactores*: larun de bestes

[160] *artavum*: knivet / *surculos*: entes / *inserat*: entet / *ligones*: picoyses / *intubas*: erbe beniés / *ervos*: everes, edres, eternues [238] / (left-hand margin) *ervus*: . . . terestre,

---

231 For *stellio* see Dief.[1] ('speech, spaich an einem rad') and the text printed by Scheler which gives 'extremitas radiorum' with a gloss *spilis* (see OED sub *spile* sb.[2] and *spill* sb.[1] & sb.[2] 'a splinter, chip, or narrow strip, of wood'). See TL 3,ii,1346 sub *estalon* and, for *paume*, FEW 7,516b ('épi de blé').

232 In the left-hand margin is the gloss 'eos: het'.

233 MS = *sultiva*. See Dief.[1] sub *succina*. MS L f.46ra has 'succina .i. pixis et dicitur a succus -ci quia ibi succi infunduntur.'

234 Corr. *carniere*.

235 Corr. *pressure*. The MS reading looks like *piccure* with a superscript *i* over the initial *p*, possibly giving the reading *prissure*. See TL 7,1829 (*presure* / *prisure*).

236 For *saticulum*.

237 See OED sub *spike* sb.[1].

238 See note 110 above. See FEW 3,243a (*ervum*), MED sub *ever* n.(2) ('darnel', only one

quikele [239] / *urticas*: urties / *lollia*: nel / *carduas*: carduns / [f.16v] *avenas*: averuns / *unco*: crok / *bubulcum*: bover / *opilionem*: bercher / *caulam*: faude / *pinguiorem*: plu gras / *stercorum*: de fens / *opulentia*: par le plenté / *tugurrium*: huelet / *transferatur*: seyt remué / *stercorationis*: de fenure / *bostar*: boverie / *agasonem*: un aner / *mulionem*: un muler / *equitio*: aras / *juvencas*: jenices / *buculas*: jenices / *bubalos*: bucles / *casses*: reis / *laquos*: laz

[161] *damas*: deymes / *capriolas*: cheveres / *cervos*: cerves / *cervas*: bises / *innulos*: founs / *odorinseca*: brachés / *leporarii*: levereres / *grande robur*: grant fust / *bifurcando*: en duble furchaunt / *binas aures*: anses / *lira*: reun / *robur*: le fust / *burim*: le handle / *capulus*: heute / *ensis*: espey / *alumnosa*: tayus / *retinacula*: les harz

[162] *stercorare*: composter / *novalia*: warrez / *fimo*: fens / *rebinare*: rebiner, sterin [240] / *veracta*: lé friches / *incensis*: enbrasez / [f.17r] *granum*: greyn / *mortifienum*: [241] mortifié / *fissum*: fendu / *herbam*: herbe / *prorumpat*: avant saliez / *calamum*: chalemel / *solidetur*: seit fermé / *tecis*: hoseus / *spicis*: espiis / *oneretur*: seit chargé / *quodammodo*: dekes en ça / *metere*: sier / *in area*: en place / *triturare*: batre / *manipulos*: gavels / *gelimas*: garbes / *submotas*: suçh mues / *collectas*: ensemle culiez / *rastro*: rastel / *mola*: muele / *eliquare*: decure / *pinsendi*: depestre [242] / *aculeum*: prikel [243]

[163] *larvam*: visere [f.17v]

[164] *proreta*: governur de le n. . . / *cancellarii*: chanceler (later hand) / *lituorum*: de greyles / *inextinguibilis*: teniable / *suppositam*: su mis / *rotabitur*: turné / *circumvolvetur*: volupi / *naute*: mariner

[165] *munita*: garni / *malorum*: de maus / *emergente*: plunga[n]t / *pice*: pige / *picata*: picure / *liniant*: seyent engluez / *livigentur* (sic): seient planiez / *haustum*: espuche-ment / *craticulis*: tres [244] / *unguine*: de gresse / *crebra*: suvenere (MS = suverene) / *velum*: sicle / *rudo*: recaner / *rudentes*: cables / *antempnis*: de cordes / *velum*: le sicle

[166] *fori*: pertuz / *funes*: cordes / *stipites*: truncs / *foratoria*: terebra, tereres / [f.18r] *podium*: poail / *scriptor*: escrevein / *rasorium*: rasur / *novaculam*: novacle / *radendum*: rere / *pumicem*: pum[i]z / *percameni*: de parchemin / *equandam*: a hueler / *lineam*: rule / *margi[n]e*: margine / *cedula*: agnice / *apendice*: idem sunt / *registrum*: seine / *puncto-rium*: puntur / *ansis*: braces / *pluteum*: la carole / *asserem*: es

[168] *centone*: par feutre / *artavum*: k[n]ivet / *ilo*: le wruet [245] / *verris*: du sengler / *liquescat*: decuret / *liturra*: defaçure / *epicausterio*: chiminé / *prunas*: breses / *attramen-tum*: arnement / *lodium*: luver [246] / *aquilonaris*: de north / *nervum*: nerf [f.18v]

---

example, c.1400) and FEW 4,396b (*hedera*). The confusion of botanical names is typical in the MSS.
239 See OED sub *quitch sb.*[2].
240 See OED sub *stir v.3.c.*
241 Scheler's text has *mortificatum*.
242 Cf. TL 7,847 sub *pestrer*.
243 See OED sub *prickle sb.*[1]1.
244 The MS reading is clear, but probably represents a miscopying of *cleis*.
245 I cannot identify this word.
246 The MS reading is a minim short.

[169] *transactionibus*: cuvenauns / *chaminum*: chiminé / *levi pulsu*: par leger debut / *folles*: lé feus / *fistillas* (sic): frestels

[170] *incus*: enclume / *bracteas*: platesz / *criseas*: de or / *laminas*: plates / *auricalceas*: de or cauke / *stagneas*: d'esteym / *cupreas*: quivré / *celtem*: chisel / *smaragdo*: emeraude / *carbunculo*: charbucle / *jaspide*: jaspe / *saphiro*: saphir / *margarita*: perle / *molam*: muele / *levigare*: planir / *polire*: polir / *extergere*: tortre / *ampullas*: ampiules (sic) / *serram*: une sye / *limam*: une file / *aurifrigium*: orfreys

[171] *consui*: estre cusu / *opere plumali*: plein overe / *opere anaglifario*: de triphure / *ductilis*: menable / *fusili*: fundab[l]e / *ceratam*: ceré / *unctam*: enoint / *inoffense*: saun curuce / [f.19r] *auricalco*: de or kauke / de *cupro*: de quivrei / *fabateriam*: la forge / *lavacrum*: lavur / *pulpitum*: lettrun / *pelves*: bacins / *sartago*: pael / *cathedra*: cheere / *thronus*: trone

[172] *absconsum*: escuns / *sacrarium*: sacrarie / *vestibulum*: vestiarie / *altarium*: altarie / *ymag[inar]ium*: imaginarie / *phiole*: vinagers / *examitum*: amice / *breviarium*: legendre / *gradarium*: grael / *manuale*: manuel / *processionale*: processional / *consuetudinarium*: ordinal / *casula*: chesuble / *superpelicium*: surpliz / *cingulum*: ceynture / *capitescium*: amuce / *fanum*: fanun / *trabes*: trefs / *acerne*: de arable / *querne*:[247] de cheyne / *tigna*: cheveruns / per *succidines*: par severundes / *cindulis*: cendlis

[173] *tintinnabula*: sunes / *pinnaculum*: bretaches / *tonus*: topet / *campanarium*: cloche / *ventilogium*: le cochet / *vectes*: vertiveles / *gumphi*: gunz / *repagula*: barres / *pessule*: loc pendaunt / *sere*: loc dedenz / *limi[n]a*: l'enterés / *cardines*: char[n]ere / *additum*: entré / *basilica*: eclise / *capella*: chepelle (sic)

Second Copy (ff.38r–54v)

[f.38r] [60] *disponere*: hordiner / *familie sue*: se mesuns / *rebus*: chosis / in *utensilibus*: en ustilmens / *quoquina*: quisine / *mensula*: petite table / *olus*: chous / *minuatur*: mincé / *lenticula*: lentisz / *pise*: peis / *pultes*: gruel / *fabe frese*: feves fresé / *fabe silique*: feves en cos / *fabe exsilique*: feves san cos / *milium*: mil / *cepe*: uniun / *legumina*: potajes / *rececari* (= resecari): trengé / *olle*: pozes / *tripodes*: treper / *securis*: cunié / *mortarium*: morter / *pilus*: pestel / *contus*: croc / *uncus*: idem / *cacabus*: caudrun / *aenum*: idem / *patella*: pale / *sartago*: paele / *craticula*: gretile / *urcioli*: peti pot / *discus*: quele / *scutella*: idem / *parapcis*: idem est / *salsarium*: saler / *artavi*: peti qutés / *exentarari*: bulés / [61][248] *coclear*: culer / *magnum*: grant / *quo*: ceste / *spuma*: spume / *ebulicio*: b(r)iulemens / *lixa*: le quiçtrun / *aquam*: euhe / *calidam*: caud / *pulli*: pucinis / *excaturisari*: chaudét / *mola*: mole / *piperalis*: pevire / *mola*: mole / *manualis*: manuale / *coquendi*: de quire / *salsamento*: saus / *sali*: scel / *mixta*: medlé / *maria*: mer / *maris*: de mer / *saporem*: sa[v]ur / *sapit*: savurit / *exprimit*: demustrit / [62] *micatorium*: miuur / *ruder*: guter / *sordes*: sulures / *defluant*: decurunt / [f.37v] [60] *gurgustio*: reis de gors / *funda*: idem, lenge /

---

247 The other MSS have: *quernule* (C), *querule* (DL).
248 The sections of text are rearranged so that the passage beginning *Item sint olle* is followed by *Item lixa* etc.

fucina: idem, elger²⁴⁹ / *jaculo*: launcet / *nassa*: bercel / in *rivario* (sic): en rivere / in *stangno*: in estaunc / [61] *archimacherus*: li mestre cu / *capanam*: petit chambere, almarie / *coquina*: quisin / *amolum*: flur / *contritum*: treblé / *pisciculos*: pesunes / *consolidandos*: a frieris / in *abditorio*: in estu / *alucia*: lavurs, guters / *volatilium*: des oues / *ancerum*: de gars / *domestica*: domeches / *lixa*: quiçtrun / *entera*: entralies / *extera*: bués / *extremitates*: lé drenertés / *crebro*: suvenerement / *competere*: acorder / *mugiles*: samunes / *amphimia*: soles / *congrus*: congre / *murena*: lampré / *musculus*: baleine / *efimera*: espreling / *gobio*: gujun / *melanurus*: dar de mer / *capito*: gurnard / *morus*: murue / *pelamides*: plais / *mulus*: mulet / *uranoscopus*: raie / [62] *megaris* (sic): machereles / *turtur*: turbut / *alecia*: hareng / *gamarus*: spinoche / *confrictus*: frit / *bocca marina*: bars de mer / [f.38v] *dispensa*: depence / *gausape*: nape / *mantile*: dubler / *manutergium*: tuahle / *pertica*: perche / *murum*: de surices / *cultellum*: cutel / *sallicium*: saler / *scultum*: entalié / *teca*: hece²⁵⁰ / *caceorum*: de furmages / *candelabrum*: chandelir / *absconca*: escu[n]se / *lanterna*: lanterne / *calathi*: baschet / *promptuario*: celer / *cadi*: barissez (sic) / *dolea*: tuneus / *utres*: buseus²⁵¹ / *ciphi*: hanapers / *cophini*: corbalis / *clepsedre*: dusilis / *cichera*: cizere / *cervis(is)ia*: serveise / *mustum*: mut / *claretum*: claré / *mulsum*: mut / *nectar*: piement / *medo*: mede / *medus*: mede / *rosetum*: roscé / *piretum*: piré / *falernum*: vin claré / *vinum garofilatum*: gilofré / *vinum feratum*: vin ferré / *lambris*: lechurs / *ydromellum*: medee / *perhenditurus* (sic): sugurnur / *jupam*: cote / *penulatam*: furré / *tunicam*: cote / *manubiis*: ma[n]chis / *birris*: gerunis / *munitam*: garnie / *laciniis*: geruns, pannes / *femoralibus*: braccis / *opus*: mister (sic) / *lateant*: tap[i]cent

[63] *caligis*: de cauces / *tibie*: jambes / *muniatur*: sit cuvirit / *estivalibus*: estivas / *calceis*: de sauleris / *laqueatis*: alacé / *camisia*: chemese / *sindonis*: de cheince / vel cirisi (for serici): u de cie / *bissi*: de blau seie / *materiam*: materi / *saltem*: suvamin²⁵² / *lini*: de lin / *penula*: la pane / *mantelli*: de ma[n]tel / ex *cicimis*: de gris, u le lace / *experioliis*: quireus / *excurellis*: quireus / *cuniculiis*: cuniis / *laeronibus*: lairuns / *urla*: urle / *sabelinis*: sabelin, oter / *matrice*: matrin / *bevero*: u de beverine / *fibre*: teysun / *vulpecula*: gupil / *roserelle*: roserel / *equitaturus*: le chevachur / [f.39r] *capam*: chape / *manubiatam*: a manches / *manuleatam*: a manches / *caputium*: caperun / *aeris*: de l'ehrir / *minas*: manaces / *ocreas*: cauces / *calcaria*: spurnnis / *ortatorios*: amonestanz / *equo*: cheval / *insidietur*: anueitet²⁵³ / *succursanti*: trotant / *cespitanti*: castans / *recalcitranti*: regibaunt / *neque stimulos neganti*: ne dure apurunt²⁵⁴ / *ambulanti*: amblant / *repedanti*: recu(c)lant / *mittendum*: enveer / *habili*: avable / *ferri*: feres / *clavis*: claus / *firmati*: enfermez / *carentivillo*: canevele / *tergum*: le dos / *coopertorium*: cuvert / *sudarrio*: suarie / *panello*: panel / *sella*: scele / *collocetur*: scet mis / *teniis* (sic): frengis / *sudari*: suer / super *clumes* (for clunes): sur la crupe / *pe[n]dentibus*: pendant / *stirpe* (for

---

²⁴⁹ See MED sub *alger* n.
²⁵⁰ See MED sub *hacche* n.3(*b*) ('cheese-rack').
²⁵¹ MS = *buscus*.
²⁵² This word, which I cannot identify, also occurs on f.39v [64].
²⁵³ See AND sub *aguaiter* (*engayter*).
²⁵⁴ i.e. *éperon*.

strepe): strius [255] / *scansilia*: idem est / *scella*: sele / *dependeant*: dependent / *arculli*: arçunes / *antella*: arsun devant / *postella*: [arsun] derere

[64] *antelas*: cordes devuat (corr. devant) / *postelas*: derere / *vestes*: vestures / sub *involucro*: desu la truse / *subponantur*: sit mis / *pectorale*: petterel / et cetere *falere*: e les auter harnés / *usui*: us / *non omittantur*: seun pas lessés / *camum*: bernac / *capistrum*: chevestre / *frenum*: fren / *habenas*: reines / *singulas*: sce[n]gles / *lingulam*: hardilun / *pusculam*: bucle / *pulvillium* (sic): bais [256] / *trussulam*: truse / *garcio*: garsun / *strigilem*: strulle / *ferat*: aportet / *camera*: chamabe (sic) / [f.39v] *ambiat*: envirunit / *parietes*: parieis / *stilis*: chapetreus / *columne*: piler / *tapetum*: tapet / *tapete*: calun quod idem est / *dependeant*: dependunt / *catthedra*: cheire / *collocetur*: sit mis / *ad bases*: ad peis / *subjuncgatur*: sei[t] mis / *scabellum*: eçchamel / *lectica*: cheer a dame, (right-hand margin) chalis, lof(if)tbed (sic) [257] / *lectum*: lite / *ponatur*: sit mis / *culcitra*: cute / *plumis*: de plume / *cervical*: oriler / *maritetur*: seit balé(r) / *culcitra*: cute / *punctata*: ponte / *vestis stracculata*: noble vesture / *pulvinas*: quisin / *capitis*: del chef / *supponende*: mettre / *supponatur*: sit mis / *linteamina*: lincheus / *sindone*: de cendel / *saltem*: suvamin / *lino*: de lin / *lodices*: langeus / *supponantur*: seun mis / *coopertorium*: cuverture / *de viridi sagio*: de vert say / *penula*: pane / *texea* (sic): teysun, broc / *boverina* (sic): beverine / *munitum*: garnie / *supponatur*: sei(n)t mis / *desit*: defaut / *purpura*: purpre / *catum*: chat

[65] *volatile*: curtine / *pertica*: perche / *insidere*: ser / *capus*: muschus (corr. muschet) / *nisus*: esperver / *herodius*: hostur / *tercellus*: tercel / *falco*: faucunt / *peregrinus*: gentil / *tardarius*: lanier / *gruarius*: gruere / *ansipiter*: ostur / *pertica*: perche / *dependeant*: dependunt / *supara*: redes [258] / *flamea*: cheinse / *flammeola*: rochet, cuverchés / *perizoma*: braes / *capa*: chape / *pallium*: mantel / *tunica*: cote / *collobium*: froc / *nimphula*: meschine / *facies*: faces / *talamum*: chanber / *serenet*: clersit / *fallat*: descevet / *mataxa*: serence, hechele (later hand) [259] / *aurifrigii*: orfreisi / *nexus*: lacement [f.40r insertion] [260] / *alietus*: merlun / *ardearius*: haeyruner / *instita matronalis*: rochet a dame / *lumbare*: vesture / *lumbatorium*: vesture de ray (sic) / *ventrale*: uardecors / *aspergines*: longe rocés / *sparta*: dras / longa *cirofea*: dras de purpure / *lodices*: laungeus / *teatrales*: deu teatre / *teristrum*: rochet a point / *collobium*: frogge [f.41r] / *tricaturas*: pliures, tressures / *explicet*: despliet / *pannos lineos*: dras de lin / *consuat*: cuset / *sarciat*: amendet / *cerotece*: gante / *digitorum*: de deis / *anputatis*: coupés / *tecam*: deel / *corigialem*: de qurt (sic) / *acus*: agulie

[66] *obviantem*: getant / *pollicium*: deel / *forficem*: forces / *filarium*: filer / *filatorium*: filer vel boyçte / *glomus*: lucel / *extricet*: treit, devodit (later hand) [261] / *varias*: divers (later hand) / *subtiles*: sutilis / *opus anaglaffarium*: subctile mester bordure / *opus plumale*:

---

255 i.e. <*estrief*.
256 See FEW 1,279b (*bastum*).
257 The word does not appear in the dictionaries, though *loftbed* is attested in MSS.
258 A miscopying of *rochés*?
259 See MED sub *hechel(e* n.
260 This is written in a later hand which is also responsible for some of the preceding interlinear glosses.
261 See TL 2,1824 sub *desvuidier*.

leger overe de ple[n] / *consuendum*: decustre / *grossas*: panis / ad *birri tricas*: a pan te
gerunis [262] / *poliendas*: p[l]anis / *laqueos*: las / *inducendos*: ameneris / *acus* . . . *grosciscimas*: tre gros acus / *illecebris*: reponttaliis / *peplo*: wimple / *intemperiem*: la deçtemperance / *coralla*: cofe de quir / *caracala*: coife de lin (later hand) / *crinali*: bende /
reticula: bende / *comarum*: chevus / *monile*: nuchet (sic), fermal / *spinter*: fiçal / *tunice*:
cote / *fustanici* (sic) vel *fustecinti*: fustanie / *camisie*: chemise / *colaria*: colers / *torques*:
bues de or / *inaures*: hournemens de orailis / [f.40v] *androchya*: dey / *gallinis*: a gelinis /
suponet: supmettit / *polificancia* (sic): pucinanz / *anceribus*: a garcis / *ascera*: curail /
sub[s]ternat: parliet [263] / *agnellos*: auniés / *morbidos*: maladis / *angniculos*: enfans de un
an. . . / *lacte*: leit / *foviat*: nuricet / in *pergulo*: paroc / *iuxta fenile*: in tas / *subrumos*:
febles, nurie le menez / *ablactatos*: deleytés / *inclusos*: enclos / *indumenta*: vestures /
matronales: cheins a dame / *cerapelline*: bifle, chenese / *colustrum*: bestingge

[67] *obsonniis*: superis / [oxi]*sigalam*: sur mac / *quactum*: crem / in *cimbiis*: en hanapes /
abditorio: cuche / *pi[n]gue*: gras / *cerum*: meche / *cum pane furfuro*: hov pan de brin /
porrigere: drecer / [f.41r] *hassa*: haste / *carnis*: car / *suille*: porche / *diligenti*: diligen /
tractatu: tret / *assata*: rocchté / *versata*: turné / *crebro*: suvenerement / *craticulam*:
gerdile / *circumvoluta*: virun turné / *alliata*: alié / *viridi*: vert / *succo*: seit jus / *racemorum*: de crapis [264] / *silvestrium*: de boys / *distemperatam*: deçtempré / [f.41v] *prunis
carbonum*: pru[n]s, carbun, bresis [265] / *condimentum*: savure / *aliut*: autre / *dedignatur*: se
deniet / *purum*: pur / *salem*: sel / *simplicem*: simple / *aliatam*: halié / *altilus* (sic): geline
/ *consiso*: cunsis / *piperis*: de piver / *aspercionem*: parpilement / *auca*: houe / *domestica*:
domeche / in *veru*: en le spoie vel broche / *scaturusata* (sic): scautdé / *membrum*: de
membre / *simino* (sic): cumin / *assata*: roste (later hand) / *guticulis*: gutis / *lardi*: de lard
/ *reficiatur*: refet / *condimentum*: savur / *aliate*: de haus / *sapidissima*: tre savuré / *cum
simplici salsa*: hov simple saus / *exenterati*: buelés / *coquantur*: seun quit / *sapore*: savor
/ *salgea*: sage / *petrosilium*: persilie / *costus*: coste / *ditanium*: ditanie / *serpillum*: peter /
alea: haus / *consumentem*: li pernant / *exillarat*: heatit [266] / *reficiat*: refeitit / se *admirari*:
admirer sey / *ciphy*: anape / *fundum*: fund

[68] *perspicuitate*: clerté / *lacrimarum*: lermis / *claritati*: clerté / *ducentis*: amenans /
virorem: verdur / *cornu*: corn / *bubali*: bugle / *decendat*: avalet / *impetuose*: hastiment /
fulminis: de fudre / *nux*: le nus / *phyllidis*: alemandre / *repens*: saliant / *experioli*: de
çcurrel / [f.42r] *gesticulans*: veysant, (original hand) vacaunt [267] / *caprioli*: cheverel /
edifiscii: de edefisç / *grisorum*: gri / *monachorum*: munis / *emicans*: pledisçable [268] /
scintille: sentellet / *parvipontane*: peti pund / *veritatis*: verité / *equiparetur*: seyt ennuueli, seit atempré / *delicatum*: clersit / *bissus*: chesil / *cristalli*: cristal / *castrum*: chastel /
decenter: avenable / *construi*: aparelé / *duplici*: duble / *fossa*: fosce / *cingatur*: seit seint,
viruné / *situm*: sé, place / *numinat* (for muniat): uarniet / *mota super nativam*: ture,

---

262 Corr. *de gerunis*.
263 For [es]*parpliet*..
264 i.e. *grapis*.
265 The glosses from here to *fudre*, below (68), are in the later (s.xiii²) hand. *Pruns* 'sloe' is a
translation of *prunus*, not *pruna*.
266 There is a superscript *e* above the second letter.
267 The MS reading is a minim short.
268 The gloss must be misplaced. To the left of the lemma has been written *vinum*.

mote desu le na. . . / *rupem*: roche / *sedem*: sege / *debitam*: due / *scortiatur*: prengis / *defectui*: a le defance / *scuccurat*: eidit / *beneficium*: benfiz / *moles*: a vense(?) / *muralis*: de li mur / ex *cemento*: de ciment / *lapidibus*: de peris / *constructa*: fet / in *arduum*: en haut / *excrescat*: cret / *erigatur*: dresé vel -ecé / *sepes orrida*: hanosue haie, hay yduse / *palis*: peus / *quadrangulis*: quarrés / *vepribus*: runces, vepres ague / *pungentibus*: runces / *vallum*: bail / *amplis*: pleins / *amplis interstitiis*: large esspaces / *fundamentum*: funde-ment / *muri*: de li mur / *venis*: a veines / *maritetur*: sit acumpanié / *eminentes*: aperysaunt / *collumnis*: de pileris / *collocatis*: esnl mez [269] / *appodientur*: seint poé, apoé / *superficies*: brutasche

[69] *trulle*: truel, plane / *cementari[i]*: di le maçun / *operam*: tente [270] / *cancelli*: carneus / *debitis*: deuues / *distinguantur*: destintes / *proportionibus*: parties / *propugnacula* (MS = propionacula): brutasches / [f.42v] *pinne*: fes / *turim*: tur / *eminenti*: aut / *loco*: lu / *desint*: defaliunt / *crates*: cleges / *castrum*: chastel / *obsidiatur*: set asegé / *defensores*: defendurs / *opidi*: de chastel / *deditionem*: a la bandesun / *cogantur*: seint constrés / *farre*: de blé / *mero*: vin / *pernis*: pernes / *baconibus*: bacon / *carne*: char / *succiduo*: sus / *posita*: mis / *hillis*: andulies / *salsuciis*: saucchus / *suilla*: sus / *ovina*: bof / *arietina*: de mutun / *leguminibus divercis*: diverce potagis / *fonte*: funtaine / *jugiter*: pardurablement / *scaturiante*: surdent / *posticis*: posternes / *subtilibus*: suttilis / *caractibus*: veies sus teris / *supteranneis*: suç la teris / *succursum*: sucur / *alaturi*: duner / *latent[er]*: celement / *lancee*: lances / *catapulte*: sete barblés / *ancilia*: escius vel rundeus / *pelte*: bockeler, talabace / *baliste*: harublaster / *fustibula*: ma[n]gu[n]és / *funde*: lenche / *sudes*: saules, peus / *ferei*: de fer / *clave*: maçue / *noduse*: plerant de nuches [271] / *fustes*: batunes / *torres*: tisunes / *sapientes*: savuranzs / *assultus*: ansuat / *obsidientium*: de seganz / *elidan-tur*: blecez / *enerventur*: seint agené,[272] seyun aneyntez / *propositum*: purpos / *conse-quantur*: seuue[n]t / *arietes*: icés estrument, berfreiis / *vinee*: pereres / *vites*: garitis / *crates*: cleyys / *balearie*: taburs de alblasteris / *machine*: mangunel, engin / *manni*: palfreis / *gradarii*: chayurus fres (!) [273] / *palefridi*: palfreys / *dextrari[i]*: destreres / *usui*: hus / *militum*: chivalers [274] / *exeuntibus*: les alanz

[70] *tube*: busines / *tibie*: gralgez / *litui*: grelles / *buxus*: flegol / *acies*: cumpanie / *cohortes*: cumpanie / *exercitus*: host / [f.44r] *tribunes*: cunestablis / *militem*: chevalerie / *ordinabuntur*: seint ordinés / *prosilient*: ors ceilent / *troiampium*: turneme[n]t / *ad troianum*: a la batayle de troye / *tornamentum*: tornement / *runcini*: runcins / *succur-saturii*: sucurable / *vernis*: a bacheleris / *vispilionibus*: robeurs / *coterellis*: garsunt a pé / *viri*: ber / *prudentes*: rusez(?) / *clangatores*: def[i]urs / *caduciatores*: criurs [275] / [f.43v] [276]

---

[269] i.e. *ensemble mis*, with nasal bars omitted by the scribe.

[270] Aphetic form of *entente*.

[271] The gloss is obscure, corr. *ple(ra)nt de nudes*?

[272] Cf. TL 3,i,1070 sub *esgener*.

[273] It looks as if the scribe has miscopied *chaçurs* and incorporated part of the next gloss [pal]frés.

[274] The MS reading is a minim short.

[275] MS = *triurs*.

[276] Folio 43v consists of a half-leaf insertion supplying a passage which had fallen out. A later hand (s.xiii[2]) is responsible for f.43r/v.

moles: aparaliement / *dispensasione*: ordenance / *mitius*: plu debonere[277] / cum *suplicibus*: of deboners / *censura*: gujement / *rigore*: par reddur / *disgressatores*: les envars, envazuris / *legirumpi*: depessans la ley / *plebicitorum*: de commune de beple / *prevaricatores*: pesuris[278] / *blebista(s)tutorum*: de stablimens / *siccarii*: murdrissuris / *multatores*: murdrus / *enectores*: occisurs / *fustigentur*: seunt batu / *puniantur*: seunt puni / *sapiat*: savuret / *frugalitatem*: esparniableté / *coniectura*: quidance / in *habundantia*: en plenté / *sensibili*: sensible / *opinio*: quidance / *clarigatores*: uereuris, diffiurus, pelur[279]

[71] *stratiles*: cunestablis, espies / *statelum*: estandart / *consequentibus*: ensuans / *committuntur*: sunt baliés / *evocati*: souderes / *milites*: chevalers / *tumultuari[i]*: fesans noyse / *sacramentales*: sures(?) / *tuba*: busine / *telorum*: quarelis / *stipendia*: soud / *stipendium*: guerdun / suis *cornibus*: par lé cornes / *strepitum*: noyse / *clangorem*: cri / *sonitum*: cri / *facientes*: feyans (sic) / [f.44r] *carceres*: prisunes / *mancionibus*: masuns[280] / *debitis*: dues / *distincti*: desti[n]gtes / *fundo*: funs / *compediti*: e[n]buez / *manicis*: manicles / *fereis*: fers / *cippi*: ceps / *columbaria*: pilleris / *excubie*: ueite,[281] getes / *vigiles*: veilable / *granario*: gerner / *hostorium*: rastre[282] / *modus*: cumb / *batus*: bussel / *frumenti*: furment / *tritici*: furment / *siliginis*: segle / *avene*: aveine / *avium*: des oisel / *cortis*: de la curt / *palea*: palie / *silique*: escos / *lolium*: nele / *avena sterilis*: wilde hote[283] / *cortis*: de la curt / *pulli*: pucinis / *galli*: coc / *galline*: gelines / *gallinarii*: cokerel / *altiles*: gelines / *altilia*: chapuns / *ansares*: houues / *annates*: hannes

[72] *cigonie*: cigoines / *ardea*: heirruns / *grues*: gruos (sic) / *mergites*: plunguns / *palustres*: moriluns / *pavo*: poun / *junonius ales*: le oyseles dame dieine[284] / *presepe*: croche (sic) / *bostar*: boverie / *are*: borgerie (sic) / *alvei*: auge, trois[285] / *strigilis*: estril / *fulica*: cote, blarie / *alunbis*: popler[286] / *altio*: uudecoc / [f.44v] *camus*: bernac / *capistrum*: chevestre / *phalere*: arneis / *enumerate*: numbrez / *cenovictorium*: civere / *textor*: tiçtur / *terrestris eques*: caball[ari]us a pé / *streparum*: estrues / *adnitens*: apuant / *apodiamento*: a le puail / *admittit*: enveyit / *exilli*: petit[287] / *dieta*: jorné / *scansilia*: estris / *fo[r]tune*: fortune / *conditionem*: la manere / *mutua*: entrechanchabel / *viscicitudine*: canjableté / *evehitur*: est sus aporté / *reliquum*: li autre / *livoris*: d'envie / *deprimatur*: seit avalé / *trocleam*: uuindas / *circumvolubilem*: avirun turnant / *pannus*: drap / *evolvendus*: a turner / *cidulas*: icés estrume[n]z / *columbaribus*: pertuz / *distintas*: divisez / *regione*: reaume / *respicientes*: regardanz / *cavillis*: cavelis / *pedorum*: crocis / *trabibus*: trefs / *tele*: teyle / *licia*: lé filis, . . . de ors / *fimbris*: frenges / *debitis interstitiis*: par du

---

277 The words appear to be followed by *lenface* (glossing *agatur?*).
278 Aphetic form of *depecëor*.
279 i.e. *guerroiers, desfiurs, apelur*.
280 The MS reading is a minim short.
281 MS = *verte*.
282 Appears to be a hapax. The lemma occasionally occurs as *rastorium*. Cf. O.F. *rastiere, rastoir(e)*.
283 See OED sub *oat sb.3*.
284 The Trinity MS has Diane.
285 See OED sub *trough sb*.
286 Apparently an error for *popel*.
287 MS = *petin*.

esspaces / *insignitis*: marchiz / *stamen*: esteim / *superponendum*: surmettre / *subponendum*: an desus metre / *trama*: strime

[73] *navicule*: spole / *transeuntis*: passant / *transmissa*: utreveié / *consolidet*: pessit / *pano*: pan, warpe[288] / *pano fereo*: broche de fer / *ligno*: de fut / *muniatur*: sit uarni / *panus*: broche / [f.45r] *spola*: spole / *penso*: filez / *glomeris*: bussel / *choperatur*: seyt cuvert / *penso*: filez / *trame*: treym / *naviculam*: navet, icel estrumen / *jaculetur*: sit juté / *remissuram*: a remetre / *frustra*: hen vein / *telam*: uuerpen[288] / *pectines ferrei*: penie de fer / *lanam*: leyne / *capillis*: cheveus / *gerentes*: aportant / *longo et reciproco*: sevenere / *sese depilaverint*: en urent(?) detret / *sincera*: clere / *abilior*: avenable / *lane*: leyne / *floccis laneis*: flocunis di la lene / *stuparum*: de stupes, erdis[289] / *superstitibus*: envirunanz / *tingtura*: tenture / *crebro*: suvener / *condimento*: savurement / *granee*: greyn / *inebrietur*: seyt enyveré / *vendiscet*: chalangit / *artificium*: engyn / *vestium*: vestures / *prorumpat*: saliet / *fullonis*: de f[u]llur / *subiciat*: suçget / *indulgentie*: a l'antente / *frequentem*: suvenir / *ablutionem*: lavement / *motus*: movement / *perduellio*: estrives / *contexere*: tissir / *abluere*: laver vel heutter / *lavamini*: lavez

[155] [*v*]*eredus*: li cartur, li gareter / [f.45v] *cuculla*: kuvle / *cucula*: cuvele / *collobium*: froge vel guliun[290] / *manubiatum*: mancé / *cum libuerit*: cum li plet / *exceat*: yt / *agacionis*: del wardant / *mul(ti)onis*: ane[r] et muler / *explere*: parfere / *aculleo*: aculyun / *flagello*: de l'ecurge / *cedat*: batit / *lenta*: flecgisable / *aurem*: orelie / *auriga*: charater / *ocreas*: hosus / *cenosas*: bouoés / *latus*: couite, side[291] / *jugum*: tertre / *lutosas*: tayuse / *plateas*: rues vel wés / *radicem*: le racin / *aptetur*: seyt mis / *carus*: char / *bige*: charet / *vias*: veis / *declives*: pendantes / *legere*: pascer / *decendo*: en dese[n]dant / *siniugi*: enscemblem[en]z / *currum*: charette / *quadrige*: li gars / *quadrige*: charette / *impetum*: e la forge vel la fole asaut / *retardare*: retardir / *sinuato*: curf / *poplice*: sun garet / *laborantem*: travaliaunt / *atestetur*: atemoniet, aforcet / *cavillam*: kevele, pin / *temonis*: temun, þille[292] / *restim*: la corde / *anteriorem*: devant / *erectam*: drecé / *epiphia*: paruns / *centone*: feutre, felte / *multiplici*: mote maneris / *sociata*: pliez / *jugum*: yioc[293] / *phaleras*: harneis / *sudarium*: suarie / *subsellium*: surcelgle (sic) / *carentivillum*: canevace / *obmitto*: passe

[f.46r] [156] *scutarium*: esquier / *equitem*: chivaler / *munivi*: uarnier / *executione*: equiciun, sute(?)[294] / *tenaciscimi*: tré flenaz[295] / *prodigi*: forilagis[296] / *interposita*: entremis / *axis*: exiltre, essel[297] / *timpano*: nave, muel[298] / *modiolo*: muel / *cavilla*: chivil / *axis*: essel / *intrusa*: buré / *radii*: les rages[299] / *cantos*: jantes / *orbite*: de la cente /

---

288 See OED *warp* sb.[1].
289 See MED sub *herd(e* n.3.
290 See MED sub *golioun* n.
291 See OED sub *side* sb.[1].
292 See OED sub *thill*.[1].
293 See OED sub *yoke* sb.
294 i.e. *porsute* with loss of prefix?
295 Corr. *tres tenanz*?
296 Scheler cites the glosses *fous larges* and *folilarges*. Cf. Gfry 4,52b.
297 See MED sub *axel-tre* n.
298 See MED sub *nave* n.
299 Cf. *cleges* below (156).

profundius: parfundement / [*in*]*scribant*: il encerchent / *vermem*: uuerm / *variationis*:[300] diverseté / *circumferensia*: circumference / *rote*: ro / *vestiatur*: sei vestir / *scrupulorum*: porez (sic), peris / *offendicula*: kurudement (sic) / *expavescat*: dutet / *aceres*: es, les es / *cratibus*: cleges / *area*: place / *quadrige*: charette / *limonibus*: bastunes / *columbaria*: pertus / *cedularum*: d'estrumen / [f.46v] *imitetur*: ensuit

[157] *vestibulo*: vestuarie / *porticus*: porche / *disposita*: ordiné / *atrium*: plaz, curt / *iuxta plateas*: jute le reale veis / *pertranseentes*: passant / *postes*: postes / *debitis*: de duis / *interstitiis*: entrepaciis / *distincti*: departés / *asceribus*: les es / *scindula*: cendlos (sic), lattis / *latis*: largis / *trapibus*: treffs, fillis / *tignis*: keveru[n]s / *parietes*: pareis / *diversa*: diverses / *regione*: manere / *remotius*: plus loins / a *fundamento*: de le fundeme[n]t / *alioquin*: atrement (MS = atre meter) / *ruinam*: trebuc / *comissura*: severunde, anglice evesbord[301] / *tota machina*: tut l'engin

[158] *crates*: walner, cleys[302] / *culmo*: caume, stubil / *calamo*: chalemel / *plaustri*: scar / *arundine*: de le rosel, red[303] / *scindulis*: cendles / *superpositi*: surmis / *lateres*: teules / *tegule*: la tys / *laquearia*: les laz / *stipitibus*: de stos, stuye[304] / *hostium*: hus / *ceram*: loc, cerure / *pesgulam*: peguns, lachet[305] / *vectes*: vertiveles / *gunfos*: guns / *repagula*: barres / [f.47r] *valve*: uicet / *bifores*: deus isues / *porticum*: portiz / *cardinibus*: cardons, herre[306] / *rusticus*: vilen / *senectute*: a la velie / *corbibus*: corbeus / *calathis*: panier / *chofinis*: corbeus / *fuscinam*: verge, funie / *hamata*: hamé, crocé / *reficere*: sauler / *ficinam*: fesel / *fisellam*: vesel / *multra*: de bucet, stoppe / *crebra coagulatione*: par suvener pressure / *casei*: furmage / *sero*: mec, quei[307] / *eliquato*: or curu / *colustrum*: colustre, meche / *reservetur*: reçue / *propinandum*: a beivre

[159] *theca*: almarie / *ex papiro vel juncis*: de junc d'entre mer / *palustribus*, palu[s]ter: dé maris / *composita*: hordiné / *coopertus*: cover / *muscarum*: mu(l)ches / *ciniphum*: de cet muche / *locustorum*: breses / *brucorum*: muche / *paleas*: palies / *ascera*: kurails / *furfur*: bren / *anatibus*: annes / *aucentibus*: anes / *aucis*: oues / *auculis*: oisilun, oysunis, goseling[308] / *cortis*: de la curt / *pollentrudium*: boletel / *taratantarum*: sarce, sife, hersive, sars[309] / *pollen*: flur / *eliquatur*: enclersit / *coletur*: colé / *specificetur*: espacefié / *frameam*: gisarme, glive, gleyve / *spatam*: besche / *tribulam*: trublu (sic), pele / *tripulos*: runce, espis / *cenovectorium*: sivere (MS = rivere) / *spatula*: le clice / *saticulum*: sedlep, corbiliun / [f.47v] *qualum*: panier / *quaxillum*: corbale, panier / *muscipulam*: surçur, rature, musfale[310] / *pedicam*: calcetrepe / *fustes*: bastu[n]s / *palos*: petis peus / *exploratos*: henserchis / *bisacutam*: besague, picheise / *eradicandam*: rater / *vepres* (MS = vespes):

---

300 MS = *variari*.
301 See MED sub *eves* n.3(*a*).
302 The MS reading is *waln*': the word remains obscure.
303 See OED sub *reed sb.*[1].
304 This form is found in several grammatical MSS.
305 The scribe seems twice to have mistaken a written s for g: read *pesuns*.
306 See MED sub *er(e* n.(*2*) and FEW 2, i, 366b (confusion of senses 'hinge' and 'thistle').
307 See OED sub *whey sb.*
308 See MED sub *gosling* n.
309 See MED sub *her(e-sive* n.
310 See MED sub *mous* n.2(*a*).

bussun / *tribulos*: runces / *centes* [= sentes]: epuges[311] / *spuria*: branches / *vitulamina*: bastardes verges / *cepes*: hayes / *incuria*: nunchaler / *subulcis*: porcher / *bubulcis*: buvers / *sopitis*: endormis / *armenta*: avers / *abducant*: aveye menent

[160] *artavum*: cutele a poynt / *surculos*: entes, greffes / *inceret*: entet / *ligones*: picoises / *tirsos*: banastu[n]s, branchis / *extirpet*: henracet / *intibas* (sic): herbe beneites / *urticas*: orties / *ervos*: ternues, bindes[312] / *lolia*: neil / *carduos*: carduns, þistles[313] / *avenas*: averu[n]s / *extirpantur*: sunt aracé / *unco*: croc / *ligone*: picoyse / *bubulcum*: bover / *opilio*: bercher / *subulcum*: porcher / *caulam*: faude / *letiorem*: plu lé / *stercorum*: de fens / *opulentia*: plenté / *tugurium*: holet / *pernoctet*: seit parnité / *mi[n]cture*: pissure / *stercorationis*: struntture[314] / *bostar*: boverie / *presepe*: creche / [f.49r] *fortune*: de aventure / *blandientis*: blandisanz / *agasonem*: asnier / *mulionem*: mulerz / *equiscio*: harraç / *equum emissarium*: estalun / *oves*: ualies / *cap(a)ras*: cheveres / *juvencas*: jenices / *tauros*: tros (sic) / *buculos*: bucles[315] / *buculos*: bufles machlees[316] / *arietes*: mutuns / *verveces*: castris / *multones*: rig-rames[317] / *casses*: reis / *reticulas*: peti rys / *laqeos*: laz / *extensos*: entenduz

[161] *circumvolvendos*: env[i]run turner / *lepores*: leve(v)res / *damas*: deyms / *capriolos*: cheverel / *cervos*: serves, cerves / *cervas*: comeles, bicis[318] / *hynulos*: founs / *arma*: les armes / *instrumenta*: estrumens / *rusticorum*: de vilens / *hodorinseci*: brachés, blod-hund[319] / *leporarii*: leverer / *aratrum*: charu / *humane vite*: de umene vye / *medium*: mecne(?) / *sortiatur*: prengit / *grande*: gref / *robur*: treph / *trabem*: tref, bem[320] / *bifurcando*: en dubele furchaunt / *procedat*: avan vent / *in binas aures*: en dubles oreiles / *liva*: reun / *latior*: plu lié / *aratrum*: carue / *una aura*: de une orelye / *contentum*: paycé / *robur*: le robeur / *curvendum*: a curver / *burim*: hard vyyie[321] / *elevatur*: est ilevé / *obliquando*: encemplie(?) / [f.49v] *capulus*: pomel / *capulus*: pin, kivil / *extremitas*: le drenerté / *libitina*: bere / *infigatur*: seun fiché[322] / *arator*: lu varur[323] / *comprehendit*: prent / *deficilis*: de gref / *regiminis*: guvernement / *antimonia*: en dure tere, dure terre / *gypsea*: arsil, cley[324] / *alumpnosa*: tayus / *sit imprescum*: est fet, enprent / *juga*: le jus / *retinacula*: retenayllis

[162] *fragantur*: seun depesez / *saligna*: fet de sauz / *suponatur*: seun su mis / *dentale*: dentel / *vomer*: le soc / *infigatur*: enfichy[325] / *sepes*: haye / *cratem*: cleye / *clavos*: cloes / *cavillas*: ch[e]velies / *restem*: corde / *cultrum*: cutre / *quonam modo*: en quele manere /

---

[311] Apparently a miscopying of *epines* (*epuies!*).
[312] See MED sub *bind(e* n.3.
[313] See OED sub *thistle* sb.
[314] Scheler quotes the gloss *estruncerie* (corr. *estrunterie*). See FEW 17,263a (*strunt).
[315] i.e. *bugles*.
[316] See FEW 6,i,425b cites *mascle* (1395) 'taureau'.
[317] See OED sub *rig* sb.3 and *ridgel* (very late dates).
[318] I do not recognise the first gloss.
[319] See MED sub *blod-hound* n.
[320] See MED sub *bem* n.2(a).
[321] Corr. *vyyte*? See note 87 above.
[322] Miscopying of *set infiché*? See *enfichy* below (162).
[323] Corr. *laburur*.
[324] See MED sub *clei* n.
[325] The final letter appears to be written over *e*.

stercorare: enfener, compoter / *oportet*: il cuvent / *agros*: lé camps / *fimo*: de feins /
pascere: pestre / *resarcire*: resercler / *cadentibus*: cheans / *novalia*: lé warez / *rebinare*:
rebiner, feleen [326] / *verecta*: warez / *renovare*: renu[ve]ller / aut *creta*: u de marle /
letificare: fere letz / *igne*: de fu / *purgare*: spurger / *stipulis*: lé stuples / *insencis*: enbracés
/ *chylindro*: quaré / *equare*: enuluier / *dentibus*: par lé dens / *cratis*: de letthe [327] / *factis*:
festes / *spinis*: de spinis / *munite*: gwrny / *cererem*: le blé / *commisscam*: balie / *trahe*: de
le erce / *beneficio*: par le benficez / *cooperire*: cuveryt / *aut grana*: u lé grens /
commendare: balier / *granum*: le gren / *mortificatum*: mort fet / *fissum*: fundu / *herbam*:
herbe / *prorumpat*: avant saliez / in *herba*: en erbe / *calamum*: chaumel, stele [328] /
solidetur: sit fermez / *calamus*: chalemel / *thesis* [= thecis]: cotelis [329] / *spicis*: heres,
spyys / *granorum*: de grey[n]is / *muniatur*: sit uarni / *honoretur*:[330] jargé / [f.50r]
oporteat: hy cuvent / *metere*: seer / *area*: place / *triturare*: batre / ab *area*: de la place /
manipulos: gaveles / *submotus*: levés / *collectas*: culyes / *horeis*: a grangis / *rastro*: rastel /
mundare: netter / *vanno*: fan / *mundificare*: netter / a *mola*: de mole, querne / *confringi*:
etre freent / *dissolui*: delyé / *sinceratum*: enclersyt / *foraminibus*: par lé pertus / *cribri*: de
cifre / *eliquare*: decurer / in *arte*: par art / *pinscendi*: de pestre / *stranfformari* (sic): ettre
furmé / *edisceranda*: a hore dire / *aculeum*: pricche

[163] *larvam*: viser / *palinodia*: chaunçun / *comprehendu[n]tur*: sunt pris / *ratem*: nef /
nauseo:[331] pucher / *vomere*: pucher / in *stransferatione*: en passage / [f.50v] *naulum*: frat
du mer / *ventose*: garuule (= Latin?) / *venor*: chace / *naturam*: nature / *innuba*:
privément eçspusé / *pronuba*: baudestrot

[164] [f.51r] *clangores*: criures / *lituorum*: greles / *halbetum*: pere / *cuspis*: la pont /
jaculo: a lussel .i. filo [332] / *orientem*: le hest / *aeris*: eyr

[165] *farre*: de blé / *mero*: de vin / *munita*: garni / *securi*: coyn / *malus*: mast / *abcindi*:
trenché / *tempestate*: tempest / *emergente*: surdant / *ultimus cumulus malorum*: drenere
cumbraunce de maul / *clavis*: clouus / *maliolis*: marteus / *concurrentibus*: curans / *pice*:
piç / *cera*: scire / *ungui[n]e*: unjment / *limantur*: planiez / *haustum*: eçpuchement /
craticulis: cleys / *compagine*: la juncture / *asceribus*: es / [f.51v] *mancionibus*: mansiuns /
erigatur: enhaucé / *velum*: sigle / *malo*: mast / *maritetur*: seyt ajoynt / *rudentes*: kables /
extremitate: a chef / *tumor veli*: bolue du sigle / *sinus*: seyn / *antempnis*: cordis

[166] *fori*: pertus / *foratoria*: uuinbel,[333] tareris / *remus*: averun / *navigio*: navie / *aura*:
vvent / *pillori*: tele cordes / *malum*: mast / *stipites*: stoc / *supodiantes*: apuans / *remus*:
averun / *tonsus*: virun / [f.52r] *podium*: royer,[334] poayl / *nauclerus*: mariner / *troclea*:
uindas

[167] *porticulus*: martel / *maleolus*: martel / *applicetur*: seit arivé / *pumice*: pumis /

---

326 See MED sub *falwen v.(1)*.
327 See MED sub *lat n.*
328 See OED sub *steal sb.*[1].
329 Cf. DMLBS sub *cotella*.
330 Corr. *(h)oneretur*.
331 In the left-hand margin 'speuue(r) quod homines nauseant'. See OED sub *spew sb. & v.*
332 The connection of gloss to lemma is unclear, though some sort of fishing net is indicated.
333 See OED sub *wimble sb.*
334 Corr. *poyer*? See Gfry 6,459c (*puier*).

planulam: plane / *plumbum*: plumet / *lineam*: reulur / *linietur*: reulé / [f.52v] *excercitus*: oste / *cedula*: angnis / *registrum*: senie / *punctorium*: pontur / *anscis*: lé brais / *pluteum*: carole monachi

[168] *scabello*: chamel / *episcatorium*: uuel / *centone*: par feutre / *artavum*: cutel / *ylo*: muel / *formet*: furmet / *pennam*: la penne / *veris*: sengler / *leofe*: de cele beste / *litura*: suachure[335] / *spectaculum*: spectacle / *clavillam*: clavun / *dispendiosam*: damajuse / *prunas*: breses, coles[336] / *in epicastorio*: in chimné / *desiccari*: estre ensecchi / *atramentum*: arlement (sic) / *lodium*: luver / [f.53r] *fenestrellam*: fenestral / *insultus*: les asaut / *aquilonis*: de nort / *inpugnet*: batit / *distincta*: departé / *disgregat*: descumfortet

[169] *fuscum*: bloi culur / *azuram*: azure / a *Salamone*: de Salamun / *repertam*: truvé / in *transaccionibus*: en cuvenant / [f.53v] *per apices*: per titelis / *aurifaber*: horfevere / *faminum*: chimné / *fumus*: fume / *per certos meatus*: par tus les issuris / *levi pulsu*: par legere bute / *folles*: belies,[337] fous / *per fistulas*: par lé fresteles / *prunas*: coles

[170] *ascendat*: enbraset / *crebra*: suvenere / *aspercio*: asparliement / *incus*: cune, stit,[338] clume / *emoliatur*: seit enmolli / *forcipis*: de tenaliis / *mallioli*: du martel / *extendi*: dettenu / *bracteas criseas*: a plate de hor / *laminas*: plate / *argenteas*: de argent / *stangneas*: plate d'esstein / *cupreas*: de cupre / *celium*: cisel / *celtem*: chisel / *preacutam*: acu / *ofelte*: pere / *marmore*: par marbre / *jacincto*: pere / *smaragdo*: smaragd / *carbunculo*: pere carbun / *margarita*: en perle / *saphyro*: presiune (sic) pere / *multiplicis*: mut de maneres / *figuras*: figurs / *sculpere*: talier / *cotim*: agesur, cote / *molam*: mole / *aciem*: aguesse / *pedem*: pé / *leporarium*: de levere / *levigare*: planier / *extergere*: suer / [f.54r] *granula*: grens / *metalorum*: de metal / *colligere*: culier / *corio*: quir / *ampullas*: ampulie / *vasa minuta*: peti vassel / *figuli*: poter / *seram*: saye / *dentalem*:[339] denté / *limam*: file / *aurifrigium*: orfreis / *filum argenteum*: fill de or

[171] *cifuli*: petit anap / *consui*: estre cusé / *in opere*: in overe / *plumali*: plen / *in opere anaglaphario*: en uverain trifure / *in opere fusili*: huveraine fusable / *in opere ductuli*: en uveraine meçnable / *rudis*: bustus / *ceratam*: en cere / *ceromate*: blanchet / *argilla*: arsil, clei / *cherusa*: blanchet / *oblitam*: enhoint / *inoffense*: nent coroucé / *casmiam*: faus argent / *litargium*: pere de argent / *ab auricalco*: de orpetre / *fabateriam*: forge / *lavacrum*: lavur, funt[340] / *mariolum*: mariole / *crucifixum*: crusifis / *pulpitum*: gres du leitrun / *anologium* (sic): lectur / *urceus*: pot / *pelves*: bachines / *tribunal*: sé / *tronus*: chairee

[172] *scamnum*: scamele / *vestibulum*: vestiarie / [f.54v] *phyole*: cruet / *pix[i]des*: bo(s)iste / *loculus*: bere / *manutergium*: tualie / *amictum*: amice / *funaculum*: lu / cum *basibus marmoreis*: hov fundement de marbre / *deaurate*: sus orés / *missale*: messel / *breviarium*: breviarie / *antiphonarum*: antefiner / *gradale*: grael / *manuale*: manuel / *processionale*: processionarie / *hymnarium*: imner / *psalterium*: sauter / *troparium*: troper / *ordinale*: hordinal / *superpellicium*: surplis / *capitecium*: amice / *alba*: aube /

---

335 For *esquachure*.
336 See MED sub *col* n.(2).
337 See MED sub *beli* n.3(a).
338 See MED sub *coin* n.(1) and OED sub *stith* sb. & *stithy* sb.
339 Corr. *dentatam*.
340 See MED sub *font* n.

singulum: senture / *zona*: senture / *blateus* (i.e. balteus): senture / *phanum*: fanun / *stola*: stole / *casula*: chesible / *trabes*: trevis / *curve*: curf / *acerne*: de arable / *querruli*: de cheçne / *tigni*: cheveru[n]s / *per succedines*: par lé cheveru[n]s / *tegminibus* sive *cidulis*: a lathis / *clavis ferreis*: clohue de fer / *ligneis*: de fut / *tegule*: tiil / *nole*: peti sen

[173] *tintinabula*: sens, belles[341] / *super turim*: sur le tur / *collocari*: estre asis / *tholus*: topet / *pinaculum*: pinacle / *campanarium*: closcher / *ventilogium*: cochet / *arduissime*: tre aut / *cheruca*: cochet / *vectes*: barres / *gumphy*: guns / *rapagula*: barre / *sere*: loc petit / *limina*: soel / *capella*: chapele / *philatorium*: boste

The commentary in this second copy of Nequam's treatise is written in a mixture of hands, beginning with the hand of the main text (s.xiii¹) and gradually giving way to a much less refined hand of s.xiii ex. It contains vernacular entries as follows:

[f.38v] hoc *ostreacium* -cii: .s. pavement de oyistris / *dolabrum*: doluer .s. bradex[342] / [f.37r] *struma*: boce in tergo / *nectar*: piment / [f.39r] *equiferus*: gallice (sic) stot[343] / *equitium*: gallice aras / *cleaca* (sic): gonge[344] / *involucrare*: (s)truscer / hoc *peditium*: pet, anglice fart[345] / *puscularius*: bucler / *succuso*: gallice trotter / [f.39v] *catum volatile*: uanerecht[346] / *falcarius*: faucuner / [f.40v] *geneceum*: bordel / *sorbet*: supen[347] / *aucionarius*: gallice regrate[r] / *labor*: hancele / *bombos*: wervel[348] / *penso*: spinle[349] / [f.41r] *pannosus*: .s. cluté / [f.41v] *gallinacium*: geliner / *refectorium*: refreytur / *nucalla*: gallice nugate / hoc *pomacium*:[350] .s. apelmos / [f.42r] *foscorium*: .i. besche / *scrobs*: .s. besche / *copa*: palleis / *armus*: espaule / *armularius*: .s. espauler / *vallum*: balie / *vallis*: valliye / [f.42v] *vinee*: hurdice / [f.43r] *eruca* (herba que stimulat luxuriam): cariloc[351] / *serapellina*: eld pilche[352] / *pero* -nis: rivelig / *glarea*: gallice gleir / *vibra*: brache tre[353] / *sicarius*: murdrissur / hoc *al(i)vieare*: gallice (sic) hivve[354] / *lisceum*: uuarp[355] / *filix*: fuger / *stigare*: gallice (sic) beitin[356] / (homo est) *simus*: cut nose (vel femina sima)[357] / *simia*: singe / *spitacus* (sic): gallice papungay / *obex*: .i. obstaculum sive barre / *colifeum*: pain alis[358] / *colum*: gallice crat(?) / *spinter*: pricche[359] / *omasus*: pudding[360] /

341 See MED sub *belle* n.(1).
342 See MED sub *brod adj.*4(d).
343 See OED sub *stot sb.*¹†1.
344 See MED sub *gang, gong* n.3(a).
345 See MED sub *fert* n.
346 The gloss runs quite clearly 'idem est quod uanerecht'. I do not recognise the last word.
347 See OED sub *sup v.*
348 Corr. *weevil* as a somewhat inaccurate gloss on *bombos* = bombyx?
349 See OED sub *spindle sb.*
350 MS = *pomamarum*. See MED sub *appel, -il, -ul* n.7(q).
351 See MED sub *cherlok* n.
352 See MED sub *eld a.* (= 'old') and *pilch(e* n.
353 See MED sub *brake* n.(1).
354 See MED sub *hive* n.(1)(b).
355 i.e. *licium* (actually 'weft' or 'woof'), see Dief.² and OED sub *warp sb.*¹.
356 See MED sub *beten v.*(1).
357 Cf. MED sub *cutten v.*(1) 2. (Ywain 260) and OED sub *cut ppl. a.* 12(b)).
358 See DMLBS sub *colyphium.*
359 See OED sub *prick sb.* V.14.
360 See OED sub *pudding sb.*

fungus et asparagus boletur tuber idem sunt: musserunes / *rubigo*: rust [361] / *sudes*: peues / *jugerum*: arpent / *sellio*: rig (terre) [362] / *upupa*: vanele / *trudes*: slide [363] / hec *cimba*: gallice chipe [364] / [f.43v] *strattilates*: gallice espies / [f.44r] *clarigo*: defier / *claricacio*: defiement / *strattilates*: espiis / *fullica*: gallice mauviz / *alimbes* (quedam avis): anglice popel / *galli palustres*: morchoc / [f.45r] *centone*: feuter / [f.46v] *specularia*: fenestre / *succina*: boyttes / *sigia*: la lye / hoc *stipatum*: stuye / *masticum*: mastiz / *popilion*: de pople / *sabuteleon*: unjment de sambu / [f.47r] *brucorum*: burdons / *tribulam*: fuel, sovele anglice, fuel [365] / [f.47v] *hervos*: gallice esternute [366] / [f.48r] *andtappoca*: cuntre-talie [367] / *appoca*: talie / *strages*: ocisiun / hec *moris*: le roge [368] / *abies*: sap, fir [369] / hec *tussis*: hoste, tuse [370] / *defidia*: peresse / *alnus*: alder / *alnetum*: aldercher [371] / *virus*: gallice venime / *virosus*: plen de venim / *gades*: merches / [f.48v] *pelex*: rivalie / *filix*: brache [372] / *frumices*: bussunes / *cilix*: robur desur la mer / *ustrina*: turail / hec *pandoxa*: gallice (sic) breuuerne [373] / *sorbilla*: sope / hec *pandoxatrix*: braceresse / *tucetum*: budding / *linere*: pursulier / *linire*: puronddre / [f.49r] *equus ducens equitium*: estalun / [f.49v] *stivarius*: charuer / [f.50r] *merenta*: gallice ruscie [374] / *coriolum*: .s. cominye / *triturator*: .s. batur / *pinso -is -sui*: .s. pestier / *rastorium*: .s. stricche [375] / *pinciculum*: .s. pester / [f.52v] *pluteum*: desche vel carole [376] / [f.53r] *ventilogium*: chote [377] / [f.53v] *auricalcum*: latun de Spanye /*aurifabriterea*: orfaverye [378] / hec *clama*: plateyn / *marmor*: marole [corr. marbre] / *smaragdus*: gallice emoroide / [f.54r] *strues*: gallice lenier .s. wodecast [379] / *barrus*: olifant

MS BERLIN, DEUTSCHE STAATSBIBLIOTHEK, PREUSSISCHER KULTURBESITZ LAT. FOL. 607 [380]

[f.1rb] [60] *pultes*: gruel / *sincopis*: gallice pamisan / [f.1rc] *mille*: gallice dicitur milier / *securis*: gisarme / *sartio -is quod est*: frire / [f.1va] *fus(c)io -is*: espandre gallice / [f.1vb]

---

361 See OED sub *rust sb.*[1].
362 See Du Cange sub *selio* and OED sub *ridge sb.*[15].
363 The Latin gloss runs 'genus curilis sine rotis ex duobus curvis lignis'. See OED sub *slid sb.*
364 i.e. *eschipe.*
365 *Tribulus, tribulum* and *tribula* are constantly confused in glosses and glossaries, *tribula* often being glossed by 'shovel' or *beche*, *tribulus* meaning 'briar', 'bramble', 'thistle', 'thorn' = *foail* (<*focale*), see Gfry 4,108b.
366 MS = *est' ernute.*
367 See DMLBS sub *antapoche.*
368 See WW 596,41 *moris: anglice a roche.*
369 See MED sub *firre n.(1).*
370 See MED sub *host(e n.(5).*
371 See MED sub *alder n.(1)1(b).*
372 See MED sub *brake(n n.*
373 See MED sub *breu-ern n.*
374 See Du Cange sub *recticinium.*
375 See OED sub *strick sb.*3. The usual lemma is *ostorium.*
376 See MED sub *deske n.*
377 Scheler's text, p.166, has 'cheruca tamen proprie dicitur ventilogium quod a Gallis apellatur "cochet" '. See TL 2,514 sub *cochet.*
378 Cf. Du Cange sub *fabrateria.*
379 See OED sub *wood sb.*[1]10.
380 It is clear from the copy of Nequam and other texts in the same MS that the scribe

[61] *species*: gallice espece / *lixivum*: anglice lec [381] / [f.1vc] *murena*: lamprie gallice / *epimera*: esperling / *gobio*: gojon / *melanurus*: uars de mer (sic) / *capito*: chabot / [f.2ra] *pelamides*: plaiz / [f.2rb] [62] *sculpo*: entalier / *bibliotheca*: almarie / *serum*: mege gallice / [f.2rc] *penula*: furrure gallice / *manubium*: ma[n]che de coutel / [f.2va] *pedes* -tis: gallice pouner / [f.2vb] [63] *ocreas* duos habet significationes: por huese vel pro chauce de fer / *equitium*: haraz / [f.2vc] *firmitor* -ris: rameur, barquier anglice (sic) / [f.3rb] [64] *stragulata*: gallice mye-[parti] / *lodices*: langeaus gallice / [65] *cata astomi*: anglice motes vel ad sordidum volans pacin(?) [382] / [f.3rc] *ardearius*: gallice haeruner / [66] *perizoma*: gallice roychet / [f.3vc] [67] *cumba*: gallice batel / [f.4rb] [68] *nugola*, *nugia*: gas gallice / [f.4vc] [70] *clangator*: crieur gallice / [f.5ra] [71] *stratellum*: estandart / [f.5rc] [72] *fullica*: mauviz gallice / *alumbos*: anglice pople / *galli palustres*: gallice mer . . .(?) anglice morkok / [f.5va] *cindulas*: lates gallice / [f.5vb] *sandux* (sic): gallice garincie / [f.6va] [158] *modulor*: atemprer / [f.6vb] [159] *locusta*, quasi longa hasta: dart / [f.6vc] [159] *tribula*: flael / [f.7ra] [160] *eruo* -is vel erceo -es, inde id posuisti in ervo pedes meos: gallice estiwre / [f.7va] [162] *manipulos*: gallice javeles / [f.7vc] [163] *piratorum*: gallice de galeys / [f.8vb] [169] *fistula*: gallice vyella (sic) / [f.8vc] [170] *celten*: gallice ciseau / [f.9ra] *anaglafario*: gallice bordeure / *obrizo*: escuré / [f.9rb] [173] *cratinabula* samer aineurs(?) / [f.9rc] *vectes*: gallice vertevel / *re(m)pagula*: barres.

MS LONDON, WELLCOME HISTORICAL MEDICAL LIBRARY, 801 [A] [383]

[f.104ra] [60] *familie*: a sa meiné / *utencilibus*: utilienens (sic) / *supellectilibus*: grans utilienens (sic) / in *quoquina*: en la quisine / *mensula*: table / *olus*: cholet / *minuatur*: seit mincé / *lentic[ul]a*: lentis / *pise*: peis / *pultes*: gruelis / *fabe frese*: feves muluis / *silique*: en cosse / *exilique*: senz ecosse / *mulium*: mil / *cepe*: uniun / *olle*: pos / *tripodes*: trepirs / *securis*: cuin / *mortarium*: morter / *pilus*: pestel / *contus*: movet / *uncus*: cros / [*pertica*]: perche / *creagra*: havet / *cacabus*: caudrun / *aenum*: poz de arein / *patella*: paele / *sartago*: grant paele / *cratic[ul]a*: gredil / *urceoli*: petis pos / *discus*: dubler / *scutella*: equele / *parapsis*: platel / *salsarium*: sausir / *artavi*: cuteus / *exenterari*: eçtre enbuelét / *gurgostio*: gorce, bernet / *funda*: lenge, dragge [384] / *fucina*: alger [385] / *jaculo*: lance / *hamice*: petite rei, angil [386] / *nassa*: berssel / in *vivario*: en vivir / in *stangno*: en stanc / *depressi*: pris

[61] *archimacherus*: mester qu / *crebro*: cribre / *cinseratum*: enclarci / *contritum*: trublé /

---

frequently did not understand what he was copying and garbled both text and glosses (a few of the latter are quite incomprehensible).

381 See MED sub *lek* n.
382 Both lemma and gloss remain impenetrable.
383 For a description of the MS see S. A J. Moorat, *Catalogue of Western MSS on Medicine and Science in the Wellcome Historical Medical Library* vol. II MSS Written after 1650 AD N–Z with Indexes, Appendix and Supplement to Volume 1 (London, 1973), pp.1464–67. Some of the commentary space is unfilled on ff.111vb, 112rb, 115rb, 115va, 116vb and 117rb. On ff.113va–vb and 114ra–rb none has been entered at all, so that these folios are blank except for a few lines of text. Most of f.117v is also blank.
384 See MED sub *dragge* n.(1)1(a).
385 See MED sub *alger* n.
386 See MED sub *angel* n.

consolidandos: a frier hu farsir / in *abditorio*: en eçtui, en forcer / *ablutia*: lawors / *ancerum*: des howes / *domesticarum*: dame, tame[387] / *entera*: buelis / *coclear*: grant culur, ladil[388] / *ebulicio*: buliement / *excaturari*: estre eçcaudi / *mola piperalis*: mole a pei[v]re / [f.104rb] *mola manualis*: meinmole / *salsamentum*: sause / *mugiles*: saumuns / *amphivia* (corrected to *amphimera*): purpeis, solis / *congrus*: congre / *murena*: lampreye / *musculus*: balayn / *epimera*: eçperlingis / *gobio*: gugun / *melanurus*: bar de mir, anglice addoc[389] / *capito*: cabot / *morus*: murue, keling[390]

[62] *pelamides*: plaiz / *mullus*: muluel / *uranosscopus*: raye / *megarus*: makerel / *turtur*: turbut / *allecia*: arreng / *gamorus*: pinoche, stanstikil (sic)[391] / *ostria*: oistris / *colchiria*: muskeliz / *micatorium*: miur, grate / *ruder*: fose / [f.104vb] in *dispensa*: en la diçspense / *gausape*: grant nape / *mantille*: petit toalie / *facitergium*: cuverchet (sic) / *pertica*: perche / *incidias*: awez / *murium*: deç suris / *cutelli*: cuteus / *salarium*: salir / *sculptum*: entalié / *theca*: kasiir / *caseorum*: furmage / *candalabrum*: chandelabre / *absconsa*: escons / *laterna*: lantre / *calathi*: paners, anglice baskés[392] / [f.105ra] in *promtuario*: en le celir / *cadi*: bariz / *utres*: buseus / *dolea*: tuneus / *ciphi*: hanaper, hanapers / *cophini*: corbeus / *coclearia*: culiers / *clepsedre*: bucins (sic) / *pelves*: basins / *corbes*: co[r]biluns / *vina*: vin / *claretum*: claré / *nectar*: piment / *sisera*: sisre / *medo*: mede / *piretum*: de piris / *rosetum*: rosé / *vinum ferratum*: vin ferré / *vinum falernum*: vin de auucerne / *vinum gariofilatum*: vin gelofré / *lambris*: a lechurs / *ambubagis*: a glutuns / [f.105rb] *perhendinaturus*: li sujurnaunt / *penula*: furet / *tunicam*: cote / *manubiis*: de manchis / *birris*: geruns / *laciniis*: paunis, goris / *femoralibus*: brais

[63] *lumbaribus*: breelles, anglice bregeldelis[393] / *caligis*: chausis / *tibie*: gambos (sic) / *estivalibus*: estuwas / *calceis*: de souleris / *laqueatis*: lacis / *consutilibus*: soulors (sic) a cureis / *sindonis*: de sondel (sic) / *serici*: seye / *bissi*: de chesil / *penula*: pane / *de cicinis*: de veir gris / *experiolis*: escureus / *cuniculis*: de cuniz / *laeronibus*: layruns / *sabellino*: sabelin / *bevere*: huttre,[394] hotere / *vulpecula*: gupyl / *roserella*: roserel, ermyn(?) / [f.105va] *capam*: chape / *manubeatam*: manché / *caputium*: caperun / *ocreas*: hoses / *calcaria*: espuruns / *stimulos*: agiliuns / *ortatorios*: amonestablis / [f.105vb] *reculanti*: reculant / *recursanti*: arere curant / *repedanti*: arere fesant / *antepedanti*: trop avant alaunt / *succussanti*: trotant / *cesspitanti*: cestant / neque *recalcitranti*: ne regibbaunt / *stimulos*: aguliuns / *neganti*: niant / *mittendo*: a lacchir / *habili*: avable / *carentivillo*: kanevas / *sudario*: huse / *panello*: panel / *sella*: sele / *teniis*: frengis, par tenges(?) / *sudari*: de suir / *clunes*: crupe / *strepe*: estrus / *arculi*: arsuns / *ansella*: arsun devant / *posstela*: arsun derere

[64] *antelas*: currey devant / *postelas*: curei derere / *involucro*: en le playe[395] / *mantica*: truse sive male / *pectorale*: peiterel / *phalere*: arneis / *camum*: bernac / *capistrum*:

---

387 Complete *damesches*? See OED sub *tame a.*
388 See MED sub *ladel n.*
389 See MED sub *haddok n.*
390 See MED sub *keling(e n.sg. & pl.*
391 Corr. *banstikel.*
392 Read 'gallice baskés'? Cf. MED sub *basket n.*
393 See MED sub *brech-girdel n.1(a).*
394 Corr. *lutre?*
395 MS = *le en playe.*

chevestre / *frenum*: frein / *lupatum*: chanfreyn / *infectum*: teint / *habenas*: reins / *singulas*: cengles / *lingulas*: hardiluns / *pluscula*: bucle / *epicingulas*: sursengles / *pulvillum*: bas / *trussulam*: truse / *pedes*: pouner / *strigilem*: estril / [f.106rb] in *chamera*: en la chaunbre / *cortina*: curtine / *muscarum*: musches / *aranearum*: iraneis / *epistilis*: de chapitels / *tapetum*: tapet / *cathedram*: chaere / *pedes*: pes / *scabellum*: eschamel, furme / *lectica*: chaere a dame / *culcitra*: quiltte / *plumalis*: deç plumis / *cervical*: oriler, piluere / *culcitra punctata*: quilte peinté / *vestis stragulata*: rayé burel / *pulvinar*: quissine, bolster[396] / *linteamina*: linceus / *cindone*: cendel / *bisso*: chesil / *lino*: de lin / *lodices*: lo[n]geus / *co[o]pertorium*: cuverture / *viridi sagio*: de vert saie / *penula*: de pane / *taxea*: de tesun, de broc / *catina*: de chat / *beverina*: de bevr, de lutre, oterene / *purpuri*: purpre / *ansellare*: truser

[65] *catum volatile*: curtine / *pertica*: perche / *capus*: muschet / *nisus*: essperver / *herodius*: girfauc / *alietus*: faucun, merenelyun (sic) / *cirri*: alowz / *tercellus*: tercel / *peregrinus*: ramage / *herodius*: ostur / *assensorius*: autein / *tardarius*: laner / *prepes*: ignel / *ardearius*: hayrun / *gruarius*: gru / *ancipister*: ostur / *supara*: cheinsis / *flammea*: cuverchif / *perizoma*: cuverture, rochet / *pallium*: mantel / *tunica*: cote / *toga*: gunele / *collobium*: frog / *antiper[a]*: escrin / the following entries are written at the top of f.106va: *instita*: cheinse / *lumbare*: curtepy[397] / *terristrum*: riveroket / *ludices teatrales*: bele vesture / *cirmata*: curte chense, sulyepeus,[398] (lunget, misplaced) they are then repeated on an extra fragment of parchment (f.106+) as follows: *instita matronalis*: cheinse a dame / *lumbare*: curtepy / *limata*: sulyepeus / *aspergines*: lunge chenses / *cirmata*: curte chenses / *longa cirophea*: purpre vestures / *ludices teatrales*: bele vesture / *teristrum*: riveroket / [f.106va] *nimphula*: mechine / *mataxa*: serence, hechele / *aurifrigium*: orfreis / *nexus*: laçuns / *tricaturas*: tressures / *compliet*: ensemble pliet / *vestes laneos*: vestures de leine / *explicet*: hor pliet / *consuat*: cusuet / *sartiat*: amendet / *ciroteca*: gans / *amputatis*: tranchis / *teca*: deel, themil[399] / *corrigiale*: de quir / *acus*: aguil

[66] *filarium*: filer, fusyl / *glomos*: luceus / *extricet*: ensemble pliet / *acus*: agulz / *opus plumale*: ofleswerc,[400] de plume / ad *consuendum*: cusyr / *biritricas*: geruns / *poliendas*: a planirs / *laques*: laz / *inducendos*: enz mettre / *acus* . . . *grosissimas*: gallice winoles / *illecebris*: les delicis / *peplum*: wimple / *intemperie*: maveyse temprure / *corrolla*: coife de quir / *coracalla*: bende de drap / *crinali*: garlande / *reticulo*: calle, crespin / *monile*: affermail, noche / *spinter*: afiçal, erpin[401] / *fuscotincti*: fustian / *camicie*: chemise / *colaria*: colers / *torques*: bende d'or / *androgia*: daye / *ova*: ofs / [f.106vb] *anceribus*: aues / *sub[s]ternat*: esparpli / *agnellos*: anieus / *morbidos*: malades / *lacte*: let / *vitulos*: ves / *ablactatos*: severez / in *perculo*: en paroc / *fenile*: fein / *maternales*: vestures de dames / *serapeline*: keinse pinché, kense ridlé / *recinium*: biphe / *terestrum*: r[i]verocat / *subulcis*: porcheris / *colustrum*: meg, best / *bubulcis*: buvers / *armentariis*: karetters

---

396 See MED sub *bolster* n.
397 See MED sub *courte-pi* n.
398 The same word appears as a gloss to *serapelline* on f.107va.
399 See OED sub *thimble sb*.
400 I cannot make sense of this word which is quite clear in the MS [*werc*² = 'work'].
401 The OED does not record 'hairpin' until the 19th C.

[67] *in obsoniis*: a supers / *obsigalam*: egre let / *quactum*: dule [= du lé?], crem / in *cimbiis*: en grans queles / *abditorio*: en cen . . . / *pingue*: gras meg / *furfure*: de bren / [f.107va] *assa*: haste / *suille*: de porc / *assata*: rosté / *diligenti*: par suvener . . . / *tractu*: turné / *prunis*: bresis / *funio*: funie / *flamma*: flamme / *condimentum*: savirement / *altile*: chapun / *conciso*: en consis / *piperis*: de peivere / *non renuit*: ne refuse pas / *asspercionem*: essparliement / *auca domestica*: owe domecche / *veru*: espee, spite / *circumvoluta*: environturné / *aliatam*: alié / *virido succo*: verjus / *racemorum*: de recins / *pomorum silvestrum*: de pomis dé bois, wodecrabe[402] / *di[s]temperata*: destempré / *galina*: gelin / *domestica*: domecche[403] / *scaturizata*: escaudé / *membratim*: de membre en membre / *cumino*: de cumin / *condiatur*: savuré / *assata*: rosté / *guttulis*: gustes (sic) / *lardi*: de lard / *reficiatur*: seit refet / *condimentum*: savourement / *aliate*: de alie / *exenterati*: enbuelis / *salsa*: sause / *cum viridi sapore*: ha verte sause / *salgea*: sauge / *petrosillum*: persil / *costus*: coste / *ditannium*: ditanie / *serpillum*: petir, pelestre / *alea*: aus / cum *pipere*: hov pei[v]re / *exilaret*: rehetet / *vinum passum*: fort vin

[f.107vb] [68] *profunditatem*: profundesse / *virorem*: verdisur / *cornu*: de corn / *bubali*: de bugle / *fulminis*: de fudre / *nux philidis*: alemande / *repens*: rampant / *experioli*: escurel / *gesticulans*: salyaunt / *caprioli*: de cheveret / *grisorum monacorum*: de gris moneis / *scintille*: de centele, sparke[404] / *Parvi Pontane*: de Petit Pont de Paris / *delicatum*: delié / *bissus*: chesil / *cristalli*: de c[ri]stal / [f.108ra] *castra*: chasteus / *desenter*: avenantment / *fossa*: fose / *citum*: le sé / *muniat*: garnicet / [f.108rb] *mota*: mote / *rupem*: roche / *debitam*: due / *muralis moles*: peysentime de murs / *cemento*: morter / *arduum*: haut / *opus*: overanie / *sepes*: haye / *horida*: hidus / *palis*: peus / *quadrangulis*: quaris / *vepribus*: runces / *vallum*: balie / *amplis*: largis / *venis*: veines / *muri*: mures / *supereminentes*: aparisauns / *columpnis*: pilers / *appodia[n]tur*: seient apeis / *superficies*: hautesse

[69] *trulle*: de le truel / *cementarii*: maçun / *operam*: entente / *cancelli*: cerneus / *proportionibus*: spaciis / *propugnacula*: bretaskes / *pinne*: cerneus / *crates*: cleis, herdles / *molares*: grant peres / *eiciendos*: hors jettre / *obsideatur*: seit asegé / *opidi*: chastel / *deditionem*: abandun / *blado*: de blé / *mero*: vin / *farre*: blé / *perniis*: pernis / *baconibus*: bacuns / *carne*: char / in *succidio*: in suse / *hillis*: anduliis, podingis / *salsuciis*: sausix / *carne suilla*: char de porc / carne *arietina*: de mutun / *leguminibus*: potages / *fonte*: fontanie / *scaturiente*: surdaunt / *posticis*: posternes / *cataractibus*: boues / [f.108va] *allaturi*: o (sic) porter / *incedant*: entrent / *lancee*: lances / *catapulte*: siete barbalé / *peltes*: targes / *baliste*: arbaleste / *fustibula*: mangenels / *funde*: fundes / *baleares*: pereres / *sudes*: peuz / *feres*: de fir / *clave*: masuis / *nodose*: nuuse / *fustes*: grant peuz,[405] bastuns / *torres*: branduns, tisuns / *asultus*: asauz / *obsidentium*: asegons / *arietes*: berfreis / *trabarie*: de trolie / *crates*: cleis / *machine*: engins / *manni*: palefreis / *gradarii*: chasurs / *destrarii*: destre[r]s / *palefridi*: pafreis / *animentur*: seint amuus

[70] *concinnant*: chasint / *tube*: busins / *tibie*: estives / *litiis*: ruez / *buxus*: flegolis / *cornua*: corn / *acies*: cumpanies / *exercitus*: host / *tribunis*: cunestablis / *militie*: chi-

---

[402] See OED sub *wood sb.*[1]10c.
[403] MS = *dommecle*.
[404] See OED sub *spark sb.*[1].
[405] MS = *pūz*.

valerie / ad *troiampium*: a turnement / *tornamentum*: burdis / *girum*: asemblé / *tiroci-nium*: burdis / *hastuludium*: burdis / *runcini*: runcine / *succussorii*: chaçurs / *vernis*: bachelers / *visspiliones*: robeurs / *coterellis*: garsuns a pé / *prudentes*: quinte bers / *clangatores*: defiurs / *caduciatores*: concordurs / *austutia*: quintise / *moles*: pesentines / *summa*: sume / *disspensatio*: ordeinement / *rigore*: redissur / *degrassatores*: envaisurs / *ligirumpi*: pesurs de lei / *plebicitorum*: del commun de pople / *privaricatores*: desusurs / *plebi statutorum*: des status de puple / *clepi*: laruns / *ablactores*: laruns de bestis / *sicarii*: murdisurs / *inectores*: occisores a la cur / [f.108vb] *antropocedi*: occisurs / *fustigantur*: fustiét / *condonentur* [= condempnentur]: condennét / *frugalitatem*: essparnance / *clangatores*: criurs / *caduciatores*: afiurs, fesaunt pes

[71] *stratillates*: cunestables / *stantelum*: estandard / *inconcussum*: nent feriz / *victoria-rum*: victores / *tumull̄tu]arii*: feisans noyse / *sacramentales*: feisant serment / *animet*: hardiet / *tuba*: bucin / *decertantis*: cumbatant / *nube*: nue / *donativa*: donablus (dona magna) / *stupendia* (= stipendia): werdun, dun / *carseres*: prisuns / *compediti*: mis en bouis / *manicis fereis*: maniclis de fer / *cippi*: ceps / *columbaris*: piloris / *excubie*: uetes / *clangorem*: cri / *strepitum*: noyse / [f.109vb] in *granario*: en grenir / *ostorium*: radure, anglice stric[406] / *conus* .i. cumba: mesure / *vanum*: fan / *batus*: bussel / *tece*: mesuris, man de grin / *frumentum*: furment / *ordei*: orge / *sigali*: segle / *avene*: aveine / *lolli*: de nele, cokil / *cortis*: de la curt / *silique*: coses / *lollium*: neel / *avena sterilis*: haverhun / *galli*: cokis / *galine*: geluns / *gallinaci(c)i*: kokereus / *altiles*: chapuns / *anceres*: gars

[72] *anates*: anes, enedes[407] / *cicones*: cigoniis / *ardee*: hairuns / *phasidis*: faisans / Libie: grues / *fulice*: maivis, (in a second hand) cotis, blerye anglice (sic) / *alambes*: poplris (sic),[408] bleries / *mergites*: divedoppis, plungés[409] / *alceones*: mowes, motes[410] / *galli palustres*: coks dé mareis / *pavones*: pouns / [f.110ra] in *stabulo*: en le stable / *presepe*: krech / *bostar*: boverie / *are*: porcherie / *alvei*: auges, troches[411] / *alveoli*: petis . . . / *strigilis*: stril / *camus*: bernec / *salivare*: chanfrein / *sonovectorium* (sic): civere, barue,[412] sivere saunz rotis / *epiredium*: idem cum rotis / *capistrum*: chevestre / *fallere*: herneis / *textor*: tistur / *terestris eques*, miles de tera: a pé / *streparum*: estrus / *adnitens*: aforsant / *apodiamento*: de le puement / *admittit*: alecchet / *exilie*: de petit / *dieta*: jurné / *scansilia*: estrus / *visci[ssi]tudine*: par entrechamgable feze / *deprimatur*: s'est abesé / *trocleam*: windas / *circumvolubilem*: envirunturnant / *evoluendus*: avirunturné / *sidulas*: laches / *columbaribus*: pertus .i. foraminibus / *regione*: manere / *cavillis*: civillis / [f.110rb] *trabibus*: trefs / *tenorem*: le urle / *tele*: teyle / *licia*: licis, fyls, hefdles[413] / *tenis*: frenges, ragges[414] / *fimbriis*: urles de la teile / in *capudio*: en caperun de teile / *intersticiis*: spaciis / *stamen*: le estaim, warp / *supponendum*: a suçmettre / *sup[er]ponendum*: de surmettre / *trama*: traim, of

---

406 See OED sub *strike* sb. 3a.
407 See MED sub *end(e* n.(2).
408 See MED sub *popeler(e* n. ('European Spoonbill').
409 See MED sub *dive-dap* n. and TL 7,1180 sub *plonget*.
410 See TL 6,108 (*möe*) and 111 (*möete*).
411 See OED sub *trough* n.
412 See MED sub *barwe* n.
413 See MED sub *heveld* n.
414 See OED sub *rag* sb.[1].

[73] *navicule*: navet, spole / *transeuntes*: tresspasant / *pano*: broche / *fenestrellas*: fenestrals / *pannus*: broche / *spola*: spolt vel horns (?) / *spola*: esspule / *penso*: de fil / *glomeris*: lussel / *trame*: tremie[415] / *sumatur*: seit afermé / *naviculam*: navet / *telam*: teile / *ordietur*: werpin, ordeyn[416] / *pectines*: penies / *resiproco*: entrechanchab[l]e / *depilaverit*: depilé / *staminis*: de steim, warp / *floccis*: flocuns / *stuparum*: de stupes / *superstitibus*: remenans / *sandicis*: de warance, anglice madder / *sindicis*: wode / *Bellivacensis*: de Beuveis[417] / *condimento*: savourement / *prorumpat*: avant saliet / *fullonis*: fulur / *abblucio*: lavement

[f.110va] [74] *solicitudo*: curuseté / [f.110vb] [73] *sindex*: warence, madder

[155] *veredus*: charetir / *ducturus*: a menir / *c(l)uculam*: cuvele / *caputio[ne]*: de caperun / *grisio*: gris / *collobium*: frog / *manubeatam*: manché / *mulonis*: mulir / officium *explere*: esspleiter, parempler / *aculeo*: agulement / *flagello*: flaol / *scorpionem*: escurge / *scedat*: batet / *auriga*: charetir / [f.111ra] *ocreas*: hoses / *tesqua*: waceus / *lutosas*: taus[418] / *plateas*: rues / *latus*: coste / *carri*: de charet / *anteriori parti*: a la parti devant / *legere*: paser / *sinuato*: turné / *poplice*: garet / *atestatur*: .i. teintet / *cavillam*: caville / *temenis* (sic): temun, thille[419] / *restem*: hard devant / *veredus*: chareter / *epispha* (= epifia): hernois, paruns[420], berec, hamis / *multiplici centone*: de mute manere de feutre / *jugum*: jug / *faleras*: hernés / *suarium*: suir, huse / *subcellium*: surcen[421], setil / *carentivillum*: canevas

[156] *scutarium*: esquir / *excecutionem*: ensuance / *rota*: roie / *axis*: de le essel / in *tinpano*: en le muel / *modielo*: muel, nave[422] / *cavilla*: cheville / *in modiolo*: en le muel / *radii*: roies, spokes / *cantos*: guntes, anglice felies[423] / [f.111rb] *stelliones*: steliuns, anglice diveles[424] / *orbite*: sente / *variis coloribus*: anglice globere[425] / *circumferentia*: circumferonce, rundesse / *fero*: de fir / *clavis*: de clouis / *scrupulorum*: de peris / *offendicula*: abusalies / *asseres*: les es / *in area*: en la place / *bastones*: bastuns / *cidularum*: rungis / *temonem*: temun

[f.111vb] [157] *vestibulo*: porche / *atrium*: place, curt / *plateas*: rues / *postes*: postes / *debitis*: dues / *intersticiis*: esspacis / [f.112ra] *asseribus*: es / *cidulis*: cendles, laces / *latis*: lés / *trabibus*: tref / *tignis*: cheveruns / *edificii*: de herbagarge (sic) / *tigillis*: de petiz cheveruns, anglice roftre, (left-hand margin) walche sparis[426] / *doma*: fes / *comissuram*: severunde, evesinge / *machina*: engin / *specularia*: fenestres / *exedre*: luvers / *orientales partes*: de le orient / *succina*: boistes / *tortiles*: aturnables / *storacis*: de ceole

---

415 See TL 10,576.
416 See OED sub *warp* v. III.20 (= *ordietur*) and *ordain* v. (= *ordinetur*).
417 The gloss adds 'ubi sunt boni tinctores'.
418 i.e. OF *täios*.
419 See OED sub *thill*[1].
420 See TL 7,339 sub *parone*.
421 Corr. *suscen[gle]*.
422 See MED sub *nave* n.
423 See MED sub *felwes* n. (pl). *Guntes* = *jantes*.
424 I do not recognise this word.
425 If this is an error for *globerd* ('glow-worm'), it may have been displaced from *stellio* which can mean 'slow-worm'!
426 See OED sub *rafter* sb.[1] and *spar* sb.[1]1. I do not recognise *walche*.

confecciun / *sigia*: lie / *corinbrum*: la baselie [427] / *popilio*: unguent de pople / *laurinum*: de laure / *sambucus*: anglice elder [428] / *epitimata*: dez flur

[158] *crates*: cleies / *calamo palustri*: chalemel de palu ou rosel de gué / *arundine*: franc ros / *cindulis*: cendles / *lateres*: teules / *laquearia*: cuples de mesun / *stipidibus*: estops / *seram*: serure, loc / *pesulam*: barre / *vectes*: vertevellis, verullis / *gumfos*: guns, hokis [429] / *repagula*: bares / *valve*: wicetz / *bifores*: duble porte / *porticum*: portis / *cardinibus*: charuns / [f.112va] *rusticus*: hum de upelond [430] / *rure*: de champ / *consulere*: consestir / *corbibus*: corbiliuns / *cumera*: heve [431] / *calathis*: baskés, panieris / *cumeris*: ruches / *vimineis*: de osiirs / *sportis*: baskis / *cophinis*: hanepirs / *fucina*: fuine, elgir [432] / *hamatam*: croké / *ficina*: chesefat / *multra*: paile, buket / *expressum*: enprent / *coagulatione*: constreinement en pressure / *sero*: mege / *colustrum*: creme, bene [433]

[159] *techa*: casiir / *iunccis palustribus*: junc dé palus, dé mareis / *muscarum*: de muchis / *cinifes*: wibet / *brucorum*: burduns / *palleas*: paile / *acera*: curalles / *furfura*: brens / *pabula*: pasturs / *anatibus*: anes / *anceribus*: anglice (sic) owes, gars / *auculis*: oiseus / *cortibus*: de la curt / *pollentridium*: buletel / *taratantrum*: sarse, her-seve [434] / *pollen*: pur (corr. flur) de furment / *coletur*: seit colé / *specificetur*: delié / *purgetur*: espurgé / *framea*: gisarme / *vangam*: besce / *tribulum*: pele, fleyl [435] / *tribulam*: truble / *tribulos*: runcis / *saticulum*: silleye,[436] sedlep / *sartionis*: de semesun / *sonovectorium*: civere, barue / *quallum*: paner, proprie hotte / *quaxillum*: petit paner / *muscipulam*: muce fal[437] / *pedicam*: pege, calketrap / *palos*: peles / *exploratos*: endurcis / [f.112vb] *bisacutam*: bisague, tuibil / *vepris*: runces / *tribulos*: carduns / *sentes*: spine / *vitulamina spuria*: brances bastardes / *sepes*: hayes / *incuriam*: nunsawance / *abactores*: laruns de bestes / *bubulcis*: bovers / *sub(ub)ulcis*: porcheris

[160] *artavi*: knivet / *surculos*: greves, (second hand) les eves / *excetat*: trenchit / *oculendas*: a musirs ensemble / *inserat*: entit / *ligones*: picoises / *cirsos*: banastuns / *intubas*: humelokis / *errvos*: [qui]chel, quechis / *carduns*: carduns / *avenas steriles*: haveruns / *opilionem*: berchir / *tigurium*: hulet / *area*: place / *micture*: pissure de la date[438] / *stercorationis*: fenture / *bostar*: boverie / *presepe*: creche / *aridieat* (pro saneat): enveiset / *prossperitas*: prosperté / *agasonem*: aner / *mulionem*: muler / in *equitio*: en (sur) haras / *emissarium*: chiva[l], estalun, stalun / *juvencas*: toreus / *tauros*: tors / *buclos*: buves / *buculas*: buveces / *bubalos*: bugle / [f.113ra] *onagros*: anis savagis / *arietes*: mutuns / *burdones*: burdu[n]s / *casses*: reis / *laques*: laz / *extensos*: estendus

[161] *ad circumvolvendum*: envolupers / *lepores*: levres / *damas*: deims / *capriolas*:

427 The same gloss, which is not in the dictionaries, is quoted by Scheler.
428 See MED sub *eller(n* n.
429 See MED sub *hok* n.
430 See OED sub *upland* sb.¹ and a.¹.
431 See MED sub *hive* n.
432 See MED sub *alger* n.
433 See note 220 above.
434 See MED sub *her(e-sive* n.
435 See MED sub *fleil* n.
436 Scheler prints a gloss *salobe*.
437 See MED sub *mous* n.2(a).
438 See AND sub *date*³.

cheveris / *cervos*: cervs / *hinnulos*: founs / *odorinse(n)ci*: brachet / *cervas*: bises / *aratrum*: carue / *grande robur*: fust / *trabem*: tref / *temonem*: temun / *bifurcando*: furchant en dus / *lira*: reun / *aure*: estapel / *robur*: fust / *stiva*: estive / *capulus*: temun / *extremitas encis*: pumel / *libitina*: bere / *alumpnosa*: tause / *salingnea*: de sa(l)uz / *retinacula*: hars, corde, hoste [439]

[162] *salignea*: de sauz / *dentale*: dental .s. soket [440] / *vomis*: soc / [f.113rb] *sepem*: haye / *cratem*: cleie, herdil / *clavos*: clous / *cavillas*: kivilis / *restem*: hart / *cultrum*: cu(r)tre / *stercorare*: enfencer / *fimo*: de fens / *resarcire*: redubir, sarclir, weden [441] / *iterando*: reherçant / *novalia*: waret / *rebinare*: rebinir / *veracta*: waret / *creta*: marl / *stipulis*: stublis / *incensis*: enbracés / *cererem*: ble / *trahe*: de herce / *fissum*: fendu / *prorumpat*: avant salie / *calamum*: chalemel / *tecis*: hosis, cotels / *spicis*: espies / *metere*: seiir(s) / in *area*: en une place / *manipulos*: gaveles / *gelimas*: gerbes / *submotas*: levez / [h]oreis: a grangis / *rastro*: rastel / *vanno*: van / *mola*: querne / *sinceratum*: enclersi / *foraminibus*: pertuz / *pincendi*: pestiir / [f.113va] *aculeum*: agiliun / *trahas*: herse

[163] *larvam*: la visere / *larvaticam*: babewere [442] / *polinodia* (sic): suvener chant / [f.114rb] *cimba*: batel / *ostrum*: hec (corr. bec) / [f.114va] *vomere*: winchir / *vomitus*: speuin [443] / *transferatione*: pasage / *naulum*: fraut anglice [444] / *veiculo*: aportement / *lolligo*: tenche

[164] *proreta*: anglice sterisman [445] / *rinna*: crevas / *carie*: purture / *tubarum*: bucins / *prorumpendo*: avant saliant / [f.114vb] *lituorum*: petis cors / *accensus*: enbracé / *acum*: agul a fil / *cuspis*: le poinz

[165] *piratarum*: de galies / *clavis*: clowis / *pice*: poie, piç / *sera picata*: sire piché / *lineantur*: sei[n]t englués / *unguine*: de hont [446] / *leviguntur*: sont planis / *unctionis*: unjement / *craticulis*: de cleies / *compaginem*: juncture / *asseribus*: des es / *velum*: sigle / [f.115ra] *zelotipus*: kukewald / *rudendo*, quod est proprium asinorum: recaner / *veli*: de sigle / *tumor*: enfleure

[166] *ventilogium*: wedirkoc [447] / *foratoria*: ter[er]es, wimmbes [448] / *remi*: hore [449] / *aura*: vent / *parastes*: cablis / *funes*: cordes / *malum*: le mast / *stipites*: estocs / *suppodientes*: supoyans / *podium*: pualie / *palme*: de la paume / *nauclerus*: mariner / *transtrum*: sege / *troclea*: windas / *aure*: vent / [f.115rb] *circumcirca*: tut envirun

[167] [f.116ra] *rasorium*: rasur / *novaculum*: novacle / ad *radendum*: rere / *pumicem*: pumiç / *planulam*: plane / *plumbum*: plum / *linula*: reule / *lineatur*: seit reulé / *margine*: ma[r]ge / *tergi*: dos / *carnis*: char / *quaternus*: quair / *cedule*: agniz / *apendice*: englu / in

---

439 I do not recognise *hoste*.
440 See OED sub *socket sb.*[2] and TL 9, 851 sub *soquet*.
441 See OED sub *weed v.*
442 Corr. *babewene*.
443 See OED sub *spewing vbl. sb.*
444 See OED sub *fraught sb.*
445 See OED sub *steersman*.
446 See TL 6,1025 sub *oint*.
447 See OED sub *weathercock sb.*
448 Corr. *wimbles* and see OED sub *wimble sb.*
449 See MED sub *or(e n.(1)*.

superiori parte: amunt / in *inferiori [parte]*: la basete / *registrum*: seine / *punctorium*: pointur / *punxi*: pointai / *non pupugi*: puniai pas

[168] *centone*: feutre / *artavi*: cnivet / *ylo*: meule / *liquescat*: decure / *littura*: equachure / *cancellaverit*: eit outé / *prunas*: breses / in *epicausterio*: en chiminé / *atramentum*: arlement / [f.116rb] *aquilonaris*: de norz / *membrana*: parchemin / *disgregat*: departet

[169] *puniceas*: vermeiles, ruges / *fuscum pulverem*: ner pudre / *azuram*: azure / [f.117ra] *aurifaber*: le horfevere / *caminum*: cheminé / *perforatum*: percé / *evaporare*: isir / *pulsum*: butement / *folles*: fous, belies / *fistulas*: tueles / *prunas*: brecis

[170] *accendat*: enbracit / *incus*: enclume, stitye [450] / *inexauste*: nent eçpuché / *malleoli*: de martel / *forcipis*: force / *malleolum*: martelet / *braceas creseas*: taches de or / *laminas*: plates / *auricalceas*: horchaut de Spaine / *stanneas*: esteim / *cupreas*: quifvre / *celtem*: chisel / *adamante*: ennont [451] / *marmore*: marbre / *cotem*: cuz / *explorat*: enserchet / *mola*: mule / *aciem*: acués / *conferant*: aportent / *pedem leporinum*: pé de levere / *levigare*: planir, saugir(?) / *extergere*: torser / *gremio*: gerun / *corio gremiali*: gerun de quir / *asceras*: boistes, sensers / *ampulas*: ampulis / *figuli*: de poter / *seram*: gallice sye, anglice file / *seram dentatam*: lime denté, sawe / *limam*: file / *filum argenteum*: fil de argent

[f.117rb] [171] *cophini*: hanepers / *ciphi*: hanaps / *consui*: estre cusu / *anag[l]afario*: bordure, trifure / *ductili*: amenable / *futili*: fundables, esspendable / *ceratam*: siré / *ceromate*: blanchet / *argilla*: arcil / *oblitam*: engluit / *inoffense*: nent cursé / *casma[m]*:[452] lie de argent / *litargium*: pur gemme / *obrizum*: or mere / *oricalco*: de orchaut / *cupro*: quivre / *auro elico*: or pur / *auricalcem*: orchaut, lie de or / *institoris*: de mercant, buscur[453] / *pellacis*: desonable / *tergiversationem*: trecherie / *fabateriam*: forge / *muniatur*: soit warni / [f.118ra] *lavacrum*: funs / *mariolum*: mariole / *pulpitum*: leitrun / *urceus*: pot, cruet / *pelves*: bacins

[172] *scamnum*: bensc / *sacrarium*: sacrarie / *vestibulum*: vestiarye, porche / *vestiarium*: vestiarie / *altare*: autir / *phiole*: phiolis / *pixides*: boistes / *loculus*: bere / *facitergium*: cuverchit (sic) / *funaculum*: sacrarie / *breviarium*: martilogie / *missale*: messel / *antifonarium*: antifenir / *gradale*: grael / *manuale*: manuel / *processionale*: procescionarie / *superpelicium*: supliz / *examictum*: aumice / *alba*: aube / *singulum*: seng[l]e / *phanum*: phanun / *stola*: estole / *casula*: chesuble / *acerne*: de arable, mapel / *querule*: de chene / *tingna*: cheverun / *tigilla*: cheveruns / *succidines*: severhunde, heveses [454] / *tegminibus*: cuverturis / *cindulis*: de cendles / *plumbeis laminis*: plate de plum / *clavis*: de clouues / *tegule*: teules / *nole*: cloket

[173] *tintimabula* (sic): petit sens a mens / *ventilogi*: koket / *vectes*: verteveles / *gunfi*: guns / *repagula*: bares / *pensula*: haspe hu loc pendant / *sere*: locs / *limina*: l'entrirs, sols

---

450 See OED sub *stithy*.
451 Scheler cites the gloss *haymaunt*; see FEW 1,28b (*adamas*).
452 See DMLBS sub *cadmia*.
453 I do not recognise this last word.
454 See MED sub *eves n.*

Vernacular glosses from the commentary in MS 801A

[60] *utensile*: gallice utiliement / *meto* -tu -sui est: seer / *puls*: gruel / *frese*: fevez muluus / *silique*: en cosse / *siliqua*: cosse / *fabe exilique*: fevez sauns eççosse / *cepe*: uniun / *tripodes*: trépés et trestel / *pilus*: pestel / *uncus*: croc / *cacabus*: caudrun de fer / *aenum*: pot de arein / *patella*: paele / *sartago*: grant paele / *craticula*: gredil / *cratis*: gallice cleie / *cratera*: hanap / *parapsis*: grant dublir / *artavi*: cuteus / [61] *spuma*: escume / *lixa*: quistrun / *exscaturizare* proprie est: ecauder hoiseus / *scaturio*: surde / *mola*: mole / *molo*: mudre / *molendinum*: mulin / *mola manualis*: mol a meyn / *mura*: sause / *micatorium*: miur / *latomus*: machun / *ruder*: fosse / [62] *manutergium*: toalie / *pertica*: perche / *incidie*: enwez / *cutellus*: cutel / *cultrum*: anglice culter [455] / *salsarium*: sausir / *sculptum*: peinture / *candalabrum*: chaundelir / *absconsa*: sconse / *dolea*: tunneus / *uter*: bussel / *crater*: hanap, bascat [456] / *cophinus*: panier et bascat vel a lite ripe [457] / *coclear*: petit culiir / *clepsedra*: dusil / *pelvis*: basin / *corbes*: gallice corbail / *cisera*: cisre / *mustum*: must / *nectar*: piment / *pigmentum*: piment / *metior*: amesurir / *medus*: mede / *rosatum*: rosé / *rosarum*: rosir / *piretum*: piré / *ydromelum*: mede / *penula*: furure, pene, bifle / *manubium*: manche / *laciniis*: paunis / *lacerna*: bifle / *femoralia*: breis / *femur* -ris: quise de humme / [63] *opus*: overanie / *caligis*: chausis / *caligo*: chause / *caligo* -gas: oscurir / *caligo*: oççurté / hoc *pede*: forstelpel [458] / *pedica*: calketrap / *estivalibus*: est[i]vaus / *cusspida*: hoce [459] / *calceus*: chausure / *calx*: talun / hec *calx*: chause / *calleo*: endu[r]cir / *laqueatus*: lacé / *laqueus*: gallice laçun, gallice laz vel surcote / *lacus*: laz de maysun / *lacunar*: post de maysun / *camicia*: chemise / *cindo*: sendel / *sericum*: seye / *bissi*: chesil / *lini*: lin / *lino* -nis: enoindre / *mantellum*: a femme / *pallium*: mantel a humme et a femme / *pirolus, speriolus, esperiolus*: idem sunt .s. esscurel / *cuniculus*: cuniz / *ferrus*: fer de chival / *ocrea*: hose / *equitium*: gallice harras / *admitto*: alecher / *ebeto*: ferit chival / *villus*: flocun / *ancellare*: truser devant / *postcellare*: trusir derere / *camus*: bernac / (top of f.106ra) *ansellare*: truser / *coxa*: quise / [65] *catum volatile*: curtine / *herodius*: ostur / *tercellus*: tercel / *falco*: faucun / *falco peregrinus*: girfauc / *ardarius*: herunir / *gruarius*: gruer / *perizoma*: cheinse / *lumbare*: vesture de reins / *ventrale*: wardecors / *limatum*: sullé / *cirma*: vesture trainant / [66] *teristrum*: riverocet / *glomus*: lissel / *serapelina*: solupé / *recinium*: keinse ridlé / *colustrum*: mege / *bubulcus*: bovir / [67] *obsonium*: supir / *oxigalla*: egre leit / *aspersorium*: wisspiliun / *admiror*: amirir u amerveliir / [68] *vallum*: bayl / *vallus*: paliz / *cancellus*: chansel / [69] *cansellus*: kernel / *hinulus*: foun / *hynulum*: escaleine / *hilla*: andulie / *tuceta*: trunsun / *posticus*: posterne / *ancile*: talevaz / [70] *salio* (-lis, -lui vel-ii vel-ivi, saltum): saliir et idem *salio* -is: chanter / *vinea*: berfroi / *tubicen*: businur / *troiampium*: burdis hu turnament / *prevarictor*: despisur / *plebi statutum*: estabelement de puples / *sicarius*: murdisur / *enector*: alasur / *frugalitas*: escarceté / [71] *stratillates*: cunestablis / *stantelum*: estandard / *tumultuarius*: feysont noyse / *stipendium*: soude / *clangator*: defiur / *caduciator*: acordur / *manice*: maniclis de fer / *excubia*: wete / *batus*: provendir / *acasciculus*: butelir / *assecretus*: chamblein / *triticum*: blé batu / *gallinarius*: chapun /

---

[455] See MED sub *culter* n.
[456] See MED sub *basket* n.
[457] See OED sub *rip* sb.[1].
[458] I do not know this word.
[459] See MED sub *hok* n.

gallinacius: kokerel / [72] *ciconia*: cigoine / *merges*: plungun / *pavo*: poun / *fulex*: mauviz / hic et hec *alimbis*: popler / *alcio*: widekoc / *alveus*: auge / *sonovectorium*: civere / *apodiamentum*: apuail / *assidue* equivocum pro 'asiduel' et pro 'eysé' / *assiduitas*: eise / *livideo*: enbloir / *troclea*: windas / [73] *sindex*: warence, mader / [74] *solicitudo*: curuseté / [155] *tesqua*: wassel / *poples*: gallice garet / [156] *cantus*: gant / *cruspulus* (= scrupulus): pere / *atrium*: gallice curt / [157] *vestibulum*: porche / *porticus*: porche / *tingulum*: gallice petit ccheverun / *doma*: gallice fest, anglice rof / *culmus*: gallice caume / *arundo*: gallice rosel / [165] *venatio*: gallice veneisun / *pireta*: robur de mir / *foratorium*: tarere / [167] *apendex*: agnice / *pluteum*: carole / *bipennis*: ache deneche / *ylum*: meule de la penne / *veres*: s[e]nglir dameche / [169] *evaporo*: yssir / *bractea*: pece / *lamina*: pece de metal

MS WORCESTER CATHEDRAL CHAPTER LIBRARY Q.50

[60] *familie sue*: a sa meyné / in *utensilibus*: en outelmens / *supellectilibus*: pety outelemens / *coquina*: cusyne / *mensula*: pety table / *olus*: cholet / *minuatur*: seit myncé / *pise*: peis / *pultes*: gruelus / *fabe frese*: fevus [m]oles (?) / *fabe silique*: ov lei cose / *exilique*: san ley cose / *milium*: mil / *cepe*: oynonus / *huiusmodi*: çou maner / *legumina*: potage / *resecari*: estre trenché / *olle*: pos / *tripodes*: trepeys / *morterium*: morter / *securis*: coyné / *pilus*: pestés / *contus*: movet / *uncus*: croc / *cacabus*: cauderoun / *aenum*: pot de arreme / *patella*: payele / *creagra*: havet / *craticula*: credyl / *urceoli*: possenés / *discus*: esquele / *par[ap]sis*: plater / *salarium*: saucer / *artavi*: knyvés / *gurgustio*: rey / *fuscina*: foyn / *hamite*: boyt [460] / *nassa*: nasse / *vivario*: viver

[61] *[amo]llum*: flur / *sincerati*: enclersi / *abditorio*: estu / *allucia*: lavurs / *entera*: les entrayls / *extremitates*: foreyntés / *proiciantur*: seynt . . . [j]etés / *coclear*: lusche / *spuma*: espume / *ebulationes*: buyluns / *excaturizata*: estre escaudez / *mola*: mole / *piperalis*: a peyvre / *mola*: mole / [f.5v] *mugiles*: sumuns / *amphinia*: porpeys / *congrus*: cungre / *murena*: laumprey / *musculus*: baleyne / *empimera*: esperling / *gobio*: gujoun / *melanurus*: bars de mer / *capito*: caboche / *ypotamus*: cheval de mer / *morus*: morue / *pelamides*: pleyz / *mulus*: muluel / *uranoscopus*: ray

[62] *dentrix*: haket [461] / *megarus*: makurel / *turtur*: turbot / *allecia*: hareng / *gomarus*: espynoche / *ostris*: oistre / *bocca marina*: buf de mer // later (s.xiv/xv) glosses which are still legible are: *caseorum*: formages / *candelabrum*: chandelabre / in *promtuario*: en le celer / *cadi*: bareles / *clepsedre*: dosels / *pelves*: bassinis / [f.6r] *lambris*: leckurrus / *sitis*: seyf / *perendinaturus*: le homme a sougurner / *birris*: gerouns / *manubiis*: maunchis / *femoralibus*: de brays / *pudibunda*: le huntose chose

[63] *caligiis*: de chauces / *calceis laqueatis*: chauces lacees / *sindonis*: sandel / *equitaturus*: a chivaucer / *capam*: chape / *manubiatam*: maunché / [f.6v] et *admittendo*: e a less[er] cure / *ferri*: ferés / *clavis*: clouuss / *firmati*: fermés / *tergum*: le dos / *coopertum*: coverét / *carentivillo*: canevas / *cella*: la cele / *collocetur*: seyt mis / *tenuis*: frengis /

---

460 See DMLBS sub *ames* ('beam, pole', 'fishing rod') and cf. Gfry 1, 676b sub *boitel* and 676c sub *boitoir*.
461 See MED sub *haket* n.

sudarii: suaere / *clunem*: croupe / *strepe*: estruus / *dependeant*: dependent / *arculi*: arsuns / *antela*: arsun devont / *postela*: [arsun] derere

[64] *antellas*: coreys devont / *postellas*: e derere(re) / *vestes*: vesturus / *sub involucro*: trossel / *in mantica*: en le trussel / *disponantur*: ordeynés / *pectorale*: peytrel / cetere *phalere*: e autre herneys / *usui equita[n]t(u)is*: a le husage de li chivauchant / *necessarie*: bossenablis [462] / *non omittantur*: ne sey[n]t pays lessez / *chamum*: bernacle / *capistrum*: chevestre / *freynum*: freyne / *lupatum*: chaunfer / *habenas*: reines / *singulas*: senglus / *lingulas*: hardeloun / *pulvillum*: hardeloun [463] / *pulvillum*: bases / *pusculas*: bucles / *trussula*: trosele / *garcio*: garsoun / *sive pedes*: hou es pé / *strigilem*: estrile / *camera*: chanbur / *ambiat*: avirounit / *cortina*: curtine / *canopeum*: coverture / a *stilis*: pilers / sive *epistilis*: hou del parti desut de p[i]ler / *tapetum*: tapé / sive *tapete*: ou chaloun / *dependeant*: dependent /

[65] [f.7r] return to interl. gl. contemporary with main text: *supara*: rochet / *perizoma*: brays / *capa*: chape / *palleum*: mantel / *toga*: gunele / *collobium*: froc / *instita matronalis*: chemyse a dame / *lumbarie*: braiel / *ventrale*: wardecors / *non limata*: vestures suylés / *aspergenes*: longe chemyse / *sparta cirmata*: vestures traylans / *longa*: lunge / *cirofea*: cheynse / *lodices teatrale[s]*: dras a puteyne / *terestrum*: rochet ridelé / *mataxa*: cerenz / *aurifrigurii*: orfreys

[66] [f.7v] *spinter*: fiçaile / *fuscotincti*: fustian / *colaria*: colers / *torques*: bues / *et inaures*: e aneles / *acera*: esquirailus / the following glosses are later and only just legible: *in festivis diebus*: en jours de festins / *matronales*: de dames / *serapeline*: . . .lleceus / *teristrum*: roket / *subulces*: porchers / *bubulces*: bovers / *armentariis*: les vachers

[67] in hand contemporary with the text: *colustrum*: busting / *occigallum*: let egre / *quactum*: crem / *in cimbiis*: en anaps / in later hand, very faint: *in obsoniis*: en sopers / *catulis*: a caelus / *pingue*: . . . mekes / [f.8r] *piperis*: de peyvre / *aspercionem*: parpilouns / *auca*: owie

[68] in large hand (s.xiiiex): *phillidis*: de alemaunder / later, pale glosses continue [67]: *dum sit tenera*: dementeris ke el set tendur / *in veru*: en spitte / *longo*: long / *circumvoluta*: environturné / *alliatam*: aylé / *fortem*: forte / *desiderat*: deseryt / *vino*: vine / *vel succo viridi*: ou de verg[us] / *racemorum*: de reccins / *silvestrum*: de bous / *galina*: gelinis / *scaturizata*: eçcaudé / *membratim*: en membre / *divisa*: devisé / *cumino*: comine / *condiatur*: savorritt / *assata*: roçté / *crebris*: sovers / *lardi*: de larde / *condimentum*: savorment / *alliate*: sause / *sapidissima*: tres savorré / cum *simplici salsa*: o simple sauce / *pisses*: pessouns / *exinterati*: debouellé / in *salsa*: en sauce / *aqua*: e de ewe . . . sount quites / cum *viridi sapore*: o verte sause / cum *pipere*: o pevere / *allea*: ayle / *salgea*: sauge / *petrosillum*: persil / *costa*: coste / *ditanium*: ditaine

[68] *conformetur*: set conformé / *color*: le colour / *claritati*: a clereté / *scintille*: de sentele / *Parvi Pontane veritatis*: de la verité de Petite . . . / *equiparetur*: set enuilé / *dilicatum*: delié / *bissis*: chaysel / *frigidatem*: freydurs / *excedat*: passet / *si castrum*: si le chaçtel / *decenter*: avenontment / *muniat*: garnet / *mota*: de la mot (sic) / *nativam*:

---

462 See AND sub *bosoignable*.
463 Presumably a scribal dittography.

natyve / *ripam* (corr. rupem): roche / *sedem*: du sege (sic) / *beneficium*: le benefet / ut *muralis moles*: ky pesauntyme de mur / *cemento*: morter, pere / *lapidibus*: de peris / *arduum*: haut / *opus*: ofrayn / *erigatur*: seit endrecé / *sepes*: hay / *palis*: peus, paleys / *quadrangulis*: quartés / *vepribus*: rounces, brer[464] / *pungentibus*: poynauns / *bene*: beyen / *postmodum*: enaprés / *vallum*: bayli / *amplis*: larges / *gaudeat*: enjoyt / *interstitiis*: espaces / *fundamentum*: le fundeme[n]t(um) / *venis*: veynis / *terre*: de tere / *supereminentes*: haus aparauns / *columpnis*: de pelers / *collacatis*: mys / *appodientur*: seint espoués / *superficies*: la somet le edefise

[69] *trulle*: de truel / *equitatem*: oueleté / *cementarii*: de masoun / *operam*: entente / *cancelli*: kerneus / *debitis*: par due spices (corr. spaces) / *distinguantur*: seint departis / *portionibus*: porceuns / *propugnacula*: britages / *pinne*: turres / *eminenti*: aparisant / *loco*: lu / *sitam*: mys / *muniant*: garnisunt / *crates*: cleys, hurdeles / *eiciendos*: or jett(r)és / *castrum*: chaçtel / *incidiatur*: seyt ensegé / *defensores*: de defendurs / *cogantur*: seyn[t] costraynt / *blado*: blé / *pernis*: pernys / *baconibus*: bacouns / *in succidio*: en sous / *hillis*: andulus / *salsuciis*: saucys / *tuscetis*: agys / *suilla*: de porc / *carne*: de char / *bovina*: de buf / *arietina*: de motoun / *ovina*: owayl / *leguminibus*: potages / *diversis*: dyvers / [f.9r] *scaturiente*: surdaunt / *posticibus*: posternes / *cataractibus subterraneis*: veis desou la tere / *opem*: eyde / *latenter*: privément / *incedant*: departont / *assint*: seynt / *lancee*: launces / *catapulte*: sete barbés / *ancilia*: rounde escus / *pelte*: talevaz / *fundibule*: mangoneus / *funde*: lenges / *baleares*: de cel lu / *sudes ferrei*: peus de fer / *baliste*: aleblaster / *clave*: maçus / *nodose*: nuouse / *fustes*: bautonus / *torres*: tourus[465] / *ignem*: fu / *obsidentium*: de preseauns / *elidentur*: seint usdés[466] / *enerventur*: seint enfeblés / *ari[e]tes*: [mo]touns / *vites*: tribuchés / *crates*: cleys / *cetere machine*: autre engynis / *manni*: palefreyus / *dextr(er)arii*: deytrerus / *gradarii*: chasurus / *usui militum*: a le usage de chival[er] / *apti*: costiabulment[467] / *exeuntibus*: hors issouns / *animentur*: seint encoragé

[70] *tube*: businus / *tibie*: estivius / *litui*: greles / *buxus*: flegés / *cornu*: corn / *acies*: cumpanye / *exercitus*: hout / *tribunis*: a coneçtables / *militie*: de chuvalerie / *ordinabuntur*: serrunt ordenés / *prosilent*: ors sailent / *troianum*: turnement / *hastuludium*: joustus / *astiledium*: burdis / *succensorii*: chasours / *vernis*: serjauns / *vispilionibus*: roburs / *coterellis*: sergauns a pé / *in castro*: en le chaçtel / *viri*: bers / *prudentes*: co[i]ntes / *inconsulte*: decounselement / *mitius agatur*: seyf [f]et / *disgrassatores*: le deverours[468] / *legirumpi*: brusourus [de] ley / *clepi*: larouns / *abactores*: larounus de beytes / *siccari[i]*: mordisurs / *multatores*: tuourus / *fustigentur*: seint bateus / *puniantur*: serrunt punys / [f.9v] *capitali sententia*: par chef sentense / *condempne[n]tur*: seyn[t] dammés / *sapiat*: savouret / *in habundantia*: en plenté / *ex signo sensibili*: en [. . .]sencible / *opinio*: quidauns

[71] *stratilates*: sergauns / *decertantibus*: estrivans / *statelum*: standart / *maneat*: mainet / *inconcussum*: ne[n]t depessé / *victoriam*: victorie / *belli*: batali / non *laudabiliter*: neun

---

464 See MED sub *brer* n.
465 An erroneous gloss which renders *turres*.
466 i.e. *ostés*.
467 I do not recognise this word.
468 MS = *le de verours*. Other MSS include the glosses *verreiurs* and *wereurs*. Cf. AND sub *guerreur*.

loiabulment / *triplex*: treble / *ordo*: order / *militum*: de chivalors / *assint*: seint / *milites*: chivalors / *decertantis*: d'eçtrivans / *telorum*: de tarces / *ducis donativa*: garsouns / *stipendium*: loiiers / *carceres*: presounes / *fundo*: fund / *compediti*: enfergés / *detrudantur*: seynt debotés / *manicis*: maunchis / *ferreis*: ferés / *positi*: mys / *cippi*: stokkes / *columbaria*: pelerus / *excubie*: waites / *strepitum*: noys / *sonitum*: soun / *facientes*: fesauns / in *granario*: en gerner / *ostorium*: strike / *corus*: mesurus / *batus*: bussel / *diverse*: diverse / *tece*: mesurus / *frumenti*: formente / *ordei*: orge / *siliginis*: segle / *avene*: aveynes / *steriles*: barrcile (?) / *pulles*: poucines / *galli*: kokes / *galine*: gelinis / *gallinacii*: kokerles / *altilia*: capouns / *anceres*: owes / [f.10r] *anates*: anes

[72] *auce*: owys / *sigonie*: sigoynis / *ardee*: herrouns / *facidos*: phaysouns / *libie*: gruis / *mergites*: plonguns / *galli palustres*: kokes de boys / *pavones*: paunus / in *stabulo*: en le çstabul / *presepe*: scrache / *are*: porcheri / *alveoli*: auges / *strigilis*: eçtrilis / *chamus*: bernacl / *cenovectorium*: sivere, barwe / *epiredium*: rongustane (?) / *capistrum*: chevestre / *phalere*: harneys / *equorum*: de chival / *textor*: tisur / *eques*: chivaler / *duarum*: deus / *streparum*: eçtrus / *adnitens*: forsouns / *apodiamento*: de l'apuement / *admittit*: lessyt / *assidue*: asiduelment / *exili*: peti / *contentum*: apayé / *dieta*: journé / *scansilia*: eçtrus / *fortune*: de aventure / *conditionem*: condissioun / *mutua*: chonchabul / *deprimitur*: sey[t] envalé / *torcleam*: windas / *circumvolubile*: environtornable / *pannus*: drape / *evolvendus*: a turner / *maritari*: eçtre reyeié [469] / *trabales*: trefus, bemus [470] / *columbaribus*: de pertus / *distinctas*: departés / *diversa*: diverse / *regione*: regioun / *respicientes*: reteysouns / *cavillis*: kyvilis / *pedorum*: de batu[n]s a berchers / *trabibus*: trevis / *tenorem*: tenur / *telem*: teyle / *ambientibus*: avirounons / *licia*: file / *teniis*: frengis / *associentur*: seyn[t] acumpanés / *stamen*: eçtaym / *deducat*: warput / *supponendum*: a sumettre / *quam superponendum*: ke a surmettur / *trama*: tremme

[73] *beneficio*: benefise / *navicule*: de navet / *transmissa*: outre veyé / *opus*: ofrayne / *consolidet*: afermet / *pano*: broche / *ferreo*: de ferse (sic) / *ligneo*: de fuçte / *muniatur*: sey[t] garny / [f.10v] *infra*: entre / *fenestralas* (sic): lé fenestres / *vestiatur*: seyt vestu / *penso*: file / *trame*: treyme / *manus altera*: autre mayn / *nav[i]culam*: nawet / *jaculetur*: jettét / in *sociam manum*: a cumpenable mayn

[161] [f.14r] glosses in red (s.xiii): *capulus*: pumel / *alumnosa*: arsilous / *retinacula*: les artus [471]

[162] *stercorare*: composter / *saligna*: de sauz / *aut fimo*: ou fen / *resarcire*: reneveler / *veracta*: warés / *rebinare*: rebiner / aut *creta*: o marle / *stipulis*: stobles / *thecis*: forés [472]

---

[469] See TL 8,1411 sub *roiier*.
[470] See MED sub *bem n*.
[471] i.e. *les harts*.
[472] The glosses in this section are entered in red.

CHAPTER NINE

JOHN OF GARLAND'S *DICTIONARIUS*

THE CAMBRIDGE, DUBLIN AND LINCOLN MANUSCRIPTS [1]

[1] [2] in *scrinio*: crofe,[3] escrene (C) en le wiche (D) [4] / de *lignis*: de fuz (D) / *tenetur*: es[t] tenu (D*) / *promtuarium*: le gerner (D*) /

[2] *calosa*: durasye (L) endurci (C) / *talus*: taloun (C) talon (D) / *rotundus*: rond (D) / *articuli*: lé ortyz (C) ortays (L) / *unguibus*: ungles (C) / *collateralis*: anfeysenable (D) / *sophena*: grosse veyne (D*) / *caville*: kyvll (C) kevil, onkele (D) [5] / *columpna*: piler (CD*) un piler (D) / *corporis edificium*: la messere (D*) / *os*: le os (C) osse (L) / *concavum*: croz (C) crose (L) croisse (D) / *medulla*: la meule (C) de mewle (D*) de meul .s. anglice maire (L) [6] / *musculus*: le muscel, le braoun (C) brahun (D) muscel, calf (D*) [7] anglice muscel (L) / *cartilago*: le tendroun, gruselbon (C) le tendrun (D) grisiler (D*) grisselir, anglice gristel, braun (L) [8] / *musculum*: a. faxwax (C) [9] braoune (D) / *poples*: garez (C) la garet (D) garet (D*) garret, anglice omme (L) [10] / *genu*: genul (C) genil (L) / *internodium*: le os de genul (C) tut la ordainement, le entrenou (D) [11] entre-ordeynement, entre-space (D*) entre-ordenement (L) / *crus*: la quise (C) la quisce (D) quise (D*) la quisse (L) / *pubi*: gallice penul, au penul (C) penele (?) (D) penuley, anglice schere (L) [12] / *marietur*: seyt baly (D*)

[3] *rusticitati*: a vilenie (D) / *tria genitalia*: tres membres gendrabel (D*) / *valva*: wiket (D) / *vulva*: cune (L) / *matrix*: la matrice (D) / *prope peritoneon*: gallice circele (proprie circulum culi rugalem) a la partye derere (C) pre du cercle de gul (D) cercel (D*) de cercel de culley (L) / *in umbilico*: umbil (C) en sun umblil (L) en le umbile (D) / *renibus*: reyns (C) / *nates*: lé nages (CD) nagis (D*) nages vel crupes (L) / *tergum*: dos (D*) / *spondilia*: lé juntures (C) ruchbon [13] et sunt iuncture: eschines (C*) lé chenez (L) [14] lé eschines (D) eschine (D*)

[4] *tentiginem*: laundeye (D) laundey (D*) laundye, kiker (L) [15] / *mempirium*: tortiz (D) torchun de cul (L) / *culum*: cul (D*) / *podicem*: poytroun (C) poytron (D) poytrun (D*) poitrun (L) / *latera*: couste (C) coutes (D) cowtes (D*) costez (L) / *lacertos*: bras (C) brays (D) bracis (D*) brace (L) / *cubitos*: coute (C) coutes (D) coutis (D*) cues (L) / *palmas*: paume (C) paumes (D) pawmis (D*) manz (L) / *pollicem*: le poz (D) poucer (D*) pocer (L) / *ungues*: ungles (C) / *indicem*: grant dey

---

1   There are two copies in the Dublin MS, see vol. 1, p.192.
2   I adopt Scheler's paragraphing, which concords with the divisions in many of the MSS, for ease of comparison (for the vernacular glosses) and reference.
3   i.e. cofre.
4   See Gfry 8,333a sub *wiche* and FEW 17,428b (*vik*).
5   See MED sub *ancle* n.
6   See MED sub *marwe* n.(1).
7   See MED sub *calf* n.(2).
8   See MED sub *crushel-bon* n. and *gristel* n. See also AND sub *braun* and MED sub *braun* n.
9   See MED sub *fax-wax* n.
10   See MED sub *hamme* n.(1).
11   MS = *le entre rou*. See FEW 7,173a which gives *entreneu* 'gros du genou' with the dates 1487 and 1530.
12   See TL 7,650 sub *penil* and OED sub *share* sb.[2]. Cf. WW 250,25 *pubes: anglice schere*.
13   See OED sub *ridgebone* and *rig-bone*.
14   L has *spondalia*.
15   See MED sub *kekir* n.

(L) demoustrer (D)[16] / *digitos*: deys (D) / *medium*: miuuel (D*) / *auricularem*: le petiz dei (D) petit dey (L) / *humeros*: les espaudles (CD) les payles (L) / *acellas*: asseles (C) esseles (C*) les asseles, harme-puttes (D)[17] esselis (D*) essel (L) / *homoplata*: grant oz de spadle (D) grant os de pys (L) / *torax*: gallice gambesoun (C) cel oz du piz (D) os de pus (L) / *munimen*: caubesun (D) / *gutture*: gorge (C)

[5] *fontinella*: fontaynele (C*) fontinele (D) f(r)ontinel (D*) / *cornua*: cornes (D) / *pirula*: bek de nez, becheroun (C)[18] le bek devant (D) pec de nes (D*) bek de nes (L) / *naris*: naril (C) narilis (D) nariel (D*) naril (L) / *colera*: colre (D) / *interfinium*: le entre-pace (D) entre-pas (D*) entr'espasce de nes (L) / *lingua*: lange (C) / *palatum*: palaht (C) le palat (D) palat (L) / *guttur*: gorge (C) jorge (D*) / *dentes*: denz (C) / *gingiva*: gensivez (C) la gingive (D) gensive (L) / *uvula*: huvel (CD) uvele (D*) uvel (L) / *gula*: gule (C) boche (L) / *labra*: leverz (C) / *mala*: joue (C) / *ysophagus*: gorgeron (C) anglice wossu[n]de, gallice gorgerun (C*)[19] le gargat, wosinde (D)[20] gorgerun (D*) / *epiglotum*: le gargat (C) le bouwel (D) buel (D*) boel (L)[21] / *palpebra*: paupebre (C) paupers (D) pauper (D*L) / *cilium*: cyl (C) cil (D) / *pupilla*: purnele (C) purnerel (D) purnel (D*L) / *tunica sclirotica*: la cotele (C) le dur pel del eul (D) pel (D*) pel dé oiles (L) / *supercilio*: au surcil (D) / circa *discrimen*: entour la greve (C) la greve (D) la greve a. sched (D*)[22] greve de chef (L) / *capilli*: chevet (D)

[6] in *cerebro*: en la servele (C) en le cervel (D) cervel (D*) / sub *craneo*: desouz la teye (C) sur (sic) la teye (D) cervelere (D*)[23] / *ymaginaria*: ymaginere (CD) pensable (DD*L) / *memorialis*: remembrable (D) remenbrable (D*) / *pulmo*: le pomoun (C) le pomun, longone (D) pomun, lungis (D*)[24] pumuun (L) / *flabellum*: le flael (C) la venetyle (D) ventilabre (D*) ventilable (L)[25] / *refrigeratur*: est refrydi (D*) seyt enfredy (L) / *decoquitur*: est defye (D*) / per *venas miseraycas*: par lé meyne veynes (D) / *mesaicas* (sic): miluel (D*)[26] / *epar*: a la feye (D) feye (D*) faye, la faye (L) / *flegbotomator*: le seynour (C) li seyner (D*) seynur (L) / cum *flegbotomo*: o le seiné (D) ov sun fleme (D*) / ab *epate*: de feye (D*) la feye, livere anglice (L)[27] / *minuit*: seynit (D*) / *originem*: nessaunce (D*) / *indigenti*: viro, abosisant (D*)[28] /

16 See TL 2,1390 sub *demostreor* and AND sub *demustrur*.
17 See MED sub *arm-pit* n.
18 FEW 1,306a cites MF *bequeron*. TL 1,894 prints only the example given by Scheler, *art. cit.*, 289 and Gfry 1,606c adds one example from an MS of *Perceval* and another from the 16th C.
19 See OED sub *weasand*.
20 The gloss *gargat* is presumably displaced from the next item.
21 Cf. the equally erroneous gloss *stomac* cited by Scheler, *art. cit.*, 289.
22 See OED sub *shed* sb.[1]2.
23 See TL 10,356 sub *toie* and 2,138 sub *cerveler*.
24 See MED sub *longe* n.
25 See Gfry 8,177b sub *ventilabre* and *ventile* and FEW 14,252a sub *ventilabrum* and *ventilare*.
26 In the text the gloss looks like *misuel*, but the right-hand margin clearly bears the entry *misaicas .s. miluel .g.* The word *miluel* appears to render *medium*, for the etymology of the lemma is given as 'a mesos, quod est medium', see Scheler, *art. cit.*, 290. Cf. the earlier gloss [4] *miluel* on *medium* = middlefinger.
27 See MED sub *liver(e* n.*(1)*.
28 A misreading of *abesognant*?

cistis fellis: pel de fel (D*) a la pel (L) / *splen*: anglice mylte (C) milte (L) [29] / *coleram*: colre (CD*) / per *cirbum et longaonem*: par (el)el boel, par autre boel (L) / *zirbum*: buel (C*) / *longaonem*: buel (C*)

[7] *splen*: esplen (C) / *ren*: renoun, kydeneye (C) [30] renun (L) in singulari numero reinun, in plurali numero reins (C*) / *lien*: bouwel (D) buel (D*) boel (L) / *lientera*: gallice menesun (D*) / *diafragma*: teye, a. midrif (C) le fresuwe, midrid (D) mid-derim (D*) midrif (C*) [31] / *dividit*: departist (D*)

[8] *urbana*: corteys (C) de burg (C*) de cité (L) / *rusticana*: de camp (L)

[9] ad *laqueos*: a laz (C) a las (L) / *liripipiis*: pigaz (CC*) pigacis (D*) pigas (L) / ad *plusculas*: a. boucles, piket (C) [32] boucles (D) bucles (D*) bukeles (L) / *tibialia*: estyveuz, estivalia idem vel hesez (C) estivés (L) stiveus (C*) / *cruralia*: quiseuz (C) quisers, huses (D) husis (D*) esses (L) [33] / *crepitas*: botez (C) botes (C*L) / *crepitas femineas*: bothes a femme (D) botis de femmis, et *monachales*: botis de moinis (D*)

[10] *corrigiarii*: ceynturers (C) lé escurreours (D) cories (C) coreres (L) / *zonas*: seyntures (C) seynturus (D) / *rubeas*: vermayles (L) / *membratas*: barrés (CD*L) barreys (D) / *ferro*: de fer (L) / *cupro*: de quyvere (C) quivre, copur (D) [34] de guivere (L) / *texta*: seyntes tysuez (C) sey tissu, de sey (L) ceynte de sceye (D*) / *stipata*: gallice barré (C) barré (D*) barrés (L)

[11] *sellarii*: celers (C) lé sellers (D) li selers (D*) celerres (L) / *sellas*: selez (C) / *panellos*: paneuz (C) panews (D*) panels (L) / *pulvillos*: baz (C) bates (C*) batis (D*) basez (D) / *pusillos*: basis (L) / *carentivillas*: kanevaz (C) canevas, kanevasce (D) canewas (D*) canefas (L) / *trusullas*: troseus (C) truses (L) / *strepas*: estrus (C) gallice estriue (C*) lé estrues (D) / *strigiles*: estrilz (CD)

[12] *scutarii*: lé escueors (D) escuers (D*) les ecures (L) / *Gallie*: Franse (D) / *scuta*: eskuz (C) scueys (L) / *tela*: teile (D) / *scuta tecta*: covertes de huge, drap (L) [35] / *coreo*: de quyr (C) / *oricalco*: orpeter, gallice orcauz (C) de fil de orochal (D) orchaut (D*) de orchat (L) / *liliorum*: de liz (C) liles (D*) de lilis (L)

[13] *plusculariii*: lé bouclers (C) buclers (C*D) bukelers (D*) buchelers (L) / *plusculas*: boucles (C) bucle (C*) bouglus (D) bocheles a talun (L) / *lingulas*: hardilonz (C) hardilionss (D) hardiluns (C*D*) ardiluns (L) / *mordacula*: mordaunz vel pendaunz (C) mordanz (C*) mordauns (DD*) pendauns (L) / *limas*: filez (C) limes, fils (D)

---

29 See MED sub *milt(e* n.
30 See MED sub *kide-nere* n.
31 See MED sub *miggern* n. The *Cambridge Nominale* ed. Skeat, 73–4 has 'Veynes rate et farsue / veynes mygge and mydreme'. Scheler, *art. cit.*, 291 gives *la fressure* as a variant gloss, see also FEW 3,778b (2a) & 814b and TL 3,ii,2293 sub *froissure*.
32 See MED sub *bokel* n. *Piket* is perhaps a gloss on *liripipium* (top of p.33) = *pigace*, see TL 7,929 'cauda caputii acuminata'.
33 See TL 4,1218 sub *huese*.
34 See MED sub *coper* n.
35 TL 4,1191 sub *houce* gives one example of the sense 'Überzug des Schildes'.

filis (D*) limes (L)[36] / *loralia equina*: loreynz de chival (C) lorey[n]is (D*) lorens de chival (L)

[14] in *foro*: en marché (L) / *acus*: agul (C) agules (L) / *acuaria*: agulers (C) aculers (D) aguere (D*) aguleres (L) / *saponem*: savoun (C) savon (D) sawn (D*) sope, savun (L)[37] / *specula*: mirours (C) mirores (L) / *rasoria*: rasours (C) rasors (L) / *fusillos*: fusils (C) fusils, anglice spindlen[38] (C*) fusilleus (L) / *cotes*: coeus (C) agezurs (D) cous (D*) cues (L) / *pirricudia*: fusils, anglice furyrn (C)[39] fusils (D)

[15] *lorimarii*: les lorimers (C) lorimers (D*) / *diliguntur*: sunt amés (L) / *calcaria*: esporounz (C) / *argentata*: surargenté (D*) / *aurata*: suzoré (D*) / *pectoralia*: petereuz (C) paytreus (D) petrerews (D*) pecterés (L) / *resonantia*: sonaunz (C) / *fabricata*: forgés (L)

[16] *institorem*: bargynour (C) marchant (D*L) / *cultellos*: coteuz (C) grant cuteus (L) / *artavos*: knyvez (C) petit chinevés (L) / *vaginas*: waynes (C) / *stilos*: poy[n]teuz (C) grefes (DL) graffis (D*) / *stilaria*: graffes (C) greffers (D) graffers (D*) greferes (L)

[17] *cumulant*: muncelent (L) / *eruginatores vel exeruginatores*: forbeours (C) furburs (D) furbeurs (D*) furborus (L) / *gladios*: des espees (C) escuez (D) des epeys (L) / *exeruginatos*: forbez (C) ben furbez (D) forbyes (L) / *tholos*: pomels (C) lé pumés (D) pomellis (D*) pomeus (C*) pomeys (L) / *capulos*: capeus (C) e lé heutes (D) hultis (D*) hautes (L)[40] / *rutilantes*: asplendizans (L) resplendisaunz (C) esplendisans (D) / *novas vaginas*: escaubercs (C) novel gains (L)

[18] *mercatores*: les merchaunz (C) marchaundurs (D) marchans (L) / *capistra*: cheveystres (C) chevestres (D) / *lumbaria*: brayels (C) braels (DL) / *ligulas*: layners (CD*) laynners (D) laneres (L) / *marsupia*: bourses (C) burs (D*) bursus (L) / de *corio cervino*: de quir de cerf (D) de quir de cerve (L) / *ovino*: de owayle (D) de owaly (L) / *porcino*: de porc (DL)

[19] *cirotecarii*: gaunters (C) gaunterres (D) gauinters (D*) ganterrs (L) / *cirothecas*: gauns (D) / *furratas*: furrés (L) / *pellibus*: de peus (L) / *agninis*: de hainesz (L) / *cuniculinis*: de cunilis (L) / *vulpinis*: de gupiles (L) de gopil (D) / *mittas*: miteyns (C) gallice miteins (C*) myteyns (D) mitey[n]is (D*) miteunys (L) / de *coreo*: de quir (DL)

[20] *capellarii*: les chapilers (C) chapelers (D) chapellers (D*) chapeteres (L) / *capellas*: lur chaupeus (C) chapeus (DD*L) / de *fultro*: de feutre (CD*) de feutre, velt (D)[41] de fetre (L) / de *pennis pavonis*: de pennis de poune (D) de pououn (C) pococ (D*)[42] / *pillea*: hurez (C)[43] hures, hamuces (D) huris ou chapews (D*) chapés (L) chapel de cotun (C*) / de *bombace*: de cotoun (C) cotun (D) de cotun (D*L) /

---

36 See MED sub *file* n.(1).
37 See OED sub *soap* sb.
38 See OED sub *spindle* sb.
39 See MED sub *fir* 4(c) *fir-iren*.
40 See FEW 16,194b sub *helt* and MED sub *hilt(e* n.
41 See MED sub *felt* n.
42 See OED sub *peacock*.
43 See Scheler, *art. cit.*, 294–5 who notes the glosses *hures, huyre* and *hurez*, but cannot find

pilleola: lé petit hurettes (D)[44] petit chapews vel huris (D*) petit chapeus (L) / de *lana*: de layne (D) / de *pilis*: de poil (L)

[21] *architenentes*: archers (CC*L) aleblasters (D) archeers (D*) / *balistas*: aleblaust (C) aleblastes (D) harbblast (D*) arblastes (L) / *arcus*: arches (L) / de *acere*: de arable (C) de arabel, mapel (D)[45] arable, mapole (D*) arable (LC*) / *viburno*: de abourne (C) de aubur (D) de aburne (D*L) auburne (C*) / *taxo*: de yf (CC*) de yfe (D) de hif (L) / *tela*: dars (DD*) darz (C) / *sagittas*: setes (CD) / *petilia*: bosouns (C)[46] / de *fraxino*: de frene (DL) de freyne (D*)

[22] *firmacularii*: fermaleres (L) / *firmacula parva*: li firmaylis (D*) fermayles petits (L) / de *plumbo*: de plum (DL) / *ferro*: fer (D*) / de *stagno*: esteym (C) de staym (D) de steym (L) / *cupro*: de quyvere (C) de quivere (D) quire (sic) (D*) quivere (L) / *monilia*: nouchez (C) nuches (D) nouchis (D*) nuches (L) / *nolas*: caumpenoles (C) clochets, lé cheles (D) campirnolis, parvas campanas, gallice cheles (D*) choletes, senes, campernoles (L)[47]

[23] *artifices*: enginurs (D*) enchinurrus (L) / de *ere*: de arem (CD) / *campanas*: seynz (C) lé sayns (D) seins (L) / *sonoro*: sonable (L) / *motu*: par le movement (D) / *denuntiantur*: denuncient / *batillorum*: des bateuz (C) du batueles (D) de batews, claper (D*)[48] de baterés (L) / *cordarum*: e de cordes (D) de cordes (L) / *attractarum*: tretes

[24] *pictaciarii*: les takoners (C) saveters, takeners (D) saveters (D*) saveterz (L) / *consuunt*: cousint (D*) cusunt (L) / *renovando*: renoveland (L) / *pictacia*: takounz (C) tacuns (DD*) tachuns (L) / *intercutia*: rivez, waltez (C) erivetes, woltes (D) rivés, walte (D*) les riveys, les erivés (L)[49] / *soleas*: semeles (DL) soles (D*) / *inpedias*: empenes (D) enpeyns, wanpeys (D*) vampes, les pinnes (L)[50]

[25] *alutarii*: les corduaners (C) lé corduaners (D) cordewaners (D*) / de *aluta*: de corduan (C) de cordeuan (D) de corduwant (L) / *calciamenta*: chaucemens (D) chacement (D*) / *formipedias*: anglice lastes (C)[51] les formes (D) formes (D*C*) lé formes (L) / *equitibialia*: jaumbeuns (C) jambel (C*) chambeus (D) jaumbés (D*) jambés (L) / *spatulas*: esclices (CD) eclisis (D*) esclice (L)[52] / *alutarii*: les corduaners (C) corduwaners (L) / *secant*: grenchent (D)[53] / *corium*: quir (D) / *ansorio*: trenket (D) / *anserio*: trenchet (D*) / *ansario*: trenke(n)t (C) / *anserio*: trenncket (L)[54] /

---

any other attestations with the sense here. See now TL 4,1233–4, FEW 4,515b note 1 and MED sub *hure* n. and *hurer* n.(*1*).

44 I can find no other example of this diminutive form.
45 See MED sub *mapel* n.
46 See Du Cange sub *petilio* and TL 1,1100 sub *bouzon*.
47 See TL 2,202 sub *champenole* and MED sub *campernole* n. See also Gfry 3,381a sub *eschele*.
48 See DMLBS sub 3 *batellus* and MED sub *claper* n.(*1*)(*a*). FEW 1,289b gives the form *batail* and (292a) *batel*. L f.102vb has *noche* in the margin beside *nola*.
49 See OED sub *welt* sb.[1] and TL 8,1335 sub *rivet*.
50 See OED sub *vamp* sb.[1] and TL 3,i,95 sub *empeigne*.
51 See MED sub *lest(e* n.
52 See Glasgow Gloss. vol. 1, p.414 and ed. Ewert in Med. Aev. 25 (1957), 158 n.32.
53 Presumably an error for *trenchent*. There is a bar across the top of the *g*.
54 See TL 10,582 sub *trenchet*.

atramentario: anglice blec (C) gallice neiret .i. blech (C*) anglice blecce, de neyret (D) [55] neyret (D*) nerete (L) / *denigratum*: aneryé (L) / *calciamenta*: soulers (D*) / *subula*: alerne (CD) halene (D*) aleyne (L) / *lineo*: lionel (L) / *licinio*: linoyl (C) linol (D*) [56] / *seta porcina*: gallice seye de porc, anglice burstel (C) [57] un sey de porc (D) seye (D*) sey de porcke (L)

[26] *pelliparii*: parmenterz (C) lé peliters (D) pelters (D*) peleters (L) / *penulas*: panes (CL) pane (D) panis (D*) / *pellicia*: pelisouns (C) pelizons (D) pelsuns (D*) / *furraturas*: fururez (C) / *catinis*: de chat (CL) / *vulpinis*: de gopil, fox (C) [58] / *leporinis*: de levere (C) / *pelliparii*: lé peleters (D) peleters (D*) / *pelles*: peuz (C) / *deliciosas*: deleyes (D*) delyes (L) / *cuniculorum*: de conyz (C) de conigus (D) cuniis (D*) / *cirogrillorum*: de grans equireus (C) escurels (C*) equrés de Spanie (= hesperica) (D) esquiews (D*) de cureys (L) / *caprillorum*: de cheverys (C) / *lutriciorum*: de loutre (C) de loutres, outur (D) [59]lotres (L) / *(h)esperiolorum, ab Hesperia, -ie*: gallice lumbardie, des esquireus (C) de ecurels (D) de scurés (L) / *cyrogrillis*: loutres (D) / *mustelarum*: belets (L) de lelés (corr. belés) (C) de belez (D) / *cisimum*: de ver et gris (C) vayr e gris (D) ver et gris (D*) vere et gris (L) / *urlas*: hourles (C) / de *sabellino*: sablyn (C) / de *laerone*: gallice rat sauvage, leeroun (C) de cat savage (D) de laerun (D*) [60]

[27] *declamatores*: criours (C) / *pelliciorum*: de pelisouns (C) de pelsuns (D*) de pelisuns (L) / *reparandorum*: a refeters (C) / *reparant*: aparailunt (L) / *plateas*: rues (C) / *furraturas*: furores (L) / *furrumturas*: furreoures (D) / *epitogiorum*: surcoz (D) de surcotes (C) surcotis (D*) sorcohes (L) / *palliorum*: mauntels (C) de mauntels (D) de manteus (L) / *furando*: en emblaund (C) en emblant (D) emblant (L)

[28] *reparatores*: lé paraylurs (D*) mendurs (D) [61] reparilers (L) / *de murinis*: gallice de maser (C) de macere (D) gallice macer (D*) macere (L) [62] / *de planis*: de plane (CD) de pleines (L) / *de acere*: arable, mapel (C) de arable (DL) arable (D*) / *bruscis*: boyl, anglice birch (C) [63] brues, warre, berich (D) gallice brus, anglice warre (D*) [64] brossis (L) / *tremulo*: tremblere, hasp (C) [65] de trenbler, abse anglice (D) trembler (D*) strembler (sic) (L) / *[a]ereo*: de arem (C) de arram, orcal (D) areyme (D*) / *argenteo*: argent (D)

[29] *precones*: bedeus, bedels (D) [66] / *hyante gula*: hovert buche (D*) abayant (D) bayant par boche (L) / *ataminatum*: atamé (C) ataminé (L) / *fusum*: versé (D*)

---

55 See MED sub *blacche* n. and TL 6,602 sub *neret*.
56 See TL 5,455 sub *lignuel*.
57 See MED sub *bristel* n.
58 See MED sub *fox* n.
59 See MED sub *oter* n.
60 See TL 5,610 sub *loir*. The forms in *-on* given in FEW 4,155a are from the 16th C. Corr. the reading of D to *rat savage*.
61 See MED sub *mendere* n. where there is only one example (1425) of the sense 'repairer'.
62 See TL 5,769 sub *madre* and MED sub *maser* n.
63 See MED sub *birch(e* n. and *bil(e* n.
64 See OED sub *warre* (found, like *boil*, as a translation of *callus*) and TL 1,1176 sub *bruis* and FEW 1,574a sub *bruscum*. *Bruscus* is also known as 'butcher's broom' or 'knee-holly'.
65 See MED sub *aspe* n.
66 See MED sub *bidel* n.

apander (sic) (L) / *in craterem*: en un hanap (D) hanap (L) / a *lagena*: du galun (D) de galun (L)

[30] *guafrarum*: wafres (C) wafrus (D) de waferes (L) / *nebularum*: de nyuweles (C) de neules (D) nulis (D*) [67] / *pronunciant*: criunt (D) / *gafras*: wafres (D) wafris (D*) wafreis (L) / *artocreas*: russeus vel russoles (C) rusceus (D) rosseus (D*) russol (L) / *nebulas*: neules (D) / in *calathis*: in lé bachés (D) / *velatis*: covertes (D) / *manutergio*: taley, de tuaile (L) / *senione*: hasart (D*) hasard (L) / *perdidi senione*: perduz hasard (D) / *calathi*: paniers (C) baniers (D)

[31] *auctionarii*: lé regraters (C) regratours (D) gratirs (D*) recrateres (L) / *servas*: chamberers (L) / *cerasa*: cyries (C) cereses (D) ciriis (D*) chireberie, cerisses (L) [68] / *pruna*: prunes (CL) pruneis (D) / *pira*: peyres (C) / *lactucas*: letusez (C) letusers (D) letuse (D*) letue (L) [69] / *nasturcia*: kressouns (C) kersuns (C*) cressuns (D) cresuns (D*) cressun, carssez (L)

[32] *placente*: symeneus (C) simenel (D) symenus (D*) simenés (L) / *ignacie*: fouaz, anglice yerife kakez (C) fuaches (D) fuascis (D*) foache (C*) foaches (L) [70] / *flamicie*: flamechez, escaudyz (C) flamiches (DL) flamicis (D*) / *auctionarium*: de grateris (D) recrateres (L) / *sulphuratis*: sufrés (D) de suphre (L) / *lichinos*: mecchez (C) candele, limilun (D) limiunt (L) [71] / *linnos* (hic lingnus): candelis (D*) /

[33] *pistores*: petours (D) pesteres (L) / *pinsunt*: peystrent (C) pestrunt (L) pestrisint (D*) petunt (D) / *cocunt*: quisun (D*) / *pastam*: pauste (C) past (L) / *furno*: furne (L) / *territorio* [corr. tersorio]: escoviluns (D*) / *tersorio*: tersour, escoveloun (C) [72] escovelun (D) tayle (L) / *acere*: de curayl (D) mestilun (D*) [73] payle (L) / *furfure*: bren (CDD*L) / *pistores*: pestrers (L) / *pollitrudiant*: boleteynt (C) bultunt (DD*) boletuder (L) [74] / cum *pollitrudio*: ov le boletel (C) boltere (D) bultere (D*) boletel (L) / *delicato*: delié (C) delee (D) deleyé (D*) delyé (L) / *fermentum*: leveynne (C) levan (D) levein (D*) leveys (L) / in *alveo*: haugis (D) in auge (L) / *archas*: huchis (D) huches (D*) wiches (L) / *costa*: ryb, grate de past (D*) ov une grate (C) doȝrib (C*) un grater de pest ou le retuer (D) grad de paste, ribcurve (L) [75]

[34] *pastillarii*: pastilers (D*) pastillers (L) / *pastillos*: pasteus (D) pastriesz (L) / *anguillis*: de angulus (D) / *pullinis*: de poucins (C) de pusig (L) / *exponendo*: avaunt

---

67 See TL 6,659 sub *nieule*.
68 See MED sub *cheri* n.
69 For various forms see FEW 5,124b.
70 See TL 3,ii,1961 sub *föace*. WW 588,39 glosses 'chesekake'. The scribe of C writes y for thorn and, apparently for other letters, so that one must interpret *þerife* = tharf, see OED sub *tharf-cake*.
71 See the different forms of *limignon* in Gfry 5,52ab and TL 5,474.
72 See TL 3,i,992 sub *escovillon* and ibid. 10,270 sub *tersoir*.
73 See TL 5,1689 sub *mesteillon*.
74 See FEW 15,i,123 et seq. The form in L is not elsewhere attested.
75 See FEW 10,89a sub *rasitoria*. Bibbesworth ed. Owen 384/8/90 has *rastuer* = ribbe (var. *douw ribbe, trowh ryb, dou rib, the dourib*), see OED sub *rib sb.³*. For grate see MED sub *grate* n.(2) and FEW 16,374a (with only modern examples).

metant (D*) / *tartas*: tartes (CD) tartis (D*) tartes, abpel-chake (L)[76] / *flatones*: flaouns (C) flaun (L) / *fartos*, repletos: de farcir (L)

[35] *coquinarii*: quisineris (D*) quisinerz (L) / *vertunt*: turnunt (D) / in *verubus*: en broche vel espeye (C) brochis (D*) broches (L) / *columis*: de coudre (CDD*) de codre (L) / *anseres*: oues (C) jars (D*) lé gars, ouwes, aucas (D) garcis (L) / *altilia*: chapouns (C) / *carnes crudas*: crue chars (L) / *salsamentis*: saue (D) / *alliatis*: aylez (C) alyés (L) / *carnifices*: les massekenes (C)[77] bucher (D) bochers (L) / *macellis*: en estauz vel en la bocherie (C) bocheries (D) en lur estaus (D*) l'oystaus (L) / *porcinas*: de porc / *lepra percussas*: sursamis (D*) surseney (L)[78] / *macheras*: cuniez (C) lé coynis (D*) cuneys (L) / *mensaculas*: grans coteus (C) grant coteus (D) grant cotews (D*) grant cuteys (L) / *incutientes*: en bochaunz (C) hocschaunt (D)[79] / *mactatores*: tuerurs (D) tuurrus (L) / *animosis*: hardiz (C) hardis (L) / *hillas*: aundules (C) andulus (D)[80] / *salsucias*: sausues (C) sausigles (D) sawcitris (D*) sasies (L) / *tuceta*: bodins (C) beus (C*) puddings, tronchons (D) poddingis (D*) podyn (L)[81] / *scruta*: tripes (C) treypis (D*) trippes (L) / *popello*: racayell (L) / *tunicato*: pover (D)[82]

[36] *trapezete*: chaunjours de deners (C) scangeours (D) chanjurs (D*) changurs (L) / *trapetam*: une plaunche (C) change (L) / *talentis*: bessant (L)

[37] *numularii*: les muneters (C) muniters (D) mineters (sic) (D*) muneters (L) / *monetent*: forgent (D) forchent (L) / *monetam*: moné (C) / ad *cambium*: a chaunche (C) gange (D) la change (L) / *cambiatoribus*: chaunjours (C) / *cambiantur*: chaungers (D) seynt changés (L)

[38] *aurifabri*: orfeveres (L) / *fornaces*: forneys (D) / *pateras*: hanap (L) / *argento*: de argent (D) / *firmacula*: fermaylz (C) formalis (L) / *monilia*: nuchis (D*) nuches (L) / *spinter*: afficayl (C) ficayl (D*) pin (L)[83] / *nodulos*: botounz (C) botons (D) botuns (D*) bodunt (L) / *eligunt*: choysent (C) / *granula*: gernés (C) gernettes (C*) gernets (DD*) pere gernete (L) / *jaspides*: japes (C) / *saphiros*: saphirs (C) saphirus (D) saphiris (L) / *smaragdos*: esmeraus (C) meraudes (C*) ssmeraudes (D) merowdis (D*) miraudes (L)

[39] *tundit*: batet (C) / *incudit*: forget (L) / *industria*: la coytise (C) la quintysce (L) / super *incudem*: sur l'enclume (C) enclune, anvelt (D)[84] clume (D*) / *incudem ferream*: enclune de fer (L) / *malleolis*: martils, marteus (D) martil (L) / *laminas criseas*: plates de or (C) platis de ors (D*) plates de or (D) de or plates (L) / *includit*: closit (D) / *argenteas*: de argent (L) / infra *anchas*: en lé fosces (D) fos (L)[85]

---

[76] Surprisingly, no such compound of apple and cake is registered in the MED or OED.
[77] Cf. MED sub *mace-gref* n. The form with -*n* is not listed in the OF dictionaries.
[78] See TL 9,924 sub *sorsemer*.
[79] See TL 6,1325 sub *oschier*, and correct C *bochaunz* to *hochaunz*.
[80] See FEW 4,652b sub *inductilis*.
[81] See OED sub *pudding sb.*I,1.
[82] See Horace, *Ep.* I,vii,65. Scheler, *art. cit.*, 302 cites the gloss 'vili, pauperi'.
[83] See OED sub *pin sb.*[1]I,1.
[84] See MED sub *anvelt* n.
[85] See DMLBS sub 2 *anca* ('bezel, setting') and Scheler, *art. cit.*, 303 who cites the gloss 'fossas anulorum in quibus sunt gemmae'.

[40] *artifices*: les enginurs (L) / *cipharii*: hanapers (C) hanapirs (D) / *incrustant*: enparaylent (C) / *vasa*: vesselles (L) / *crustis aureis*: pesez (C) peces (D) pesis (D*) de peses de or (L) / *crateribus*: a hanaps (C) hanaps (L)

[41] *pannarii*: les drapers (C) draperis (D) draperes (L) / *albos*: blankeis (D*) / *camelinos*: de camelot (C) de camelin (DL) / *blodios*: de blu (C) bluis (D) / *burneticos*: burnet (CL) / *virides*: vers (C) vertes (L) / *scarleticos*: escarlez (C) scarlet (L) / *radiatos*: rayés (CL) rais (D*) / *stanfordeos*: estaunfordeis (C) de Estaford (D) / *ulnando*: en mesurant (C) / *ulna*: aune (L) / *pollice*: powce (D*) pocir (L)

[42] *usurpant*: mespernu[n]t (L) / *mapeas*: naps (L) / *manutergia*: tuales (L) / *lintheamina*: linchés (L) / *teristra*: riverochet (D) rochis vel chemis (D*) / *supara*: rochés (C) roket (D) rochis (D*) rochet (L) / *stamineas*: estamin (D*) astem (L) / *pepla*: gymples (C) uimplis (D) / *telas*: teyles (L) / *flammeola*: keverechefs (C) corchif (D) keverechisy (L)

[43] *apotecarii*: les especers (C) lé spicers (D*) aspiacores (D) apissorus (L) / *electuaria*: letuarie (CL) letuaries (D) / *radices*: rasines (C) / *zedoarium*: zedewal (C) zedewale (D) cedewarie (D*) citheuuant (L)[86] / cum *zinzibero*: gingivere (C) ov chingivre (D) gingiver (D*L) / *cumino*: comyn (C) comint (D*) cumyne (L) / *piper*: peivere (C) / *gariophilos*: glous de gilofre (C) glou de gilofre (D) clow de gilofre (D*) clous de gilovere (L) / *cinamono*: kanel (C) canele (D) canel (D*L) / *anisum*: anyz (C) anis (DL) anise (D*) / *maratro*: semense de fenul (C) semense de fenil (D) semen de fenoly (L) / *zucaram*: soucre (C) zucre (D) succre (L) / cum *liquiricia*: ov licorise (D) regalise, regalis (L)

[44] *apotecarii*: espicer (C*) espicosoures (D) / in *apotheca*: en le espicerie (D) espicerie (C*) / *zinziberum*: gingevere (C) zinchivre (D) gingivere (L) / *conditum*: sauverré (D) / *alexandrinum*: alexandre (C) alesandre (L) / *elleborus*: eble (sic) (C) marsere (D) marcir (D*) marcerer (L)[87] / *diaprunis*: leteuarie (D*) / *diagragantum* (corr. diadragantum): diagranfeyt (D*)[88]

[45] *carpentarii*: chapenters (L) / *fabricant*: forchunt (L) / *cupariis*: couvers (C) cupers (D*) cuperes (L) / *cupas*: cuvez (C) cowis (D*) vateis, cuves (L) / *dolea*: toneuz (C) toneus (L) / *onophora*: costereus (CD*) buscellos (D) costrey (L) / *cados*: barils (C) baryl (L) / *cavillis*: chevile, pinnis (D*)[89] chevel (L) / *cuneis*: cownis, anglice pennis (D*)[90] cuneys, qunus (L) / *cupariorum*: cupers (L)

[46] *rotarii*: les reers (C) lé rouis (D*) roiers (L) / *fabricando*: charpentant (C) / *plaustra*: charz (C) char (C*) uaynis vel chars (D*)[91] chars (L) / *canti*: jauntes (CL)

---

86 See TL 2,451 sub *citoval* and OED sub *setwall*. The commentary in L has *chichenuant*.
87 See TL 4,1285 sub *ieble*.. The *Alphita* (ed. Mowat) has (p.51) 'ebulus vel ebula . . . angl. welleuort [vel licheuurt]'. Scheler, *art. cit.*, 305 notes the gloss *masaire*, see TL 5,769 sub *madre* and MED sub *maser n.* Such confusion of botanical names eg. ebulus and elleborus is commonplace in glossed texts.
88 Corr. de dragan feyt (?)
89 See OED sub *pin sb.*[1]I,1.
90 See preceding note.
91 See OED sub *wain sb.*[1].

gauntis (D*) / *radii*: spokes (C) [92] / *axes*: essels (L) / *timpana*: mowel (D*) moels (L) / *modii*: lé moueles, anglice naye, tympana idem (C) mowellis, nayis (D*) [93] / *axes*: le essele (C) / *caville*: kiveles (C) couvilis (D*) / *limones*: lymouns, yilles (C) [94] limonz (D) limuns (D*) bastuns (L) / *juga*: les jus (C) jus (D*) / *themones*: temouns (C) temouns, willes (L) / *arquillis*: hames (ham berewes expunged, C) torturs (D) tortuys (D*) boȝes (C*) tortues (L) [95]

[47] *carucarii*: les caruers (C) caruers (D*) jaruers (L) / *stivam*: la mance (C) la manicle (D) estive, le manche, andel (D*) [96] manet (L) / *dentem*: dental (L) / *dentem* sive *dentalia*: le dentau (D*) / *trabem*: le tref (D*) / *jugam*: jus (D*) / *corbes*: corbilon (D) corbaylis (D*) / *flagella*: escurge (D) flaels (C) flaeus (D*L) / *vannos*: vanz (C) vans (D*) vauns (L) / *sarcula*: serclers (C) sarceus (D*) sarcluris (L) [97] / *cultros*: coutres (D) cutris (D*) / *uncos*: croks (C) / *tribulas*: trible (D) trubles (C) trublus (D*) peleys (L) / *vangas*: beches (C) beche (C*) beschis (D*) beges (L) / *marras*: pigoyses (D) owe (L) [98] / *sarpas*: sarpes (C) sarpis (D*) sarps (L) / *ligones*: picois (C) hous (D) pycoys (D*) pigosce (L) / *colaria equorum*: ham-berewes (C) [99] / *collaria equina*: colers a chyval (L) / *epifia*: paruns (D) [100] harneis (C) herneys (D*) harnés (L) / *scope*: baleis (C) baleys (D*) / *scobe*: baleys (D) / *rastra*: rastele (D) rausteus (C) rasteus (D*) rastel, rake (L) [101] / *flagella*: flaels (C) / *manutentum*: hantstaf (C) [102] manuel (D) maunchel, anstaf (D*) mangel (L) / *virga*: wipel (C) scungil (D*) [103] / *cappa*: cappe (CD*) copele (D) / *furce*: furchis (D*)

[48] *molendinarii*: moners (L) / *farricaptias*: gallice tremuz (C) trameus, binnes (D) lur trameus, bynnis (D*) trameus (L) gallice ecluses (C*) [104] / *rotas versatiles*: res (C) reus turnables (D) rowis (D*) reres [sic] turnables (L) / *aquaticas*: ewieys (L) / *fusos*: fusils (DL) fuciles (C) fusilis (D*) / *scarioballa*: anglice kogges (C) cogges, alisons, aleçuns (D) lé nouis, coggis (D*) noys radii (L) [105] / *cinoglocitoria*: le encluse (D) anglice yutil (C) les clusys, flodwayis (D*) suttleys, cluses (L) [106] / *molares*: granz peres (C) peris de molin (D*) grant peres (D) / in *farricaptia*: tremuz (C) en le

---

92 See OED sub *spoke sb.*
93 See MED sub *nave n.*
94 See OED sub *thill 1.* The scribe of C regularly uses y for thorn.
95 See MED sub *boue n.(1)7(d)* (*arquillus* = an ox-bow), *hame n.(2)* and *ham-berwe n.* See also TL 10,460 sub *tortoir.*
96 See MED sub *hondel n.*
97 See TL 9,176 sub *sarcel.*
98 See TL 4,1124 sub *höe.*
99 See note 95 above.
100 See Gfry 5,785a sub *paronne.* and TL 7,339 sub *parone.*
101 See OED sub *rake sb.¹.*
102 See MED sub *hond(e 8.(a).*
103 See OED sub *swingle* and *swipple.*
104 See Du Cange sub *faricarpstia* and FEW 13,ii,275b (*trimodia*) and cf. Gfry 8,9a sub *tramalie.* For the definition of the gloss ('illud quo ponitur bladum molendini') see MED sub *binne n.* The gloss *ecluses* is evidently misplaced (see *cinoglocitoria* later).
105 See MED sub *cogge n.(2)*, TL 1,316 sub *aluchon* and FEW 24,285a. In L f.104vb the commentary has 'quidam nodi in rota interiori qui movent fusum molendini'.
106 See OED sub *shuttle sb.³* and cf. MED sub *flod-yate.*

tramas (D) trameu (D*) in l'entramés (L) [107] / *batillo*: baterel (D*) sclaps (L) [108] / *alveum*: auge

[49] *antemuralia*: barbekanes (L) barbekans, berfrays (C) barbecans (C*D) barbekans (D*) / *sedato*: peysé (D*) / *tumultu*: la noys (D) noyse (D*) / *licias*: granz fosses (C) lices, focis (D) fossys (D*) / *superfossata*: double fosses (C) duble fosse (D*L) / *crates*: cleis (D*) / *propugnacula*: bretaches (CL) bretases (D) bretachis (D*) brutasches (C*) / *tabulata*: plaunchés (CD) planchis (D*) pl[a]ngés (L) / *craticulata*: enchins (C*) hurdis (C) [109] hordis, clayis (D) engyn de cleis (D*) chin de cleys (L) / ex *cratibus*: de cleys (D) de treuis [110] (D*) / *erecta*: adressé (D*) / *cestus*: talevaces (C) talevas (DL) talevace (D*) / *clipeos*: escus (C) escu (D) escuis (D*) / *targeas*: targes (CD) targis (D*) / *brachiola*: bracerole (C) braceroles (D) bracerolis (D*) brassenoles (sic) (L) [111] / *pesundedit*: trebuchat (C) trebucha (D) mit suz pé, trebucha (D*) trobechat (L) / *perrarias*: pereres (C) perers (DL) pereris (D*) / *Simonem comitem Montis Fortis*: Leycestre anglice (C) [112] / *mangonalia*: mangoneus (CD) mangeneus (D*) / *arietes*: motouns (C) mutuns (DL) motuns (D*) / *fustibula*: befreys vel foundeles (C) [113] berfrays (D) fundis (D*) / *trebucheta*: trebuchés (C) trebechet (C*) trebuchets (D) trebuchez (D*) / *sues*: truies, minors (D) meyners (D*) miners (L) [114] / *vineas*: garites (C) vines (D) garrytis (D*) garrites (L) / *catos*: chaz (C) / *cados*: barrilis (D*) barrel (L) / *versatiles*: turnable (L) / *secures*: coynés (C) hache denays (D) coyneyis (D*) quniués (?) (L) / *dacas*: hache daneche (C) haches (D) gallice hache danehache (D*) hache danaches (L) tuybil (D*) [115] / *bipennes*: besagu (C) bessuaguis (D*) bessague (L) / *gesa*: gysarms (C) gisarme (C*) gisarms (D) gesarmis (D*) guishames (L) / *Galliorum*: de franceys (D) / *sparos*: fauchouns (C) fauchun (C*) fauçuns (D) / *sparthas*: fausars (D*) [116] / *Hyspanorum*: de spaynels (D) des espayneus (C) panciels (L) / *cateyas*: gaveloks (C) dars (D) hantes (D*) hantes, lances (L) / *pugiones*: misericordes (C) espeys, misericordes (D) misericorde (L) / in *dolonibus*: en escabers (C) en geynes (D) escaubers (D*) en kauberces (L) / *Teutonicorum*: de tyeys (C) de tyays (D) teys (L) / *anelacias*: anleys (C) anelacis (D*) anelaces (D) anelacis (D*) anelas (L) / *Anglicorum*: de englays (D) / *pila Romanorum*: pilez dé romayns (D) / *sarillas*: talevaz (C*) ascues (L) / *sarisas*: escus (D*) / *Macedonum*: dé troyens (D) / *peltas*: talevas (C) targes (D) eschus (L) / *Tolosanorum* (corr. tolosanarum): damis de Tolet (D*) / *arcus Trojanorum*: ars dé gregays (D) / *palos*: peuz (D) peus (D*) / *malleos*: marteus (D*) / *ligones*: pycoys (D*) / *clavas*: masues (C)

---

107 See FEW 13,ii,276b (*entremuie*) and 236b sub *tremaculum*. The sense of lemma and glosses is 'mill-hopper'.

108 See MED sub *clap(pe* 3(*a*) (citing *Parv. Prompt.* 79 'clappe, or clakke of a mylle: taratantara, batillus'). Cf. AND sub *baterel*.

109 See TL 4,1166 sub *hordeiz*.

110 Corr. *trellis*? Cf. FEW 13,ii,266b.

111 See Scheler, *art. cit.*, 311 where the lemma is *peltas*. The sense 'small shield' does not seem to be attested in the dictionaries.

112 See Scheler, *art. cit.*, 310.

113 See TL 3,ii,202b sub *fondel*.

114 FEW 6,i,642b gives *miner* 'saper (une muraille) à coups de boulets'.

115 See OED sub *twibill, twybill*.

116 See TL 3,ii,1643 sub *fauçart*.

massuis (D*) massues de fer (L) maces de fer (D) / *jacula*: darz (C) / et *cathapultas*: e
setes barbelez (D) / *galeros*: heumes, chapel de quir (C) heumis (L) heymes (D)
heumis (D*) / *conos*: creystes (C) creytes (D) crestis (D*) crestes (L) / *toraces*:
wambesouns (C) gambaysuns (D) gambisum vel uardecors (D*) wadesuns (L) /
bombacinia: aketun (C*) haketouns, purpoyns (C) aketuns (D) purpoyntis (D*) /
galeas: haumes (D) coyphe de quir (L) coyfis de quir (D*) / *galeis*: coyfes de quir (C) /
loricas: haubers (C) hauberks (D) hammes (L) / *ocreas*: heses (C) hoseus (D) chausis
de fer (D*) esses (L) / *femoralia*: quiser (C) quisers (DD*) quisses (L) / *cruralia*:
quisers (C) / *genualia*: genulers (CDD*L) / *lanceas*: lances (CD) lances de fer (L) /
hastas: hantez (C) hauntes (D) hantes (L) / *contos*: perchez (C) perges (D) perchis
(D*) perches (L) / *uncos*: crocs (C) crokis (D*) croc (L) / *cippos*: ceps (CDD*L) /
cathenas: chaynes (D) cheines (L) / *barrarias*: barres (CL) bareys (D*) / *ignem pelas-*
gum: fu gregis (D*) fue gregos (L) / *pelasgum*: gregés (D) / *vitrum*: verre (C) veir (D)
veyr (D*) verre (L) / *liquefactum*: enclarsi vel fundi (D*) / *fundas*: linges (C) lenkes
(D) fundis (D*) fundes (L) / *glandes*: plates de plom (C) platis de plum (D*) plate de
plum (L) / *balistas*: arblas (D) arbelasts (L) / *trocleatas*: torkeis (C) a troil (C*) de
troyl (D) a trayl (D*) troclé (L)[117] / *materaciis*: materas (CL) materacis (D*)

[50] *fullones*: lé fulurs (D) folurs (D*) folours (C) / *nudi*: nus (D) / *pilosos*: veluz
(DD*) velus (L) / *alveo*: auge (L) gallice auge (C) / *sufflantes*: sufflauns (C) / *fullant*:
foulent (C) / *concavo*: crocu (C) cros (D*) croz (L) / *argilla*: arzil (C) argil (D*) arsyl
(L) / *lotos*: lavez (D*) lavés (L) / *cardinis*: charduns (D*L) / *radunt*: reent (C)

[51] *tinctores*: les tey[n]tours (C) tenturus (L) teinturs (C*) / *rubea*: wayd (C)[118] en
brasil (D)[119] / *majore*: greyn (D) / *gaudone*: wede (D*L) de gayde, wed (D) warance,
meder (C*)[120] / *sandice*: wode (C*) warence (CD) wede (D*) / *rubea*: de uarence, de
vermayl (D*) vermayl, ruge (L) vermayls (D) vermail (D*) / *ungues*: les ungeles (D)
/ *pictos*: peyns (D*) / *numismatis*: de moneye (D*)

[52] *cerdones*: les taneurs (C) lé tanurs (D) tannurs (D*) / *frunire*: tanner (CD*L):
tannir (D) / *coria equina*: quir de cheval (D) / *taurina*: de tore (D) de tor (L) / in
truncis concavis: en truns croys (D) trouncs (C) trunks (D*) / *scalprum*: une gratte,
grattur (D) grate (D*) gradde (L)[121] / in *frunio*: tan (C) en le tan (D*) tanne (L) /
cruditas: la cruezce (D*) crués (L)[122] / *fetida*: solé (D*L)

[53] *fabri*: lé fevers (D) les feveres (C) / super *incudem*: l'enclume (C) sur une
enclume (D) enclume (D*) / *malleos*: martews (D*) / *forcipibus*: tenayl (C) tenayls
(D) tenel (L) / *ventilatione*: soflement (D*) sufflement (L) / *follium*: de fous (C) de
suflez (D*) de sufeles (L) / *cultros*: cutres (DL) / *vomeres*: sokes (D) soc (L) / *ferros*
equinos: fer de cheval (D) / *ferrum ad vangam*: le fer a beche (D) / *vangam*: beche
(CD*L) / *tribulam*: gallice pele, anglice houwe (C)[123] trible, pele (D) a un pele (D*)

---

117 See FEW 13,ii,172a sub *tragula* and 313b sub *trochlea*. See also Gfry 7,763b sub *torquer*.
118 See OED sub *woad sb.*[1].
119 See TL 1,1135 sub *bresil* and FEW 1,506a.
120 See MED sub *mader(e n.*
121 See MED sub *grate n.(2)*.
122 FEW 2,ii,1368b does not give an example of this form earlier than the 14th C.(*cruesse*).
123 See MED sub *houe n.(2)*.

pelys (L) / *falces*: faus (CDL) / *sarcula*: serclers (C) sarceus, wed-hokis (D*) sarceus, serclors (D)[124] / ad *prata*: a prés (D) / *ligones*: pichoys, houes (D) picoyis (D*) / *facillas*: faucils (C) fauciles (D) petite facilles (L) / ad *messes*: a blés (D)

[54] *coci*: lé cues (D) / *cacabos*: caudron (D) / *urceos*: pocenez (C) pocenet (D) pot (L) / *patellas*: payles (DL) / *sartagines*: granz paelz (C) grant payls (D) grant paeyl (D*) pale a chars (L) / *pelves*: bacins (CD) bassin (L) / *mortaria*: mortirs (D) / *scutellas*: equeles (D) / *idrias*: pot a ewe (D) seylis (D*) soles (L) / *rotundalia*: platenis (D*) salers (D) plates (L) / *acetabula*: sauser (C*) saucer (D) sauceris (D*) sausers (L) / *olla*: pot ad spicer (C*) pots (D) / *coclearia*: equilers (D) quilers (C) culers (L) / *scutellas*: esqueles (C) / *scaphas*: cates (C*) gates (CD) gatis (D*) g(r)at (L) / *micatoria*: miours (C) miurs (D*)[125] grates (L) / *craticulas*: gredils (CD) gredilis (D*) / *creagras*: havés (CDD*L) / *clibanos*: furnays (D) furneyis (D*) fornes (L) / *epicausteria*: les austres (C) chymeneye (D) chimen(en)eyis (D*) chimenés (L) / *fornaces*: forneis (C)

[55] *mappa*: nape (D) / *fimbriatum*: frengé (CL) frengés (D) / *tripodes*: trepés (C) treves (L) / *trestelli*: tresteus (C) trestel (L) / *torres*: tysouns (C) tisuns (D*) tysun (L) / *cremalia*: cremelers (D*) ardable (C)[126] cremalirs (L) / *focalia*: fouail (C) buche (C*) fuayls (D)[127] buches (L) / *stirpes*: souches (C) suches (C*) stoc (L) / *cippi*: ceps (D) troncs (C) cep (L) / *vectes*: barres (C) vertiveles (D) verules (L) / *sedilia*: banks (C) seches (D) formt (L) / *sponde*: chaslit (C) forme close (D) chalys (L) / *cathedra*: cheere (C) chayer (D) chaflit (sic) (D*) / *fercula*: faudestole (C) chayer paiable (D)[128] segis (D*) fadestoles (L) / *culcitre*: coyltes (C) quilte (D) / *levigatis*: planiés (L) / *cervicalia*: orilers (C) oryler (D) orireis (D*) orrilet (L) / *pulvinaria*: quissers (sic) (C) quisines (D*) quisin (D) quissun (L) / *cribrum*: cribre (CD) / *haustrum*: boket (CD) bochet (L) / *taratantarum*: sarce (CD) sarcer (D) saz (L) / *casearium*: casiere (C) casier (D) cheser (D*) chesyr (L)[129] / *muscipula*: ratuere (CD)[130] rate (L) / *multra*: boket a let (D)

[56] *pulpita*: lettrouns (C) lectron (D) letrun (L) / *crucibolum*: crucel (C) / *creta*: creie (C) creye (DD*) / *sepo*: syu (C) seu (D) suze (L)[131] / *asser*: un asser (D) esse (L) / *absconsa*: escons (C) / *speculum*: mirewer (C)[132] / *pumex*: pomiz (C) pomyce (D)

[58] *giga*: la gige (C) gige (D*)

[59] *indumenta*: robes (D) afublement (L) / *tunica*: cotez (C) cotes (D) / *supertunicalia*: surcotez (C) ascurtores (sic!) (L) / *scapularia*: escapeloris (C) aspalerus (L) / *pallia*: maunteuz (C) / *renones*: tabars (CD*L) / *coopertoria*: covertures (C) couvrelit

---

124 See TL 9,176 sub *sarcel* and OED sub *weed-hook*.
125 See FEW 6,ii,72b and TL 3,i,1124 sub *esmiëoire*. See also MED sub *miour(e n*.
126 The scribe has confused the lemma with *cremialis*!
127 See Gfry 4,108b sub *foail*.
128 Presumably an error for *pliable*. See TL 3,ii,1650–1 sub *faudestuel* and MED sub *folding ppl.* (e).
129 The form *cheser* is not in MED or OED. Cf. FEW 2,i,456b et seq.
130 See FEW 10,123a and Gfry 6,619c sub *ratoire*.
131 See FEW 11,358b sub *sebum*.
132 See MED sub *mirour n*.

(D) / *lintheamina*: lincheuz (C) tabars (D) / *sarabarre*: esclaveyns (C) esclavines (D) esclavens (D*) asclaviyns (L) / *bombacinia*: aketounz (C) aketuns (D) aketun (D*L) / *tapete*: tapez (C) / *cuculli*: coulez (C) cuuelis (D*) couelon, monek (D) [133] cules (L) / *stragule*: les estreyls, rays (D) / *camisie*: chemises (D) / *collobia*: frocs (C) frokes (DL) / *lacernis*: biflez (C) bifles, yenne mantil (D) [134] mauntel de bifle (D*) bife, mantel (L) / *trabee*: vesture de rey (D) / *paludamentis*: mantil de pourpre (D) mantel de pupre (D*) dra de purpre (L)

[60] *missale*: messal (C) / *gradale*: grael (C) / *troparium*: troper (C) tropir (D) / *antiphonarium*: antifiner (C) / *letaniam*: letenie (C) letanie (D) / *breviarium*: breviarie (C) brevir (D) / *martirologium*: martelogie (C) martiloge (D) / *bibliotecam*: bible (C)

[61] *catholice*: leaument (L) / *figurative*: fugurablement (L) / *ypotetyce*: persunament (L) / *prophonetice*: criablement (L) / *simboletice*: reconsilaument (L) unde simbolum -li, escot de taverne (C*) / *presagoreutice*: coyntement (C) / *presagoretice*: sachabelement (L) / *silogistice*: conclusament (L) / *trenetice*: laumentusement (L) / *erotice*, ab *eros*, erois: barun (C*) / *gratificative*: merciablement (D) / *lamentatorie*: plorablement (D) / *palinodice*: rechauntablement (D) rechantablement (L) / *apostolice*: amonestablement (L) / *responsorie*: respondablement (D) / *suasorie*: amonestablement (D) / *antipodice*: respunablement (L) / *didascalicon*: au manere de metre (L)

[62] *superpilicio* vel *superlicio*: surplis (C) / *phanula*: phanoun (C) phanon (D) phanun (L) / *alba*: aube (C) / *talari*: a talouns (C) vesture geke au pé (D) [135] / *stola*: estole (CDL) / *thiara*: mitre, amite (C) amite (DD*) / *amictum*: amite (C) amit (L) [136] / *infula*: chesuble (CD*) chessubal, chesubel (D) chesible (L) / *cinctorio*: ceynture (C) senture (D) zenture (L) / *pedum*: sa cros (D) / *podere*: aube (D) / *mitra*: mitre (CL) / *anulo*: anel (C) / *pedum*: gallice croce (C) la croce (D) cros (D*)

[63] *aspersorium*: wispiloun (C) wispilum (D) juttuer (D*) wispilun (L) [137] / *vexillum*: baner (D) / *campana*: sane (D) seyn (L) / *campanario*: clocher (C) chochir (L) / *turribulum*: encencer (C) ensenser (D) e[n]sens (L) / *phiala*: cruest (D) viele cruet (C) fyole (L) / *analogium*: lectern (C) / *pixis*: boyste (D) / *hostiarum*: de obleis (C) hoytes (L) de obblés (D) [138]

[64] *strigilet*: estrilit (D*) estrilet (D) / *batis*: boseus (C) [139] provenderis (D*) / *presepia*: cretches (C) crecchis (D) crechis (D*) / *fimos*: les fens (C) lé fyens (D) fens (L) / *strigilibus*: estrils (C) / *cinovectorio*: civere (C) baruwe, severe, cure (D) [140] cever (L) / *transfert*: oustre portet, portent (D) / *inpinguendos*: au drecer, a composters (D)

[65] *forcipes*: forces (D) / *theca*: deel (C) del (DL) deyel (D*) / *fusus*: fucil (C) fusel (D) fusil (D*L) / *vertebrum*: peysoun, werve (C) pesun, werve (D) pesun, zewel (D*)

---

133 *monek* = monk, the rest of the gloss ('cowl') having apparently dropped out.
134 *yenne* = þenne ('thin').
135 The commentary in D f.21rb has 'talaris est longa vestis usque ad talos'.
136 See TL 1,355 sub *amit*.
137 See FEW 17,599b sub *wisp and Gfry 4, 271c sub *getoir*.
138 See TL 6,942 sub *oble*.
139 See TL 1,1035 sub *boissel*.
140 See FEW 2,ii,1575 sub *currus* and MED sub *barwe n*.

pessun (L)[141] / *colus*: conyl (C) cunoyl (D) conil (D*) cunnylle (L) / *mataxa*: serence
(CDD*) / *trahale*: trael, rel (C) trahale, rel anglice (D) rel (D*) traés (L)[142] /
girgillum: voyder, rarwindel (C) devoyturs (D) wtuarie (D*) vuedefori, varwindle
(L)[143] / *excudia*: escuche, swigleand (C) escuce, swengle (D) eclise (D*)[144] / *linipulus*:
brittel (sic) de lin, strike (C) britil de lin, anglice bete (D*)[145] un serjon (D)[146]
brstel de lin, anglice bete (L) / *rupa*: rippecomb (C) rupeye (D) grate (D*) ruperer
vel grad (L)[147] / *feritorium*: bateldore (C) gallice batuer (C*) batuer (D) batildore,
bature (D*)[148] batuer (L) / *cupatorium*: couvere, boukfat (C)[149] la covere (D) cuver
(C*) cuvere (D*) cuvir (L) / *lexiva*: lessive (D) / *lixivatorio*: la buwe (D) buket (D*)
boket (L)[150] / *calotricatorium*: la ridewere (C) riduer (DL) riduere (C*)[151] / *collotrica-*
torium: riduer, sclicebrede (D*) / *licinitorium*: liche (CC*) liche, sclikeston (D) lige,
anglice sclikeston (D*) lige, anglice sclicston (L)[152] / *lucibruciunculum*: liche (C)

[66] *textrices*: teytreis (D*) / *pectines*: lahaniurs, peynis (D*) lannirus (L)[153] / *stamina*:
esteyme (D) files (D*) / *trama*: off (D) treyme, of (D*)[154] / *a spola*: de le espole (C)
espole (D) spole (D*) / *pano*: del broche (C) brochet (D) broche (D*L) / *lama*: lame
(DD*) slay ou la leme (C) lame, scle (L)[155] / *in troclea*: en le tramel (C) vindeyse
(D*) tramer (L)[156] / *globorum*: de luceus / *orditur*: warpet (C)[157] / *tramam*: treyme
(D*) / *ductione*: par l'amene[men]t (L) / *orditur*: uerdir (D)[158]

[67] *serica texta*: seynt de seye (D*) de seye (DL) tysues (C) seius (L) / *textrices*:
tytresses (D) / *cavillarum*: cavellis (D) / *caville*: cevilus (D*) / *subtegmina*: lur tremes
(C) tramels (D) treymis, of (D*) tremes (L) / *cum lignea spata*: ov le clise de fusz,

---

141 See OED sub *wharve sb.* and TL 7,840 sub *peson. Zewel* remains obscure. MS C p.40 offers
as a second meaning of *vertebrum* 'rotundum os in genu'. Scheler, *art. cit.*, 320 cites *wervel* and
Gfry 8,214a has *vervellon* = *internodium*.
142 See Du Cange sub *trahale* and TL 10,534. See also OED sub *reel sb.*
143 See FEW 14,594ab and TL 2,1824 sub *desvuidëor*. See also OED sub *yarnwindle.*
144 See FEW 3,290a and OED sub *swingle-hand* (1825 'a swingle-hand or scotcher') and
scutch.
145 Scheler, *art. cit.*, 321 cites the glosses *betil* and *butel*, see MED sub *betel n.* See also MED
sub *bete n.(3)* and OED sub *strike sb. 3a.*
146 See A. Thomas, 'Anc. Bourg. *sergeon*', *Romania* 39 (1910), 253–4 and FEW 2,i,709–10.
147 See TL 8,1552 sub *rupe* and OED sub *rib v.*[2].
148 See MED sub *batildore n.*
149 See MED sub *bouking ger. (b).*
150 See FEW 15,ii,7a (*buka*) and TL,1195 sub *buie* and 1202 sub *buquet.*
151 See TL 8,1276 sub *rideoir.*
152 See OED sub *sleek v.* and *sleekstone*, Gfry 4,774c sub *liche* and FEW 17,146a (*slikien*).
Although Scheler, *art. cit.*, 321 gives the gloss *sclikenbrede* it does not appear in the English
dictionaries.
153 Cf. MS Oxford, Bodleian Library, Rawlinson G 99 f.160vb '*pectines*: laniurs, anglice
slayes' and see FEW 5,148–9.
154 See OED sub *woof sb.*[2].
155 See OED sub *slay sb.*[2]. See also OED sub *reed sb.*[1]10 and TL 5,111 sub *lame* ('instrumentum quod percutit filum'). Scheler, *art. cit.*, 370 cites the variant *leine.*
156 See FEW 13,ii,195b which gives *trameour* (1364) and Gfry 8,9b sub *trameure.* Scheler, *art.*
cit., 370 gives the gloss *trameor.* See also OED sub *windas.*
157 See OED sub *warp sb.*[1]III.
158 corr. *urdir?*

espeye de fust (D*) speye, esclyce (C)[159] spey de trefe (L) / *de textis*: de seyus (L) / *cingula*: seyntes (C) / *crinalia*: garlaundeches (C) garlunndis de hechis (D*)[160] garlandeges (L) /

[68] *pictrices* (sic): peyneressis (D*) / *cloacam*: foreyne (C) longan (D) chaubre de lungayne (D*) / *monperia*: torchouns (C) / *menperia*: torchunnis (D*) / *memperia*: torcheruns (D) / *menperia*: torchun du cul (L) / *pelliciis*: pelesuns (D*) pelisuns (L) / *fedis*: soylés (D*) / *velaminibus*: curverturs (D) / *carpent*: escharisent (D*) / *carpunt*: charpis sunt (L) / *villosas*: veluzs (D*) / *pectinibus*: peynes (C) / *depilant*: detrehent (C)

[69] *devacuatrices*: les devoideresses, þe wynderes (C)[161] devotueres (L) / *devastatrices* (sic): voyderesse (D*) windestren (C*)[162] / *devacuant*: voydint (D*) / *aurisece*: trencheresses de or (D) trenchaunz or (C) trenchent or (D*) trenchan or (L) / *marsupia*: les bourses (C) bursis (D) / *coitu frequenti*: sover lescherie (D*)

[70] *platea*: rue (D) / ante *paravisum*: devant le parvys (C) parvis (D*) / *anseres*: howis (D*) / *galli*: cos (L) / *perdices*: perdriz (C) perdrisis (D*) / *phasiani*: fesaunz (C) phesans (D*) fessans (D) / *alaude*: alouez (C0 alowis (D*) / *passeres*: mossouns (C) mochons (D) musserunis (D*) mussun (L)[163] / *anates*: anes (D*) / *plumarii*: plovers (CD) pluvers, hulsterris (D*)[164] / *ardee*: herouns (C) heyron (D) hayruns (D*) / *grues*: grues (C) / *signi*: synes (C) / *pavones*: poouns (C) / *turtures*: tourtres (C) turtus (L) turteris (D*) / *turdi*: tourdes (C) turnes (L) / *anses*: oues (C)

[71] *auceps*: le oysilers (C) / *nemore*: bos (L) / *aquila*: egle (CL) / *herodius*: herouner, gyrfauc (C) hayrun (D*) herunner (L) / *ancipiter*: goshawke (C, s.xv hand)[165] oustur, goshauec (D) girfauc (D*) girfac (L) / *capus*: muscat (D) muschet (D*) muchet (D) / *sturnus*: estornel (C) kestrel (C, s.xv hand)[166] esturnel (D) le creterel (D*) creterel (L) / *falco*: faucoun (C) / *merulus*: meryloun (C) merulon (D)[167] / *maviscus*: mauvuis (D) mawisse (D*) maviz (L) / *psittacus*: papejay (CL) papejoy (D) papinjai (D*) / *philomena*: rusinole (C) nytyngale (C, s.xv hand)[168] russenol (D) rossenole (D*) ruscinole (L) / *lucinia*: chardenerole, anglice goldfinch (C) carderole, goldfinc (D*) chardenrole, goldfing (D)[169] / *liricina*: jardunoyl (L) / *milvum*: coufle (DD*) / *muluum*: le coufle (C) / *milium*: cufle (L) / *cornicem*: cornil (C) cornayl (D) corf (D*) cornile (L) / *corvum*: corf (CD) / *bubonem*: huan (CL) houwane (D) huant (D*) /

---

[159] See TL 3,i,924 sub *esclice*.
[160] Cf. MED sub *hacche* n. For *garlande* = *crinale* = 'sorte de peigne' see Gfry 4,232a.
[161] See OED sub *winder* sb.[1] and cf. FEW 17,588a sub *winde*.
[162] See OED sub *windster* sb.
[163] See TL 6,158–9 sub *moisseron* and *moisson*.
[164] Cf. MED sub *holste*? Cf. Hunt in *Notes and Queries* 28,1 (Feb. 1981), p.15a 'plumuarius: un plover, a ulnester'.
[165] See MED sub *gos-hauk* n.
[166] See OED sub *kestrel* and FEW 2,ii,1321ab.
[167] See TL 3,i,1120 sub *esmerillon*, FEW 17,157ab and cf. MED sub *merlioun* where the confusion is noted with the heraldic *merlete* (martlet). *Merulus*, of course, means blackbird, but confusion is commonplace in the glosses.
[168] See MED sub *night-ingale* n.
[169] See MED sub *gold-finch* n and AND sub *charderole*.

vespertilionem: chautsoriz, anglice backe (C)[170] cauve sorice (D) chau sorice (D*)
cauvesors (L) / *nicticoracem*: nit raven (C)[171] corf de nuth (D) freyseye, corf de nut
(D*) / *pellicanum*: pellican (CL)

[72] *salmones*: saumons (D) / *trutas*: troutes (CD) trutis (D*) trutes (L) / *murenas*:
lampreyis (C) lampreie (C*) lamperyes (D) lanpreyis (D*) lamprees (L) / *morium*:
morue (C) muluel (C*) moruwe (D) morue, muluel (D*)[172] / *pectines*: plays (LCD)
plais (D*) / *anguillas*: anquiles (sic) (D) / *lucii*: luz (C) le luz (D) / *rochie*: roches (CD)
rokis (D*) / *rosee*: roches (C*) / *stincii*: stenches (D) tench (C) espinoshis (D*)
pinoches (L) / vel *tenci*: tenches (L) / *stincii*: espinochis, anglice banett (D*)[173] /
stincti: tenches (C*) / *ragadie*: rays (C) lé reys (D) rayis (D*) raies (C*) rays (L) /
allecia: harans (D) hareyns (C) / *mulli*: molez (C) petiz molets (D) mulés (L) / *hamis*:
croks (C) crocs (D) hevis (L)[174] / *retibus*: reys (C) / *percas*: perches (C) le perche (D)
/ *gobiones*: gojouns (CD) / *gamaros*: espinoches (C) espinocles (C*) esperling, espinoches (D) / *megaros*: makereus (C)

[73] *capros*: chevres (D) chevers (D*) / *capras*: bises (D*) / *capellas*: gallice cheveres
(D*) / *edos*: bokereus (C) bokerels (D) bukis (D*) chiveres (L) / *mulos*: mules (C)
muls (L) / *pullos*: puleyns (C) / *equabus*: jumentes (C) / *burdones*: burdounz (C)
burdons (D) burduns (D*)[175] / *camelos*: chameus (D*) / *dromedarios*: rabitis vel
dromedarie (D*)[176] teu manere corous, a dromos quod est cursus (D)[177] / *porcas*: lé
estrues (D) trueys (L) / *porcellis*: cheiuns (L)

[74] *silvestria*: sawagis (D*) / *cervi*: cerfs (C) cerf (D) / *cerve*: bises (C) bices (D) bisis
(D*) bisse (L) / *dami*: deyns (C) / *dame*: deymes (C) deyme (D) daimis (D*) / *hinnuli*:
fououns (C) founs (D) fowns (D*) fouuns (L) / *capre*: chevre (D) chiveres sauvage
(L) / *caprea*: roe, cheveryl (C)[178] / *taxi*: tesouns (C) tesuns (D) tessuns (D*) / *linces*:
linces (DL) / *apri*: senglers (CDL) sengelers (D*) / *leones*: leouns (C) liuns (D) /
tigrides: tigres (D) / *pardi*: pardes (D) lepardis (D*) pars (L) / *esperioli*: esquireus (C)
escureus (D) escurés (L) / *ursi*: urses (C) urs (D) hurs (D*) / *urse*: hurses (D*) /
cuniculi: conys (C) cuniges (D) / *lepores*: leveres (C) / *simie* (sic): singes (D) / *simie*,
hec: femele (D) / *simei*: synges (C) / *simee*: chingessis (D*) / *lutricii*: loutres (C)
lutres, otur (D) lutris, oteris (D*) lutres (L)[179] / *linces*, hic linx: anglice ylouworm
(C)[180] / *vulpes hastute*: gupils quayntes (D) coyntis (D*) / *pitoydes*: putoys (C) puteys,

---

170 See MED sub *bakke* n.
171 See MED sub *night* n. 6 (*a*).
172 Some MSS have *morum*. See MED sub *mulwel* and TL 6,315 sub *moruel*.
173 Cf. MED sub *ban-stikel*.
174 See TL 4,1040 sub *havet*.
175 See Gfry 1,688a and FEW 1,632b.
176 See OED sub *rabite*.
177 There seems to be confusion with *dromonarius* (= 'dromones, naves cursoriae'). FEW
     2,1571b records *corau* etc. in the 16th C. designating a boat and *courir* with the sense (from
     the 11th C.) 'aller vite sur l'eau (d'un navire)'.
178 See OED sub *roe*[1].
179 See MED sub *oter* n.
180 Presumably for *glouworm* (Dief.[1] has *linx vel linca, lintwurm*), an obviously erroneous gloss.

bulmerdes (corr. fulmerdes) (D) putois, fulmard (D*) [f]ulmert, pitoyes (L) [181] /
galinarum: de chelinis (L) / in stagnis: en eu esteant (D)

[75] salvia: sauge (CDD*L) / petrosillum: persil (CDL) percil (D*) / dictanus: ditayne
(C) ditoyne (D) ditan (D*) ditane (L) / ysopus: ysope (C) isop (D) ysop (L) /
celidonia: celidoyne (C) celidone (DL) celedon (D*) / feniculus: fenil (CL) fenuil
(D) fenul (D*) / piretrum: petre (C) pelestre (C*) peletre (DD*L) / columbina:
columbine (CD) / viola: violettes (C) violete (D) viol (L) / rosa: rose (D) / urtica:
ortiz (D) hurtie (D*) / lilium: lile (D) / carduus: chardon (C) charduns, þistels [182] (D)
carduns (D*) kardun (L) / saliunca: calketrappes, anglice blindenetle (C) [183] rosa
bastarde (C*) chauchetrape (D) calketrap (D*) kalketrape (L) / malua: mauve (C)
hocke, mauwe (D) mawe (D*) hoclef, mauve (L) [184] / agrimonia: agrimoyne (CD*)
egremoyne (D) / solatro: morele, docke (C) morel, souredocke (D) morele (C*D*)
morel (L) [185] / solsequio: seusikel (C) goldes ou solsecle (D) solsequiel, golde (D*)
solscegle, glode (sic) (L) [186] / mercurialis: daisezen (C*) [187]

[76] ortolanus: cortiler (C) le gardiner (D) / colit: cutivet (D) / olus: cholet (C) chous
(D) / caulis: cholet (DL) / borago: borage (CDD*) burrage (L) / beta: bethe (C) bete
(D*L*) betes (D) / allia: ayle (C) aws (D*) / porrum: poree (D) porreus (D*) porrey
(L) / sinapis: senevé (C) semens a mustard (D) seed de mustard (D*) senefey (L) /
sinapium: moustard (CD) mostart (L) / porreta: pore (CD) porree (L) / civolli: civoles,
chessebolle (C) [188] cyvous (D*) civos (L) / cepule: oynounz (C) honiuns (D) hununs
(D*) / hinule: escaloyns (C) scaluns, ekaloynes (D) eschaluns (D*) ascalun (L) /
pimpinella: pimpernele (CD) primerole (D*) premeroel (L) [189] / pilosella: philesole
(C) piloselle (D) piroche (D*) pilocke (L) [190] / sanicula: sanicle(le) (C) sanigle (D)
sanicle (D*L) / buglossa: plantayne, manfelun (D*) madefelun (L) [191] / lancea:
launcelé (CD) lancelé (D*) lanscelés (L) matefelun (C*) matefeloun (C) [192]

[77] cerasus: ciresere (C) cereser (D) ceser (L) / cerasa: ceriez (C) cirises (D) cerisses
(L) / pirus: perer (DL) / pira: peyres (D) pers (L) / pomus: pomer (L) / poma: pomus
(L) / prunis: pruner (L) / pruna: prunes (D) prunus (L) / coctanus: coynere (C)

---

[181] See MED sub fulmard n.
[182] See OED sub thistle sb.
[183] See TL 2,320–1 sub chauchetrape and chauchetrepe, FEW 2,i,65ab, MED sub calketrappe
and OED sub caltrop. See also MED sub blind adj. 5(a).
[184] See MED sub hokke n. (1)a.
[185] See MED sub dokke n. The glosses docke / souredocke are erroneous.
[186] See MED sub golde n.
[187] See MED sub daies-ie n. The gloss seems quite arbitrary.
[188] See MED sub ches-bolle n. (= papaver). There seems to be confusion with a form like
chibolles (MS Oxford, Bodleian Library, Rawlinson G.99 f.161va).
[189] The gloss primerole is a mistake, though the vagueness of its early use is commented on in
OED sub primerole. See, too, the range of meanings in OED sub pimpernel.
[190] C has philosella and D* pirosella. The Alphita ed. Mowat, p.144 calls it 'pelosee vel
peluette'. Cf. TL 7,606 (pelosele) and FEW 8,504a. The forms in D* and L do not seem to be
attested elsewhere.
[191] See MED sub mate-feloun n. and FEW 6,i,519b. Again the gloss seems arbitrary. Cf.
Alphita, p.83, 1.18.
[192] Mate-felon properly translates iacea, here confused with lancea. Scheler, art. cit., 372 has
the gloss plantaine rendering lancea.

quincer (D) coyner (D*) coyne (L)¹⁹³ / *coctana*: coyns (CL) quinces (D) / *mespilus*:
la medlere (C) meddler (C*) medler (D) nefler (D*) mestler (L)¹⁹⁴ / *mespila*: medles
(C) nefles (D*) meles (L) / *pessicus*: peychere (C) pecher (D) peschis (D*) peches
(L) / *pessica*: peyches (C) peches (D) / *castanea*: chanteyn (D) chastaunyer (L) /
castaneas: chasteynes (C) chanteynes (D) / *nux*: noyer (D) coudre (C*) nuer (L) /
avellana: noer (C) couder (D) nosyler (D*) codre, nusiler (L) coudre (C*) / *avellanas*: nugagis (C)¹⁹⁵ petite noys (D) nusilles (L) / *ficus*: figer (CD) fykyr (L) / *vitis*: la
vine (C) / *uvas*: graps (CL) / *pampinos*: foyles de vines (L) / *palmites*: lé braunches
(C) braunches (D) branches (L) / *antes*: rasins (L) / *phalangas*: forches (D) furchez
(D*) furches (L)

[78] *luco*: boys (CL) / *quercus*: cheyne (CD) / *fago*: fou, anglice behc (C) fou (D) fou,
bech (D*) foye (L)¹⁹⁶ / *pinus*: pin (L) piner (D) / *pirus*: perer (D) / *lauro*: lorere (C)
lorir (D) lorrirer (L) / *celsus*: morere, bribbel-tre (C) le frang morir, mulberietre (D)
alier (D*L) franc more (C*)¹⁹⁷ / *celsa*: morues, salics (D)¹⁹⁸ alies (L) / *corno*:
hebe-tre (D)¹⁹⁹ / *corna*: cornes (L) hebes (D) / *cinus*: cenelere (C) haȝþorn, aubepine
(C*)²⁰⁰ ceneler (D*L) / *cina*: ceneles, haues (C)²⁰¹ seneles, hauþorne (D) cynelis
(D*) ceneles (L) / *husso*: houz (C) hus (C*) huez, holine (D)²⁰² hous (D*) holin (L)
/ *rupnus*: runce (D*) / *rumice*: runce (D) / *rampnus*: grosinere, yeveyort (C) grosiler
(C*) griselir, þeveþorn (D)²⁰³ chrosiler (L) / *bodegar*: le eglenter (C) eglenter (D*) /
bedegar: anglentere (D) / *bodelgar*: englenter (L) / *populus*: pepler (C) popolir (D)
peplir (L) / *salice*: sauz (C) sauz, wu (?) (D) saws (D*) saus (L) / *tremulo*: tremblere,
aps (C)²⁰⁴ trembeler (D*) tremlir (L) / *pepulus*: bolaser (DD*) bolacer (L)²⁰⁵ / *tilia*:
linde (D)²⁰⁶ / *pepula*: peple²⁰⁷, anglice bolaces (C) bolases, purneles (D) purnelis
(D*) bolas, purneles (L)

[79] *architectari*: estre covert (C) estre forgé (D) estre ch[ar]penté (D*) estre charpunter (L) / *trapetas*: plaunches (CD) planchis (D*) planches (L) / *solivas*: sulle, les
solives (C) sulives (L) / *lacunaria*: vousurus (D) / *tingna*: cheverouns (C) chevron
(D) cheveruns (D*L) / *lodia*: lover (D) lovers (CD*L) / *laquearia*: laz (C) cowplis
(D*)²⁰⁸ laces (L) / *trabes*: trefs (C) grant tres (D) / *latas*: lazes (C) / *epistilium*: somet

---

¹⁹³ See TL 2,824 sub *cöoignier* and *cöoing*.
¹⁹⁴ See MED sub *medler* n. and FEW 6,44b.
¹⁹⁵ Scheler, *art. cit.*, 373 cites the gloss *nugakis* without commentary.
¹⁹⁶ See MED sub *beche* n.
¹⁹⁷ See TL 6,273 sub *morier* and MED sub *brembel* n. See also MED sub *mul-beri(e* n., TL
3,ii,2201 sub *franc* and ibid., 1,303 sub *aliier*.
¹⁹⁸ See DMLBS sub *celsus* 2. Corr. *morues* to *moures*? *Salics* must be misplaced and may have
arisen from a misreading of the lemma *salice* later.
¹⁹⁹ See MED sub *eben tre* and *eben(us* n.
²⁰⁰ See MED sub *hau(e-thorn* n.
²⁰¹ See MED sub *haue* n.(*2*).
²⁰² See MED sub *holin* n.
²⁰³ See OED sub *theve-thorn* and correct the reading of C accordingly.
²⁰⁴ See MED sub *aspe* n.
²⁰⁵ See MED sub *bolas* n. and Gfry 1, 618b.
²⁰⁶ See MED sub *lind(e* n.
²⁰⁷ MS = *speple*.
²⁰⁸ See AND sub *couple* and MED sub *couple* n.(*3*).

(D) sumet (L) / *epistilus*: chapestel (D*) / *columpna*: pelir (D) / *basis*: fundement (CD) / *stilus*: meyne partie (D) / *dolabra*: doluer, brodax (D) [209] doluere (C) doleuers (L) / *bisacuta*: bisague (D) / *rosticutio*: besacuz (C) besague (L) / *resticutio*: besague (D*) / *acia*: asze (C) adese, aze (D) hassze (D*) asce (L) [210] / *securi*: coynyé (D*) / *bessuacuto*: twbyl (D*) [211] / *terebro*: tarere (C) navegar (D) [212] terere (D*) terire (L) / *cuneis*: wengez (C) weg (D) coynis, ueggis (D*) [213] / *celte*: chicel (C) chisel (D) cicel (D*) scicel (L) / *plana*: plane (CD*) / *cavillis*: kevil (D) / *calce*: chauz (C) cauce (D) caws (D*) / *lathomus*: massun (L) / *latomorum*: du machun (D) / *latomi*: del machon (C) / *lathomega*: ston ax (C) [214] trouel, trulle (D*) truel (L) / *amussi*: esquire (CD*L) / cum *perpendiculo*: livel (C) o le level (D) penderol (D*) perendurel (L) [215] / *ponderoso*: chargus (L)

[80] *peregre proficiscens*: en pelerimage (sic) (D*) perlinage (L) / *proficiscens*: espleyt-ant (D*) / *galeas*: galies (D*) / *galeis militaribus*: heumes de chivalers (C) hewmis de chevaler (D*) / *lembos*: petit nefes (D) bateus (C) petit nefis (D*) petit nefes (L) / *triremes*: snages, cogkes (C) coggis (D*) cocgnes (L) [216]

[81] *neufragia*: perul de mer (D*) / *carcerem*: prisun (D*) / *supplicia*: lé tormens (C) / *crucem*: croys (D*) / *patibulum*: gibet (CD*) chibet (L) / *calofurcium*: galewes (C) [217] fu[r]chez (D*) furche (L) / *fustes*: bastun (DL) peuz (C) bastuns (D*) / *eculeos*: chewaws de fust (D*) / *serras*: saues (C) [218] scies (L) / *laminas*: plates (C) platis (D*) / *quadragenas*: scourgis (D*) / *sarras*: sawis, seyis (D*) [218] / *ungulas*: croks (C) crokis de fer (D*) ungles (L) / *scorpiones*: escorges (C) escorpiones (D*) eschurges (L)

[82] *liricines*: arpurs (D*) harpurs (L) / *tibicines*: businurs (D*) bussiners (L) / *cor-nicines*: cornurs (D*) / *vidulatores*: vielours (C) viulurs (D*L) / *giga*: gige (C) gigye (D*) / *vidulis*: vieles (CL) veylis (D*) / *sistro*: cutel (D) cutel volable (L) / *symphonia*: symphan (C) / *cithola*: sitole (C) citole (D*) cithoyel (L) / *psalterio*: sautrie (C) sauterye (D*) / *cymbalis*: cymbeus, simbyrnes (C) [219] chimbes (D*) chims (D) cim-bees (L) / *choro*: croude (C) [220] / *tympano*: tabour (C) tabur (D*) / *tripudiatrices*: trecheresses (D) treschereschis vel espringurs (D*) [221] aspinguoresses (L) / *aspis*: serpent (D*)

[83] *nuptis*: mariés (L) / *modulis*: motes (C) modes (D) chaunsuns (D*) petit chan-suns (L) / suis *tripudiis*: lur treyches (C) / *coream*: la carole (D) karole (L) / *canticis*:

---

209 See MED sub *brod adj. 4(d)*.
210 See FEW 1,152ab and OED sub *adz, adze*.
211 See OED sub *twibill, twybill*.
212 See OED sub *auger* and MED sub *nauger n.*
213 See OED sub *wedge sb.*
214 See OED sub *stone-ax.*
215 FEW 8,176b has forms like *pandarel, pandourel* with quite different meanings.
216 See AND sub *coge*, MED sub *cogge n.(1)* and OED sub *snack sb.¹*.
217 See MED sub *galwe n.*
218 See OED sub *saw sb.¹*.
219 I have found no other example of this form.
220 See MED sub *croud n.(2)*.
221 See TL 3,i,1257.

grant chansuns (L) / *tripudiis*: caroels (L) / *cataracte*: fenestre (C) / *cathaduppe*: lé conduit de la ter (D) condut (C) cundyes (L)

Glosses from the commentary in MS C [222]

[4] *thorax*: hauberc / [7] *ren*: gallice renon / *renes*: gallice reyns / [11] *pulvillos*: gallice baz / [14] *pirricudium*: fusil / [18] *mercator*: marchaund / *mercimonium*: gallice marchaundise / *ligulas*: layners / [19] *cirotecarii*: gaunters / [20] *bombace*: gallice cotoun / *bombacinium*: gallice purpoynt / [21] hec *taxus*: yf / *taxus*: gallice teson / hoc *taxum*: gallice lard / [22] *firmacularii*: brochemaker (s.xvi hand) [223] / *stamum*: gallice estem / [24] *pictacia*: takun / *inpedia*: empeyne gallice / [25] *equitibiale*: gallice jambel / *atramentum*: gallice arnement / *licinium*: liniel / *subula*: gallice alerne / [30] hic *arthocasius*: gallice flaon / [32] *lichinus*: mecht / [33] hic *acus*, aceris: gallice mestilon / *furfur*: bren / [36] *trapezeta*: gallice gangeor / *talentum*: gallice besant / [38] *pateras*: gallice coupe / *spinter*: gallice ficayl / *nodulus*: gallice botun / *granula*: gallice gernez / *jaspides*: gallice japes / *saphiros*: safir / [39] *laminas*: gallice plate / [42] *supara*: roket / [45] *onoforum*: gallice busseuz / [46] *canti*: gallice jaunt / *tympanum*: gallice tabour / *arquillus*: quedam ligna in collo equi, gallice halsteuz,[224] vel arquillus est circulus qui circuit collum bovis vel porci ne intret sepem; bene dicitur isti porci sunt *arquillati*: gallice juchez [225] / [47] *stivam*: gallice maunche / *tribulus*: gallice rounce / *vanga*: beche / [48] *farricapa*: gallice brauce, anglie hotte [226] / *cynociglocitorium*: yutil [227] / [49] *antemurale*: gallice barbecan / *toraces*: gallice gambeysons / *uncinus*: petit croc / *cippus*: gallice cep / hii *barri*-orum, sine singulari numero est genus ludi: barrez [228] / hec *vitrea*: gallice verryne / *troclea*: gallice wyndaz / [52] *cerdo*: gallice tanour / [62] *alba*: aube / [65] *theca*: gallice deel / *funus*: gallice fusil / *vertebrum*: pesun / *trahale*: gallice trahul / *girgillum*: vouders / *feritorium*: gallice batuer / *lucibruciunculum*: ylicston / *retropofocinium*: yolstoc [229] / [67] *caville*: gallice caveles / [74] *simea*: syne / [75] *viburnum*: gallice auborne / *saliunca*: gallice cauketrappe / [78] *fagus*: gallice fou / *bodegar*: gallice eglenter / *murra*: gallice mazer / [79] *trapetas*: planchiz / *soliva*: anglice grontsulle [230] / *securis*: gallice coyne / [81] *patibulum*: gibet / [82] *tripudiare*: gallice trecher / *tripudium*: espringerie / [83] *chorea*: gallice carole

Glosses from the commentary in MS C*

[11] *pulvilli*: gallice bates / *strepes* (corr. strepas): gallice estriue / [13] *pluscula*: gallice bucle / [17] *erugino*: gallice furber / hic *tolus*: gallice pumel / *capulos*: gallice houtis,

---

222   I do not repeat references already given for identical forms in the main text.
223   See MED sub *broche* n.(1)2(d).
224   A form of halter?
225   Scheler, *art. cit.*, 308 cites the gloss *jujez* (= 'yoked').
226   See MED sub *hotte* n. Scheler, *art. cit.*, 308 cites the glosses 'gallice dicitur braute et anglice dicitur hoc [corr. hot]'.
227   See note 106 above.
228   See TL 1,851 sub *barre* (jöer as barres).
229   This obscure gloss is added at the top of p.40 over the sentence 'Ego sedi retro retropofocinium et commedi meum lucibruciunculum'. A later hand has added a final *k* to *yolstoc*.
230   See MED sub *ground* n. 15(b) (gronsel, grounsel).

anglice hilte / [18] *capistrum*: chevestre / *lumbare*: gallice brael / *ligulas*: lainers / [20] hec *pilea*: gallice chapel de cotun / *fultrum*: gallice feutre, anglice velt / [21] *acer*: gallice arable / *vibumus*: auburne / hic *taxus*: gallice dicitur tessun / *taxum*: lard, yf / [24] *pictaciarii*: gallice tacuners / *intercutia*: gallice rivez / *solea*: semele / *inpedia*: enpeine / *spatula*: gallice esclices / [25] *alluta*: cordiwan / [26] *pellipirii* (sic): gallice peleters / *lutricorum*: gallice lutres / [27] *epitogiorum*: gallice surecoz / [28] *murinis*: gallice mazere / *bruscis*: gallice brus, anglice warres / *tremulus*: trembler / [29] *precones*: gallice criurs / [30] *artocrea*: gallice russole / *senio*: gallice asard / [31] *auxionarii*: gallice regrateres / [32] *flamicie*: flamiche / *lichnus*: meche / [33] *furfur*: bren / [35] *columus*: gallice coudre / *altile*: chapun / [36] *trapezete*: chanjurs / *talentum*: besant / [38] *patera*: hanap / [42] *teristra*: geinse a dam / *stamineas*: gallice stamin / [44] *cinamomum*: gallice canele / [45] *onofora*: gallice coffres / [48] *liscia*: gallice lices / *bracteolas*: gallice braceroles / *scarioballum*: gog [231] / [49] *tabulata*: planchés / *anelacia*: anelaz / *jesum*: gisarme / *bombacinia*: gallice aketuns / *bombax*: gallice cotun / *toraces*: gallice gambeisuns / *trocleatas*: windas [232] / *contos*: gallice perches / [52] *cerdones*: gallice tanurs / *cedo*: trencher / *frunire*: gallice taner / *frunium*: gallice tan / hic *fallis*: gallice faus / [54] *rotundalia*: gallice taillurs / *clibanus*: furn / *epicausterium*: astres / *fornax*: gallice furs / [55] *vectis*: gallice barres / hii *barri*: gallice barres / *pulpitum*: leitrun / *retrofocinium* vel *lignificum*: treffuer [233] / [59] *lacernis*: gallice bifle / [62] *infula*: cheisible [234] / [65] *techa*: gallice de la chesir / *fusum*: gallice fusel / *colus*: gallice cunoyle / *mataxa*: cilence (sic) / *trahale*: treiues [235] / *girgillum*: gallice devoideresse / *excudia*: gallice escoinche [236] / *rupa*: gallice rupe / [66] *trama*: gallice treyme / *troclea*: gallice windas / [67] *crinalia*: gallice gerlande / [71] *auceps*: oysylur / [81] *calofurcium*: gallice gibeth / *lamina*: gallice plate / *serra*: gallice sye / *serra*: gallice serure / [82] *tripudium*: tresch / *tripudiare*: trecher / *amussis*: gallice esquire / *timpanum*: gallice tabur / *vidula*: gallice viele / *chorea*: gallice carole / *tripudium*: gallice tresche

Glosses from the commentary in MS D [237]

[2] *pubem*: penul / [3] *matrix*: matrice / [5] *gingiva*: gencive / *ysophagus*: gorge / [9] *plusculas*: gallice buches (corr. bucles) / *tibialia*: estivaus / *crepitas*: gallice bothes / [10] *stipata*: barré / [11] *pulvilli*: gallice baz / *carentivilla*: gallice canevas / *strepe*: estru / [13] *pluscularii*: gallice bukelers / *lingulas*: hardeluns / *mordacula*: gallice mordant / *loralia*: gallice loraus .i. paytreus / *equicium*: gallice haraz / [16] *artavus*: gallice knivet / [17] *exeruginare*: furbir / *tholos*: gallice pumés / *sapulos* (= capulos): gallice heutes / [18] *mercor, -ris*: gallice marcandes / *mercimonium*: gallice marcandise / *capistra*: gallice

---

231 i.e. cog.
232 See OED sub *windas* and TL 4,789–90 sub *guindas*.
233 See Gfry 8,35c–36a sub *treffouiere, treffouyer, trefouel*, TL 10,570 and FEW 13,ii,183. Cf. WW 607, 33 'repofocilium: anglice an hedbronde' and MED sub *hed* n.(1)7(b).
234 Also on p.148 of the MS are the following two notes: 'erotice, ab eros -erois, barun' and 'simboletice, a sin, cum, bolus, unde simbolum -li, escot de taverne'.
235 Corr. *treules*?
236 See note 144 above. MS Rawlinson C 496 has *soienge* and MS Bern 709 *eschoange*.
237 To save space I have omitted the word *gallice* (which precedes most of the glosses in the commentary) except where confusion or doubt might arise.

chevestre / *ligulas*: hardeluns, laners / [19] *mitas*: gallice mitayns / [20] *fultro*: feuter / *pilleus*: capel de cotun / *bombacinium*: gallice parpoint / [21] *architenentes*: gallice areblaster / *balistas*: gallice aleblast / *acere*: arabel / hec *acerra*, -rre: gallice navet (et est vas in quo ponitur thus super altare) [238] / hec *taxus*: yfe / hic *taxus*: tessun / hoc *taxum*: lard / [22] hoc *stannum*: gallice estayn / *nola*: gallice clochet / [24] *pictaciarius*: saveter / *pictacia*: gallice tacuns / *intercutia*: gallice rivés / *inpedias*: empenes / [25] *alluta*: gallice corduuan / *formipedias*: gallice furmes / *equitibialia*: gambaisuns / *spatulas*: esclices / *atramentarium*: arnement / *subula*: alayne / *licinium*: anglice liniol [239] / *gernobodum*: gernun / [26] *cirogrilli*: escureus / hic cismus est illud animal quod defert vayr et gris / [27] *epytogium*: gallice surcot / [28] *murrinis*: gallice mazer / *bruccus*: gallice brois / hec *acer*: arable / [30] *artocreas*: gallice russoles / *calathus*: gallice paner / *senio*: gallice hasard / [31] *pruna*: gallice brese / *pruina*: gallice gelé [240] / *nasturcium*: cressun / [32] *placente*: gallice symenés / *flamicie*: flaumeches / *ignacie*: gallice fuaz / *lichinus*: gallice meche / [33] *torsorium* (for tersorium): escuvelun / *ordior*: ordir / hic *acer*: gallice bren / *furfur*: gallice bren / [33] *pollitrudiant*: bulleter / *pollitrudium*: buletel / [34] *spurius*: gallice bastard / [35] *verua*: espeye / *columis*: de couder / *altile*: gallice capun / *alo*: nurrir / [36] *trapezete*: scangure / *trapeta*: gallice planche / *talentis*: besans / *bisantius*: besauns / [38] *pateras*: hanaps / *spinter*: gallice espinel [241] / *jaspis*: gallice jape / *smaragdus*: gallice meraude / [39] *laminas*: gallice platayns / [42] *teristra*: cheynse / *supara*: gallice rochet / *stamen*: gallice stamines / *flameola*: gallice cuvercheves / [43] *gariophilus*: clou de gelofer / [44] *apothecarii*: espiceres / *apotheca*: espicerie / *eleborus*: gallice marsere / [45] *carpentarius*: gallice carpunter / *cuppas*: gallice cuves / *cupa* cum unico 'p': gallice cupe / *dolea*: gallice tuneus / *onophora*: gallice bucés / *colum*: gallice tunur [242] / [46] *canti*: gauntes / *limones*: gallice limune / [47] *stiva*: manche / *tribulus*: runce / *tribula*: pele / *vangas*: beches / *epiphia*: gallice hames [243] / [48] [*faricapsias*]: gallice trameus, hoper [244] / *scarioballa*: anglice cogges / [49] *antemuralia*: gallice barbecans / *liscias*: gallice lices / *propugnacula*: bretases / *tabulata*: gallice planchés / *craticulata*: clays / *ancile*: gallice talevas / *clepsedra*: dusyl / *targias*: gallice targes / *brachiola*: gallice braceroles / *perarias*: gallice peres (sic) / *mangonalia*: mangoneus / *fustibulum*: berfrays / *sparus*: fauchun / *dolo*: doler / [*cathapultas*]: setes barbelés / *thoraces*: gallice gambaysuns / *bombacinia*: gallice aketun / *bombax*: gallice cotun / *ocreas*: hoseus de fer / *genualia*: gallice genulers / *uncos*: gallice croc / *cippos*: gallice ceppes / *ignem pelasgum*: fu gregeays / *vitrea*: verre / *balistas trocleatas*: aleblaz de trolle / *troclea*: gallice windas / *materaciis*: gallice materas / [51] *tingo*: gallice tainder / *gaudone*: gallice gayde / [52] *cerdones*: gallice tanur / *frunire*: tanir / [54] *coquina*:

---

[238] See DMLBS sub *acerra* (*a*) 'incense-boat' (the ME gloss 'a shyppe' is quoted). Gfry 10,194a sub *navette* cites a document of 1380 giving the definition 'une navette d'or a mettre l'encens' and a similar one of 1353.

[239] See MED sub *linyolf n*.

[240] See TL 4,225 which cites *gelé* for *gelee* in Bibbesworth, though the editor prints *gele*.

[241] Cf. TL 3,i,1208 sub *espincel* (citing the gloss 'spinter: espinchel') and *ibid*., 1211 sub *espingle*. See also *Olla patella* ed. Scheler, p.188.

[242] See FEW 13,ii,415a (*entonedoir, entonnoir*) which does not give the forms *tunur, toneour* found elsewhere in the present study.

[243] See TL 4,861 sub *hame*.

[244] See MED sub *hopper(e n*.

quisine / *cacabus*: gallice caudrun / *urceos*: gallice poz / *pelves*: gallice bacins / *ollas*: gallice pot a spicer / *rotundalia*: gallice salers / *acetabula*: gallice sauser / *acetum*: aysil / *scaphas*: gallice gates / *craticulas*: gallice gredil / *micatoria*: gallice miur / *creagras*: gallice havés / *clibanos*: gallice furnays / *ephicausteria*: gallice aster / [55] *incus*: enclune / *vangas*: beche / *tribula*: pele / *ligones*: haue / *sarcula*: gallice sarceus / *retropoficinium*: gallice trefuer / *cremale*: gallice cremeler / *focalia*: fuale / *stirpes*: suches / *cippi*: gallice ceppes / *vectes*: gallice barres / *barri*, -orum sine singulari genus ludi est: gallice barres / *sedilia*: seges / *scanna*: gallice baunke / *sponde*: gallice chaliz / *fercula*: gallice chaer, anglice faudestole, alio modo dicitur *ferculum*: carnis gallice mes / *culcitra*: gallice cute / *cervicalia*: gallice orler / *pulvinaria*: gallice quissin / *multra*: gallice seyle / *haustum*: gallice espucher[245] / *mulcipula* (corr. muscipula): gallice ratoir / [56] *pulpitum*: gallice letrun / [58] *giga*: gallice gige / [59] *renones*: gallice tabard / [60] *missale*: gallice messel / [61] *herotice*, ab *heros*, -is: gallice barun / [62] *alba*: aube / *pedum*: gallice croce / [63] *vexillum*: gallice baner / [64] *batum*: gallice bussel / *cenovectorium*: gallice civer / [65] *theca*: gallice dele / *fusus*: gallice fusel / *vertebrum*: gallice pesun / *mataxa*: serence / *trahale*: gallice trahal, anglice rele[246] / *girgillus*: devoiturs / *excudia*: escuce / *rupa*: gallice rupe / *ferritorium*: batuer / *calotricatorium*: riduer / *licinitorium*: gallice liche / [67] *cavillarum*: gallice caveles / *lignea spata*: espeye de fute[247] / *crinale*: gallice garlandes / [66] *trama*: gallice trayme / *troclea*: gallice tremer / *lama*: gallice lame / *ordiri*: urdir / [68] *carpentum*: gallice charet / [69] *devacuatrices*: devoideresses / *aurisece*: trencheresses de or / *marsupia*: gallice burses / [70] *anseres*: oues / *anates*: anes / *perdices*: gallice pertriz / *phasiani*: gallice fesauns / *passeres*: gallice mussuns / *plumarii*: gallice pluvers / *grus*: gallice grues / [71] *cornicor*: gallice gangeler / [72] *pectinibus*: gallice plaices / [74] *hinula*: escalun / *esperioli*: escureus / *sima*: gallice pentiz / *putoydes*: gallice (sic) fulmard / [77] *virgultus*: verger / [78] hii *antes* sine singulari, gallice wiles[248] / *fagus*: fou / *bedegar*: eclenter / *hussus*: gallice huse[249] / [79] *tigna*: cheverun / *lodia*: gallice luvel (sic) / *securis*: gallice cuné / *dolabra*: anglice bradax / [80] *triremes*: gallice goges[250] / *galea*, media producta est: gallice galé[251] / *galea*, media correpta instrumentum est militis: gallice haume / [81] *laminas*: gallice platains / *sera*: serure / [82] *vidula*: gallice viel / *tympana*: gallice tabur / *tripudiare*: trecher / *tripudium*: treche / [83] *tripudium*: treche / *tripudiare*: espringer / *cathaduppa*: gallice condute

Glosses from the commentary in MS D*

[2] *pubem*: gallice penul / [5] *uva*: grape / *ysophagus*: anglice wolende[252] / [9] *p[l]uscula*: gallice bucle / *tibiale*: gallice estivaus / *crurale*: gallice house / *crepitas*: botis / [11]

---

245 See TL 3,i,1265 sub *espuisëor*.
246 See OED sub *reel sb.*[1].
247 The commentaries have 'instrumentum mulieris'.
248 See FEW 14,552a (*veilles*).
249 See TL 4,1193 sub *housse*.
250 i.e. *coges*.
251 *galé* for *galee*.
252 Corr. *wosende*.

pulvilli: bates / *carentivillum*: gallice canule²⁵³ / *strepis*: gallice estruis / [12] *scutare*: ascuter / [13] *plusculus*: gallice buclir / *lingula*: gallice hardilun / *loralia*: gallice lorens de peterel / [16] *artavus*: knivet / [17] *eruginare*: gallice furber / *tolos*: gallice pomel / *capulus*: gallice heute / [18] *lingula*: layner / [20] *fultrum*: feutre / *pilea*: chapel de cotun / *bombace*: cotun / *bombacineum*: gallice porpunt / [21] *balista*: arblaster / *acere*: gallice arblat²⁵⁴ / hec *taxus*: gallice arbor, yf / hic *taxus*: gallice tessun / hoc *taxum*: gallice larde / [24] *pictacia*: gallice tacuns / *intercutia*: gallice rivet / *soleas*: semele / *inpedias*: empeinnes / [25] *alluta*: gallice cordewan / *formipes*: gallice formes / *equitibiale*: jambel / *spatula*: esclise / *atramentarium*: neiret / *subula*: aloyne / *licinio*: linoys / [26] *cuniculi*: cunis / *cirogrillus*: equireuus / *sabelinum*: sabeline / *cismus* animal quod fert vers et gris (on f.181v: hic *cicimis* (sic) animal quod defert ver et greys) / *laerone*: laerun / [27] *epitogiorum*: surcote / [28] *murinus*: gallice macere / *brucis*: gallice brois / hic *acer*: gallice arable / [29] yo, -as: abaier / *lagena*: gallice galun / [30] *artocreas*: russoles / *calathus*: paner / [31] *auctionarius*: regraters / *pruna*: brese / [32] *place[n]tes*: symenus / *f[l]amicie*: flaunes / *ignacie*: fuaches / *lichinos*: mesches / [33] hec *acus*, -ceris: mestilun / *furfur*: bren / *pollentriduum* (sic): poltel / [35] *columis*: coudre / *altile*: chapun / [36] *trapete*: chanjurs / *trapeta*: gallice planchis / [42] *supara*: chemise, rochet / [46] *canti*: lé jauntis / [47] *tribula*: pele vel truble / *tribulus*: runce / [48] *faricapsie*: tremie / [49] *cestus*: talavace / *clepsedra*: buche vel dosil / *periaria*: perer / *trocleatas*: areblat de troia / *troclea*: vindase / [52] *cerdones*: tanur / *frunire*: gallice taner / [53] *ligones*: gallice howe / [55] *torres*, item truncus, retropohomitum vel lignificum: gallice tresuer²⁵⁵ / *stipes*: stock / [59] *renones*: gallice tabard / *tyara*: gallice hure / [62] *pedum*: gallice croce / [64] *cenovectorium*: civer / [65] *vertebrum*: vertoyl / [69] *devacuatrices*: gallice minters²⁵⁶ / [75] *salamica* (corr. saliunca): calketrappe sed calcaneus est calketrappe de ferro / hic *malus* est ille qui non habet patris hereditatem: gallice bastard / *vibranum*: aburne / [78] *bodegar*: englenter / [82] *vidula*: gallice viele / *tripudium*: treche

Glosses from the commentary in MS L

[5] *gengiva*: gallice dicitur gencive / *ysophagus*, gula stomachi: anglice wosende / [12] *strepas*: gallice estrues / *carentivillas*: gallice dicunt canavaces / [14] *piscularii* (corr. pluscularii): buch[el]ers / *p[l]usculas*: gallice bucles / *loralia*: gallice lorens / *agularia*: aguler / [16] *artavus*: cnivet / [17] *eruginare*: gallice furber / *tholos*: gallice pumel / *capulos*: cusis / [18] *mercor*: gallice marchandise / *capistrum*: gallice chevester / *lingulas*: gallice lorens / [20] *fultrum*: gallice feutre / *pillia*: gallice chapel de cotun / *bombace*: gallice cotun / *bombacineum*: gallice purpoint / [21] *architenentes*: gallice archer / *balistas*: gallice arblaster / *arcus*: gallice arcke / hic *taxus*: teysun / hoc *taxum*: gallice larde / [24] *pictaciarii*: gallice zavaters / *pictacia*: gallice tacun / *intercutia*: gallice rivales²⁵⁷ / *soleas*: gallice semeles / *inpedias*: gallice vampes / [25] *alluta*: gallice

---

²⁵³ For *canevel*? See Scheler, *art. cit.*, 292.
²⁵⁴ An error for *arable*.
²⁵⁵ Corr. *trefuer* and see note 233 above. The MS appears to read *significium*, where other MSS have *lignificium* or *ignificium*.
²⁵⁶ This appears to be a misplaced gloss on *nummularii* [37], see MED sub *minter n.*
²⁵⁷ Cf. Gfry 7,204b sub *rival* (revel) (sorte de filet) and FEW 10,412a (*rivetoire* 'sorte de filet

cordeuan / *formipedias*: gallice formis / *spatula*: esclice / *ansorio*: gallice trenket / *atramento*: nereyt / *subula*: alene / *licinio*: linoyl / *seta*: see / [26] *pelliparii*: pellitir / *pellicia*: gallice pelisuns / *penulas*: panes / *furaturas*: furures / *cuniculi*: chunicgs / *lutriciorum*: lutre gallice / *mustelarum*: beletres, anglice uuesle [258] / *epitogiorum*: de sukoz / *palliorum*: maunteus / [28] *ciphorum*: de hanaps / *murrinus*: mazre / *acer*: arable / *tremulo*: tremble / *bruscis*: broys gallice, anglice burche [259] / [29] *hyante*: abaer gallice / *lagena*: galun / [30] *nebularum*: de niules / *artocreas*: russoles / *calathis*: paners / *senione*: hasard gallice / [31] *auctionarii*: regratirs / *narstucia*: cressun / [32] *placente*: simeneus / *ignacie*: fuas / *flamicie*: flamiches / *lichinos*: limiuns / [33] *pistores*: gallice bolengurs / *pinsunt*: pestrisunt / *tersorio*: tuayllun / *siligine*: segle / *acere*: mestulun quod eicitur a vanno / *furfure*: bren / *politrudiant*: buletent / *politrudium*: buletel / [34] *pastillarii*: pasteyrs / *pastillos*: pasteys / *farcio*: gallice farsir / [35] *verubus*: broche / *columis*: de codre / *altilia*: chapunz / *carnifices*: buchirs / *macellis*: estaus / *lepra*: sursemeys / *mensaculas*: grant chuteus / *truceta* vel *tunseta*: gallice puddins / *popello*: racaylle / [36] *trapezete*: chanjurs / *talentis*: besauns / [37] *nummularii*: munetirs / [38] *fornaces*: furnases / *pateras*: hanaps / *monilia*: nuches / *spinter*: efficayl / *nodulos*: butuns / *granula*: gallice guernetes / *jaspides*: japes / *smaragdos*: emeraudes / [39] *industria*: quinntise / *tundit*: bate / *incudem*: enclume gallice, anglice stiþee vel anvult [260] / *malleolas*: petiz marteus / *laminas*: plates / *criseas*: oreis / *anchas*: fosses quibus ansis ponuntur gemme / [41] *pannarii*: drapirs / [42] *usurpant*: mespernent / *mappa*: naps / *manutergia*: tualles / *braccas*: bracce / *teristra*: chenses / *supara*: rochet / *staminas*: estamin / *flammeola*: kevrechisy / [43] *apothecarii*: espicir / *apotheca*: especerie / *confectiones*: confectiuns / *electuaria*: letuaries / *zedoarium*: citheuuant / *zinzibero*: ginguivre / *gariophilos*: clous de gilofre / *cynamomo*: canele / *maratro*: semense de fenoyl / *luiquiricia*: [r]egalise / [44] *zinsiberum*: gallice genguivre cunduyt [261] / *alexandrinum*: alesandrin / *elleborus*: marcire gallice / [45] *cupas*: cuwes / *dolea*: tuneus / *onophora*: costireus / *cados*: barils / *cavillis*: kivilles / *cuneis*: qunus / [46] *rotarii*: ruyrs / *quadrigas*: charettes a quatre reus / *plaustra*: chers / *conti*: gallice jauntes / *modii*: moel / *limones*: limuns, bastuns / *radii*: raes, anglice spokes / *themones*: themuns anglice yilles / *juga*: jus / *arquillis*: rotres / [47] *carrucarii*: charuyr / *stivam*: maunche / *flagella*: flaeus / *sarcula*: sarceus / *runco*: sercler / *uncos*: cros / *vomeres*: socus / *tribulas*: peles / *vangas*: beches / *epiphia*: gallice bureus [262], anglice hame / [48] *farricapsas*: trameus / *versatiles*: turnables / *fusos*: fusiyls, anglice spinles [263] / *scarioballa*: lé nus de la re, anglice cockes / *cynoglocitoria*: cluses, anglice sutteles / *molares*: les pires de mulin / [47] *scobe*: balés / *rastra*: rasteus / *furce*: furkes / *manutentum*: manchel, anglice hanstaf / [49] *antemuralia*: barbekanes / *licias*: lices / *superfossata*: duble fosses / *propungnacula*: bretages / *tabulata*: plaunchis / *craticula*: engyn de clees / *cestus*: talevas / *bracheola*: braceroles / *parrarias*: perires / hoc *perarium*: gallice quariie /

de pêche'). One expects *rivet*, which has apparently been confused with another derivative of *ripa*, *rival*.

258 See OED sub *weasel sb*.
259 The gloss seems to be faulty, see MED sub *birch(e n*.
260 See OED sub *stithy sb*. and MED sub *anvelt n*.
261 *Conduyt* < *conditum*, see FEW 2,ii,1021b.
262 Corr. *hureus* and see TL 4,1172 sub *horel*.
263 See OED sub *spindle sb*.

mangonalia: manguenés / *fustibula*: slinge [264] / *trebucheta*: trebechés / *arietes*: mutuns / *sues*: minires / *vineas*: garites / *machine*: engins / *secures*: quinnes / *bipennis*: besagues, anglice tuybile / *dacas*: haches danaches / *gesa*: guisharmes / *chateyas*: hauntes / *pugiones*: misericordes / *dolonibus*: eskauberges / *anelacias*: anelas [265] / *sarillas* (sic): echus / *peltas*: eschus / *palos*: bastuns de fust / *malleos*: marteus / *clavos*: masues di fer / *cathapultas*: setes barbilees / *galeros*: heames / *conos*: crestes / *thoraces*: gambesuns / *bombacina*: parpuyns / *galeas*: cayfas / *loricas*: haubers / *ocreas*: hesus / *femoralia*: quissirs / *genualia*: genulirs / *contos*: perches / *cathenas*: chennes / *cyppos*: ceps / *ignem pelasgum*: fu gregés / *liquefactum*: fundeys / *fundas*: fundes / *glandes*: plates de plum / *balistas trocleatas*: arbelastes de truyl / *troclea*: anglice windase / *materaciis*: materays / [50] *fullones*: fulere / *pilosos*: velus / *alveo*: gros auge / *argilla*: arsile / *cardinis*: chardruns / [51] *tinctores*: teynturs / *rubea*: ruget / *majore*: warrence, anglice mader / *gaudone*: wede / [52] *cerdones*: tannurs / *cedo*: trencher / *scalprum*: g[r]ate / [53] *inc(l)udem*: enclume / *forcipibus*: tanaylles / *ventulatione*: suflement / *follium*: suflez / *ferros equinos*: fers de chival / *vangam*: beche / *tribulam*: pele, angl. sovule [266] / *ligones*: picoses / *sarcula*: sarceus, wed-hoc anglice / *falces*: faus, anglice syes (?) / [54] *cacabos*: chaudruns / *urceos*: pot / *sartagines*: grant paeles / *pelves*: bacyns / *idrias*: seyllas / *ollas*: pot / *rotundalia*: plateus / *acetabula*: saucirs / *sapphas*: gates / *eppicausteria*: astres vel chiminees / *fornases*: furs / [55] *fimbriatum*: frengé, anglice ragguede [267] / *tripodes*: gallice treveitis / *trestelli*: trestés / *torres*: tisuns / *cremalia*: cramallires / *focalia*: buche / *stirpes*: gallice suches / hic *stirpis*, -pis: estoyc [268] / *retropoficinium*: gallice trefuer / *cippi*: ceps / *vectes*: veruyls gallice / *sedilia*: bans / *scanna*: furmes / *sponde*: chalit / *levigatis*: plainees / *culcitre*: quiltes / *pulvinaria*: quisins / *cribrum*: cribre / *haustrum*: buket / *taratantarium*: saz / *casanium* (corr. casiarium): chesire / *muscipulam*: lachure [269] / [59] *perca*: perche / *indumenta*: afeblemenz (corr. afublemenz) / *supertunicalia*: surkoz / *scapularia*: espaulires / *pallia*: mauntelis / *coopertoria*: chuvrechifs / *lintheamina*: linceus / *sarrabarre*: sclavines / *bombacinia*: aketuns / *tapete*: tapiz / *cuculli*: cuulet / collobia: froc / *lacernis*: bife / *paludamentis*: maunteus de purpre / [60] *missale*: mesel / *gradale*: greel / *martilogium*: martiloge / *bibliotecam*: une bible / [61] *chatholice*: leaument / *tipice*: figurablement / *pragmatice*: demandablement / *ypothetice*: persunaument / *paranetice*: entremetauntument / *prophonetice*: criablement / *proseutice*: prechaument / *herotice*: amablement / *diastolice*: deparaiblement / *antisiastice*: encuntre sé memes / *simboletice*: reconsilaument / *presaugoretice*: avantsachablement / *silogistice*: conclusament / *largetice*: gratiusement / *trenetice*: waumentusement / *palinotice*: rechanturablement / *apostolice*: amonestablement / *antipodice*: respunablement / *tropice*: conversablement / *ethice*: moraument / *satirice*: reprisablement / *cinice* .i. canine: chinablement / [62] *supercilia* (corr. superlicio): surplis / *alba*: aube / *phanula*: phanun / *stola*: estole / *thiara*: mitre / *amictum*: amit / *infula*: chesible / [63] *aspersorium*: vispilun / *vexillum*: banire /

---

[264] See OED sub *sling sb*.
[265] The commentaries derive *anelacia* 'ab Alano inventore, qui fuit pirata regis Ricardi' and cite the epitaph to Richard I which is printed by William Camden, *Remains concerning Britain*, repr. London, 1870 (Library of Old Authors), p.401. See also Scheler, *art. cit.*, 311.
[266] See OED sub *shovel sb*.
[267] See OED sub *ragged a.*[1].
[268] See TL 3,ii,1397 sub *estoc*.
[269] See Gfry 4,690b sub *laceure*.

campana: seyn / *campanario*: clochir / *turubulum*: sensir / *phiala*: fiole / *hostiarum*: de hoytes gallice vel blees[270] / [64] *dentatis*: edentees / *batis*: provendirs / *presepia*: creches / *cenevectorio*: civire / *inpinguendos*: engressir / [65] *forfices*: forces / *theca*: deel / *vertebrum*: pesun / *colus*: cunuylle / *mataxa*: serence / *trahale*: trahul / *girgillum*: devudores / *excudia*: eschuce, anglice syngle / *linipulus*: bristel de lin / *rupa*: rupire, anglice rib / *feritorium*: batuer / *cupatorium*: cuvir / *lixivatorio*: buket / *calotricatorium*: asser rugosus, gallice riduer, ridlingbret[271] / *linitorium*: gallice lige, anglice slicston / [66] *textrices*: tesires / *pectines*: laniurs, anglice sclees / *stamina*: stayms / *trama*: treme / *spola*: espole / *pano*: broche / *lama*: lame, anglice slebret[272] / *troclea*: gallice tramer / *globorum*: lusseus / [67] *texta*: tissus, seyus[273] / *serica*: de seye / *cavillarum*: de chivilles / *spata*: espee / *crinalia*: garlaundeches / [68] *focum*: fue / *pelliciis*: peliçuns / *velaminibus*: cuverturs / *carpunt*: charpis sunt / *villosam*: velue / *depilant* .i. detrahunt: gallice depeignunt / [69] *devacuatrices*: devuderesses / *auricece*: trencheresses de or / [70] *perdices*: perdris / *phasiani*: phesans / *alaude*: aloes / *passeres*: mussuns / *plumarii*: pluvirs / *ardee*: haruns / *pavones*: pouns / *turtures*: turtres / *turdi*: esturnel / [71] *auceps*: osilur / *insidiatur*: enguetit / *herodius*: herunnir / *ancipiter*: girfac / *capus*: muschet / *sturnus*: crestuler[274] / *merulus*: merulun / *mavicius*: mauviz / *psitacus*: papegai / *philomena*: ruscinole / *liricina*: chardunerole / *milium* (corr. milvum) cuffle / *cornicem*: cornile / *vespertilionem*: cauvesurise, anglice bacche / *nicticoracem*: corf de nuyt / *pellicanum*: pellican / [72] *piscatores*: peschurs / *salmones*: samuns / *trutas*: trutes / *murenas*: lamprees / *morium*: murue / *pectines*: plais / *rocie*: roches / *stinchi*: epinoches, anglice stichulus[275] / *tenci*: tenches / *ragadie*: raes / *allecia*: arenns / *mulli*: mules / *hamis*: havus / *rethibus*: rees / *percas*: perches / *gobiones*: gujuns / [73] *capros*: bucs / *edos*: chivereus / *burdones*: burduns / *camelos*: chameus / *dromedarios*: dromedaries / [74] *dami*: dayms / *hynuli*: founs / *capree*: chevereus sauvage / *taxi*: tessuns, anglice broces[276] / *linces*: linces / *apri*: senglirs / *pardi*: pars / *cuniculi*: chunigs / *esperioli*: esqureis / *simei*: singes / *lutricii*: lutres, anglice hotur / *stangnis*: estange / *pytoides*: putoys / [75] *orto*: curtil / *salvia*: sauge / *petrosillum*: persil / *dictanus*: ditayn / *celidonia*: celidone / *piretum*: peletre, anglice petir[277] / *urtica*: ortie / *carduus*: kardun / *saliunca*: caucutrappe / *malva*: mauve, anglice hoclef / *agrimonia*: agrimuine / *salatro*: morele, anglice sur-docke / *solsequio*: solsequie, anglice golde / [76] *ortulanus*: churtilir / *caulis*: cholet / *borago*: gallice borage / *beta*: gallice bete[278] / hic *maurer* est ille qui non habet patris hereditatem: gallice bastar / *porrum*: porreus / *allia*: aus / *sinapis*: senevee / *sinapium*: mustarde / *porreta*: poree / *cyvolli*: cyvoys / *hynule*: eskalunes / *pimpinella*: premerole / *pilosella*: piloche / *sanicla*: sanicle / *buglossa* .i. bovis glossa .i. lingua bovis: gallice mautefelun / *lancea*: launcelee / [77] *virgulto*: vergir / *cerasus*: cerisir / *serasa*: serises /

---

270 *blees* = *oblees*.
271 See OED sub riddle v.².
272 See OED sub *slay sb.*¹ 2 (*slay-bred*).
273 FEW 11,50a dates *soyeux* to 1549.
274 The origin of English *kestrel* and the forms of OF *crécerelle* remain unclear, cf. FEW 2,ii,1321ab. I have not found the form *crestuler* elsewhere.
275 See OED sub *stickleback*.
276 See MED sub *brok n.(1)*.
277 Corr. lemma to *piretrum* and see MED sub *peter n. 3* and TL 7,867 sub *petre*.
278 See MED sub *bete n.(1)*.

pirus: perir / *pira*: peres / *pomus*: pumir / *poma*: pummes / *prunus*: prunir / *pruna*: prunes / *coctanus*: quuynnir / *coctana*: quuyns / *mespilus*: neflir / *mespila*: melles / *pessicus*: peschir / *pessica*: pesches / *castanea*: castaynnir / *castaneas*: castanes / *nux*: nuir / *nuces*: noys / *avellana*: nusillir / *avellanas*: nusilles / *ficus*: fikir / *ficus*: fikes / *uvas*: grapes / *pampinos*: f(r)olies de viinnes / *palmites*: branches / *antes*: raysins / *phalangas*: furchez / [78] *silvestrium*: sauvages / *fago*: fo, anglice behec / *pinus*: pin / *lauro*: lorir / *celsus*: aliers / *celsa*: alies / *corno*: cormir / *corna*: cormes / *cinus*: cenilis, anglice hay yord²⁷⁹ / *cina*: cineles / *husso*: huus, anglice holin / *rumpnus*: gersilir / *bodelgar*: englentir / *rumpnice*: runce gallice / *populus*: poplir / *salice*: saus / *tremulo*: tremlir / *pepulus*: bulacir / *pepula*: purneles / [79] *trapetas*: planches / *solivas*: sulives / *lacuna*: fosse / *tigna*: cheveruns / *lodia*: luvires / *laquaria*: laces / *basis*: fundement / *epistilium*: sumet / *dolabre*: doleure / *rosticutio*: bisague / *acia*: ace / *terebro*: terire / *celte*: cisel / *terebellum*: forrer gallice / *cavillis*: kivilles / *calce*: caus / *lathomi*: massun / *lathomega*: truel, anglice trulle²⁸⁰ / *amussi*: esquire / *perpendiculo*: perendurel / *ponderoso*: chargus²⁸¹ / [80] *dromones*: dromuns / *lembos*: petites neist . . .²⁸² / *triremes*: anglice cocgnes / [81] *califurcium*: gibet / *lammas*: plates / *serras*: syes / *scorpiones*: eschurges / [82] *tibicines*: businirs / *cornicines*: cornurs / *vidulatores*: viulurs / *timpano*: tabur / *cimbalis*: cimbeus / *tripudiatrices*: espinguoresses / *tripudiare*: trecher / *tripudium*: treche / [83] *choream*: karole / *tripudiis*: espingueries / *chatadippe*: gallice chunduyt

MS WORCESTER CATHEDRAL CHAPTER LIBRARY Q.50

[f.20v] commentary [s.xiii]: [24] *pictaciarii*: gallice [sic] cobelers²⁸³ / *pictacia*: gallice tacun / *solee*: gallice soles / *inpedia*: gallice empinis / [22] *firmacularii*: gallice fermey-lers / [17] *eruginatores*: gallice fourbur / *tholus*: gallice pomel / [18] *capistrum*: gallice chevestre / *ligula*: gallice layneris / [19] *mite*: gallice mitayns / [20] *fultro*: gallice de feutre / *bombex*: gallice cotoun / [21] *architenentes*: gallice archers / *baliste*: gallice alblastre / *acer*: gallice arable / *taxum*: gallice lard / *taxus*: gallice if / [f.21r] [25] *alluta*: gallice corduuian / *formipedia*: gallice furme / *spatula*: gallice esclicez / *atramentario*: nert, enke / *licineo*: gallice lincel / [26] *cuniculorum*: gallice conigeus / *sirogrillorum*: gallice ecquer(er)us / *lutriciorum*: gallice loutres / *sabellino*: gallice sabelin / *laerone*: gallice laerunt / [28] *murrinus*: gallice de macere / *acer*: gallice arable / [38] *arthocreas*: [ru]soles

On f.21r there are a few interlinear glosses of s.xiv/xv as follows:

[26] *lutricorum*: oters / *cirogrulos*: scorelis / *urlas*: rewers²⁸⁴ / *sabelino*: blamier (?) /

---

²⁷⁹ Corr. *hayporn*, cf. WW 572,45 *cinus*: *haythorn*.
²⁸⁰ See OED sub *trowel sb*.
²⁸¹ FEW 2,i,419a gives only *chargeable* ('lourd, pesant'), but see AND sub *chargeous* ('hard, grievous').
²⁸² The MS appears to read *neist'*, a misreading of *nefes*?
²⁸³ See MED sub *cobeler(e n*.
²⁸⁴ If the meaning appears to be hems trimmed with fur, then it is an early anticipation of the modern meanings registered in FEW 10,357a ('bout retroussé de la manche d'un habit', 'les deux parties d'un habit qui, se croisant sur la poitrine, sont repliées').

laerone: menener (?) [285] / the same hand continues on [f.21v] [30] *arthocreas*: ha-chewes / *senione*: hazardiye / [32] *placente*: simenelys

[f.21v] commentary: [32] *lichinis*: gallice meches / *ignacie*: gallice flass (sic) [286] / *flammicie*: flemcis gallice / [f.22r] [35] *veru*: gallice espeie / [37] *numularii*: gallice moners / [38] *pateras*: gallice hanappers / *interlinear glosses (s.xv)*: [35] *macheras*: flessch ax [287] / *hyllas*: puddinggs

[f.22v] in hand of s.xiv, interlinear glosses: [39] *industria*: la qeyntise / *incudit*: batet / super *incudem*: le encikeloun de fer / *malleolis*: petys martels / *subtilibus*: sotils / *laminas*: plates / *includit*: encloset / infra *ancas*: deens pertus / *quibus*: de lé quel / *generose*: gentils / commentary (s.xiii): [42] *terristra*: gallice chemis / *supara*: gallice rochet / *stamen*: gallice eçtayme / *pepla*: gallice wimple / [43] *apotecarii*: gallice eçpisers / *apoteca*: gallice eçpisery / [f.23r] [45] *cuppas*: gallice cuyfus / *cados*: gallice barels / *dolea*: gallice tonels / *onofora*: gallice costrels / [47] *tribulum*: gallice rounce / *vanga*: gallice beche / [48] *faricaptie*: gallice tramels / interlinear glosses (s.xiv): [45] *anofora*: costrez / *cavillis*: chevils, pin / *cados*: barel / *cuneis*: par echels, weg / [46] *modii*: mowels / *limones*: limouns / *temones*: temouns / *juga*: yok, juges / *arquillis*: hames, estels [288]

[f.24r] (s.xv) [47] *ligones*: picousche / [f.27r] [78] *silvestrum*: wode / *fago*: besc / *husso*: holu / *salice*: salw / *tremulo*: hasp / *bedegar*: hepe brer [289] / *tilia*: ly[n]de

MS BERLIN, DEUTSCHE STAATSBIBLIOTHEK, PREUSSISCHER KULTURBESITZ LAT. FOL. 607 [290]

[2] *tibia* (quodam instrumentum): estive / *tuba* gallice appellatur busyne . . . anglice appellatur trompe / *cavilla* (illud instrumentum): gallice kevyl appellatur et anglice a weuge / *musculus*: gallice braune de la . . . anglice miff [291] / *cartilago*: gallice appellatur crussel et anglice a gristel bon / *internodium*: gallice la verrepne du genuyl [292] / *pubex*: gallice dicitur penul / [3] *peritoneon* (circuitus cunium): anglice a wiulbon et gallice

---

[285] This gloss and the preceding one are uncertain and obscure.

[286] Corr. *flanss*.

[287] See MED sub *flesh n.2c(b)*.

[288] See TL 3,ii,1372 (*estele*).

[289] See MED sub *hepe n.(2)e*.

[290] The evidence of this MS must be treated with the greatest caution. It is clear that the scribe has misplaced items and frequently did not understand what he was copying. It would therefore be unwise to place any reliance on forms and equivalents in the MS which are not corroborated from other sources. There is a garbled *accessus*, different from the one printed in Vol. 1, in which we are told 'Magister Johannes de Garlandia . . . composuit hunc libellum ad commoditatam discipulorum suorum ad reprehensionem Alexandri Nequam de quo dicit "Nigrior esse potes, nequior esse nequis" '.

[291] Corr. *riff* or *midriff*.

[292] It seems likely that the meaningless *verrepne* (MS *v'repne*) is a miscopying of *entreneu*, or conceivably, assuming the scribe's eye wandered from the French to the English equivalent, of *knepane* (see WW 590,19).

appellatur cercele de cul [293] / [5] *pirrula*: gallice apellatur le bec du nes / *gingiva*: gallice gummus [294] / *huvula*: gallice dicitur uvet et anglice molo [295] / *epiglotum*: . . . anglice wesond [296] / *sclironta* (infirmitas oculorum): gallice la male . . . / [6] *craneum*: gallice sumet de le chef / *cistis*: gallice dicitur ceste et anglice milte [297] / *cirrare*: gallice taburner / *cirrator*: taburneur / *cirra*: taburn / [7] *diafragma*: gallice dicitur cerepne et anglice mideride [298] / *budegarium* (fructus): anglice appellatur aepe [299] / *budegar*: eglentere / [12] *corinda*: anglice dicitur a dagker [300] / *celilium* (siccisolium): anglice interpretatur dayshewe [301] / [15] *frena* componitur efreins et dicitur de freno -es, myen [302] / [17] *eruginatores*: gallice vocantur furbeurs / *erugo*: gallice dicitur ruyhle / *tholus*: gallice pumun appellatur / [21] *prurigo*, prurigaris: gallice dicitur quitre [303] / *taxus*: gallice appellatur tesun et anglice a broc / [22] *lamina*: gallice pece / *laminatim*: gallice dicitur de pece en pece / *insicla* (instrumentum textricis): anglice appellatur a glay [304] / *fulligo*: anglice soth et gallice suye / [27] *toga*: gallice appellatur gune / *pallus* dicitur: mantel / [28] *reparatores*: li rep[ar]aylhers / *ciphorum*: des enapes / [33] *polentridium*: gallice dicitur balutel / *fermentum*: gallice levayn / *alveum*: gallice auge / *arcugerium* (vehitur super arcos): proprie gallice appellatur wousur / *costa*: gallice appellatur scravillun et anglice a ribbe [305] / [34] *collustrum*: gallice kalleboz / *verubus*: gallice dicitur espey / *corulus*: gallice codre / *incudis*: gallice dicitur englume / *hilla*: gallice anduhle / *illusa*: gallice anguilpart (?) / [42] *sistra*: gallice aketune / *supara*: anglice a rive rochet [306] / *peplum*: gallice guinple / *flameola*: gallice dicitur a cuvre-chiep (sic) / [49] *arietes*: gallice pereres / *gesa*: gallice dicuntur gisermes / [*spartas*]: gallice feuchur / *catapulta*: gallice dicitur sete barbelé / *bonbacinea*: gallice vocantur purpoins / *glandes*: gallice stapilhuns [307] / [50] *argilla*: gallice dicitur arsil et anglice rochestre herthe [308] / [51] *gaudo*: anglice dicitur wod / *sandix*: gallice dicitur warence / *blodium*: gallice dicitur bluet / [52] *corinda*: anglice dicitur a last [309] / *equitium*: gallice

---

293 For the English gloss see OED sub *whirl-bone* 2. It is not appropriate to the lemma and may have been displaced from *internodium* (see WW 590,19).
294 Actually English 'gums'!
295 It looks as if *molo* is a miscopying of *uvola*.
296 See OED sub *weasand*.
297 Displaced from *splen* presumably. Cf. DMLBS sub *cystis* ('gall bladder, scrotum, cyst'). FEW 2,ii,1615b gives no medieval reflexes of this word.
298 See MED sub *mid-rid(e* n.
299 See MED sub *hepe* n.(2).
300 The gloss seems to be an error (see MED sub *daggere*), for *corinda* reappears in [52] as 'a last'.
301 See MED sub *daies-ie* n.
302 There is confusion with *frio*, see MED sub *mien* v.
303 The MS appears to read *quitur* which implies that the scribe took *prurigo* as a noun, see FEW 2,ii,1166a (*cuiture* = 'brûlure d'une plaie').
304 Corr. lemma to *insubula* and gloss to *slay*.
305 The French gloss represents *escov(e)illon*. See OED sub *rib* sb.³.
306 The MS appears to read *kive rochet*.
307 I can find no other example of this form. See OED sub *staple* sb.¹ and FEW 17,221b (*estaple* f. 'pieu' (1361)). Du Cange glosses *glandis* 'pars superior valli in munitionibus urbium'.
308 I do not know what is meant by 'Rochester earth'.
309 See MED sub *lest(e* n. The usual lemma is *calopodium*.

dicitur aras / [53] *follinacium*: gallice dicitur folenet[310] / *falx*: faussil gallice / [55] *tresticula*: gallice dicitur treteus / *cremium*: gallice dicitur karboneis et anglice a colleop[311] / *sedilia*: dicitur gallice a foustrimitol[312] / *multorium*: gallice dicitur la bivre de la vache et anglice hudur de la vache[313] /[56] *pulpita*: gallice dicitur letrun / [62] *talare* -aris: gallice dicitur parure / *poder[is]*: gallice bassures / [65] *liquibricium* (sic): anglice a sliqueston[315] / *ferritorium*: dicitur gallice karole / [72] *gobiones*: gallice gujuns / *gamerus*: gallice vocatur tenche / *ephimera*: gallice / [74] *linces*: anglice werewlves[316]

---

310 I have not encountered the lemma or gloss elsewhere.
311 See MED sub *collop(pe* n.
312 An uncomprehending attempt to copy *faudestol*?
313 The MS has *biv'* which I do not recognise. For the English(!) see OED sub *udder*.
314 The gloss does not seem to be attested elsewhere.
315 See OED sub *sleekstone*.
316 See OED sub *werewolf, werwolf*.

CHAPTER EIGHTEEN

JOHN OF GARLAND'S *UNUS OMNIUM*

THE CAMBRIDGE AND DURHAM MANUSCRIPTS [1]

[A] [2]

arculus: arsun (C) gallice arçun (D) / *artavus*: knivet (C) / *celle*: gallice de la sele (D) / *clitella*: gallice cofre (D) / *vielle*: viele (CD) / *artocrea*: gallice russel (D) gallice russeus (D) / *artocepta*: gallice lavurs (C) [3] / *artus*: gallice ortil (C) / *arcubulus*: gallice archer (D) / *architesis*: fure (D) / *articuli*: urtiz (D) / *architenens*: archir (C) / *sollertia*: gallice coyntise (D) / *arcubium*: wayte (CD) / *abigo*: envee chacer (C) / *ambactus*: truflur (C) treflur [sic] (D) / *ambages*: trufles (CD) / *ambago*: trufle (C) / *ambiguosas*: dutusis (D) / *amiculum*: keverchif (C) / *amictina*: anglice tike (C) [4] / *mitra*: coyfe (C) / *amictus*: covertur (C) / *alteror*: entrechanger (C) entrechaunger (D) / *adultus*: gallice parcru (D) / *aluta*: cordiwan (C) / *alcedo*: anglice meu (C) [5] / *alietus*: merilun (C) in gallico dicitur merilun (D) / *alutarius*: gallice cordewaner (D) / *auriga*: gallice chareter (D) / *obaudis*: beshoyes (D) [6] / *avicipula*: anglice putfalle (C) [7] / *aqualiculum*: lavur (C) / *aries*: mutun (C) / *arrabo*: ernis (D) [8] / *avena*: avayne (C) / *avia*: forveable (CD) / *avias*: fables (C) / *glaucessit*: devent jaune (D) / *aucipitis*: de un ostur (D) / *acer*: gallice arable (CD) / *acredula*: gallice sorele (C) avis que alio nomine dicitur lucuna [sic] vel philomena gallice russinole, anglice nutegale (D) [9] / *alcedo*: .i. meora, gallice maue de mer (D) / *acesso* (= acesco): gallice enegrir (C) / *acerbus*: egre (D) / *acinacina*: drasche de grache [corr. grape] (C) [10] / *acroma*: .i. pomum silvestre, anglice wodecrabbe (D) [11] / *aleator*: hasardur (D) / *aleo*: hasardur (D) / *albicat*: emblancher (C) / *albor*: blaunchure (D) / *albumen*: gallice blaunchure de le uf (D) / *area*: place (C) / *ambro*: gallice glutun (C) / *arena*: gravele (CD) / *arista*: areste (C) / *atramentarium*: gallice arnement (C) / *atramen* .i. nigredo sutoris .s.: blachhe (C) [12] / *auleum*: gallice curtine (CD) / *aristor*: glaner (C) / *aristoforum*: anglice trunke (D) [13] / *auxion-*

---

1 I print the vernacular glosses from MSS Oxford, Bodleian Library, Rawlinson G 96 and Corpus Christi College (D) 121 in *Revue de Linguistique Romane* 43 (1979), 162–78.

2 I print the glosses according to the alphabetical sections in which the *Unus omnium* is organised (strict alphabetical order is not adhered to within each alphabetical section).

3 MS D f.125r has 'hoc artoceptum est vas artificialiter factum et dicitur artoceptum quasi habens duo cepta .i. principia artificiosa composita quasi lavacrum'.

4 See OED sub *tick sb.*[1]. The marginal commentary gives *amictinum* as 'pediculus', so that the sense 'cover' given in OED sub *tick sb.*[2] and which might have been expected here is not relevant.

5 See MED sub *meue* n.(2) and DMLBS sub *alcedo*.

6 The text reads 'Si bene non audis, ea que dicuntur obaudis' and the gloss is 'obaudire est male audire, ut quando aliquis fingit se non audire'.

7 See OED sub *pitfall sb.*

8 See MED sub *ernes* n.

9 At the top of f.39r in C a fifteenth-century hand (or later?) has added 'acredula: gallice sorele, anglice golfinhc' and, in the right-hand margin, 'hic renunculus, kedeney'.

10 The commentary in C f.39v has 'hoc acinacinum sive acinacium'. See DMLBS sub *acinaceum*. MS Oxford, Corpus Christi College 121 f.85v has 'hoc acinacium sive asinacinum est cossa uvarum'.

11 See MED sub *crab(be* n.(2)a.

12 See MED sub *blacche* n.

13 The line in the text runs 'Hinc aristoforum vas dicunt piscibus aptum' and the marginal

ator: regratur (C) regrater (D) / *apostata*: le renéé (D) / *ardea*: hayrun (C) / *arceda* (stella in celo): Charles Wen (C)[14] / *arcedia* (quedam stella): Charles Wel (C) / *atomus*: gallice putye, anglice mote (D)[15] / *liceor, -eris*: gallice preiser (D) / *liceo, -es*: gallice est preisé (D) / *anticopa*: kontretalie (D)[16] / *aranea*: yrayne (C) / *alapam*: buffe (C) / *alveus*: auge (C) anglice trou (D)[17] / *alvarium*: rusche (C) / *antetica*: trusse (C) une truse (D)[18] / / *amussis*: gallice esquire (D) / *minium*: gallice vermilun (C)

[B]

balbus: anglice wlaffin (D)[19] / *bolus*: mossel [sic] (C) / *balo*: blete (C)[20] / *balearius*: arblastir (C) / *balena*: balene, wal (C) anglice wal (D) / *balista*: arblast (C) alblast (D) / *bisulcus*: gallice duble reuun (D) / *bitumen*: arsil (C) / *antibulum* .i. pignus: gage (C) / *bubastis* (musca bovina)[21]: une grosse musche (C) / *bacca*: gallice perle (CD) / *bullio*: gallice bulier (D) / *bulla*, nodulus: gallice botun (D) / *lanista*: mace[c]rin (C) / *bullicio*: biollun (C) / *brachiale*: bracerole (C)

[C]

cantus: jaunte (C) anglice feluhe (D)[22] / *cantus*: chaunsun (D) / *cicuta*: gallice humbeloc, anglice herbe beneyt [sic] (D) / *canabs*: cambre, hanep (C) / *colo*: gallice culer (C) / *colum*: colur (C) / *incus*: encluyn (C) / *candidarius*: parmuntir (qui dealbat coria) (C)[23] / *candor*: gallice blaunchure (D) / *calcitro*: recuyller (C) / *calx*: talun (C) / *corea*: carole (C) / *caverna*: crevesce (C) / *cophinus*: corbail (C) corbayl (D) / *caldarium*: gallice cauderun (C) / *canna*: gallice rosele, anglice spir (C)[24] / *corista*: gallice queristre (D) / *culmus*: chaume (D) / *culponeus*: riveling (CD) / *culmen*: hautesce (D) / *caveam*: fosse (D) / *culcitra*: qulte (C) coylte (D) / *concaccus*: gallice perle (D) / *cuniculus*: cunil gallice (C) / *cullum*: une kuele (D) / *cunabula*: bers (C) berce (D) / *columpna*: pilir (C) piler (D) / *cune*: gallice borz [sic], cradel anglice (C)[25] / *cereus*: cirge (CD) / *cassis*: haume (C) / *colum*: tuneur (D)[26] / *ceroma*: blaunchet (D)

---

commentary in C f.39v has 'quoddam vas in quo conservantur pisces' and D f.127v explains 'de hec arista, -e et foros, ferre, quia deferuntur pisces aristas habentes'. These notes confirm the gloss *trunke*, see OED sub *trunk sb.II.8*. A different meaning is given in DMLBS sub *aristophorum*.

14   See MED sub *Charle-wain*.
15   See TL 7,1672 sub *poutie* and MED sub *mot n.(1)*.
16   See DMLBS sub *anticopa*.
17   See OED sub *trough sb.I*.
18   In the right-hand margin of C f.40v is the gloss 'minium: gallice vermilun'. A fifteenth-century hand has added on the same folio 'inarro, subarro: hernescher, anglice 3irni' and 'hic arrabo, arrabonis: hanselle'.
19   See MED sub *blaffard n.(1)* and OED sub *wlaffe v*.
20   See MED sub *bleten v*. In C f.41r a later hand (s.xv) has added 'boatus -tus -tui, anglice noyse'.
21   Cf. DMLBS sub *buprestis*.
22   See MED sub *felwes n.(pl)* where the singular form is described as 'rare'.
23   See MED sub *parmenter n*.
24   See OED sub *spear sb.[2] 2b and 3*.
25   corr. *berz*. See MED sub *cradel n.(1)a*.
26   C f.42v also has a gloss on *colum*, 'tunidor, gallice tunur'. See OED sub *tunder[1]*. The form *tunedore* is found in MS Cambridge, Gonville and Caius College 136 p.61 (Serlo of Wilton,

/ *tholomeum*: anglice tolselde (C) [27] / *cadus*: baril (C) / *cribro*: cribler (C) [28] / *recidigna*: anglice riveroket (C) rochet (D) / *succiduus* .i. caducus: cheable (C) / *caducus*: cheount (D) / *recidivus*: recheable (C) / *offa*: supe (D) / *collibium* (est cibus delicatus, quodam genus oleris): gallice joute (C) [29] / *cophinus*: gallice hanaper (D) / *vas panis*: gallice corbayl (D) / *carex*: anglice star, seg (D) [30] / *calvus*: gallice caut [corr. cauf] (D) / *casona* .i. vestis .i. spinter: afiçal (C) / *cepum* (confectio ex cepis): gallice hunioné (D) [31] / *callidus*: gallice koynte (D) / *percontor*: gallice ensercher (D) / *clavis*: clef (D) / *claudico*: clocer (C) / *claudus*: clop (C) cloc (D) / hec *claudes*, claudis .s. inclusorius: anglice hayward (C) [32] / *claudes* .i. claudicatura: closure (C) / *crasso*: engreser (D) / *clatrus*: barre (C) / *secors*: gallice coard (C) / *secordia*: cowardise (C) / *coredulus*: faucun (C) / *exclusor* .i. limitor vel janitor: portir (C) [33] / *lacesso*: detrere vel entarier (C) gallice entarier (D) / *condilus* (est nodus percutiens in digitis): anglice knekeles (C) [34] / *cuneus*: gallice kivil (D) / *circinus*: cumpas (C) cunpas (D) [35] / *cecus*: auwgle (D) / *carminor*: gallice charmer (C) / *caprea*: gallice cheverul, anglice ro (D) / *carbo*: charbun (C) / *coritus*: furel de le arc (D) / *celtes* (<celtis): chisel (C) gallice chisel (D) / *clipeus*: eschu (D) / *clunaculum*: un cruper (D) / *ceculto*: enwgler (D) / *clunes*: crupe (CD) / *campso*: chavager (C) / *canistra*: rosel (C) / *canna*: rosel (C) rosele (D) / *camus*: bernak (CD) / *cerdo*: tannur (C) tanur vel pelter (D) / *capistrum*: chevestre (C) / *capsa*: hucche (D) [36] / *capus*: muschet (C) / *cippus*: cep (C) / *cicuta*: bebe [corr. herbe] beneyt (D) / *centuplus*: duble cent (D) / *ancile*: bucler (D) / *caupo*: taverner (D) / *caupona*: taverne (D) / *cinctoria*: centure (C) / *crudeo*: devenir cruel (C) / *capito*: gallice caboche (C) [37] / *saxa*: roches (C) / *muscipula*: ratunel (C) ratuere (D) / *coculus*: quistrun (C) / *anticipare*: awaunt prendre (D) / *conquestrius* (qui facit gafros): wafrur (C) / *caprona*: de chif (C) / *crudelis*: cruel (D) / *camera*: chaumbre (D) / *apoteca*: gallice gerner (D) / *elistropheum*: cunsode (C) / *cubatoria*: dortur (C) / alauda *cirrita*, gallina cirrita: gallice koppid (D) [38] / *crudeo*: devenir cruel (C).

De differenciis) and Berlin, Deutsche Staatsbibliothek, Preussischer Kulturbesitz, lat. fol. 607 f.18r 'cola: tunudors'.

27 See OED sub *tolsel*.

28 In the right-hand margin of C f.43r has been added 'cribro, -bras, est farinam sincerare, gallice cribler, anglice sufte'. See OED sub *sift v*.

29 See TL 4,1812 sub *jote*.

30 See OED sub *star sb.*[2] and *sedge sb.*[1].

31 In the right-hand margin of C f.43r *cepicium* ('vinum aliquod confactum ex cepe') is glossed 'gallice hyonet'.

32 See MED sub *hei-ward n.*

33 In the left-hand margin of C f.43v is the entry 'monoceros . . . gallice unicorn'.

34 See MED sub *knokel n.*

35 On f.44v of C a fifteenth-century hand has added the glosses 'nativus: vilayn, cicuta: gallice aloyne, anglice weremod'.

36 See MED sub *huche n.*

37 On C f.45v a fifteenth-century hand has added the glosses '*cenovectorium*: dreye, scario-ballum: anglice a clacce of a melle, morum: blakeberie, pinna (pars piscis): vin'. See MED sub *draie n.*, *clak(k)e n.(2)* and *fin n.(1)*.

38 See MED sub *copped ppl. 1(b)* ('crested of bird').

[D]

dica: gallice talie (D) / *domesticus*: privé (C)[39] / *dedico*: dedier (D) / *ductilis*: amenable (CD) / *clepsedra*: dusil (C) / *donativum*: gallice werdun (D) / *dedo*: abaundoner (C) / *abdo*: muscer (C) / *crucido*: gallice decoper (C)[40] / *domicilium*: gallice severunde, anglice evesinge (D)[41] / *dolo*: doler (D) / *dolimen*: hache (C) / *dolium*: anglice azze (D)[42] / *dolabra*: anglice bradax (D) / *dolatura*: dolure (C) / *deterio*: emperer (C) enpeirer (D) / *dissipo*: deseverer (C) / *diaria*: menisun (C) / *dumus*: bussun (C) / *ditare*: enricher (D) / *dureo*: endursir (D) / *denseo*: espesser (D) / *densus*: espés (D) / *spina*: gallice eschine, anglice rigbon (D)[43]

[E]

edus: bukerel (C) / *esculus*: gallice mellir (C) gallice metler (D) / *exesus*: envirun rungé (D) / *semesus*: demi mangé (D) / *edulium*: pan (C) cumpanage (D) / *comedo*: glutun (C) / *emax*: achatable (C) / *interimo*: tuer (C) / *redimo*: rechater (CD) / *aenum*: cauderun (C) / *erro*, erroris .i. scurra: anglice harlot (C) / *estus*: chaline (D) / *egestudo*: busuiner (D) / *accessus*: aprussement (C) / *perrectos*: gallice avançable (C) / hic *iter*, iteris (ponitur pro quadam ave que flava est tota et crocea): gallice oriole, anglice wodewale (C)[44] / *exta*: buelis vel entrailles (C) / *reditio*: repeyranse (C) / *reditus*: repeyr (D) / *census*: de rente (D) / *census*: rente (D) / *venum*: vendable (C) / *excreo*: gallice ascracher (C) / *fiscedula*: gallice oriole (D)

[F]

facundus: renable (D) / *fatiscor*: estre las (C) / *offa*: supe (C) / *coapto*: gallice affaytes [corr. affayter] (C) / *fabulor*: mentyr (D) / *letificor* vel ludificor, -aris: gallice degabber (C) / *infantia*: enfaunce (D) / *fax*: tisun (C) / *falcastrum*: faucil (C) / *falco*: faucher (D) / *facitergia*: tuaylle (C) / *fascia*: bende (C) / *fele* (idem quod hec cerva): gallice bisce (C) / *fasciculus*: petit fes (C) / *fibula*: tache (D*) / *fibulo*: tacher (D*) / *effibulo*: destacher (D*) / *proditio*: gallice treysun (C) / *fiber*: gallice tessun, anglice broc (C) / *effibulo*: gallice detacher (C) / *fibula*: tache de mantel (C) / *fidentia*: leuté (C) / *figulus*: potir (C) / *ferina*: venisun (C) / *effert*: encroullez (C) / *justa* (olla monachorum): juste gallice (C) / *fissilis*: fendable (D) / *filix*: anglice brake (D)[45] / *trifidus*: fendu en treys (D) / *ferus*: fors (D) / *feretrum*: bere (CD) / *frutex*: bussun (C) / *fuco*: gallice fardeer (D) / *fruges*: blé (D) / *fucus*: anglice dran, ez (C)[46] / *fructuarium*: fruture (C) / *fulica*: gallice blarie (CD) / *fuligo*: suhe gallice, sot anglice (C) / *apis*: un hé (D) / *fragor*: noyse (CD) / *caverna*: crevesce (C) / *fraxinus*: frenne (C) frene (D) /

---

[39] In the right-hand margin of C f.46r a fourteenth-century hand has provided the gloss 'yris, -dis: anglice reynbowe'.

[40] At the bottom of f.46v in C a fifteenth-century hand has added 'nuclius: gallice noel, anglice curnel'.

[41] See MED sub *evesing n.*

[42] See MED sub *adese n.* and OED sub *adz, adze.*

[43] See MED sub *rigge-bon n.*

[44] See OED sub *woodwall*. At the top of f.48v C has 'hec ictericia dicitur morbus quando aliquis flavescit, gallice jaonis' and at the bottom of the page 'perrectus -ta -tum gallice avançable'.

[45] See MED sub *brake(n n.*

[46] See MED sub *drane n.*

furfur: bran (C) / *defuco*: furbeer (C) / *furtivus*: gallice larcinus (C) / *furca*: furche (C) / *poples*: garet, anglice hamme (D) / *fragum*: gallice freyse, anglice strauberie (C) / *flagellum*: flael (C) anglice scurge (D) [47] / *inflat*: enfler (C) / *abscindula*: spone (C) [48] / *fusco*: enbrunir (C) / *fuscus*: brun (CD) / *fuscamen*: brunissement (C) brunisement (D) / *flammea*: kuverché (D) / *fuligo*: sue, anglice sod (D) / *fuscotinctum*: gallice fustiani (C) / *farcino*: farcer (C) / *farcimen*: farsure (D) / *fartor* vel farsor: gallice farsur (C) / *farrago*: furage (C) / *formicales*: tenaylles (C) / *fornax*: furneys (D) / *forulus*: furel (CD) / *fomentum*: nurisement (D) / *fomes*: nurisement (D) / *forpex*: sisurs (C) cisurs (D) / *defensorius*: defendable (C) / *fetus*: feonissement (C) founisement (D) / *formosus*: bel (D) / *forus*: pertus (D) [49] / *foramen*: pertus (D) / *forum*: marché (D) / *confuga*: futif (C) / *cumfuga*: futif (D) / *fugitivus*: futif (D) / *fermento*: leveyne (C) / *fautor*: otreur (C) / *placitat*: pleset (D) / *poples*: garet, anglice hamme (D) / *frigella*: finche (C) anglice finch (D) / *frugella*: rusche (C) gallice frue, anglice rok (D) [50] / *favus*: rey de mil, anglice hunicom (C) / *frondator*: titemus anglice (C) / *cumulosus*: gallice muncelus (D) / *coxa*: quise (D) / *fiscedula*: gallice oriole, anglice wodewale (C) / *frixura*: fruture (D) / *fossor*: anglice delvere (D) [51] / *fossorium*: anglice delvere (D) beche (D) / *fetidus*: sulie, puaunt (D) / *fetosus*: puant (D) / *fungus*: musserun (D) / *fibula*: tache (D) / *fixus*: fiché (D) / *fixura*: fichanse (D) / *fenero*: gabler (D) / *phenerator*: gallice usurer (D) / *fastidio*: gallice enhorgulher (D) / *verber*: bature (D) / *funda*: lenge (D) / *fons*: fonteyne (D) / *fluvius*: flot (D) / *deflorat*: roumpit flurs (D) / *fornacilia*: hublez (D) / *confiteor*: reloyer (D) / *fornacio*: anglice bath [52] / *febriato*: enfeverir (D) / *framea*: gisarme (D) / *fremitus*: fremisement (D) / *defrautor*: trahir (D) / *fagus*: gallice foue, anglice bech (D) / *fragrasco*: reflerer (D) / *flaveo*: enbloyer (D) / *flavus*: bloye (D) / *fulvius*: bloysant (D) / *phicedula*: gallice oriole vel piscis qui alio nomine dicitur runbus, esturgun (D) / *tortor*: peynur (D)

[G]

maxillaris: de joewe (C) / *genu*: genuyl (C) / *degenero*: forliener (C) / *gerulus* est equs: gallice sometir (D) / *genitura*: gendrure (C) engendrure (D) / *gentilis*: payn (C) / *gerulus*: portable (C) / *gerusia*: escurge (CD) / *germina*: estren (C) / *suggero*: entiscer (C) enticer (D) / *congeries*: muncelement (C) / *gerra* (nuga inepta): trufle (C) / *gesum*: gisarme vel ges, anglice tapul (C) [53] / *gravitas*: grevance (D) / *suggestus*: entisement (C) / *digerere*: defier (C) / *gurgulio*: gallice mulet (C) / *gesticulor*: sailler (C) / *gulosus*: glutun (C) / *gulo, -onis*: glutun (C) / *gressutus*: takun (C) / *globosus*, plenus globis: gallice de muns (C) / *glabrio*: teynne (C) / *glaber*: teynnus (C) / *granum*: greyn (CD) / *galea*: heume (D) / *gazophilacium*: tresorie (C) / *glaucus*: bloy (C) / *gluticus*: tranglutè (C) / *glutino*: engluer (C) / *regiro*: returner (C) / *glis* (herba adherens vestibus): gallice gletunire (C) / *gravia* (macula in oculo): anglice hawe (C)

---

47   See MED sub *scourge n.*
48   See OED sub *spoon sb.1.*
49   C f.51v has 'forus est foramen in navi ubi ponitur remus, anglice þe hore'.
50   See TL 3,ii,2313 sub *fru* and MED sub *rok(e n(2)*.
51   See MED sub *delver n.*
52   See MED sub *bath n.2(a)*.
53   Cf. OED sub *tubbal?* See also OED sub *tapul.*

[H]

humido: enmustir (C) enmoyster (D) / *exheredo*: deshereyter (C) / *predia*: gallice
riche maneres (D) / *edera*: gallice [sic] yvu (C)[54] / *hereticus*: eretik (C) / *honusto*:
charger (CD) / *exhilaro*: aveser (C) / *hilaramen*: aveysure (C) / *honorus*: honorabil (C)
/ *abhortator*: desamonester (C) / *hortarius*: amonestable (C) / *hippotamus* (quasi equus
marinus): anglice a sele (C) / *hio*: abayr (C) / *hyatus*: abaissement (C) / *haustum*:
espuchement (D) / *hirna*: saucich, pudding (C) / *hircus*: bukerel (CD) / *hinulus*: foun
gallice, est fetus servi et serve, deyme (C) / *hilia*: gallice aundulie (D) / *lacivus*:
enveysé (D) / *hostilis*: enemiable (D) / *hirna* (hec hirnea dicitur illa pellicula in qua
ponitur salsucia vel hirna): gallice sauchich (C) / *hostorium*: estric (D) / *ybernus*:
yvernayl (D)

[J]

jugulus: gallice gorge (D) gorge (C) / *jugulo*: estrangler (C) / *jurgare*: tenser (C) /
ydraula (genus organi): anglice floytes (C) anglice floute (D)[55] / *jactulo*: gallice
dinner (C)[56] / *jaculum*: gaveloc (C) / *jaculor*: lancer (D) / *jactacula*: gallice gez (C) /
juvenca: gallice jenice (D) / *injuria*: gallice tord (D) / *injurius*: gallice tortenus (D)
torcinus (C) / *juba*: gallice creste (D) / *jagatia* (ani fissuras vates dicunt jagatias):
arshol (C)[57] / *ymbrex*: gallice guter (D) / *ymbricium*: lovir (left-hand margin, gallice
lovir vel gotir) (C)

[L]

allego: alegger (C) gallice alleger (D) / *Litana* [? for *Latina*]: gallice Lumbardie (D) /
Latium: Ytalia, Lumbardie (C) / *legumen*: potage (C) / *pulpita*: deske (C) / *litura*:
defauçure (C) / *legat*: gallice deviset (C)[58] / *labo*: chaunceler (C) gallice chanseler
(D) / *ludarius*: gallice hasard (D) / *lubrico*: gallice esclicer (C) / *labrico* (sic): gallice
escliser (D) / *labina*: gallice mareys (D) / *lapsio*: escolurjous (C) / *utris*: costret (C) /
luxus: loche (C) / *dilato*: enlargir (C) / *lamina*: plate (C) / *lancino*: gallice launcer (C)
/ *libricus*: esclisable (D) / *lamentum*: waymissement (C) / *lacinia*: (a) faudure (C) /
lamia (quasi lama): anglice mare (C)[59] / *ortus* .i. tensa: gallice une teyse de tere (C) /
limax: gallice limazun (C) / *limus*: tay (C) / *lima*: file, anglice vile (C) / *elimatus*:
gallice furbé (C) / *elimare*: furber (C) / *elemator*: furbur (C) / *pelex*: rivayle (C) /
levitonaria (collobia): gunele (C) / *levio*: gallice picoyse (C) gallice pikoyse (D) /
lenio: gallice asuager (D) / *leno*: gallice leschur (D) / *allevo*: gallice alleger (D) / *lorum*:
gallice rene (D) / *lingula*: hardilun (C) gallice hardiliun, anglice tunge (D)[60] /
lingulata: gallice tenaylles, anglice tonge (C) anglice tunge (D) / *licium*: hevele (D)[61]
/ *ligulam*: laynir (C) gallice laner (D) / *ligustrum*: primerole (CD) / *levionem*: gallice

54   English 'yvy'(?).
55   See MED sub *flouten*.
56   See Du Cange sub *jantaculum* and TL 2,1950 sub *disner*.
57   Written in a fifteenth-century hand. See MED sub *ars* n.2(a).
58   The line of text runs 'Qui mittit legat moriens sua munera *legat*'. MS Oxford, Corpus
Christi College 121 f.102r glosses '.i. delegat et dividit'.
59   See MED sub *mare* n.(2).
60   See OED sub *tongue* sb. 14a.
61   See MED sub *heveld* n.

pikoyse (D) / *liquamentum*: decuranse (C) / *deliquium*: decuranse (C) gallice degutement (D) / *liquo*: gallice dekure (D) / *laquear*: gallice lace (D) / *exlicitor*: bargayner
(C) / *lentiscus*: anglice burche (C) anglice birch (D) / *lentigo*: lentille (C) / *liceor*:
gallice preyser (D) / *laurus*: lorir (C) / *conspersa*: rusee (C) / *licitatum*: bargayn (C) /
licito: gallice bargayner (C) / *lardus*: lard (C) / *focus*: astre (C) / *lumbus*: reyns (IC) /
marmor: marbre (C) / *lima*, limatis (illa pellis quam faber habet ante se): suyllepel
(C) gallice soliepel (D) / *lotrix*: laundire (C) / *lotorium*: lavur (C) / *lodix*: gallice
laungel, witel (C) langele, anglice witil (D) [62] / *labium*: livre, lippe (C) levere (D) /
liricen: harpur (C) / *liveo*: embloir (C) enbloyer (D) / *collivesco*: comencer de embloir
(C) / *lividus*: bloy (CD) / *proseuca*: bordel (D) / *lato*: gallice enlargir (D) / *lanx*: gallice
balaunce (D) / *lamentor*: gallice waymenter (D) / *lamia*: anglice strie (D) [63] / *lacinia*:
gallice paun, anglice sclitte (D) [64] / *lacerta*: gallice lesarde, anglice evete (D) [65] / *lanio*
.i. macellarius vel carnifex: mascecrin (C) / *lentiscus*: anglice birch (D) / *libo*: guster
(C) / *libum*: wastel (C) / *colludo*: degaber (D) / *laqueo*: gallice alacer (D) / *laquear*:
gallice lace (D) / *lacunar*: gallice summet (D) / *detero*: tribler (D) / *lingo*: gallice
lescher (D) / *litigium*: gallice tensun (D) / *laurus*: lorere (D) / *limite*: sente gallice (D)
/ *lumbus*: reyns (D) / *laqueo*: lacer (C) / *lactes*: letenges (D) / *lapista*: mortir (C) /
lapidicina (idem quod lapicidium): quarire (C) / *libitina*: bere (C)

[M]

memoralis: remenlbrable [sic] (C) / *mantica*: trusse (C) gallice truse (D) / *manutergia*:
tuaylle (C) / *mancipo*: abaundoner (C) / *sporta*: corbayl (C) corbiliun (D) / *manubium*: maunche (C) / *emendo*: gallice amender (D) / *mirtus*: anglice gohel (C) [66] /
motio: gallice movance (D) / *meritorium*: gallice leude, anglice schoppe (D) [67] /
mercatum: marchié (C) marché (D) / *merx*: marchandise (C) gallice marchaundise
(D) / *malus*: gallice mast (C) / *mercenarius*: gallice marchand (D) / *mordax*: mordable
(C) / *molosus*: brachet (C) limer (D) / *morsuo*: morder (D) / *mula*: mule (C) / *murena*:
lampré (C) lampreye (D) / *modulus*: gallice motet (D) / *modulor*: gallice chanter (D)
/ *mando*: gallice glutun (D) / *muscipula*: ratur (C) [68] / *monilis*: de fiçayl (C) / *antemurale*: gallice barbecane (C) / *permeo*: gallice passer (D) / *medico*: gallice mediciner
(D) / *missale*: gallice messale (D) / *messor*: seur (C) / *polimita*: gallice pipelori (C) /
minium: vermilun (C) vermiliun (D) / *emissarius*: gallice estalun (D) / *musculus*:
gallice braun (D) / *munio*: gallice garnir (D) / *murmur*: grundiliement (D) / *multi-
cium*: rochet (C) / *ydromel*: boschet (C) / *mustum*: gallice must (D) / *mucidus*: muselé
(D) / *mergus* (vas aptum puteo):[69] buket (C) / *mergus*: plungun (C) / *marcor*: flestisur
(C) / *mitigo*: gallice assuager (D) / *minio*: de vermiliun (D) / *miniographus*: gallice
alumenur (D) / *maceo*: gallice enmegrir (D) / *maceries*: gallice megresse (D) / *macero*:

62   See OED sub *whittle sb.*[1].
63   See OED sub *stry*.
64   See OED sub *slit sb.1*.
65   See MED sub *evete n.*
66   See MED sub *gail(e n.*
67   See OED sub *shop sb.*
68   In the right-hand margin of C f.61v a fifteenth-century hand has added 'hec ansa: an
     hop'. See OED sub *hope sb.*[2] 3.
69   The gloss to *hoc mergus, mergoris* runs 'est situla cum qua trahitur aqua a puteo'.

gallice enmegrir (D) / *macilentus*: megre (C) / *macellum*: gallice macecrenerie (D) / *macellarius*: macecrin (C) / *cediculati*: gallice chiselés (D*) / *minctus*: gallice pissé (D) / *mando*: gallice maunder (D) / *metior*: mesurer (D) / *monedula*: gallice choue, anglice ko (D)[70] / *medulla*: gallice meule (D) / *multipes*: gallice clouport, anglice lukechest (D)[71] / *monacha*: gallice nuneyne (D) / *remoramen*: gallice targaunce (D) / *matertera*: gallice aunte (D) / *merulus*: gallice merle (D) / *mulgeo*: gallice leter, anglice milkin (D) / *marceo*: anglice welkid (D)[72] / *marcor*: efflettrisyre (D) / *milleus* (pelo): gallice rivelink (D)[73] / *merges*: gallice plungun (D)

[N]

navigo: sigler (C) / *navica*: marnir (C) / *nato*: noer (CD) / *natrix*: noeresse (C) / hic *nator*: gallice nour (D) / *navigo*: gallice noer (D) / *natatus*: rowinge (C) / *nautabilis*: noable (C) / *strix*: estrie, mare (C)[74] / *strigem*: gallice pesarde (D)[75] / *nexo*: gallice alacer (D) / *nexus*: lassure (C) / *nothus*: bastard (CD) / *ignotescere*: pardoner (C) / *naris*: naril (C) / *nasturcium*: anglice curse (C)[76] / *nasturcia*: gallice cressuns (D) / *novale*: waret, et alio nomine dicitur veractum .q. vere actum, anglice walghe (C)[77] / *nutamen*: ensenement (C) / *nonus*: neufme (D) / *nigro*: gallice enneyrer (D) / *nota*: gallice note et merche (D) / *ignosco*: perduner (D) / *natus*: gallice nesaunce (D) / *renuo*: gallice refuser (D) / *abnuo*: gallice refuser (D) / *nuo*: gallice asener (D) / *nutus*: gallice asenement (D) / *obnubo*: gallice kuverir (D) / *numella* (cathena in numerosis maculis contexta): anglice sakel (C)[78] / *tempora*: les templus (C) gallice templis (D) / *nugor*: gallice trufler (D) / *fulcio*: gallice suppoer (D) / *netus*: anglice spinninge (D) / *nodo*: gallice noer (D) / *naucipendo*: gallice nent preyser (D)

[O]

opilo: estuper (CD) / *ocillum*: braundele, tetere anglice (C)[79] gallice brandel (D) / *exosus*: heynus (C) / *olus*: cholet (C) / *olor*: cigne (C)[80] / *ortus*: gallice nesaunce (D) / *batus*: curalie (D) / *opulentus*: gallice plentivus (D) / *abhominor*: anglice wlatin (D)[81] / *ostorium*: gallice radure (D) / *ordior*: gallice urder (C) / *testam*: escale (C) / *rastrum*: herse (C) / *occo*: gallice hercer (D) / *occa*: gallice herce (D) / *pixis*: boyste (C) / *ostra* (notat testam): gallice escale (D) / *hostorium*: estricl (C)[82]

---

70 See MED sub *co* n.
71 See MED sub *loc-chester* n. and Gfry 9,113c sub *cloporte*.
72 See OED sub *welk* v.[1].
73 See MED sub *riveling* n. The lemma *pelo* is an error for *pero*.
74 See MED sub *mare* n.(2).
75 See FEW 8,192a (*pensare*) which gives *pesard* as 'cauchemar'.
76 See MED sub *cresse* n.
77 See MED sub *falwe* n.
78 See OED sub *shackle* sb.[1].
79 See OED sub *teeter* sb.
80 On f.65v C has the line 'Venditor est oleris olitor vel ductor oleti / .i. stercoris / with the gloss 'funi [= foin?] waye' and another line 'Hinc avis et fetor equivocatur olor'.
81 See OED sub *wlate* v.
82 Cf. OED sub *strickle* sb.

[P]

procus (qui petit novos amores): dauneer (C) / *procor*: dauneer (C) / *procus*: gallice
douneur (D) / *primulas*: gallice auke primer (D) / *papula*: gallice berbulette, anglice
welke (C) [83] / *culicem*: gallice wibet (C) / *papilla*: anglice wirte of te teyt (C) [84] /
pullus: gallice puscynt (D) / *pullulo*: gallice burguner (D) / *pulvinar*: quissir, anglice
bolster (C) gallice quisine (D) / *impluvium*: lovir (right-hand margin gallice lover)
(C) gallice luver (D) / *polimita*: gallice pipelori (C) [85] / *polipus*: anglice crabbe (C) [86] /
propudiare: ribauder (C) gallice ribauder (D) / *oportunus*: gallice kuvenable (D) /
lollium: anglice cokkel (C) / *panulea*: broche (C) gallice broche (D) / *propero*: gallice
haster (C) / *propio*: gallice aprocer (D) / *panus*: la brache [sic] (C) / *pexus*: pyenné
(C) / *pectino*: pynner (C) gallice peynner (D) / *tempestivus*: seysonable (C) / *intem-
pestivus*: deseysonable (C) gallice nent sesunable (D) / *pestis*: gallice pestilence (D) /
pollex: puz (C) / *pollen*: flur (C) / *pictacium*: anglice clotes,[87] gallice tacuns (C) /
membranula: petite escroette (C) / *plectrum*: pletrun de harpe (C) gallice plectrun de
harpe (D) / *patinam*: gallice paele (D) / *plexus*: gallice puni (D) / *pendulus*: pendable
(C) / *penna*: gallice latte (C) / *piscina*: gallice viver (D) / *puteo*: gallice puer (D) /
penula: furure (C) / *pensum*: fusil (C) gallice fusil (D) / *pondus*: gallice peys (D) /
pensio, -onis: pensiun (C) / hic et hec *pensilis*, et hoc *pensile*: pendable (C) gallice
donable (D) / *pensum*: gallice fusil (D) / *pensum*: gallice peys (D) / hec *panduca*,
genus organi, hoc *panducar*: anglice baggepipe (C) / *flectipendo*: vil presir (C) / *predo*:
robeur (D) / *predor*: robeer (D) / *predatus*: robbé (C) robé (D) / *interpres*: gallice
latemir (C) / *pedicam*: pantir (C) / *compes*: firge (C) / *predia*: gallice richesse, manere
(D) / *preditus*: gallice enrichi (D) / *tripos*: trestel (CD) / *lauce*: leument (C) / *pelex*:
rivayle (C) / *apello*: ariver (C) / *pilus*: peyl (C) / *pessulum*: cliket (C) / *pelta*: talevas
(C) / *podium*: gallice apoalie (D) / *punctim*: de puynt en puynt (C) / *multipes*: gallice
clouport, anglice lukecheste (D) [88] / *pomacium*: gallice pomaz (C) / *plaustrum*: wan
(C) [89] / *pulpita*: letrun (C) / *privignus*: filastre, anglice stupsune (C) / *plumacium*:
orelir (C) / *pulvis*: gallice pudre (D) / *pelex*: rivalie (D) / *repello*: gallice debuter (D) /
pungnus: gallice puyn (D) / *postremus*: gallice dreyn (D) / *deplumo*: oster pennes (C) /
prestigium: geglerie (C) / *prestigiator*: juglur (C) / *paulominus*: un poy meyns (C)
gallice poy meyns (D) / *pirus*: perir (C) gallice peyrere (D) / *pirum*: pere (C) / *pirgus*:
gallice cheker (D) / *plaustrum*: gallice karre (D) / *pannuceus*: gallice cluté (D) / *pix*:
gallice peys (D) / *tessera*: gallice dé (D) / *plausus*: gallice enjoy (D) / *exprobro*: gallice
reprucer (D) / *opprobrium*: gallice repruce (D) / *pirata*: gallice robeur de mer (D)
pedium (calciamentum in superiori parte pedis): gallice enpeyne (D)

---

83 See OED sub *whelk*[2] and AND sub *borbelette*.
84 See OED sub *wart sb*[2]. and *teat*.
85 Cf. TL 7,966–7 sub *pipoler*. MS Oxford, Corpus Christi 121 f.106v has the gloss 'vestis
pluraliter radiata vel guttata'.
86 See MED sub *crab(be n.*(1). C f.67r has the gloss 'pisces plures habens pedes, idem quod
cancer'.
87 See MED sub *clout n.*(1).
88 See note 71.
89 See OED sub *wain sb*.[1].

[Q]

quaternus: quair (C) gallice quayer (D) / *quadragies*: karaunte fiz (C) quaraunte fyeche (D) / *quinquagies*: sinkante fiz (C) cinckaunte fyeche (D) / *quadringenti*: gallice quatre cent (D) / *quindecies*: gallice quinse fyeche (D) / *quadriga*: carette (C) / *quincenti*: sink cent (C) / *questorius*: cumpleynable (C) / *quadruplo*: gallice quadrubler (D) / *quanto*: gallice de comben (D)

[R]

rupes: roche (C) gallice roche (D) / *roro*: ruser (C) / *rumino*: runger (C) / *rumo*: runger (C) / *rumor*: novele (C) / *rumex*: gallice fauchun (C) / *rumorizo*: runger (C) / *ruder*: gutire (C) gallice guter (D) / *ramex*: gallice runce, anglice brambel (C) / *fragum*: gallice frese, anglice streuberie (C) / *rabies*: rage (C) / *rabulus*: raluys (C) (?) / *rancida* (vel rancidula): anglice wlat (C) [90] / *raptim*: celement (C) / *rostrum*: bek (C) / *ramale*: ramil (C) / *mentula*: cuyllun (C) / *ramale*: braun[che] (C) / *remex*: guvernayl (C) / *remillus*: gallice [sic] hore (D) [91]

[S]

statura: gallice estat de cors (D) / *statera*: gallice balaunce (D) / *stipulam*: gallice chaume (D) / *prostibulum*: gallice bordel (D) / *lena*: gallice puteyne (D) / *stamen*: esteym (C) anglice warp (D) / *extasis*: paumisun (CD) [92] / *sensus*: sentement (C) / *socors*: coard (C) gallice kuard / *spurius*: bastard (CD) / *nothus*: bastard (C) / *surdus*: gallice surd (D) / *surdesco*: devenir surd (C) / *conscio*: gallice cunsacher (D) / *socordo*: gallice kuardise (D) / *sagum*: say (CD) / *suasor*: gallice amonester (D) / hic et hec *sualis* et hoc -le: amonestable (CD) / *satio*: semaunce (D) / *serum*: meg (C) gallice mege (D) / *speculator*: wayte (C) gallice weyte (D) / *consutilis*: asemble cusable (C) / *sulcus*: reun (C) / *sulcator*: reunir (C) / *seminarium*: anglice sedelep (D) [93] / *subula*: aleyne (C) / *sura*: gallice estrumel (C) anglice scinebon (D) [94] / *succina*: suz de char e de pessun (C) / *succinum*: suz (C) / *succina*: tripe (D) / *sumen*: gallice grase de porc (D) / *salsus*: salé (C) / *saltus*: launde (C) gallice launde (D) / *desolo*: desconforter (C) / *solor*: gallice conforter (D) / *consolor*: gallice conforter (D) / *serra*: gallice [sic] saue (D) / *salaria*: gallice saler (D) / *exsilium*: issil (C) / *sanguino*: sayner (C) / *sanguisuga*: samsue, leche (C) [95] / *siliqua*: escoce (C) eschose (D) / *solium*: gallice soler (D) / *solsequium*: solsicle (D) / *sinum*: buket (C) fesele (D) / *desino*: finir (C) / *sinus, -nui*: seyn (C) / *dissimulo*: deguiser (C) / *saturo*: ensauler (C) / *sextarius*: sestir de vin (C) / *suggo*: leter (D) / *solium*: gallice soler (D) / *proseuca*: bordel (D) / *senio, -onis*: hasardur (C) / *squalidus*: suyllé (C) / *sexagies*: sesante fiz (C) / *sexagenus*: sesantime (C) / *rosus*: rungé (CD) / *scansile*: estrif (C) estru (D) / *sigalum*: segle (D) / *signo*: mercher (D) / *signum*: signe (D) / *sigillum*: sel (D) / *scaphium*: gallice une gate, anglice

---

90   See OED sub *wlat a.*
91   See OED sub *oar sb.*
92   An addition to C f.71v in a fourteenth-century hand runs 'surio [= curio], -onis: gallice scyrun, anglice hondwerm'. The lemma often appears as *subcreo* in medieval MSS. For the English gloss see MED sub *hond(e* n.8(i).
93   See OED sub *seed-lip.*
94   See OED sub *shin-bone.*
95   See OED sub *leche* n.(4).

mele (C) [96] creye (D) / *scaphus*: espaule (D) / *scapularis*: scapelori (D) / *scapula*: espaule (C) / *scalpo*: grater (C) / *signarius*: baneur (D) / *scansio*: muntaunce (D) / *scamellum*: fourme (D) / *scamnum*: schaere (D) / *scopo*: baler (C) / *scopa*: balene, besme (C) [97] / *spatula*: esclisse (C) sparre (D) [98] / *scabo*: grater (D) / *scabidus*: roinus (D) / *spuo*: escoper (C) cracher (D) / *spumo*: escumer (C) / *sputus*: craché (D) / *spurcus*: bastard (D) / *pumex*: pumiz (C) / *pumico*: pumicer (C) / *spurius*: bastard (CD) / *spacior*: dedure (D) / *servitus*: servage (C) / *sartor*: redubur (C) / *soleo*: soleer (D) / *scrutinium*: encerchement (D) / *septuagesimus*: sesantime, setantime (C) / *scrutum*: tripe (D) / *sileo*: teyser (D) / *silex*: cailonc (D) / *silentia*: teysaunce (D) / *sinus*: seyn (D) / *sinum*: fesele (D) / *similo*: sembler (D) / *dissimilo*: degeser (D) / *saturo*: sauler (D) / *satur*: wodewose (D) [99] / *panis*: payn (D) / *ignobilis*: bastard (D) / *septiginti*: set cent (C) / *sopitilis*: dormable (C) / *sonorus*: sonable (C) / *consonat*: acordet (C) / *septemtrio*: gallice north (D) / *subtus*: desuz (C) / *sanctimonialis*: noneyne (C) / *sudes*: suer (C) / *septulus*: set duble (D) / *sextarius*: sester de vin (D) / *strido*: fere noyse (C) / *strigilis*: estrille (C) / *splen*: esplin (C) / *scaturigo*: surse de ewe (C) / *scatebrosus*: gallice pleyn de surse (D) / *scatebra*: surse de ewe (C) / *affluere*: decure (C) / *scortum*: bordel (C) / *sevius*: gallice cruel (D) / *desevio*: endeveer (D) / *serpillum*: peletre (C) gallice pelestre (D) / *supremitas*: gallice hautesce (D) / *aspersorium*: wispilun (C) / *squama*: eskerde, scale (D) [100] / *circum*: environ (D) / *spina*: eschine (C) / *spica*: espi, anglice ir (C) [101] / *seminecis*: demi mort (C) / *semo*: neym (C) / *scintilla*: anglice sparc (D) [102] / *scutica*: escurge (CD) / *sido*: gallice abeser (D) / *scurra*: harlot (C) / *situla*: buket (C) / *surculus*: greffe (C) gallice ente (C) / *sera*: lok (C) / *stirpo*: arasser (C) / *obserat*: barret (C) / *stupor*: abaysure (D) / *sculpo*: entayller (C) / *sculptilis*: tayllable (C) gallice entaliable (D) / *scalpurio*: gallice runjer (D) / *strepo*: fere noyse (C) / *serus*: gallice tardis (D) / *strepor*: noyse (C) / *celare*: entayller (D) / *strepa*: estrif (C) estru (D) / *aturmen*: plane (C) / *singulto*: trangluter (C) / *obses*: ostage (C) hostage (D) / *sussuro*: gallice grundiliur (D) / *squaleo*: waxen reu (D) [103] / *scaphus*: espaule (D) / *stillicidia*: gallice guter (D) / *struma*: gallice bose (D) / *singulto*: gallice saungluter, anglice sobbin (D)

[T]

tentorium: pavilun (C) gallice pavilhun (D) / *tuber*: musserun, paddukmete (C) [104] / *tendicula*: gallice pantir (C) / *teges*: bordel (CD) / *tugurrium*: hulet (C) / *tussicula*: gallice tuss, anglice kouin (D) [105] / *tentoria*: gallice pavilhun (D) / *tonsito*: gallice tunder (D) / *tintinabula*: campernole (C) / *trabs*: gallice treyf (C) / *area*: place (C) / *todus, todulus*: gallice kurlu (D) / hic et hec *tritilis*, hoc *tritile*: desolable (C) / *tritura*:

---

96 See MED sub *mele* n.(2). C f.73v has 'hoc scaphium est locus ubi arma reponuntur et etiam vas in quo pedes lavantur'.
97 See MED sub *besm(e n.*
98 See OED sub *spar sb.*[1].
99 See OED sub *woodwose*.
100 See OED sub *scale sb.*[2].
101 See MED sub *er(e n.(2)*.
102 See OED sub *spark sb.*[1].
103 See OED sub *wax v.*[1] and *row adv.*
104 Neither OED sub *paddock sb.*[1]. nor MED sub *paddok(e n.* records this compound.
105 See MED sub *coughing ger.*

bature (C) / hec *terranea* (locus in civitate): une mise (C) / *trapete*: a la mule (C) / *tributum*: truage (C) / *zelotipus*: gelus (C) / *tolus*: tupet (C) / *talaris*: talun (C) / *talis*: li dez (C) / *taxillus*: petiet (sic) dez (C) / *tessara*: dez (C) / *talus*: un dez (C) / *taxus*: yf gallice (C) / *tessella*: petit dez (C) / *trucido*: defuler (C) / *trutina*: balanze (C) / *tonitrus*: gallice tuneyr (D) / *trudarces*: gallice estrumel (C) / *tirocinium*: burdiz (CD) / *tantillus*: petit (C) / *traha*: gallice herce (D) / *torcular*: gallice pressur (D) / *titillo*: catiller, tikeli[n] (C) catiller, anglice tikelin (D)[106] / *titillicus*: enveysé (C) / *torta*: turtel (D) / *trituro*: gallice batre (D) / *terebrum*: wimbel (C)[107] / domus *tricantium*: gallice treschauns (D) / *tribus*: lynie (D) / *detrecto*: gallice manyer (D) / *zelotypus*: gallice kuperel, anglice kokewald (D)[108] / *trutina*: gallice balaunce (D) / *turgor*: gallice emflure (D) / *tenea* (impedia): gallice vampie (C) / *tendicula*: gallice pantir (C)

[V]

vibro: gallice croller (C) / *viror*: verdisur (C) / *bivarium* habet duos sensos, ponitur aliquando pur vivire, et aliquando pro fraunc; unde Oratius 'Excipiant pro senes quos in vivaria / en lur franciz / mittunt'[109] [*Ep*. I,1,79] (C) / *vitulor*: anglice starte (D)[110] / *vitellus*: gallice muel de le huf (D) / *vitamen*: le moel del uf (C) / *vibex*: anglice wale (C)[111] / *versor*: gallice turnur (C) / *vertigo*: gallice turnure (C) / *veternum*: jauniz (C) / *exvigilo*: deveiller (C) / *verecundia*: verguyne (C) / *voluptuose*: delitusement (C) / *uter*: buceus (C) / *veniale*: pardonable (CD) / *ventilo*: suffler vel enchacer (C) suffler (D) / *vena*: veyne (D) / *ventrale*: brael (C) / *venabulum*: borsper (C)[112] / *venor*: chacer (CD) / *vimen*: gallice hosyere (D) / *vado*: je way (C) / *conventus*: covent (D) / *vadio*: je engag (C) / *advena*: estraunge (D) / *vador*: waer (C) / *vadator*: wayur (C) / *invado*: asailer (D) / *vespa*: waspe, anglice waps (C) waspe (D) / *usito*: frequentatum u sove[ne]l (D) / *redunco*: recouper (D) / *variatim*: diversement (C) / *vicie*: fyeche (D) / *vicecomes*: vescunte (D) / *vitta*: bende (C) / *vafer*: vesie anglice vel dicens rumores (C)[113] / *verbosor*: janglur (C) / *urcheus*: picher (C) / *viaticum* est victus qui defertur in via et Corpus Christi: gallice liveresun (C) / *ulcus*: boce (C) / *vallis*: valee (C) / *valva*: wyket (C) / *vallum*: bail (C) / *probra*: r(e)epresse (C) / *vectes*: barre (C) / *viola*: violette (D) / *violo*: honir (D) / *vestibulum*: vestiarie gallice porche (D) / *ustio*: arsure (D) *usturamen*: ars, anglice brend (D)[114] / *viscus*: englu (C) / *zelotipus*: gelus (C) gallice cuperel (D) / *ustilamen*: arsure (D) / *agrestis*: de cuntré (D) / *vicus*: rue (D) / *vicinus*: veysin (D) / *villus*: flocke (D)[115] / *vario*: diversefier (D) / *vindemio*: sarcler (D) / *unuo*: asembler (D) / *urceus*: pot (D) / *ulcus*: boce (D) / *vallum*: bayl (D) / *valva*: gallice wiket (D) / *viciam*: vesce (C) gallice ves, fecches (D) / *vexillum*: gallice banere (D) / *vapulo*: gallice batre (D) / *umbilicus*:

---

[106] See OED sub *tickle v.*
[107] See OED sub *wimble sb.*
[108] See MED sub *cokewald* n. and Gfry 2,334b sub *coupereau.*
[109] See TL 3,ii,2203 sub *franc.*
[110] See OED sub *start v.*
[111] See OED sub *wale sb.*[1] 2.
[112] See MED sub *bor* n.5.
[113] See OED sub *wise a.*
[114] See MED sub *brand* n.
[115] See MED sub *flok* n.(2).

anglice novele [sic] (D)[116] / *involucrum*: gallice trusse (D) / *veruca*: gallice verue, anglice warte (D)[117] / *papula*: anglice welke (D)[118] / *visco*: gallice gluer (D) / *veracta*: gallice waret (D) / *vere*: veyr (D) / *epimena* (corrected from *ypomena*): anglice sperling vel smilte (D)[119]

[Y]

ydromellum: mede (C)

[Z]

zelotipus: gallice cuperel (D) gelus (C)

MS LONDON, LAMBETH PALACE LIBRARY 502

[A]

[f.15r] *arculus*: arsun / *artoceptum*, vas habens duo cepta .i. duas ansas, est enim artoceptum vas artificialiter factum: gallice [cor]baylun / [f.16r] *niocharistim*: nowendun (?) / *alietus*: gallice merilun / *alluta*: cordewan / *aculeus*: gode, pricche[120] / [f.16v] *anachorita*: recluse / *epar*: .i. giser / *armenta bovum*: vacherie / *inarro*: bargayner / *angina*: bolle de le çen (?)[121] / [f.17r] *acinacina*: drache / [f.17v] *area*: place / *aristoforum*: a fislep[122] / *atramentarium*: arnement / *auxianator*: grater / [f.18r] *ardea*: hayrun / *arceda* (stella): Carlewayn / *alapam*: bufe / [f.18v] *antidotum*: triacle

[B]

balatus: blating de berbys[123] / *biclivium*: gallice duple pendant

[C]

[f.19r] *clepsedra*: gallice dusil / *capo*: le chapun / *camus*: barnac / [f.20r] hec *creditaria*: chambere

[D]

[f.20v] *dominus*: dicitur gallice daunz / [f.21r] *obdo*: gallice estuper

[E]

[f.22v] *esculus*: mellir / [f.23r] *estuo*: bruler / *erro*: harlet / [f.23v] *exta*: buez

[F]

[f.24v] *falx*: sikel / *fibula*: tachet / *figulus*: potir / [f.25r] *ferina*: gallice veneysun / [f.25v] *frangmentum*, idem est quod residuum: gallice relef / *fraga*: gallice frese,

---

116 See OED sub *navel sb.*
117 See OED sub *wart sb.*
118 See OED sub *whelk.*[2]
119 See OED sub *sparling* and *smelt sb.*[1].
120 See MED sub *gode* n. and OED sub *prick sb.13.*
121 i.e. 'angina pectoris'.
122 See MED sub *fish* n.5 (o).
123 See MED sub *bletinge ger.*

strowberie / *poples*: gallice hamme / *flagellum*: gallice scorge / [f.27v] *frigo*: gallice frier / [f.28r] *fodio*: gallice fouer / *figo*: gallice ficher / *fibula*: tache / *verber*: gallice bature / *flagellum*: gallice flael / *coxa*: la quysce / [f.28v] *faginentum*: locus est ubi crescunt fagi, anglice beschc / *frico*: froter

[G]

[f.29r] *degenero*: forligner / [f.30r] *grando*: grisyle / *granarium*: gerner / [f.31r] *girgillum*: wyndas / [f.31v] *hirsutus*: gallice erumflé [corr. eruplé?]

[H]

hostorium: gallice stric / *ybernaculum*: pawelun / *Ybernia*: gallice hyrlonde / *hortator*: desamoneçter / *horologium*: gallice horloge / *hoccrea* .i. pellicula illa in qua ponitur salsucia: .s. pudding / *hima* .i. salcicia: anglice saucikyl [124] / [f.32r] *recondit*: musez

[I]

elixatura .i. brodium: anglice brroz [125] / *precor*: le meyir / [f.32v] *ydolum*: gallice maumeht / *ydraulas*: pipe, floute [126] / *jaculor*: lancer / *jactacula*: gallice gees / [f.33r] *ymbricium*: luver

[L]

allego: playder / *lectisternium*: gallice aurnement de lit / [f.33v] *litura*: defaçure / [f.34r] *lusito*: degabber / *ludarius*: hasardrie / *labina*: mareys / *proluvies*: gallice ordure / *lenio*: losenger / [f.34v] *lucubra*: crusil / [f.35r] *ligulam*: layner / *subligas*: layner / *laquear*: cople / *deliquium*: gallice degutement / [f.35v] *lupanar*: gallice bordel / *latus*: cotthe / *lamia*: gallice strie, gallice [sic] wyche [127] / *lacertam*: gallice lesarde / *limula*: gallice [sic] fil-hyren [128] / [f.36r] *limus* .i. oblatus: oclong [sic] ut strabo, anglice purblent [129] / *limen*: soyl / *lodix*: strayles [130] / [f.36v] *libum*: gallice gattel

[M]

[f.37v] *mango*, mercator, quia manu tangit equos: gallice romongur [131] / *manubria*: gallice monche / *sporta*: gallice corbayl / *manile*: gallice tuoayle / *mirtus*: gallice genet / *mala*: gallice jhoue / [f.38r] *mullus*: gallice mulet / [f.38v] *lacerti*: gallice braz / *munimen*: garnisement / *muccipula*, instrumentum ad mures capiendos sic docta quia mures stringat: gallice arblayt / *munero*: rewerduner / [f.39r] *macies*: megresse / *macus*: megre / *maceria*: pareye / *macerarium*: de mesere / [f.39v] *vesica*: gallice [sic] bladdre [132] / [f.40v] *mergite*: anglice gav[r]el [133] / *situla*: gallice bochet / [f.41r] *marcor*: gallice flettrisur

---

[124] This form does not appear in the dictionaries.
[125] See MED sub *broth* n.
[126] See MED sub *floute* n.
[127] See OED sub *witch* sb.
[128] Cf. MED sub *file* n.(1).
[129] See OED sub *purblind.*
[130] Cf. TL 3,ii,1472 sub *estrel* and FEW 12,284b which gives 'estreille' from 1377.
[131] See MED sub *ro-mongour* n.
[132] See MED sub *bladdre* n.
[133] See TL 4,300 sub *gevrel.*

[N]

noctua: anglice nitrawen [134] / *nuo*: gallice cener / *numella*: anglice sakel [135] / *nastusia*: gallice cyhirsons / [f.42v] *papille*: gallice mamele / *nervus*: anglice senewes

[O]

os[c]ito: anglice gonen [136] / [f.43r] *exossare* .i. laniare: gallice deramer / [f.43v] *testam*: anglice scale / *occa*: gallice sercler

[P]

pixis: gallice buçte / [f.44r] *procor*: gallice dauner / *procavus*: wouté / [f.44v] *lodium*: gallice luver / [f.45r] *pecten*: gallice peyne / *convicia*: ledenges / *penum*: celer / [f.46v] *pedena*: vecer / *pedia*:[137] gallice patyns / [f.47r] *apello*: gallice ariver / *pultes*: gruel / [f.48v] *palistra*: place /

[R]

[f.49v] *rumex*: runce / [f.50r] *fibula*: tachet

[T]

[f.51v] *tuber*: musserun / [f.52v] *timpana*: tabur / [f.53v] *calathum*: gallice panier

[V]

[f.55r] *villus*: floc / *vitta*: bende / [f.56v] *ventilare*: chascer

[Y]

[f.58r] *ypemenia*: sperling

---

134 See MED sub *night* n.6(*a*)
135 See OED sub *shackle sb.*[1].
136 See MED sub *gonen v.*
137 Read [*calo*]*pedia*?

INDEX OF MANUSCRIPTS USED

BERLIN (W. Germany)
Deutsche Staatsbibl. (Preuss.
Kulturbesitz)
   lat. fol. 607 57ff, 108f, 154ff

CAMBRIDGE
University Library
   Oo.6.110 21ff, 159ff
Gonville and Caius College
   136 (76) 37ff, 65ff, 125ff
   385 (605) 81f, 125ff
Peterhouse
   207 9
   215 5ff, 23ff
Trinity College
   0.7.9 (1337) 37ff, 86ff

DUBLIN
Trinity College
   270 15ff, 26ff, 37ff, 65ff, 125ff

DURHAM
Cathedral Libr.
   C.IV.26 15ff, 26ff

EDINBURGH
Nat. Libr. of Scotland
   Advocates 18.4.13 85f

LINCOLN
Cathedral Libr.
   132 3ff, 37ff, 65ff, 125ff

LONDON
British Library
   Arundel 394 15ff, 26ff
   Harley 683 90ff
        4967 9ff
   Additional 8092 37ff
        10089 11
        16380 5
        41476 12
Lambeth Palace Library
   502 171ff
Wellcome Historical Medical Library
   801^A 109ff

OXFORD
Bodleian Library
        Auct. F.5.6 (2195) 11f
   Rawlinson
        G 99 (15462) 37ff

WORCESTER
Cathedral Library
   Q.50 62, 119ff, 153f